Studies in the Gospels

ROBERT HENRY LIGHTFOOT, 1883–1953

STUDIES IN THE GOSPELS

ESSAYS IN MEMORY OF
R. H. LIGHTFOOT

Edited by D. E. NINEHAM

Professor of Biblical and Historical Theology in the University of London
at King's College

OXFORD

BASIL BLACKWELL

1955

PRINTED IN GREAT BRITAIN
BY WESTERN PRINTING SERVICES LTD., BRISTOL
BOUND BY KEMP HALL BINDERY, OXFORD

Contents

Robert Henry Lightfoot

1883—1953

ROBERT Henry Lightfoot was born at Wellingborough on 30th September 1883, the youngest son of the Reverend R. P. Lightfoot, at that time vicar of Wellingborough and subsequently rector of Uppingham, Archdeacon of Oakham and prolocutor of the Lower House of the Canterbury Convocation. His forbears had been for centuries farmers at Moreton Hampstead, near Exeter, and the succession was first broken by his great-grandfather, who deserted farming for an academic career and matriculated at Balliol in 1790. His son followed in his footsteps and became eventually Rector of Exeter College. Lightfoot himself was educated at Uppingham and then at Eton, and at both schools impressed the masters as a boy of great promise, though physically he was far from robust. But when, in 1902, he went up as an exhibitioner to Worcester, he found his work hampered by certain nervous troubles which were to dog him throughout his life, and he obtained only a second in Mods and a third in Greats. Despite this discouragement, he was persuaded by C. F. Burney to read for the Honour School of Theology and in 1907 he obtained a first class in it; he also won the Liddon Studentship and, in the following year, the Senior Septuagint and Senior Greek Testament Prizes. Immediately after he went down, the generosity of friends made it possible for him to travel extensively and the long letters he wrote at the time show how greatly he appreciated the opportunity and how much enjoyment and interest he derived from it.

On his return, after a period of training at the Bishop's Hostel, Farnham, under B. K. Cunningham, he was ordained to a curacy at Haslemere in 1909. He himself always looked back on his three years there as some of the happiest in his life; he took a full part in the various activities of the parish and seems to have enjoyed them all. His ministry is still remembered in the village with gratitude and affection. But much though he enjoyed parochial life, he seems never to have given up the hope of academic work; in 1909 he was an unsuccessful candidate for the Chaplain Fellowship at Exeter* and in 1912 he accepted the invitation of R. G. Parsons, then Principal of the Theological College at Wells, to serve on his staff. At Wells too Lightfoot was happy; he was always keenly appreciative of natural beauty and conceived a lasting affection for Wells itself and the surrounding countryside. The students found him the most approachable member of the staff and the innumerable lectures he was called upon to give—on subjects as diverse as Christian ethics and liturgiology—were always thoughtful and crystal clear, if not perhaps strikingly original. When war came and Parsons went off to other work, Lightfoot became effective head of the College, and in 1916, when Parsons finally resigned, Lightfoot was appointed as his successor. At Easter 1917 it became necessary to close the College for the duration of the war and Lightfoot became domestic Chaplain to the Bishop of Winchester. Rather to his surprise he discovered something of a taste for administrative work and he enjoyed the insight he got into the practical workings of the Church of England and the entrée he was given into the interesting society the Talbots attracted to Farnham Castle even in wartime. In February 1919 Wells re-opened, but after less than a year Lightfoot left on being appointed "Visitor's Fellow" of Lincoln College, Oxford.

The two years he spent at Lincoln were probably the happiest in his life. In the intimate society of a small and sympathetic Common Room his natural shyness was easily overcome and his considerable gifts as a mimic and raconteur could be displayed to advantage;† he had indeed, as the Fellows of Lincoln discovered, a keen eye for the foibles and and pretensions of others, and his anecdotes almost always had a sting in the tail, though they were never malicious. He also found satisfaction in his work among the undergraduates; "Flossie," as they affectionately called him, was certainly something of a figure of fun, with his extreme formality—his way of dealing with his shyness—and his rather pedantic manner, but his essential friendliness and exceptional kindness quickly endeared him to everyone, though then, as always, it was the public-school men who found it easiest to get to know and understand him. At this period it was as a pastor

---

* N. P. Williams was the successful candidate.

† These never deserted him; even at the end of his life he could readily be persuaded to do superb imitations of various people he had known. His imitations of the late Dean Armitage Robinson, for example, are never to be forgotten.

rather than a scholar that he was principally known in the University, and when in 1921 New College was looking for a chaplain, the Fellows took the rather unusual step of inviting Lightfoot to transfer to them from Lincoln. After much thought he felt bound to accept the invitation, which he saw as a call to greater responsibilities and wider opportunities. That decision, as he himself was inclined to think later, was probably a mistake. The Common Room at New College was very much larger than the one he had been used to at Lincoln and its ways necessarily more formal; moreover, many of its members at that time were far from sympathetic to organized Christianity, and Lightfoot, almost morbidly sensitive and still very conscious of his "failure" in Mods and Greats, was not the man to stand up easily to their indifference or hostility. Determined to justify his position in a tangible way, he undertook an extremely large share of the administrative work of the College, until in 1929 he held concurrently the posts of Junior Bursar, Dean of Divinity, Sub-Warden, Tuition Secretary and Tutor for Admissions, Secretary of the Benefices Committee, Tutor and Chaplain, as well as being a pro-proctor in the University, Speaker's Lecturer in Biblical Studies and an Examining Chaplain to the Archbishop of Canterbury.* This was perhaps an excess of zeal, for he was not particularly well-fitted, by temperament or experience, to deal tolerantly with the high-spirited undergraduates of the post-war generation. But he laboured most diligently among them as chaplain, and if he worked through social contacts and the building up of personal friendships, rather than by more direct and formal methods, everyone recognized that it would have been quite contrary to his character to speak easily about the things of the spirit, and his pastoral endeavours were in fact widely respected and appreciated. As far as theology went, he gave himself out, or at any rate allowed himself to be thought of, as a rather "hack" scholar, competent at most to pass on in clear form the discoveries and insights of others. He attended both Turner's and Streeter's seminars and, as his private papers now reveal, pondered deeply on the issues raised in them; but at the time even his colleagues hardly suspected that he had much original contribution to make.

But those who listened with a discerning ear to his lectures on the Gospels must have detected that deep thought had gone to their preparation and that Lightfoot was increasingly dissatisfied with the critical account of the origins and nature of the Gospels

---

* A post he held from 1913 almost to the end of his life. From 1948 he was a Six Preacher at Canterbury Cathedral.

then dominant in English theological circles. This became clear when in 1928 he was appointed to the Speaker's Lecturership in Biblical Studies and delivered what must have seemed at the time a rather odd course of lectures. They do indeed make rather strange reading; halting and tentative, developing, and some-times changing considerably, in view-point as they go along, often fanciful and even bizarre in their interpretations, they can yet be seen in retrospect to have marked an important change. In his contribution to the Modern Churchmen's Conference at Girton in 1921* Lightfoot had indeed pointed out very clearly certain difficulties and apparent inconsistencies in the synoptic accounts of Our Lord's life and ministry, but he had not seemed to feel that they provided any serious obstacle to a fairly full and accurate knowledge of the historical facts, and he had concluded by agreeing with Weinel, against Burkitt, that "we know Jesus right well."† Meanwhile, he had, for all his disclaimers, been working steadily on the texts, and, as a result, certain questions had defined themselves in his mind, particularly with regard to the literary form of the Gospels, the kind of information an evangelist sought to convey and the methods he used to convey it. For example, he asked himself whether the juxtaposition of events in the Gospels was meant to convey the evangelists' belief that they happened in chronological succession, as had been widely assumed, or whether it was rather intended to point to some *theological* con-nexion between them. Or, to put the same point in another way, had the differences between the Fourth Gospel and the Synoptic Gospels been exaggerated and were the Synoptists perhaps not so far from St. John in their intentions and literary methods? Lightfoot's Speaker's Lectures will be best understood if they are seen as a first tentative, and largely independent, attempt to inter-pret the Gospels in the light of such considerations. In places he is still very much under the sway of the older presuppositions, and where he breaks away he is often still very uncertain what herme-neutic principles the Gospels do in fact demand. At the end of the lectures he himself was far from satisfied with the solutions he had propounded, though as clear as ever about the centrality and importance of the problem.

A hint from C. H. Dodd determined him to learn German and see what light he could get from German scholarship, and in 1931 he went to Germany and made contact with Bultmann, Dibelius and others. This visit marked a turning point in his

---

* See *The Modern Churchman*, Vol. XI for Sept. 1921, pp. 223 ff.

† See Burkitt's Preface to the English translation of Schweitzer's *Quest of the Historical Jesus*, p. v.

academic career. For he saw that the conclusions of the *Form-geschichte* school fully justified the suspicions he had already formed about the older, liberal, interpretations of the Gospels, and so they gave him confidence to go on with his own investigations. At the same time they provided him with a more objective and satisfactory basis from which to carry on his search for non-historical principles of interpretation. A further, and unexpected, result of the visit was to give him a sense of mission to the English theological world. Form-criticism was then little known—or at any rate little appreciated—in England, and, as one who had accidentally stumbled on it and its significance, as he modestly put it, he felt bound to bring it to the notice of English students; for he was convinced that they would not get much further with their interpretation of the Gospels until they took it into account. He realized very fully, indeed he probably exaggerated, the misunderstanding and unpopularity he was likely to incur, but he felt the task to be so imperative that he overcame his shyness and sent in his name as a candidate for the Bampton Lecturership in 1934. When he was elected, his natural diffidence reasserted itself and it was only after a considerable struggle with himself that he delivered and published the lectures.* Originally intended, as the title and preface make clear, as a consideration of Gospel interpretation in general, they had, in the event, to be chiefly confined to the Gospel according to St. Mark. At the time Lightfoot himself regarded them as little more than a work of popularisation, designed to familiarise English students with the methods and conclusions of the form-critics and the implications of their work. And in the much-quoted final paragraph he seemed largely to accept Bultmann's very negative assessment of the historical value of the Gospels as seen through form-critical eyes.† In fact, as he himself realised later, his lectures were far from being a slavish reproduction of continental conclusions. He had gone to Germany in 1931 to find answers to certain questions about the purpose and literary methods of the evangelists, and his interest in the new

---

* *History and Interpretation in the Gospels* (Hodder and Stoughton, 1935). Many were the friends who helped him in the days just before the delivery of the lectures when his paralysing nervousness had prevented the completion of even one lecture. If rumour is to be trusted, the expert in such matters might even detect several different hands in the first part of the first lecture!

† This paragraph attained great notoriety; it proved to have been very unfortunately phrased, coming, as it did, with all the emphasis of a peroration. Lightfoot expected that the allusion to Job 26^{14} (R.V.) would be more widely recognised than it was and so his words were frequently understood in a sense rather more extreme than that intended (see Lightfoot's own statement in *The Gospel Message of St. Mark*, p. 103*n*). In any case he subsequently modified his views on this subject.

methods he found there never succeeded in driving these questions from his mind; on the contrary, his interest in the new methods was at least partly due to the recognition that they put his original questions in a new light and helped towards a solution of them. In the account of Gospel origins given by Bultmann, Dibelius and Karl Ludwig Schmidt, the personality and intentions of the individual evangelists counted for very little; the Gospels were almost represented as having composed *themselves* under the impersonal forces of community need and tradition. This seemed to Lightfoot a very dangerous half-truth. Taking a hint from H. J. Cadbury, whose book on Luke-Acts, published in 1927, he greatly admired, he made it his aim to discover why St. Mark selected and arranged his material in just the way he has, and what form and aspect of the Christian gospel he sought to convey by so doing. The form-critical insight that the material when it reached St. Mark had virtually *no* order or arrangement seemed to him to make imperative the question: What sort of order then has the evangelist imposed upon it and what sort of truth about the Incarnation can be derived from a careful study of that order? And once that question was asked, the differences of arrangement between the various Gospels were seen to ac-quire a new significance as suggesting a possible difference of theological interpretation, or at any rate emphasis. In the Bampton Lectures this last fact received such recognition as was possible in a work concerned mainly with a single Gospel. In many ways *History and Interpretation* may not have been a very good book, but it was an important book inasmuch as it opened up these new ways of approach to the study of the Gospels, and it was throughout pervaded by an earnestness and concern for truth which did not always characterize the reviews and criticisms of it. In certain respects *Locality and Doctrine in the Gospels*, which followed, largely derivative though it is, is a better book. It is a kind of appendix to the Bampton Lectures, seeking to show how the geographical data in the Gospels should often be treated as vehicles of theological insight rather than of topo-graphical information for its own sake. The opening section of this book—whatever may be thought of its conclusions—is a good example of the way Lightfoot's use of form-critical methods was controlled by his concern with the evangelist's total purpose, as well as being an outstanding instance of his meticulous and accurate treatment of linguistic detail.

During these years Lightfoot had, as we have seen, come to believe that he had a contribution to make in the scholarly world, modest and unoriginal though he felt it to be. Accordingly, he decided to devote himself to his studies, giving up most of his administrative work in College and even retrenching somewhat in his pastoral work, though he never ceased to be an active member of many bodies connected with the University.* In 1934 he was elected to the Dean Ireland's Professorship of Exegesis of Holy Scripture, then a part-time chair which he was able to hold without giving up his fellowship at New College, and from then on he devoted himself almost exclusively to his New Testament studies, though he continued as Chaplain of New College and took his share in College administration during the war period. In 1936 his work was recognized by the award of an Honorary D.D. from the University of Aberdeen and in 1938 he became a D.D. of Oxford and also an honorary fellow of his old college. In the last year of his tenure of it, the Dean Ireland's Chair became a full-scale professorship and Lightfoot was elected to an Emeritus Fellowship of New College, which he held till 1950 when, to his great joy, Lincoln renewed his association with it by making him an Extraordinary Fellow.

In 1950, he published, under the title *The Gospel Message of St. Mark*, a number of lectures and papers which he had written on previous occasions and which all alike bear witness to the meticulous and detailed accuracy of his scholarship. But his principal occupation in the last four or five years of his life was the composition of a commentary on St. John's Gospel which was almost complete at the time of his death and will soon be published. When it is, it will be seen to be very characteristic of its author. Based on Inge's dictum that: "the Fourth Gospel is so complete and coherent in itself that for the careful student it will be found to answer all the questions which it raises, so far as such questions are answerable,"† it expounds each passage on the basis of a minute and thoughtful comparison with other relevant parts of the Gospel and the rest of the New Testament. The result betrays an exhaustive knowledge of the texts and years of pondering on them and is usually highly illuminating without

---

* He was, for example, then or later, a member, and later chairman, of the Board of the Faculty of Theology, a Curator of the Bodleian Library, a Delegate of Privileges, a Delegate of the University Press, Secretary of the Oxford Society for the Study of Theology, Treasurer and Chairman of the committee responsible for the Lexicon of Patristic Greek, a Vice-President of the Origen Society and Senior Treasurer of the Oxford Union Society. These and a number of other bodies have testified how much they owe to the careful and conscientious interest he took in their affairs.

† Lightfoot himself, in a paper read to the Origen Society on Feb. 23rd 1944, said that he took this to mean 'that the key to any particular passage in the book lies in the consideration of the work as a whole or of other sections of it with which the particular passage has affinities', It might perhaps be said that Lightfoot extended the dictum to apply to all the Gospels.

being fanciful. It is also typical of Lightfoot that the scope of the book is strictly limited. We look in vain for enlightenment on the relations between the Fourth Gospel and religious literature from contemporary non-Christian sources (a subject on which he often lamented what, by his standards, was his ignorance), or for any of those reflections on the relation between the thought of the Fourth Gospel and the thought and language of to-day which make Hoskyns's commentary, for example, so profound a contribution to the philosophy of religion.

But the absence of such reflections, here or in his other writings, should certainly not be taken to suggest any lack of concern with contemporary religion. Lightfoot was a deeply religious man; no one who knew him could doubt that, and to hear him celebrate the Holy Communion was to be made immediately aware of it. But a number of causes combined to keep such concerns out of his published writings. Reticent by temperament, he had been brought up in an age and tradition which did not encourage public discussion of personal religion. And religion to him was essentially personal; for he was deeply influenced by the "liberal" belief that religion is an affair between a man and his Creator, to which dogma, whether ancient or modern, is an irrelevance. His earlier lecture notes show how concerned he was about the relation between the historic religion of the New Testament and the religious belief of to-day, and his deep and sustained interest in the Johannine writings was largely due to his belief that they, more than any other New Testament books, were relevant to the problem.* His own thinking on the matter was determined to a very considerable extent by the views of two men, the late Dean Inge and the late Professor C. C. J. Webb. The former in particular he regarded as an almost infallible guide,† and from him he learned what amounted almost to a *gnosis*, a doctrine of unmediated mystical approach to God which largely by-passed the problems of historic New Testament Christianity and made questions of dogmatic definition, churchmanship and ceremonial seem almost indifferent. To these last he himself sat

* In his earlier lectures he often spoke of the Fourth Evangelist as 'universalising' Christianity and liberating it from the particular Jewish-eschatological form in which it still appeared to a large extent in the Synoptic Gospels.

† It was discovered after his death that he had formed a complete collection of Dean Inge's writings; through the services of a press-cutting agency, even the most fugitive newspaper and magazine articles had been included. The collection is now in the possession of Prebendary A. F. Judd.

It may well have been lack of confidence in himself as a philosopher engendered by his third in Greats that led him to place such overwhelming reliance on the views of others about the *philosophical* aspects of Christianity. He was always very willing to acknowledge the authority of the expert in spheres where he regarded himself as inexpert; "our best guides tell us" was a favourite phrase with him.

very loose and he was apt to get impatient when others attached greater importance to them. Whatever the merits of such a position, it enabled him to achieve a great measure of objectivity in his view of New Testament problems and to face with comparative equanimity the rather negative conclusions about the Gospels to which at one time he felt driven.* It also had the rather curious effect of making him divide off his critical studies sharply from his preaching; "congregations", he would say, "are not interested in dogma—and that is as it should be." His own sermons were concerned almost always with what he regarded as the timeless truths about the relation of God and the human soul and as a result he was able to preach them repeatedly over the years without serious alteration, despite the considerable change that came over his critical views about the New Testament.† All this might easily convey the false impression that Lightfoot did not ascribe any very high *religious* value to the Bible, but viewed it mainly as an object for critical and historical research. Nothing could be further from the truth. It was in fact one of the most striking things about him that with his rigorous critical approach to the Bible he combined an attitude of deep reverence and humble expectancy towards it. It was from this that his great influence as a teacher of theology largely sprang. To generations of students apt to be bewildered by the implications of Biblical criticism, he showed, by the very reverence and excitement with which he approached the sacred text, that, even at its most stringent, it is quite compatible with a lively appreciation of the Bible as the Word of God. And if at times his own conclusions seemed somewhat radical—perhaps more radical than they really were—his friends always knew that that was not due at all to any lack of concern at the ultimate implications of what he wrote; on the contrary, it was precisely because he regarded the study of the Bible as too serious and sacred a sphere for anything but the most searching honesty.

The secret both of his excellence as a New Testament scholar and of his influence as a teacher could hardly be better set out than it was in the editorial with which *Theology* greeted the publication of his last book.‡ 'One knows,' the editor wrote, 'that behind everything Dr. Lightfoot writes there are years of patient

---

* More than one reviewer of his Bampton Lectures raised the question of their implication for religious faith to-day and of Lightfoot's failure to deal with the problem.

† In the last years of his life he was able with complete sincerity to preach, unmodified, sermons he had first composed before the first great war, a remarkable indication surely both of the scrupulous care that had gone to their original composition and of the stability of his religious, as opposed to his critical, opinions.

‡ *Theology*, Feb. 1951.

reflection during which every detail has been attended to and all the evidences have been weighed with scrupulous honesty. He does what it is very difficult for anyone nowadays to do, not least for any theologian: he comes to the Gospels without presuppositions about what he is going to find in them and so he genuinely lets them speak for themselves and shine in their own light. Moreover he has, and communicates, the conviction that they are terribly and mysteriously alive, and even verbally inspired in a sense other than the wooden one. No one has seen more clearly that to go to the Gospels—or simply to Mark and Q—for a biography of Jesus, or for that picture of the "Jesus of History" which the piety of fifty years ago discovered and delighted in, is to go for what they do not, and were never intended to, provide. On the other hand, no one has done more than Dr. Lightfoot to help students to read the Gospels as they were read by those for whom they were originally written, and to find that so read they are the records of a weight of glory beyond all comparison.

'At many points Dr. Lightfoot shows that strange conclusions, to which he finds himself led on critical grounds, bring into relief unheeded aspects of the Gospel of salvation and are important for the preacher as well as for the scholar.'

Two further tributes remain to be paid. The first is to Lightfoot's editorship of the *Journal of Theological Studies*. He was indefatigable in seeking out and assessing contributions, in encouraging and assisting young and inexperienced contributors and in ensuring that what was printed was as clearly and cogently set out as his experience and unstinted efforts could make it. No one who saw the great work and patience that went into its production could be surprised that, at the time of his death, the *Journal of Theological Studies* had such a high reputation throughout the world.

The last tribute, and the hardest to formulate, is the personal one. On first acquaintance the impression he gave was of being formal and precise almost to the point of pedantry; 'meticulous' is a word which leaps to the mind in connection with his character as well as his lecturing and writing.* Sensitive, essentially reticent and readily offended, he was not the man to form many lifelong friendships of a really intimate kind. But he fully made up for that by his great interest in, and kindness to, his pupils and other young workers in the theological field, and the other younger people with whom his various activities brought him into contact.

* So far as his writing goes, this sentence is a gem too precious to be omitted: 'I must be allowed to say dogmatically that in the fourth gospel Judas is probably "the man of sin," the "anti-Christ".' (Quoted, *Theology*, Feb. 1951.)

His pupils in particular are conscious of a very special debt to him; for it was peculiarly in his teaching that his real greatness was shown. His deep belief in the importance of his subject and his whole-hearted devotion to it were such as could hardly fail to communicate themselves to those who attended his lectures or 'read with him', as he modestly liked to put it, in tutorials. And his influence was the more effective because of the great personal interest he always took in all those with whom his various activities brought him into contact. From those who needed help with the elements of New Testament Greek to those engaged on the most erudite research, any serious student of theology could always be sure of his sympathy and help, often help of a severely practical kind which must have consumed many hours of his time. Younger theologians especially could always rely on his encouragement to persevere in any worthwhile scholarly undertaking and in particular they were welcome—if they could face the discipline!—to have their English style clarified and simplified by his exacting but penetrating criticism.

We who benefited from all this are deeply conscious of our debt to him and this book* is some acknowledgement of it. We are only sorry that various unavoidable delays prevented its publication in time for us to present it to him in person.

D. E. N.

* It was originally planned, on the suggestion of the Reverend J. C. Fenton, as a tribute to Lightfoot from a group of his former pupils. But when it became clear that a wider circle of scholars would like to express their admiration of Lightfoot by contributing to it, their co-operation was naturally welcomed as making the tribute more representative and comprehensive.

The Septuagintal Background
to the New Testament use of ΔΟΞΑ

by

L. H. BROCKINGTON

'. . . When he that hath bidden thee cometh, he may say to thee, Friend, go up higher: then shalt thou have glory in the presence of all that sit at meat with thee,' Lk. 14^{10}: 'And an angel of the Lord stood by them, and the glory of the Lord shone round about them,' Lk. 2^9. These two quotations taken from the same gospel illustrate the wide range of meaning which δόξα is capable of expressing in the New Testament. It ranges from the honour men accord their fellows to the glorious presence of God himself. The word, in use, has its overtones and undertones which reflect its Old Testament background. Its normal classical meaning, 'opinion', does not occur anywhere in the New Testament, but, on the other hand, a whole range of theological usage in the New Testament is not found in classical Greek. In this it is almost entirely dependent on the Septuagint where there is one passage only in which δόξα can properly bear the meaning 'opinion' (Ecclus. 8^{14}) but where, on the other hand, δόξα regularly translates the Hebrew כָּבוֹד in reference to God's glorious presence and activity and to the honour ascribed to him by men. The Septuagint, indeed, uses δόξα in this sense more frequently than the Hebrew uses כָּבוֹד. Other Hebrew words for honour, majesty and dignity are also rendered by δόξα in the Greek Bible and furthermore it is added to the text in a number of passages by way of interpretation.*

The dependence of the New Testament on the Septuagint in its use of δόξα may readily be shown by reference to the direct use made of Septuagint passages in which δόξα occurs. There is one quotation: 'All flesh is as grass, and all the glory thereof as the

* Cf. II Chron. 2^6, Isa. 4$^{2-6}$, Exod. 33^{19}.

flower of the grass'* which is closer to the Septuagint than to the Massoretic text and retains the use of δόξα for *ḥesedh*. II Thess. 1⁹ may perhaps also be regarded as a quotation, since it virtually repeats the refrain of Isa. 2¹⁰, ¹⁹, ²¹ in the form it has in LXX.† Further allusion to LXX usage may perhaps be seen in the coupling together of 'power' and 'glory' in a number of New Testament passages.‡ They may be dependent on Ps. 63 (62)². Similarly, Dan. 7¹³ᶠ· in the LXX version may have influenced the use of ἐξουσία in close connection with δόξα in Lk. 4⁶§ and Jn. 17², ²², ²⁴. The dependence on Dan. 7¹³ᶠ· goes much further, of course, than this linguistic echo and may be seen in the reference to the coming again of the son of man in Matt. 16²⁷, 24³⁰, Mk. 13²⁶, Lk. 21²⁷. An interesting point of exegesis is raised by the apparent use of Gen. 1²⁷ 'God created man in his own image' in I Cor. 11⁷ 'forasmuch as he is the image and glory of God; but the woman is the glory of the man'. It may well be that δόξα is here virtually a synonym of εἰκών seeing that δόξα translates *t^emunah* 'form' in Num. 12⁸ and Ps. 17(16)¹⁵.‖¶ We shall examine other passages later in this essay in which δόξα refers to the external form or shape (Rom. 1²³, II Cor. 8²³, Jn. 17²², ²⁴).

In addition to these resemblances and allusions the claim may be made that the New Testament takes over the characteristic LXX use of δόξα and builds upon it. What, then, is the *characteristic* use of δόξα in the Septuagint? We may answer: its use to express the *effect* of God's presence, that is to say, his power and

---

* I Peter 1²⁴: Isa. 40⁶.

† 'From the glory of his majesty' is translated by LXX 'from the glory of his strength'.

Hebrew: מֵהֲדַר גְּאוֹנוֹ

LXX: ἀπὸ τῆς δόξης τῆς ἰσχύος αὐτοῦ.
Cf. also Jn. 9²⁴ (Josh. 7¹⁹), Rom. 1²³ (Jer. 2¹¹ and Ps. 106²⁰).

‡ (Matt. 6¹³), 24³⁰, Mk. 13²⁶, Lk. 21²⁷, Rev. 4¹¹, 7¹², 15⁸. A. M. Ramsey, *The Glory of God and the Transfiguration of Christ*, p. 30, n. 1, draws attention also to the connexion between δόξα and βασιλεία in Mk. 8³⁸ to 9¹ and connects it with Ps. 145¹¹.

We may note also that Ramsey, in a note on p. 41, draws attention to the use of ὑψωθήσεται and δοξασθήσεται in Isa. 52¹³ and indicates a possible background here to the Christian conception of the sufferings of Christ as the means of his exaltation and glorifying, with special reference to Jn. 12³¹ ᶠ· (p. 68). This appeal to the Old Testament may be strengthened, perhaps, by reference to some other places where the two verbs occur together in the LXX: Isa. 4², 33¹⁰, Ecclus. 43³⁰ and (differently) Ps. 36²⁰. But these may also do little more than serve to show that the two verbs were readily associated in speech and their coupling may therefore have little exegetical significance.

§ Cf. Matt. 4⁸ which has a shorter text and no reference to δόξα.

‖ See the article 'The Greek Translator of Isaiah and his interest in ΔΟΞΑ', by the present writer in *Vetus Testamentum*, I, i (1951) p. 27. Cf. also v. Gall, *Die Herrlichkeit Gottes* (1900), pp. 92 f.

¶ Other passages dependent on, or showing knowledge of LXX are: Heb. 1³, cf. Wisd. 7²⁵ᶠ·; II Pet. 1¹⁷ and Ps. 145 (144)⁵; Rev. 15⁸ and Isa. 6⁴, Exod. 40³⁴ and Hag. 2⁷ (the smoke from Isa. and the glory from Exod. and Hag.); I Cor. 2⁸ and Ps. 24 (23)⁷⁻¹⁰; Rev. 18¹ and Ezek. 43².

activity. This represents a somewhat different shade of meaning from that which the Hebrew equivalent *kabhodh* exhibits. In the Hebrew the emphasis falls on the *fact* and *apprehension* of God's presence but in the Greek the translators moved away from the idea of the knowledge of the presence of God to that of the saving power of his presence.

Since the purpose of this essay is to show how the Septuagint has influenced New Testament usage, it is not intended to make an exhaustive treatment of the way in which δόξα is used in the New Testament.*

There are four ways in which δόξα is used in the New Testament which may be said to be directly due to corresponding usage in the LXX. (1) The conception of brightness. (2) The power and wonder-working activity of God. (3) The saving power of God. (4) The conception of God-likeness.

1. The conception of brightness in the word δόξα. This was already present in Hebrew usage, not so much in the etymological significance of the word *kabhodh* as in its use in describing theophanies. The LXX emphasis on the radiance of God's presence may be seen in the narrative of Exod. 34²⁹ ᶠᶠ· where the phrase 'the skin of his face had horns' (meaning, presumably, sent out rays like horns) is rendered 'the appearance of the skin of his face was *glorified*'. But it is in the LXX of Isaiah that this trait emerges clearly.† The most direct reference to the radiance of δόξα in the New Testament is in Acts 22¹¹, 'And when I could not see for the glory of that light'. This occurs in the description of the encounter of Paul with the risen Christ, the Christ 'in glory', on the Damascus Road. Verse 6 mentions the 'great light' (φῶς ἱκανὸν) whilst other references to the vision all show the same element of brightness and light—Acts 9³, 22⁶, 26¹³.

As in the Old Testament, so in the New Testament, brightness is a standing accompaniment of all direct revelation from heaven: the word for it is δόξα. At the Annunciation (Lk. 2⁹) 'the glory of the Lord shone round about them'.‡ At the Transfiguration Matthew and Mark both mention the change in our Lord's appearance, and the conversation with him of Elijah and Moses, but it is Luke, who uses δόξα with a frequency comparable with that of John's Gospel, who reports that Moses and Elijah appeared 'in glory', and that the disciples 'when they were fully

---

* This is fully discussed in A. M. Ramsey's book: *The Glory of God and the Transfiguration of Christ* (1949).
† Isa. 2¹⁰· ¹⁹· ²¹; 4²; (9¹); 30²⁷; 40⁵; 58⁸; 60¹ ᶠ·· ¹⁹; cf. also Bar. 4²⁴, 5⁹; Wisd. 7²⁵ ᶠ·· See *Vetus Testamentum*, I, i, 28 ff.
‡ Cf. Isa. 4² (LXX), 9¹.

awake . . . saw his glory'. There is more than mere brightness here, for we may think of it as a full revelation of God on behalf of Jesus, but the immediate *effect* was that of great and dazzling light. When the angel appeared to John (Rev. 18¹) 'the earth was lightened with his glory' with which we may compare the description in Ezekiel (43²) of the coming of the glory of the Lord 'and the earth shined with his glory'.* The glory of God will illumine the new Jerusalem (Rev. 21²³). In the New Testament the light of God's glory is often associated with Jesus Christ as the saviour of mankind. The Nunc Dimittis hails him as 'salvation' which is then further elaborated by two appositional phrases: 'a light for revelation to the Gentiles, and the glory of thy people Israel'. Light and glory are both in apposition to salvation and may be regarded as virtually synonymous with it and with each other in this passage.† The phrasing recalls several passages from Deutero-Isaiah: 'a light to the Gentiles' 42⁶; 'a light to the Gentiles that my salvation may be to the end of the earth' 49⁶; 'In the Lord shall all the seed of Israel be justified, and shall glory', 45²⁵; 'and I will place salvation in Zion for Israel my glory (LXX for my glory)', 46¹³; 'all the ends of the earth shall see the salvation of our God', 52¹⁰. Thus this passage, with its apparent dependence upon Deutero-Isaiah, establishes a strong association of glory, light and salvation. The association of glory with salvation is one that the Septuagint makes firmly, and which, as we shall see, is continued in the New Testament. Two familiar passages may serve to summarize what has been said of the element of brightness and radiance in δόξα: Heb. 1³: 'the effulgence of his glory' which would recall to readers the passage in *Wisdom* (7²⁵ᶠ) 'a clear effluence of the glory of the Almighty . . . for she is an effulgence from everlasting light': and II Cor. 4⁶: 'Seeing it is God, that said, Light shall shine out of darkness, who shined in our hearts, to give the light of the knowledge of the glory of God in the face of Jesus Christ'.

2. A rapid glance over the passages already mentioned will show that the New Testament, like the LXX, does not use δόξα merely to convey the idea of the brightness of God's presence but as a kind of token word for a larger whole of which the major element is that of the salvation of men. Before considering the soteriological element in particular we may first note, as an inter-

---

* LXX: καὶ ἡ γῆ ἐξέλαμπεν ὡς φέγγος ἀπὸ τῆς δόξης κυκλόθεν. Cf. Rev. 15⁸: 'And the temple was filled with smoke from the glory of God'.

† So Ramsey, *op. cit.*, p. 39: 'It is not certain whether "light" and "glory" are both in apposition to "salvation", or whether "revelation" and "glory" go together in dependence upon "light". But the former seems more probable.'

mediate link, the use of δόξα and cognate words in the LXX to express the power and activity of God, especially as displayed in his 'wonderful acts' on behalf of his people. Some of the evidence here is to be found in the use of the adjective ἔνδοξος and the verb δοξάζω: e.g. LXX rendering of Exod. 34[10], 'I will do marvels (נִפְלָאוֹת)', LXX: 'I will do glorious things' (ἔνδοξα). Compare also Exod. 15[1], [21] where for the Hebrew 'he hath triumphed gloriously', LXX has 'he is glorified gloriously', and Exod. 15[11] where for the Hebrew נוֹרָא תְהִלֹּת 'fearful in praises' LXX has θαυμαστὸς ἐν δόξαις which might mean either 'in honours' or 'in glorious works'. There are other examples of the translation of the root פלא (or even פלה, Exod. 33[16]) by the root δοξάζω (Deut. 28[59], Job 5[9], 9[10]). ἔνδοξος also represents נוֹרָאוֹת in Deut. 10[21], עֲלִילוֹת in Isa. 12[4] and תְּהִלָּה in Isa. 48[9]. Thus it is unmistakably clear that the translators of LXX used δόξα, ἔνδοξος and δοξάζω to convey the idea of God's miraculous, awe- and worship-provoking activity on earth.

This usage is continued in the New Testament as in Lk. 13[17]: 'the multitude rejoiced for all the glorious things that were done by him'. Luke, both in the Gospel and in Acts regularly speaks of men glorifying God on account of the miracles wrought by Jesus. In Acts 3[13] it is Jesus himself who is glorified by reason of the power which continued to be exercised by his disciples.* The breadth of view thus displayed is limitless. God, all glorious in himself, is gloriously active in the world on man's behalf through the mediation of his Son to whom, to borrow a phrase from the fourth Gospel, he has given glory. After the death of Jesus the glorious activity is mediated by the disciples. For all the glorious deeds thus spread abroad God receives the glory due to him from men. It is tempting to see an obverse and a reverse in Lk. 4[6] and Jn. 17[2], [22], [24]. In Lk. 4[6] the devil offers to give to Jesus 'all this authority (ἐξουσία) and the glory of them' probably echoing Dan. 7[13] f. In Jn. 17 Jesus acknowledges the authority (ἐξουσία verse 2) and also the glory (verse 22) which he has received from God and claims to have transmitted to his followers. Perhaps it may not be thought unduly fanciful if we regard this transference of authority and glory as the sequel to the renewed temptation immediately prior to his arrest. The story of the raising of Lazarus again shows the connotation of power underlying glory. Jesus says that the death has happened for the sake of God's glory 'that the Son of God may be glorified thereby' (Jn. 11[4]) and later

---

* Luke 2[20], 5[25, 26], 7[16], 13[13], 17[15], 18[43], 23[47]; Acts 4[21], 11[18], 13[48], 21[20]. Cf. also Matt. 9[8], 15[31]; Mk. 2[12]; Jn. 11[4] (17[4]).

(verse 40) he confirms this in the words, 'Said I not unto thee, that, if thou believest, thou shouldest see the glory of God?' The glory of God manifested itself in the miracle of restoration to life. For that matter, all the miracles wrought by Jesus were manifestations of his glory (Jn. 2[11]). It is in this sense that we may perhaps interpret a number of Pauline references to the glory of God.* In some of them, however, there is room for a different exegesis: Rom. 3[23]—'Saint Paul is no doubt here alluding to the rabbinic idea that Adam was created with a ray of the divine glory on his face, and that this was one of the six things lost at the fall';† '. . . all alike feel themselves far from the bright effulgence of God's presence';‡ Rom. 6[4]—'. . . it has been suggested that Saint Paul is thinking here of the radiance of the Shekinah piercing the gloom of Sheol, an idea found amongst the Rabbis'.§

3. The saving power of God. In LXX usage this may be best illustrated by Isa. 40[5] where, for the Hebrew 'The glory of the Lord shall be revealed and all flesh shall see (it)', the LXX has 'The glory of the Lord shall be revealed and all flesh shall see the salvation of God'.|| If proof were required of the New Testament interest in salvation we might use the evidence of Lk. 3[4-6] where the evangelist quotes part of Isa. 40[3-5]. The other synoptic gospels (Matt. 3[3] and Mk. 1[3]) quote only verse 3. Luke extends the quotation to take in verse 4 and the *second* half of verse 5 in its Septuagint form. Ramsey, commenting on the omission of 5a writes:¶ 'Luke extends the quotation to include its "universalist" conclusion, but it is curious that he omits καὶ ὀφθήσεται ἡ δόξα κυρίου'. But, we may ask, is it really curious? The glory is not necessarily for *all* to see, whereas Luke is interested in salvation, and, moreover, when he uses δόξα he mostly uses it in a different sense from that of the quotation. The omission, of course, may be simply due to lapse of memory, if he was quoting from memory, but, if so, his memory was governed by his soteriological interest. In the light of what has already been said above, about the wonderworking power of the glory, he could not fail to recognize that with the revelation through Christ Jesus the exercise of God's power was for the salvation of men. In that respect the New Testament fully continues the emphasis already made by the Septuagint, namely that the glory of God is the salvation of men,

---

* Rom. 3[23], 6[4], 9[23]; Eph. 1[6, 12, 14], 3[16]; Col. 1[11, 27].
† Ramsey, *op. cit.*, p. 46, n.
‡ Sanday and Headlam, *Romans*, p. 81.
§ Ramsey, *op. cit.*, p. 31, n.
|| See *Vetus Testamentum*, I, i, 30 f.
¶ *Op. cit.*, p. 37, n.

particularly the salvation of Israel. In the New Testament this is
virtually put the other way round. The glory was first manifested
in the salvation of Israel but is now more particularly concerned
with the salvation of the Gentiles. Many of the passages which can
be used to illustrate this theme have already been used above, so
we may here limit attention to Rom. 9²³, '. . . that he might make
known the riches of his glory upon vessels of mercy, which he
afore prepared unto glory' on which it has been claimed that
8²⁸⁻³⁰ is the best commentary:* 'And we know that to them that
love God all things work together for good, even to them that are
called according to his purpose. For whom he foreknew, he also
fore-ordained to be conformed to the image of his Son, that he
might be the firstborn among many brethren: and whom he
fore-ordained, them he also called: and whom he called them he
also justified: and whom he justified them he also glorified'. We
have already noted the virtual equation of salvation, light and
glory in the Nunc Dimittis and we may perhaps see yet a further
instance in Luke's use of δόξα in his story of the acclamation of
Jesus on Palm Sunday. Whereas Mark 11⁹, ¹⁰ in citing Ps. 118²⁵ f.
transliterates the Hebrew *Hosanna*, Luke (19³⁸) has 'Blessed is the
king that cometh in the name of the Lord: peace in heaven, and
glory in the highest'. 'Glory in the highest' takes us back in one
leap to the praises of the angel host at the Annunciation (2¹⁴) and
sets the whole gospel in a framework of saving glory.†

4. The conception of God-likeness. There are a few places in
the Septuagint where the word δόξα seems to bear the meaning of
'form' or 'image'. There are four passages where this meaning
seems pretty certain: Num. 12⁸ and Ps. 17 (16)¹⁵ in both of which
it renders the Hebrew word *tᵉmunah* 'form'; Isa. 52¹⁴ where it
translates *to'ar* 'form', 'figure', 'outline' (of which 53² may be an
echo, although δόξα here renders *hadhar* quite naturally) and
finally Isa. 43⁷ where, for the Hebrew 'whom I have created for
my glory', LXX has '*in* my glory (? image) did I prepare him'.

Several New Testament passages need to be reconsidered in the
light of the possibility that δόξα may mean 'image', 'likeness' as in
these four passages in LXX. I Cor. 11⁷: 'For a man indeed ought
not to have his head veiled, forasmuch as he is the image and glory
of God: but the woman is the glory of the man'. Rom. 1²³: 'and
changed the glory of the incorruptible God for the likeness of an
image of corruptible man': this is dependent upon Jer. 2¹¹ and

---

* Sanday and Headlam, *Romans*, p. 263.
† Cf. Ramsey, *op. cit.*, p. 40. 'In the highest' offers yet another link with the LXX
in Ps. 148¹. The following passages should also be noted as evidence of the salvation
content of δόξα: Jn. 11⁴, ⁴⁰; Rom. 3²³, 6⁴; I Cor. 2⁷; Eph. 1⁶, ¹², ¹⁴, 3¹⁶; Col. 1¹¹, ²⁷.

Ps. 106 (105) [20]. Rom. 9[4]: 'whose is the adoption, and the glory, and the covenants, and the giving of the law. . . .' δόξα immediately follows υἱοθεσία and belongs more to that word in sense than it does to διαθῆκαι which follows it. Perhaps we may translate: 'whose is the sonship, and the god-likeness, and the covenants'. In II Cor. 8[23] Paul speaks of brethren who are messengers of the churches and the glory of Christ. That is to say, they are regarded as representing Christ in the churches, as being his image or likeness. Is it in this way that we must interpret the glory which Jesus received from God and passed on to his disciples (Jn. 17[22, 24])? Whether this be so or not, there are other places in the fourth Gospel where the meaning 'god-likeness' or 'divinity' best suits the context. The incarnate Word shared God's glory as an only son. He resembled his Father in glory and men beheld his glory (1[14]). He partook of the essence of Godhead before the world was (17[5]) and was able to communicate it to his immediate followers (17[22, 24]).

The use of the verb 'glorify' in John makes this the more certain. Until Jesus had been restored to his full divine state* the spirit could not be given (7[39]). The disciples did not understand all that had taken place in Jesus' lifetime, but when he was 'glorified' they remembered the things that were written (12[16]). The resumption of his divine state would follow his passion (12[23], 13[31, 32], 16[14], 17[1]).

* 'Resumed the fulness of Divinity', Plummer, *Greek Testament: St. John*, p. 179.

8

The Appearances of the Risen Christ: An Essay in Form-Criticism of the Gospels

by

C. H. DODD

THE form-critics distinguish with some unanimity two main types of narrative in the Gospels. Their nomenclature differs, but if we say that there is a concise and a circumstantial type of narrative, we shall beg no questions. There are no doubt types which do not readily fit either category; there are border-line cases, and it may not be easy, or even possible, to draw the line quite definitely; but anyone can feel the difference in character between, let us say, the story of the Withered Hand or of the Blessing of the Children, and the stories of the Epileptic Boy and the Gadarene Swine. The latter trace the course of an incident from stage to stage with heightening interest, and make it vivid to the reader by means of arresting details, and traits of character in the actors and interlocutors. In the story of the Epileptic we are shown, for example, the embarrassment of the disciples, the alarming symptoms of the boy's disease, the pathos of the father's repeated appeals, the pressure of the crowd, and the suspense created by the difficulty and apparent initial failure of the cure. In the story of the Gadarene Swine we have the horrifying description of the manacled maniac among the tombs, his grotesque fantasy about a legion of devils, the wild stampede of the pigs, the alarm of their owners, and finally the telling contrast of the restored madman, now 'clothed and in his right mind', aspiring to be one of the disciples of Jesus. All such details are a part of the art and craft of the story-teller, who, himself excited by the story he tells, seeks to kindle the imagination of his auditors. These stories are sometimes labelled 'Novellen', for which, perhaps, the best English equivalent is 'Tales'.

9

In sharp contrast to these 'tales', the 'concise' type of narrative tells us nothing which is not absolutely essential to a bare report of what happened or what was said. It observes the unities of time and place, and takes no account of development. The situation presupposed is depicted in the fewest possible words ('He went into a synagogue and taught', 'It happened that he was in the house', or the like). Then follows the word or action which set things moving ('There was a man with a withered hand', 'They brought children to him', etc.) and this evokes the significant act or word of Jesus, after which the narrative ends by indicating the response of the interlocutors, or the effect produced upon spectators. This extremely concise and economical style of narrative has been shown by comparison with similar 'forms' elsewhere, to be characteristic of folk-tradition, in which an oft-repeated story is rubbed down and polished, like a water-worn pebble, until nothing but the essential remains, in its most arresting and memorable form. And it is a form which makes it possible for the story to be told as a self-contained unit, without any necessary direct link with what precedes or follows. The inference is that narratives of this 'concise' type (which should be made to include not only 'Pronouncement-stories' or 'Apophthegms', but also stories of action, such as 'Miracle-stories', cast in a similar mould) are drawn directly from the oral tradition handed down by the corporate memory of the Church, and consequently that they belong to a deposit which was deeply cherished and constantly repeated because it was bound up with the central interests of the Christian community.

The 'Tales' on the contrary allow more room for the taste and ability of the individual narrator. They are closer to the 'unformed', or free, body of reminiscences which must have floated about in early Christian circles. That they were in consequence more exposed to alteration or 'improvement' is no doubt true; but I can see no cogent reason for accepting the view that the 'Tales' as a body represent a later, or secondary stage of the tradition.* If they are said to include 'worldly' traits, were the Christians so insulated from the world, even in the earliest days, that they had no interest in a well-told tale?

These two types of narrative which have been distinguished in

---

* Contrast the relatively 'concise' narratives of Matt. 8^{28-34}, 9^{18-26}, with the 'circumstantial' narratives of Mk. $5^{1-20, 21-43}$. Few critics would assign the former to an earlier date. If Matthew, in 9^{27-31} and 20^{29-34}, has taken over two forms of a story, the one more 'concise' and the other more 'circumstantial', there is no ground for making either the one or the other 'primary' or 'secondary': they are simply variant forms which the tradition assumed.

the evangelical records of the ministry of Jesus may be recognized also in those parts of the Gospels which follow upon the account of the discovery of the empty Tomb on Easter morning. Here we are given a number of narratives of appearances of the risen Christ to certain of His followers. Some of these narratives have a character similar to that of the 'Tales'. For example, the stories of the Walk to Emmaus in Lk. 24, and of the meal by the Sea of Galilee in Jn. 21, are full of the kind of dramatic detail, and characterization, which we have noted in such stories as those of the Epileptic Boy and the Gadarene Swine. On the other hand there are other narratives which equally clearly show the traits of such 'concise' narratives as the Withered Hand and the Blessing of the Children.

It will be well to start by analysing these 'concise' narratives. If we take, to begin with, the appearances of Christ to the Women in Matt. 28⁸⁻¹⁰, to 'the Eleven Disciples' in Matt. 28¹⁶⁻²⁰, and to 'the Disciples' in Jn. 20¹⁹⁻²¹, it is easy to recognize a common pattern, which we may analyse as follows:

A. The situation: Christ's followers bereft of their Lord.
B. The appearance of the Lord.
C. The Greeting.
D. The Recognition.
E. The Word of Command.

I shall label narratives of this type, Class I, and those of the 'circumstantial' type, Class II.

Class I

We must now examine the three examples of 'concise' narrative, to see how the common pattern is variously developed. Using the index letters employed above, we get the following scheme:

	MATT. 28⁸⁻¹⁰	MATT. 28¹⁶⁻²⁰	JN. 20¹⁹⁻²¹
A.	The Women were on the way from the Tomb to the Disciples.	The Eleven Disciples went to Galilee, to the Mountain appointed as rendezvous.	Late on Sunday evening the Disciples were gathered with closed doors [for fear of the Jews].
B.	Jesus met them.	Jesus approached.	Jesus stood in the midst.
C.	He said Χαίρετε.*	—	He said Εἰρήνη ὑμῖν.*

* Χαίρετε is the normal, everyday, greeting in Greek; εἰρήνη ὑμῖν represents the normal greeting in Hebrew or Aramaic. If we may suppose an Aramaic tradition underlying, the word might well be the same in both.

| D. | They approached, grasped His feet, and did Him reverence. | When they saw Him they did reverence, though some doubted. | The disciples were very glad when they saw the Lord. |
| E. | Go and announce to my brothers that they are to go to Galilee and they will see me there. | Go and make disciples of all nations ... | As the Father sent me, so I send you. |

It is to be observed that the bare pattern is expanded at certain points, but in so brief a way as not to alter the character of the *pericopé*. The expansions add nothing fresh, but emphasize what is already present in the pattern, though scarcely explicit. Thus, in all three *pericopae* there is at least a hint of an element of doubt or fear. In Matt. 28[17] it is explicit: 'some doubted'. In Matt. 28[10] it is implied in the words, 'Fear not'. In Jn. 20[20] nothing is said of any doubt in the minds of the disciples, but the Lord 'showed them His hands and His side', thus setting at rest, by proof tendered, a doubt which was there though unexpressed. Neither of the Matthaean *pericopae* has any such explicit tender of proof. In 28[18] the words of the Lord, 'All authority is given to me', seem sufficient to set all doubts at rest, but in 28[9] the fact that the women touch His feet may be held to carry an implicit assurance that there is a real Person before them. It is, perhaps, legitimate to say that this type of resurrection narrative carries within it, as an integral element, a suggestion that the appearance of the Lord does not bring full or immediate conviction to the beholders, who require some form of assurance: the sight of His wounds, contact with His body, or His word of authority.

Each *pericopé* works up (like the 'Paradigms' or 'Pronouncement-stories') to a significant word of the Lord. In Matt. 28[10] it is no more than an injuction to the disciples to keep their rendezvous in Galilee. In Jn. 20[21] it is a formal commission to the apostles, in its simplest form: 'As the Father sent me, so I send you'. After this a second incident is added: the 'Insufflation', accompanied by a further charge. This however is strictly not a part of the narrative of the appearance of the Lord: the gift of the Spirit is a separate incident, even though, in John's setting of the story, it follows immediately upon the Christophany. In Matt. 28[18-20] the commission is given a more extended form, covering a wider field: the mission to the nations; the ordinance of baptism; the threefold Name; the promise of the Lord's perpetual presence. Here the standard pattern of resurrection-narrative has been used to introduce a kind of 'church-order', which may be compared with the 'church-order' of Matt. 18[15-20].

Allowing, then, for these minimal supplements, we may recognize a standard pattern of resurrection-*pericopé* which is analogous to that of the 'concise' narratives in the accounts of the Ministry, and like them bears the marks of a tradition shaped, and rubbed down to essentials, in the process of oral transmission. Two of them are so formed that they are complete in themselves. 'The Eleven went to a mountain in Galilee' is just such an opening as 'They entered into a synagogue', or 'He went to Capernaum'; and 'On Sunday evening when the doors were shut where the disciples were . . .' is comparable with 'In those days when there was a great crowd and they had nothing to eat'. In Matt. 28[8] there is no similar beginning: a connexion exists with what has preceded; yet the *pericopé* might have stood alone, and comparison with Mark shows that there has in any case been some editorial manipulation hereabouts.

We must ask later whether there are any other *pericopae* which, though not reproducing the pattern in so pure a form, properly belong to the same class; but for the moment it will be better to turn to those which clearly belong to a different class, that of 'circumstantial' narratives.

Class II

Here we have two obvious examples to start with: the Walk to Emmaus in Lk. 24[13-35], and the Appearance by the Sea in Jn. 21[1-14].

1. The Walk to Emmaus is a highly-finished literary composition, in which the author, dwelling with loving interest upon every detail of his theme, has lost no opportunity of evoking an imaginative response in the reader. The pace of the story is leisurely, and the lapse of time is marked. The walk, enlivened by absorbing conversation, continues until we find that time has slipped by and the day is far spent. The return journey to Jerusalem is felt by contrast to be hurried, and interest passes at once to the reunion of the travellers with the Eleven, and the interchange of startling news. The changing moods of the two companions are convincingly rendered; their encounter with the unknown Stranger and their invitation to him to break his journey are managed with admirable naturalness; the scene of recognition at the supper-table, with the immediate disappearance of the mysterious Guest, is dramatically effective. We observe also the precise identification of persons and places: the name of one of the travellers, Cleopas; the village of Emmaus, sixty *stades* from Jerusalem. All these are no traits of a corporate tradition. They

are characteristic of the practised story-teller, who knows just how to 'put his story across'.

But further, the writer has used the captivating narrative as a setting for a comprehensive treatment of the theme of Christ's resurrection in its character of a reunion of the Lord with His followers. The dialogue is so managed that it leads up to a basic programme for the study of 'testimonies' from the Old Testament, which was the foundation of the earliest theological enterprise of the primitive Church.* The recognition of the Lord at table carries a significant suggestion to a community which made the 'breaking of bread' the centre of its fellowship. Not only so: the narrative is so contrived as to include, by means of 'flash-backs', the discovery of the empty Tomb, the angelic announcement, and the appearance of the Lord to Peter (24[22-24], [34]), so that the *pericopé* as a whole forms a kind of summary 'Gospel of the Resurrection'.

It is clear, then, that we have no mere expansion of the general pattern, but a carefully-composed statement, which, in the framework of a narrative of intense dramatic interest, includes most of what needs (from this evangelist's point of view) to be said about the resurrection of Christ. It is however worth noting that here, as elsewhere, the story begins with the disciples feeling the loss of their Lord, that Jesus takes the initiative, and that the dramatic centre of the whole incident is the ἀναγνώρισις—for it seems proper in this case to use the technical term applied by ancient literary critics to the recognition-scene which was so often the crucial point of a Greek drama.†

2. The account of the appearance of the Lord to seven disciples by the Sea of Galilee, contained in the appendix to the Fourth Gospel (Jn. 21[1-14]), is recorded within the framework of a complex narrative, covering a considerable lapse of time, from the evening of one day, all through the night, to the morning of a second day. The narrative comprises two distinct but interlocking incidents: the fishing of the disciples and breakfast on the shore. Each is told with a wealth of picturesque detail. The incidents are dramatic, the dialogue lively and in character. There is abundant detail. We learn, for example, not only that

---

* Cf. 24[46-47], Acts 26[22-3], where we have a primitive scheme for biblical research. It is scarcely accidental that Cleopas is represented as having sought in Jesus the fulfilment of the (political) hope of the ἀπολύτρωσις of Israel, and that he learns instead that it is through suffering that the Messiah must enter into a glory which is clearly not of this world.

† See the admirable discussion of forms of ἀναγνώρισις in Aristotle, *De Arte Poetica*, 16, pp. 1454b 19–1455a 21. Aristotle's distinctions of various methods of recognition may be aptly applied to the New Testament material.

Peter impulsively leapt into the sea, but that he first put on his coat; not only that a fire was kindled on the beach and breakfast prepared, but that it was a charcoal fire and that bread and fish were supplied. We are told the number of the company, five of whom are identified, the distance of the boat from shore, and the number of fish,* which strained the net but did not break it. All this is strictly unnecessary to the main theme. It is characteristic of the story-teller, and reflects his interest in the story and his mastery of his craft. The centre of interest is the recognition of the risen Lord, but here the recognition is not immediate but spread over an appreciable period. It begins with the dramatic exclamation of the beloved disciple, which impels Peter to jump overboard, but it is not complete until the party has landed and Jesus, having invited them to breakfast, distributes bread and fish. The motive of the breaking of bread appears once again, as in the Emmaus story. There is evidence in early Christian art that the meal of the seven disciples was treated, along with the Feeding of the Multitude, as a symbol of the Eucharist.

Unlike Lk. 24$^{13-35}$, the *pericopé* does not embody didactic passages in the story itself, which is a straightforward, uninterrupted, dramatic narrative. But it is made to lead up to a significant dialogue, in the course of which Peter receives his apostolic commission. Thus the motive of Matt. 28^{19} and Jn. 20^{21} reappears in a different setting. In spite of the marked contrast in form and pattern, we are still in close contact with the fundamental motives which underlie the concise narratives of Class I.

We have now established the fact of two clearly distinguishable types of resurrection narrative. We must next examine the remaining such narratives in the Gospels, which appear to be doubtful or intermediate types, to see to which of the two main classes they are more akin. They are as follows:

1. The appearance to 'the Eleven' in the Received Text of Mk. 16$^{14-15}$.
2. The appearance to 'the Eleven and those with them' in Lk. 24$^{36-49}$.
3. Mary Magdalen at the Tomb in Jn. 20$^{11-17}$.
4. Doubting Thomas. Jn. 20$^{26-29}$.

1. The so-called 'Longer Ending' of Mark must no doubt be regarded as 'spurious' in the sense that it formed no part of the

---

* Fantastic applications of *gematria* to the number are out of place, but it is probably significant that some zoologists of the period computed the number of species of fishes as 153.

Gospel according to Mark as it originally appeared; but as a rendering of the early Christian tradition of the resurrection appearances it demands consideration on its merits. On the face of it the *pericopé* conforms fairly closely to the type of Class I.

A. As the Eleven were sitting (at table) cf. Lk. 24^{30}, Jn. 21^{13}.
B. Jesus appeared to them.
C. (In place of Greeting.) He reproached them for incredulity.
D. [The Recognition is wanting, though implied.]
E. He said 'Go into all the world and preach the Gospel. . . .'

The *pericopé* thus culminates, like Matt. 28$^{16-20}$, Jn. 20$^{19-21}$, in a commission to the apostles, which is also represented in the dialogue which follows on Jn. 21$^{1-14}$; and here, as elsewhere, it develops beyond the immediate situation into a more general instruction to the Church, with the promise of divine assistance.

The question may be raised, whether this *pericopé* is based (as parts of the 'Longer Ending' almost certainly are) upon the narratives in the canonical Gospels. That the Eleven were at table when Christ appeared to them is a trait which does not appear elsewhere: in Lk. 24^{30} it is two disciples (apparently alluded to in Mk. 16^{12}), neither of them belonging to the apostolic body, to whom He is known in the breaking of bread; and in Jn. 21^{13} it is a body of seven disciples, two of whom are unidentified, to whom He distributes bread and fish. It is therefore no more likely that the author of the Longer Ending took this trait from the canonical Gospels than that it is an independent rendering of a traditional motif. The incredulity of the Eleven—or rather of some of them—is referred to in Matt. 28^{17}, and, as we have seen, it may be taken to be implied in the tendering of proofs in Jn. 20^{20}. But nowhere else does Christ, instead of greeting His disciples, reproach them. Thomas indeed is reproached, by implication, in Jn. 20$^{26-27}$, and the two companions in Lk. 24^{25}, but the (rest of the) Eleven are not implicated. Thus it is not improbable that we have, here again, a generalized trait in the current tradition finding independent expression in a particular formulation of the tradition. In short, it appears reasonably likely that Mk. 16$^{14-15}$ is to be added to Class I, as another example of the formulation of tradition in a 'concise' narrative. In that sense it would be a 'genuine' record, in spite of its dubious credentials, since it adheres closely to the general traditional pattern without slavishly following any other written account known to us.

2. Lk. 24$^{36-49}$. We have here a *pericopé* of mixed character. The

main items in the pattern of 'concise' narratives re-appear, though much modified:

A. They were talking together.
B. Jesus stood in the midst (cf. Jn. 20[19]).
C. [He said 'Peace to you', as in Jn. 20[19]; but not in the 'Western Text'.]
D. The process of recognition is greatly spun out: at first the disciples are terrified (cf. Matt. 28[10]), and think they are seeing a ghost: Jesus tenders proof by pointing to His hands and feet (cf. Jn. 20[20]) and invites them to touch Him (cf. Jn. 20[27]). They are still incredulous, and He tenders final proof by eating in their presence.
E. The concluding word of command is here replaced by a longish address consisting of (*a*) instruction regarding the use of testimonies from the Old Testament (cf. Lk. 24[26-27]), (*b*) a commission to preach (cf. Matt. 28[19]), and (*c*) the assurance of the help of the Spirit (cf. Jn. 20[22-23], Matt. 28[20], where the presence of Christ is equivalent).

It is clear that we have here an extensive working-over of the common pattern. In most of the *pericopae* that we have studied, the proofs of identity are hardly more than hinted at. Only in Jn. 20[20] are we explicitly told that Christ pointed to His wounds. In the present *pericopé* the corresponding statement (Lk. 24[40]) is not certainly part of the original text, but there is a formal pronouncement of Christ which makes the point far more emphatic: 'Look at my hands and feet [and convince yourselves] that it is I myself'. And whereas in Matt. 28[9] the women clasp the Lord's feet in a spontaneous gesture of devotion, here He bids them 'Feel me, and look; a ghost has not flesh and bones, as you see that I have'. Again, whereas in the 'Longer Ending' of Mark the Lord appears to the Eleven at table, and in the Emmaus story and the Appendix to the Fourth Gospel He is known to His followers in the breaking of bread, here He asks for food, and clinches the proof that a real Person is before them by actually eating broiled fish in their presence—a unique feature in the Gospel narratives, though it may be intended by the not quite clear statements of Acts 1[4], 10[41].

The *pericopé* is thus no longer a simple, traditional story of the appearance of the Lord: it is a piece of controversial apologetic set in the framework of such a story. The simpler narratives conveyed something of the naive, spontaneous sense of the primitive believers that something almost too good to be true has happened. Here we are aware of something different: the faith must be defended by argument, not against the natural doubts of simple people, but against a reflective and sophisticated scepticism. Yet it would not be right to class this *pericopé* with the 'Tales'. There is no detail in the narrative (with one exception) which is not strictly necessary to it as a *piéce justificatif*. The one exception is the statement that the Lord ate broiled fish.* It would have been sufficient for the narrator's immediate purpose to affirm that Christ ate food in the presence of His disciples. The added detail is the kind of trait that marks the story-teller. For the rest, it is enough to compare the details of this *pericopé* with those of the Walk to Emmaus and the Appearance by the Sea of Galilee to be convinced that it does not belong to Class II. It may perhaps best be characterized as an example of the 'concise' type of narrative in which apologetic motives have caused everything else to be subordinated to an elaborate presentation, not indeed of the ἀναγνώρισις itself, but of the grounds upon which such recognition was based.† It is certainly more remote from the original tradition, orally handed down, than the typical narratives of Class I, but the obvious work of an author has not altogether disguised the form of the tradition which underlies.

3. Jn. 20$^{11-17}$. The story of the appearance of Christ to Mary Magdalen at the Tomb on Easter morning is told briefly and with great economy of words. So far it would seem natural to include it among the 'concise' narratives of Class I. The evangelist has indeed so woven the theme of the appearance with that of the angelic announcement that the kind of opening which is normal in narratives of this class is obscured, but apart from this, it is easy enough to recognize the typical pattern.

 A. Mary stood by the Tomb.
 B. Jesus appeared.
 C. He greeted her.
 D. She recognized Him.
 E. He gave her a command.

But when we have said this, it obvious that we have something very different from the regular examples of 'concise' narrative. In spite of all the brevity and economy, the narrator has succeeded in conveying, not so much incidents as psychological traits, which are not necessary to the presentation of the main theme, but appeal

---

* Some MSS, entering into the spirit of the scene, add 'and honeycomb'.

† The production of multiple proofs of identity is a familiar accompaniment of the ἀναγώρισις motive in Greek drama, both tragic and comic.

to the imagination. Mary stood weeping. She turned suddenly round and saw a Figure whom she took for the gardener. The reader's attention is at once arrested. There follows a dialogue as richly suggestive as it is brief. The two speeches with which it ends, one from each of the interlocutors, consist of one word each: 'Mary'—'Rabbuni!' Yet they are laden with meaning. The words which Christ then utters have the character of Johannine theology, as the distinctive use of the verb ἀναβαίνειν* sufficiently indicates. In their present form, at least, they are no doubt the composition of the evangelist. But in this John has done no differently from the other evangelists, who, as we have seen, hold themselves free to expand or develop the concluding utterance of the Lord, in order to make it a vehicle for some significant summary of His purpose for His Church. Yet even so, the 'Touch me not!' has a dramatic value in the story quite independent of its theological import.

These features all tend to associate the present *pericopé* with the 'circumstantial' narratives of Class II. They are quite alien from the ethos of folk-tradition, to which belongs a certain naïveté evident in all our 'concise' narratives. There is nothing naïve here, but a reflective, subtle, most delicate approach to the depths of human experience. This story never came out of any common stock of tradition; it has an arresting individuality. We seem to be shut up to two alternatives. Either we have here a free, imaginative composition based upon the bare tradition of an appearance to Mary Magdalen, akin to that represented by Matt. 28⁹⁻¹⁰, or

---

* This verb has a special significance in the vocabulary of the Fourth Gospel, e.g. 3¹³⁻¹⁷, 6⁶²⁻⁶³. So pregnant is it that there is reason to suspect that even where, ostensibly, it means no more than the journey of a pilgrim to the Holy City, it is intended to carry overtones. If so, then it is not altogether unlikely that the message to the 'brothers' of Jesus here intentionally alludes to what He is recorded to have said to His 'brothers' in 7³⁻⁸. They have urged Him to go to Jerusalem to make a public appeal. He replies, 'My time is not yet here. . . . I am not "going up"—οὐκ (or (?) οὔπω) ἀναβαίνω—to this feast, because my time is not yet ripe'. With that in mind, we might read the message which Mary is to carry to the 'brothers' as meaning, 'My time is now ripe; I am "going up"—not to Jerusalem, but to my Father'. It is perhaps significant that it is only in the accounts of the appearance to Mary Magdalen here, and to the women (one of whom, at least editorially, is Mary Magdalen) in Matt. 28⁹⁻¹⁰, that account is taken of the 'brothers' of Christ in recounting His resurrection. In Mk. 16⁷ the message is sent to 'His disciples and Peter'. In Lk. 24³³⁻³⁵ the news is given to 'the Eleven and those with them'. In Lk. 24²² the 'we' who receive the angelic announcement from the women are indeterminate, and equally indeterminate are the expressions used in the 'Longer Ending' of Mk. 16¹⁰, ¹³. Now in the early Church the 'brothers' of Jesus were a well-recognized group (cf. I Cor. 9⁵), who long enjoyed a special position in the Church as Founder's kin. The leading member of the group was James. We know from I Cor. 15⁷ that an appearance of the Lord to James was affirmed in the primitive tradition, though it is nowhere recorded in the canonical Gospels. Is it possible (this is pure speculation) that the report of an appearance to Mary Magdalen and other women was especially associated with the tradition of James and his circle, and that this tradition was largely eclipsed by the tradition preserved in the circle of Peter and the Twelve? Cf. also Ac. 1¹⁴.

else the story came through some highly individual channel directly from the source, and the narrator stood near enough to catch the *nuances* of the original experience. It would be hazardous to dogmatize. The power to render psychological traits imaginatively, with convincing insight, cannot be denied to a writer to whom we owe the masterly character-parts of Pontius Pilate and the Woman of Samaria. Yet I confess that I cannot for long rid myself of the feeling (it can be no more than a feeling) that this *pericopé* has something indefinably first-hand about it. It stands in any case alone. There is nothing quite like it in the Gospels. Is there anything quite like it in all ancient literature?

4. Jn. 20$^{26-29}$. The story of Doubting Thomas is a pendant to the 'concise' narrative of the appearance to the Disciples in 20$^{19-21}$ (see pp. 11–13 above). It hardly forms a separable *pericopé*, for it is not fully intelligible without the connecting narrative of 20$^{24-25}$. Its theological and apologetic motives are obvious. Its broad pattern scarcely differs from that of our typical 'concise' narratives of Class I, and there is little in the way of picturesque detail (not directly demanded by the main motive) to associate it with the 'circumstantial' narratives of Class II. Thomas is hardly an individual as Mary Magdalen is; he is a type of the 'some' who 'doubted', according to Matt. 28^{17}. We should not be far wrong in saying that John has chosen to split up the composite traditional picture of a group, some of whom recognize the Lord while others doubt, and to give contrasting pictures of the believers and the doubter, in order to make a point which is essentially theological. The Thomas-*pericopé* has its nearest analogue in Lk. 24$^{36-43}$, but it is at once farther removed in character from the primitive tradition and far more delicate and perceptive in approach.

We have now surveyed all the narratives of appearances of the Lord in the canonical Gospels, which seem to have any claim to be treated as separate units of tradition, whether they belong to the class of 'concise' narratives reflecting directly the corporate tradition of the primitive Church, or to the class of 'circumstantial' narratives allowing more scope to the individual author, or whether they diverge in various ways from both types.

Outside the canonical Gospels there is little that we can bring into comparison. We have three accounts of the appearance of Christ to Paul, but none of the three constitutes a narrative unit comparable with those which provide the material of the Gospels. The narrative, in all its forms, resembles those of the Gospels in so far that the word of Christ initiates the transaction, that the recognition is the central feature, and that the scene ends with a command of Christ. But the whole situation is so different* that the comparison is of little significance.

In Rev. 1$^{10-18}$ we have an 'appearance' of Christ to John in Patmos described in apocalyptic terms, with all the usual imagery. Comparison with the Gospel narratives is not profitable, except to underline the fact that the latter are entirely free from these apocalyptic traits. Even where, as in Matt. 28$^{16-20}$, the intention is clearly to introduce the risen Christ as King of the World, seated upon the throne of His glory (cf. Matt. 25$^{31-34}$), there is no attempt to suggest that glory through the conventional symbolism of apocalypse. The Gospel narratives, indeed, are notably sober and almost matter-of-fact in tone.

Outside the New Testament there is little of which we need take note. The Gospel according to the Hebrews, so Jerome informs us, contained an account of an appearance to James. The fragments he quotes are not sufficient for any complete reconstruction of the narrative. The situation presupposed appears to be different from anything contemplated in the canonical Gospels, for the first fragment reads, 'When the Lord had given the linen cloth to the servant of the priest, He went and appeared to James'. It is then explained that James had taken a vow not to eat bread until he should have seen Jesus risen from the dead, and the narrative goes on to tell how the Lord 'took bread and broke and gave it to James the Just; and said to him "Eat your bread, my brother, for the Son of Man has risen from them that sleep" '. The association of the appearance of the Lord with a meal, and in particular with the breaking of bread, we have already noted as a feature of several of the canonical narratives, but for the rest this narrative has little in common with them. Clearly it had more of the character of a 'tale' than of the 'concise' type of narrative drawn from the common oral tradition.

The Gospel of Peter evidently contained at least one narrative of an appearance of the risen Lord. The longest extant fragment (in the Akhmim MS.) ends with what was clearly the beginning of a story about an appearance to Peter and others, who have taken their nets and gone to the sea. We can only conjecture that something similar to Jn. 21 followed, but to which type of narrative it would conform we have no means of knowing.

* The story of the conversion of Paul is avowedly an episode in the life of an individual who has a biography of his own. Of the persons recorded as having followed Jesus in His lifetime, the only one who is (in even approximately the same sense) an individual with a biography is Peter, and the appearance to Peter is nowhere described.

The material outside the canonical Gospels, then, whether in the New Testament or in apocryphal gospels, is of no great importance for our purpose, but it does give a little help, by comparison and contrast, towards defining the forms in which the tradition of appearances of the risen Lord was preserved. We should now have a fairly clear idea of these forms—of the two main types and of the range of variation from them.

It should have become clear that the skeleton outline which we noted for the 'concise' narratives of Class I remains valid, on the whole, for all the varieties: the 'orphaned' disciples (cf. Jn. 14^{18}); the appearance of the Lord, usually with some word of greeting; the process of recognition; the final word of command. All the additional material in the narratives of Class II is little more than expansion of this general outline. The expansion is usually related either to the plight of the disciples, or to the process of recognition, or to the content of the final word of command, or to two or all three of these. Of actually extraneous matter there is little or nothing.

By this I do not mean that we are to suppose the writers of the 'circumstantial' narratives to have had before them as sources existing narratives of the 'concise' type, which they set about elaborating. To attempt to extract from the story of the Walk to Emmaus or the Appearance by the Sea some original nucleus which would conform to the pattern of Class I would be an unprofitable task. I conceive Class I to represent the 'formed' tradition, stereotyped through relatively long transmission within a community, and Class II to represent a freer and more individual treatment of the still 'unformed' tradition consisting, we may suppose, of things that various people remembered to have seen or to have been told, and in their turn related in a spontaneous and unconstrained fashion. Comparison with material outside the Gospels has tended—for what it is worth when there is so little such material—to emphasize by contrast the broad, basic similarity of the Gospel narratives among themselves.

There are no further such narratives to be examined. But there are certain *pericopae*, incorporated in the portions of the Gospel dealing with the Ministry of Jesus, which have been more or less widely regarded as representing traditions referring originally to post-resurrection appearances of the Lord. It will be of interest to test such *pericopae* by the standard of the established scheme which we have recognized.

   1. Lk. 5$^{1-11}$: the miraculous Draught of Fishes and the Call of

Peter. The resemblance of this whole *pericopé* to Jn. 21 has led many critics to suggest that it was originally a post-resurrection narrative, as it is in the Fourth Gospel, and that Luke (or his immediate authority) transplanted the incident into the context of the Ministry—as others have suggested that John transplanted it in the opposite direction. There is certainly a problem here, but it is one which our form-critical study of the post-resurrection appearances does not greatly help to solve. For supposing the story to have referred, in the original tradition, to the period after the resurrection, practically every *formal* feature of post-resurrection narratives has been eliminated. There is no initial separation between Christ and His disciples, no unexpected appearance, no recognition: only the commission to Peter remains as representing the word of command with which such narratives commonly close. The features which are common to Lk. 5 and Jn. 21 (with this one exception) are those which, even as they occur in John, are not *characteristic* of post-resurrection appearances. The problem, therefore, of the true relation between these two narratives must be solved, if at all, by different methods.

2. Jn. 6¹⁶⁻²¹, Mk. 6⁴⁵⁻⁵¹: the Walking on the Water. This *pericopé*, in its Johannine form, shows many of the features of post-resurrection narratives, as will be clear if we try to apply to it our formal scheme.

A. The disciples were at sea and Jesus was not with them.
B. They saw Jesus walking on the sea.
C. (They were afraid, but) Jesus hailed them with a word of reassurance.
D. They were willing to receive Him into the boat (i.e. they recognized Him).
E. (The word of command is missing: instead, the voyage ends.)

What we have to observe is that this narrative, just as it stands, *could* have occurred among the narratives of the appearances of the risen Christ. It has some similarities to the story in Jn. 21: the disciples are at sea without Jesus; the reunion takes place (apparently) on shore—assuming, that is, that the words ἤθελον λαβεῖν αὐτὸν εἰς τὸ πλοῖον imply that their intention to take Jesus on board was not fulfilled because they found that they were already in a position to disembark.* Nor is there any feature which would

* If it were legitimate to bring Matthew into the comparison, we should observe that in both stories Peter plunges into the sea to join the Lord, Matt. 14²⁸⁻³¹, Jn.21⁷. The reason why he failed (in Matthew) is that he 'doubted', for Jesus asks, εἰς τί ἐδίστασας; cf. Matt. 28¹⁷ (of the Eleven after the resurrection) οἱ δὲ ἐδίστασαν. It is difficult not to suspect that there had been some obscure kind of contact between the two traditions at an early stage.

necessarily be out of place in a post-resurrection narrative—unless we are to understand that the disciples actually did receive the Lord into the boat; but John does not in any case say so.

So far, therefore, as the formal character of the *pericopé* goes, it would be possible to regard it as a post-resurrection narrative displaced. It conforms in the main to the type of Class I of such narratives, but the description of the violence of the wind, and the measurement of the distance from shore (cf. Jn. 21⁸), might be regarded as approximating to the form of the 'circumstantial' narratives.

It is, however, to be observed that the Marcan rendering of this incident is farther away from the type of the post-resurrection narratives. In Mark we are not presented at the beginning with the picture of the 'orphaned' disciples. Instead, we are told that *Jesus* took leave of them and went to the mountain, from which point *He saw them* in trouble, and so *went to meet* them and proposed to pass them by. So far the whole story is told from the side of Jesus, as it is in no post-resurrection narrative except that of the appearance to James in the Gospel according to the Hebrews. Again, Mark says definitely that He entered the boat, as John does not, and this would be a trait alien from the general character of the post-resurrection narratives. If we are to assume that Mark represents the earlier stage of this narrative, we should be disposed to infer that John had assimilated it to the form of the post-resurrection narratives. But does Mark, necessarily, in every case, represent a more primitive stage of tradition than John? I doubt it. There are in this case some grounds (which I will not here discuss) for believing that John is following an independent tradition which is in some respects more original than Mark's.

The conclusion we should draw, it appears, is that there is so striking a similarity between this *pericopé* and the general type of post-resurrection narrative that it may well be either (*a*) that a traditional narrative originally referring to an appearance of the risen Lord has been transplanted, whether intentionally or not, into a different context, or (*b*) that an incident which originally belonged to the Galilaean Ministry of Jesus has been influenced by the post-resurrection narratives, and has been, particularly in the Fourth Gospel, assimilated in large measure to their form. In coming to a decision between these alternatives, we should have regard to the fact that in Mark and John alike (though in different ways) the incident is firmly welded into its context, more firmly, indeed, than most of the *pericopae* belonging to the Galilaean Ministry.

3. Mk. 9^{2-8}, and parallels. The Transfiguration. Among critics of a certain school it has become a dogma that this is an antedated post-resurrection appearance of the Lord. On formal grounds this theory has no support whatever. On the contrary the *pericopé* in question contrasts with the general type of post-resurrection narrative in almost every particular. Let us go through it point by point. (To save space, I shall use the symbols 'T', for the Transfiguration-*pericopé*, and 'R' for the general type of post-resurrection narrative.)

(i) Whereas R invariably starts with the disciples 'orphaned' of the Lord and records a reunion, in T they are together throughout. If the Evangelists were making use of a form of tradition which began with a separation, it would have been easy enough to contrive a setting for it (cf. Jn. 6^{15-16}, Mk. 6^{45}).

(ii) In R, a word of Jesus always has a significant place, either as greeting, or as reproach, or as command, or as any two or all three of these. In T, He is silent throughout.

(iii) In T, a voice from heaven proclaims the status and dignity of Christ. There is no voice from heaven in R. Only in Rev. 1^{10-11} is there a voice (apparently) from heaven, drawing the seer's attention to the vision which he is to see. In the accounts of the appearance to Paul the voice from heaven is that of Christ Himself.

(iv) In T, Christ is accompanied by Moses and Elijah; in fact the 'appearance' (ὤφθη αὐτοῖς!) is that of the two personages of antiquity and not of Christ Himself (who is there all along). In R, Christ always appears alone (never accompanied, e.g., by the angels who figure as heralds of the resurrection).

(v) In T, Christ is seen by His disciples clothed in visible glory. This trait is conspicuously absent from R in the Gospels. Only in Rev. 1^{16} is He described as 'shining like the sun in his power', and this, as we have seen, stands quite apart from the Gospel tradition. Its absence is perhaps the more remarkable because a dazzling light provides the visible form in which Christ appeared to Paul according to Acts; and since Paul himself includes his own experience in the list of appearances of the risen Lord, there may well have been a temptation to colour other forms of R accordingly. If so, the evangelists have resisted the temptation.

To set over against these points of difference I cannot find a single point of resemblance. If the theory of a displaced post-resurrection appearance is to be evoked for the understanding of this difficult *pericopé*, it must be without any support from form-criticism, and indeed in the teeth of the presumption which formal analysis establishes.

4. Some critics have proposed to interpret the story of the Stilling of the Storm in Mk. 4³⁵⁻⁴¹ and parallels by a similar hypothesis, but once again the hypothesis finds no support in form-criticism. It might be held that, since the raging ocean out of all control is a symbol of primaeval chaos, and so of returning chaos at the end (cf. Lk. 21²⁵), and 'the voice of the Lord upon the waters' (Ps. 29³) is a symbol of the divine sovereignty asserted over all rebellious powers, a scene in which Christ reduces the raging sea to submission by His word is a kind of '*parusia*'-scene; and if it be true (as Dr. Lightfoot has taught us, and as I believe) that Matt. 28¹⁶⁻²⁰ is a kind of *parusia*-scene, it might be argued that the two scenes are in some sort equipollent. But it is precisely the apocalyptic imagery associated with the *parusia*-idea that is absent from Matt. 28 and present (on this hypothesis) in the Storm-*pericopé*. There is therefore no probability in the view that the Stilling of the Storm was in the original tradition a post-resurrection narrative. We may, however reckon with the possibility that the tradition which underlies this *pericopé* had at some stage been influenced by apocalyptic conceptions, and had absorbed some of their imagery.

We have now exhausted all the passages in the Gospels where the traditions regarding the appearance of Christ to His followers after His resurrection have been formed into narratives of the event, concise or circumstantial.* But there is another form in which such traditions were handed down, containing no such description of any single incident, but either offering a list of such incidents, or else summarizing the whole series in a comprehensive statement. We must now turn to passages of this kind.

Summaries and Lists

1. In Acts 1³⁻⁴ we have a comprehensive summary of all that followed the resurrection of Christ. It runs as follows: 'He presented himself to the apostles alive after his Passion by means of many proofs,† appearing to them over a period of forty days, and speaking about the Kingdom of God; and then, while he was eating with them (?),‡ he instructed them not to depart from

---

* I have not included the story of the ascension, which is of a different character. In the 'Longer Ending' of Mark (16¹⁹) and the Received Text of Lk. 24⁵¹, it is scarcely more than an editorial winding-up of the series of incidents following the resurrection. In Acts 1⁹⁻¹¹ alone it is shaped into a real narrative, the main motive of which seems to be given in the concluding words of the angelic pronouncement.

‡ The meaning of the word συναλιζόμενος is very uncertain. See Cadbury's excellent note *ad loc.*

† Ἑν πολλοῖς τεκμηρίοις: cf. Aristotle's category of recognition διὰ σημείων (proofs of identity) (*De Art. Poet*, 1. 1). Aristotle might have said that Luke used the term

Jerusalem, but to await the promise of the Father. . . .' We are here at a wide remove from the living tradition. The summary is a literary composition by an author who looks back to what he has himself written in the first volume of his work (Lk. 24).

2. It is otherwise with the summary statements contained in the outline form of apostolic *kerygma* given in certain chapters of Acts. In chapters 2, 3, and 5 we are told no more than the bare fact that the apostles are witnesses to the resurrection of Christ. But the form of *kerygma* attributed to Peter in 10$^{34-43}$ is rather more explicit: 'God raised him up on the third day, and permitted him to become visible, not to all the people, but to witnesses previously chosen by God, namely to us, who ate and drank with him after he rose from the dead; and he instructed us to proclaim to the people. . . .' Similarly in the *kerygma* attributed to Paul in 13$^{16-41}$ we read, 'God raised him from the dead, and he appeared for several days to those who had accompanied him from Galilee to Jerusalem, and who are now his witnesses to the people'. (The change from 'us' to 'those who accompanied him' is dictated by the fact that this speech is assigned to Paul and not to any of the original apostles.)

If these forms of *kerygma* in Acts may be accepted as representing with reasonable fidelity the general type of early preaching, as I believe they may, then the Gospel narratives which we have been examining would readily serve the purpose of exemplifying or illustrating the statements made in general terms in the *kerygma*. The 'concise' narratives would be precisely (in Dibelius's sense of the term) 'paradigms' for the use of the preacher.

3. In I Cor. 15$^{3-8}$ we have something still more particular. After reporting the death, burial and resurrection of Christ, Paul adds a formal list of appearances of the risen Lord to various persons:

'He appeared to Cephas,
    then to the Twelve.
After that he appeared to more than 500 brethren at once.
After that he appeared to James,
    then to all the apostles.
Last of all he appeared to me.'

This list of Christophanies Paul declares to form part of the *kerygma*, as it was set forth by all Christian missionaries of whatever rank

---

loosely, since he elsewhere distinguishes τεκμήριον from σημεῖον (e.g. *Anal. Pr.* xxvii, especially p. 70b2). But Luke perhaps knew what he was about: a τεκμήριον, in the Aristotelian use of terms, is a more *certain* kind of proof.

or tendency (15¹¹), part of the 'tradition' which he had received (15³), part of the 'Gospel' which the Corinthians had accepted when he evangelized Achaia (15¹). No statement could be more emphatic or unambiguous. In making it Paul is exposing himself to the criticism of resolute opponents, who would have been ready to point to any flaw in his credentials or in his presentation of the common tradition. Exactly how much of the list comes directly out of the common form of *kerygma* is not quite clear. The appearance to Paul himself is obviously not part of what he 'received'. The parenthetic remark that most of the 500 are still alive may well be an addition to the received formula, since it refers to a definite point of time—that, no doubt, at which the apostle was writing. The rest of the list, it appears, we must accept as part of the common and primitive tradition.*

We seem to have a further trace of the same formula in Lk. 24³⁴. Luke intends here, as we have seen, to present a kind of comprehensive 'Gospel of the Resurrection' within the framework of a single narrative. In pursuance of this intention he makes 'the Eleven and those who were with them' cap the remarkable news which Cleopas and his companion have brought from Emmaus by announcing, 'The Lord has indeed risen, and he appeared to Simon'. It is impossible to miss the close parallel with I Cor. 15⁴⁻⁵:

Lk.	I Cor.
ὅτι ὄντως ἠγέρθη ὁ κύριος	ὅτι ἐγήγερται τῇ ἡμέρᾳ τῇ τρίτῃ †
καὶ ὤφθη Σίμωνι	καὶ ὅτι ὤφθη Κηφᾷ.

It is hardly doubtful that the evangelist was familiar with a formula practically identical with that which Paul 'received' and 'transmitted'. We should not miss the significance of the fact that he is content to report the appearance to Peter in this jejune kerygmatic form. However ready he may have been to 'write up' traditional material which had reached him, and however great the skill he displays in doing so, he was clearly not willing to create a whole story out of a bare statement like this: otherwise, what a

---

* It has been suggested, and not without some plausibility, that the balanced statements, ὤφθη Κηφᾷ, εἶτα τοῖς δώδεκα· ὤφθη Ἰακώβῳ, εἶτα τοῖς ἀποστόλοις πᾶσιν, may derive from two separate lists, the one current in the tradition sponsored by Peter, the other in a tradition sponsored by James and the 'brothers' of Jesus (see note on p. 19). This is possible, but in that case we must certainly take it that the two lists had been combined before the formula was transmitted to Paul, since he expressly says that the list, as he gives it, was common to all Christian missionaries; and this was of controversial value to him, because it was representatives of the party of James who were his principal opponents within the Church.

† The Lucan form naturally does not include 'the third day', for *ex hypothesi* it is on 'the third day' that the words are spoken; the reader already knows that from the very emphatic statement 24²¹: σὺν πᾶσιν τούτοις τρίτην ταύτην ἡμέραν ἄγει.

story we might have had of the appearance of Christ which was (to judge from various indications) crucial for the whole history of the Church, but which has inexplicably failed to enter into the Gospels!

It is indeed a remarkable fact that the narratives in the Gospels are far from covering the whole ground of the list given in the Pauline *kerygma*. We might regard Matt. 28^{16-20}, Lk. 24^{36-43}, Jn. 20^{19-21}, Mk. 16^{15-14}, as representing the appearances to 'the Twelve' and to 'all the apostles', without being in a position to distinguish precisely which is which. It has been suggested that Jn. 21 represents the appearance 'to Cephas', but it is certainly not an appearance to Peter alone, perhaps not chiefly to Peter, since it is the beloved disciple who first recognizes the Lord. The appearance 'to James' appears only in an apocryphal gospel. That the appearance 'to above 500 brethren at once' may be represented by the account of Pentecost in Acts 2, the descent of the Spirit being a surrogate for the presence of the Lord (perhaps in the sense of Jn. 14^{16-19}, or even of II Cor. 3^{17}), was a suggestion which at one time commanded some favour, but it remains a pure speculation.

It appears, then, that the narratives in the Gospels were not produced as expansion, by way of commentary or 'midrash', of the list of appearances in the primitive tradition; while it is quite certain that the list was not compiled out of the Gospels. We must conclude that the list of successive appearances on the one hand, as we have it in I Cor. 15, and as it is implied in Lk. 24^{33-34}, and on the other hand the different types of narrative in the Gospels, are independent of one another, and represent alternative methods of supplementing the simple statements of the *kerygma* in its baldest form, that Christ rose from the dead and that the apostles were witnesses to the fact, since He appeared to them after His Passion.

The motives underlying the two different methods may perhaps be distinguished by examining the forms. In the Gospel narratives of Class I, which, we have reason to suppose, represent most closely the corporate oral tradition of the primitive Church, the witnesses are usually the apostolic body as a whole (whether identified as 'the Eleven', or 'the Eleven and those with them', or in other ways). Names of individuals are not mentioned. An apparent exception is Matt. 28^{9-10}, where, in view of 28^1, the reader identifies the women as Mary Magdalen and 'the other Mary' (whoever she may have been). But if we were right in isolating 28^{9-10} as an independent *pericopé*, the individual names may not have been present originally. In any case, the intention in general seems to be to present the facts as attested corporately by the apostolic body (using that term in the widest sense), in the spirit of I Jn. 1^{1-3}. Credence is invited, not on the testimony of a given witness, but on the authority of the apostolic tradition embodied in the Church. Where we have apologetic expansions of the narrative, they are directed towards meeting the objection that the apostles themselves may have had insufficient grounds for making the claims they do make. Various τεκμήρια are adduced, but these still rest upon the corporate testimony of the apostolic body. In the end it all goes back to the affirmation of that authoritative group, who say, in answer to questions raised, 'That which we have seen, that which we have heard with our ears and our hands have handled, we declare to you'. Either their word is to be accepted, upon the whole matter, or there is nothing further to be done.

In the formula of I Cor. 15, on the contrary, there seems to be an attempt to meet a possible objector to some extent by defining more precisely the source of information, so as to put him (in theory at least) in a position to question the witness. There can hardly be any purpose in mentioning the fact that most of the 500 are still alive, unless Paul is saying, in effect, 'the witnesses are there to be questioned'. And it is not the same thing to appeal to the authority of 'the Eleven and those with them' or the like, and to mention Cephas and James as individuals. Cephas was well-known to the Corinthians, whether directly or not; James was a name to conjure with among many who belittled Paul himself. Certainly Paul appeals to the consensus of all Christian missionaries: this is the same appeal to a generalized apostolic authority that underlies the forms of 'concise' narrative in the Gospels. But it is of advantage to him that he can adduce an agreed statement which particularizes the authorities.

In the 'circumstantial' narratives of the Gospels also individual names are introduced; but the motive here is the enrichment of the story rather than the strengthening of the evidence. The introduction of names into a story which was originally anonymous is noted by the form-critics in general as a feature of 'legend'. It by no means follows that the names are unhistorical, but it is probably true, here as in analogous cases, that the main reason why the names are given is that they lend greater interest and vividness to the narrative. To recognize this is to underline the entirely different purpose of the mention of names in the *kerygmatic* formula of I Cor. 15.

4. There is one more passage which should be placed alongside Paul's list for comparison—the 'Longer Ending' of Mark, part of which we have already considered. Mk. 16¹⁴⁻¹⁵ seemed on examination to be a fairly typical example of a 'concise' narrative based upon the common oral tradition. Yet it appears here as the climax of what looks like a list not altogether dissimilar from that of I Cor. 15:

> 'He appeared first to Mary Magdalen . . .
> After this he appeared to two of them as they were journeying into the country . . .
> Later, he appeared to the Eleven themselves as they sat at table. . . .

The sequence, πρῶτον . . . μετὰ δὲ ταῦτα . . . ὕστερον, recalls the εἶτα . . . ἔπειτα . . . ἔπειτα . . . εἶτα . . . ἔσχατον πάντων of I Cor. 15³⁻⁸. We must therefore examine the passage more closely.

If this was a list analogous to that of I Cor. 15, it must have had a rather fuller form, since in each case we are told something more than the bare fact that the Lord appeared to such-and-such a person. But apart from that, the list does not seem calculated to serve the precise purpose which we inferred to have been in view in the construction of the Pauline list. The latter, as we saw, reinforces the statements of the *kerygma* by particularizing the sources of evidence, especially by singling out the great names of Peter and James. In Mk. 16 the appearance to 'the Eleven' may be taken to represent what I have called the generalized authority of apostolic tradition. It goes no further. The appearance to two unidentified persons on a journey to some unnamed place adds nothing to the evidence, for the purpose in view. Only Mary Magdalen is specified by name. It is doubtful whether for the wider public her name would carry much weight. Indeed the writer himself goes on to say that 'those who had been with Him' did not believe a word she said. There would seem to have been some reluctance on the part of the Church or its spokesmen, to place much weight upon her evidence. That is perhaps why her name does not figure in the official list adopted, as Paul declares, by all Christian missionaries. It does not appear, then, that the list in Mk. 16 was shaped by the same motives as that given by Paul.

Then should we conclude that the appearances to Mary Magdalen in 16⁹⁻¹¹ and to the two companions in ¹²⁻¹³ are, like the appearance to the Eleven in 16¹⁴⁻¹⁵, forms of 'concise' narrative in a highly concentrated form (though scarcely more concentrated

31

than Matt. 28$^{9-10}$)? Against that view there are the following considerations: (*a*) the narratives, though extremely brief, contain details not essential to the main theme, similar in character to those which appear in the 'circumstantial' narratives: the description of Mary Magdalen as one 'out of whom he had cast seven devils'; the Eleven 'lamenting and weeping' (an unparalleled trait); the appearance of the Lord 'in another form'; (*b*) the longest and most emphatic parts of these little stories are those which describe, not the appearance of the Lord itself, nor the recognition of Him by His followers, but the reporting of the incident to others and its unfavourable reception (16$^{10-11,13}$). There is therefore no such specific formative motive at work as we can recognize elsewhere. It is only when we look at the list as a whole that a possible guiding idea may be discerned. The whole stress is laid upon the appearance to the Eleven, which serves to introduce the Lord's command to His Church (which in some MSS. is greatly expanded), His ascension, and the summary of the early Christian mission which concludes the passage. The two incidents briefly touched upon in 16$^{9-13}$ serve only to introduce the main incident, and to exhibit the unbelief with which the reports of Mary Magdalen and the two companions are received, as a foil to the faith of the Church. The contrast of belief and unbelief is in fact a prominent theme of 16$^{14-20}$.

While we saw no definite reason to conclude that the narrative in 16$^{14-15}$ was derived from any of our canonical gospels, it does appear that verses $^{9-13}$ may be derivative. Mary Magdalen 'out of whom he had cast seven devils', is almost verbally after Lk. 8^2. The reception of her report recalls the statement of Lk. 24^{11} that the report which she and other women brought about the empty Tomb was similarly received: 'They thought they were talking nonsense, and disbelieved them' (ἠπίστουν αὐταῖς in Lk., ἠπίστησαν in Mk.). With these echoes in mind, we shall be disposed to think that the appearance to the two companions came out of Lk. 24 rather than directly out of oral tradition. The appearance to Mary Magdalen however cannot itself have come from Luke. It may have been derived from John or from Matthew (by singling out one of the two women of whom Matthew speaks). The 'Longer Ending' does not otherwise show any clear mark of dependence on John, while the command to go and preach to all the world, and the institution of baptism (16$^{15-16}$), resemble Matt. 28^{19} fairly closely. The record of the ascension, on the other hand (16^{19}), being entirely in biblical language (II Kgs. 2^{11} LXX + Ps. 110^1), does not appear to depend on Acts 1^9.

The most probable conclusion seems to be that the author of the 'Longer Ending' is in the main composing freely out of current tradition, but drawing upon Matthew and Luke for part of his material.* As a summary of what happened after the discovery of the empty Tomb it carries no independent authority.

We may now summarize the conclusions to which the investigation seems to have led, and draw some corollaries.

1. The earliest extant form in which the appearance of the risen Lord are reported is an ordered list of such appearances to specified individuals and groups, which was included in the *kerygma* of the early Church as it was communicated to Paul. Its purpose seems to have been to provide interested enquirers with a guaranteed statement of the sources of evidence upon which the affirmations of the *kerygma* were grounded.

2. Perhaps equally early in origin, though transmitted to us in a later document, are the bare statements contained in other forms of the *kerygma*, to the effect that the apostles are witnesses to the resurrection, inasmuch as Christ appeared to them alive after death. Here there is no attempt to deploy the sources of evidence: the statement is made, like the *kerygma* as a whole, upon the collective authority of the apostolic body.

3. In the Gospels there is a series of concise *pericopae*, bearing the marks of a corporate oral tradition, in which the appearances of Christ to individuals and groups are briefly described. The points upon which emphasis is laid are (*a*) the recognition of the Lord by His disciples, almost always with the implication that such recognition was neither immediate nor inevitable; and (*b*) the word of command given by Christ to His followers. These two elements are apt to be expanded in more-developed examples of this type of *pericopé*, (*a*) by the tender of proofs of the reality of the Person who appeared, and of His identity with the Crucified, and (*b*) by the introduction of further material appropriate as a final charge to the apostles. These *pericopae* do not mention individual names. They put forward their statements, like the forms of *kerygma* under 2, upon the collective authority of the apostolic body, and may well have served as 'paradigms' or illustrative examples for preachers. They show no sign of having been derived from the authorized list of appearances under 1. Their

---

* For another example of the combination of material drawn from a canonical gospel with an independent rendering of oral tradition I should wish to refer to the fragment of an unknown gospel in Egerton Papyrus 2, the composition of which may well be nearly contemporary with that of the 'Longer Ending' of Mark; see my argument in the *Bulletin of the John Rylands Library*, vol. 20, No. 1, Jan. 1936. But not all critics take that view of Eg. Pap. 2.

formative idea we may take to be: The Christ who died is the living Guide and Ruler of His Church; Matthew adds, the Lord of heaven and earth.

4. There are other *pericopae* in the Gospels which give a more circumstantial narrative of the appearances. The added matter is almost entirely of the nature of dramatic or picturesque detail, especially in the presentation of the recognition of the Lord by His disciples. A marked feature is the introduction of a common meal at which the risen Lord 'breaks bread' for His disciples. The resurrection is thus associated with the eucharistic ideas and practice of the early Church. For the rest, it cannot be said that these circumstantial narratives alter the perspective or the implications of the briefer type of narrative.

5. Negatively, the Gospel narratives, of whatever type, are entirely free from the conventional apparatus of apocalypse. There are no supernatural signs accompanying the appearances,* and the risen Christ communicates no revelations of the secrets of the other world as He is often made to do in later apocryphal works. Even though in Matthew Christ appears as Lord of heaven and earth, His lordship is not signified by any kind of portent: His word is sufficient.

6. For some other forms of tradition which enter into the Gospels the form-critics have been able to adduce analogies from other fields, as, for instance, the Epidaurus inscriptions for some of the healing-stories, and rabbinic aphorisms and dialogues for didactic *pericopae*. It is more difficult to find any such analogies for the post-resurrection narratives. In certain respects the more circumstantial narratives recall accounts of theophanies in the Old Testament and in profane literature, especially those in which at first the Visitant is not recognized for what He is, but when recognized imparts some solemn instruction, promise or command (e.g. Gen. 18, Jud. 6, 13). But the points of difference are more numerous and striking than the points of resemblance. In particular, in theophany-stories proof is usually offered of the supernatural or divine character of the Visitant: in the Gospel stories the proofs tend to show His real humanity (He has flesh and blood, bears wounds in His body, even eats human food). In some ways we might find a nearer analogy in the ἀναγνώρισις-scenes of Greek drama, but again the analogy is by no means close.

---

* It is, of course, true that the risen Christ is visible or invisible at will, and that closed doors are no bar to His entrance. This feature is a necessary *datum* of the situation, and though it is, no doubt, abnormal or praeternatural, it has little in common with the stuff of apocalyptic visions. With the narrative of the Ascension we pass into the sphere of apocalypse.

surely intended to be understood as contrasts to events in the life.

7. It has been not unusual to apply the term 'myth' somewhat loosely to the resurrection-narratives of the Gospels as a whole. The foregoing investigation will have shown that, so far as the narratives of the appearances of the risen Christ are concerned, form-criticism offers no ground to justify the use of the term. The more circumstantial narratives certainly include traits properly described as legendary,* but 'legend' and 'myth' are different categories, and should not be confused. *Formally*, there is nothing to distinguish the narratives we have been examining from the 'Paradigms' and other concise narratives on the one hand, and the 'Novellen', or 'Tales', on the other, which occur in other parts of the Gospels, and they merit the same degree of critical consideration, not only in their aspect as witnesses to the faith of the early Church, but also as ostensible records of things that happened.

---

* The term 'legend', as a formal category, does not carry any necessary judgement about the factual truth of the story. It refers to a manner of telling the story. The relation of legend to fact is different from that of (let us say) a chronicle or a letter from someone concerned, but the relation exists, and should be investigated.

The Central Section of St. Luke's Gospel

by

C. F. EVANS

IN the Westcott and Hort text of the New Testament, in which the editors made their division of the text after 'examining carefully the primary structure of each book', a small space is left after Lk. 9⁵⁰ and again after 13³⁵ and 17¹⁰, presumably on the supposition that more than one journey to Jerusalem is being described; a similar space is left after 19⁴⁸ to distinguish the teaching given on these journeys from that given in Jerusalem itself. The larger space used by Westcott and Hort to indicate major divisions is found in this Gospel after the Preface, after the Birth Narratives, and after 21³⁸ to mark the beginning of the Passion. It is also found after Acts 1¹⁴ to denote the period brought to a close by the Ascension. It is questionable, however, whether this arrangement does justice to the importance in this Gospel of the section beginning at Lk. 9⁵¹,* an importance which is made clear both by the manner in which its material is presented, and by the style of its opening sentence.

Ἐγένετο δὲ ἐν τῷ συμπληροῦσθαι τὰς ἡμέρας τῆς ἀναλήμψεως αὐτοῦ καὶ αὐτὸς τὸ πρόσωπον ἐστήρισεν τοῦ πορεύεσθαι εἰς Ἰερουσαλήμ, καὶ ἀπέστειλεν ἀγγέλους πρὸ προσώπου αὐτοῦ. (Lk. 9⁵¹⁻⁵².)

These verses are surely as remarkable as any in this Gospel. Bengel comments upon them, 'Instabat adhuc passio, crux, mors, sepulcrum: sed per haec omnia ad metam prospexit Jesus, cujus sensum imitatur stilus Evangelistae'. The construction of ἐγένετο with ἐν τῷ and the infinitive followed by καὶ (αὐτός) and a verb in the indicative, which is almost peculiar to Luke in the New Testament, is characteristic of the narrative style of the LXX.

* Wherever it is rightly held to end.

Συμπληροῦσθαι is not generally used with a temporal sense,* and is perhaps chosen here as a sonorous word fitting an important moment; it recurs with this meaning only, and perhaps significantly, in the almost identical words (ἡμέραν for ἡμέρας) with which the story of Pentecost is introduced. Στηρίζειν τὸ πρόσωπον is an expression confined to the LXX, where it is always followed by ἐπί with the meaning 'to set against', 'to oppose'; its use with the infinitive of purpose is called by Dalman 'an inexact application of a Hebraism known to him (Luke) through the Greek Old Testament'.† The corresponding phrase in 9⁵³, τὸ πρόσωπον αὐτοῦ ἦν πορευόμενον εἰς 'Ιερουσαλήμ Dalman also calls 'a Hebraism incorrectly used, and incapable of imitation in Hebrew'. The expression ἀπέστειλεν ἀγγέλους πρὸ προσώπου αὐτοῦ is strongly biblical, and it suggests that something more is intended by the words ὥστε ἑτοιμάσαι αὐτῷ than simply the preparation of a lodging, just as the similar expression at 10¹, which is modelled upon it and looks back to it (cf. ἑτέρους ἑβδομήκοντα), is more than a preface to a mission charge, since in this latter case the Lord is himself to follow on behind the missionaries, and to come in person to all the places to which they have been sent in advance (οὗ ἤμελλεν αὐτὸς ἔρχεσθαι). Taken together, 9⁵¹⁻⁵³ and 10¹ suggest a situation analogous to that of Moses who, in leading Israel towards the Promised Land, sends out one emissary from each tribe 'to search the land for us, and bring us word again of the way by which we must go up, and the cities unto which we shall come', and who appoints seventy elders to receive of his spirit and to share his work.‡

Stylistically, therefore, the aim of the writer seems to have been to sound an especially solemn note by an unusually strong concentration of biblical idioms. The most important word, however, has still to be considered. Using a turn of phrase which he has employed elsewhere, the evangelist here characterizes a period of time and its fulfilment by reference to the event which is being expected throughout that period and which brings it to a close.§ The remainder of what is to be narrated concerning the days of

* MM give instances in the papyri of the verb and the noun used in a temporal sense. In the LXX there are three cases of the noun and one of the verb, all of the completion of the seventy years captivity in Babylon.

† *The Words of Jesus*, p. 31. But cf. IV Bas. 12¹⁷: ἔταξεν 'Αζαὴλ τὸ πρόσωπον αὐτοῦ ἀναβῆναι ἐπὶ 'Ιερουσαλήμ. J. Starcky in a study of the phrase in *Recherches de Science Religieuse*, Tome xxxix, 197 ff., argues that Luke altered the construction deliberately, perhaps with reference to Isa. 50⁷: ἔθηκα τὸ πρόσωπόν μου ὡς στερεὰν πέτραν, in order to express the firm resolution of Jesus in going to Jerusalem, and that Jerome's rendering 'obfirmavit faciem suam ut iret Jerusalem¹ has caught the right meaning.

‡ Deut. 1²¹⁻²⁵; Num. 11¹⁶ ff.,

§ Cf. Lk. 1⁵⁷, 2⁶, ²¹, ²², Acts 2¹. 2*Vide* Zahn, *Kommentar* on Lk. 9⁵¹.

the Lord's flesh is placed under the sign manual of his ἀνάλημψις. How is ἀνάλημψις to be understood here? Not of the act of ascension simply, for this would require ἡμέραν rather than ἡμέρας, as in Acts 1²¹⁻²² (cf. Acts 2¹). The word is absent from the LXX, but the corresponding verb is used there, not only with its customary senses, but also as a semi-technical term, synonymous with μετατιθέναι, in connexion with the translation of certain Old Testament saints to heaven before death.* The themes of translation, assumption and heavenly journeys, which are found so frequently in ancient literature in general, became especially common in Jewish apocalyptic, and in the opinion of Charles the Greek word which lies behind the Ethiopic, Syriac, Slavonic and Latin versions in which such apocalypses have been preserved is ἀναλαμβάνειν.† In the New Testament the verb is used with this meaning three times in Acts, in the longer ending of Mark, and at I Tim. 3¹⁶, the noun only in the Lucan passage under discussion. Its earliest occurrence is in Ps. Sol. 4²⁰, where Ryle and James explain its use in the neutral sense of 'death' by the desire of the translator to render the double meaning of 'uplift' and 'remove' in the original Hebrew word, and they argue for a date early in the first century A.D. for these Psalms precisely on the grounds that no translator could have used the word in such a sense in the later years of the century, for by that time it had become a technical term for the assumption of the blessed.‡ An instance of the transition from the sense of 'death' to that of 'assumption' is probably to be seen in the Latin fragment of the Assumptio Moysis. In the opinion of Charles and others this fragment forms part of an original Testament of Moses (Διαθήκη Μωυσέως) written between A.D. 7 and 29, in which Moses predicts to Joshua the future history of Israel as far as the reign of Herod, instructs and encourages him, and appoints him as his successor. Moses is here represented as dying an ordinary death (1¹⁵), and the Latin translator rendered ἀνάλημψις in the Greek version by 'mors'. Later this work was combined with an Ἀνάλημψις Μωυσέως, which was concerned with the circumstances of the mysterious death of Moses, and which came to give its name to the whole book. The editor who joined the two works together rendered ἀνάλημψις by 'assumptio'.* The

* Of Elijah—IV Bas. 2¹¹: ἀνελήμφθη Ἠλειού . . . . ὡς εἰς τὸν οὐρανόν. So too I Macc. 2⁵⁸. Ecclus. 48⁹: ὁ ἀναλημφθεὶς ἐν λαίλαπι πυρός. Of Enoch—Ecclus. 49¹⁴: καὶ γὰρ αὐτὸς ἀνελήμφθη ἀπὸ τῆς γῆς. Such men are described in IV Ezra 6²⁶ as 'qui recepti sunt homines, qui mortem non gustaverunt a nativitate sua'.

† *The Apocalypse of Baruch*, p. 73. Gr. En. 12¹ has ἐλήμφθη of Enoch.

‡ Cf. also Test. Levi 18³—but the word is not in all the MSS. *Irenaeus, Adv. Haer.*, I, ii, and III, xii, 5, show that the word has become an ecclesiastical term for the Ascension.

* Charles, *Apoc. and Pseud.*, ii, 408. Kautzsch, *Pseud.*, p. 312, thinks that the strange

date at which such a combination was made—if indeed it was made*—is uncertain, but if the dispute over the body of Moses referred to in Jd. 9 is derived from this source, then it will have taken place prior to the writing of that epistle, as there are fairly clear reminiscences of the Διαθήκη Μωυσέως in the same epistle. It is thus possible that Luke was acquainted with the book in its final form. There is a striking resemblance between the statement in the speech of Stephen in Acts 7[36]: οὗτος ἐξήγαγεν αὐτοὺς ποιήσας τέρατα καὶ σημεῖα ἐν γῇ Αἰγύπτῳ καὶ ἐν ἐρυθρᾷ θαλάσσῃ καὶ ἐν τῇ ἐρήμῳ ἔτη τεσσαράκοντα and Ass. Moys., iii, II: Moyses . . . qui multa passus est in Aegypto et in mari rubro et in heremo annis xl,† and there are other similarities between the Assumptio and Luke-Acts.‡ If the evangelist knew the work in its composite form, then he will have been acquainted with a document which under the title of 'Ανάλημψις comprised not only the passage of its subject from earth to heaven by a mysterious death, but also a series of addresses and injunctions delivered in Amman beyond Jordan to his successor whom he is leaving behind. This might go some way towards explaining why the evangelist, after an introduction in solemn biblical tones, chose to place under the head of an approaching ἀνάλημψις not only the Passion, Resurrection and Ascension of Jesus in or near Jerusalem, but also a mass of teaching delivered in the course of a journey thither.

If this estimate of Lk. 9[51-53] is at all acceptable, then the problem presented by the whole section Lk. 9[51]-18[14] becomes particularly acute. This section makes up almost one-third of the entire Gospel, a good deal of its material is not found elsewhere, and it contributes not a little to the total picture which emerges from Luke-Acts. Yet, the very variety of names given to it—the Travel Document, the Peraean Section, the Samaritan Document, etc.— shows that commentators have been at a loss what to make of it. It is the perplexity of the harmonist, as A. Wright observed, 'Our contention is', he wrote, 'that it is entirely unchronological, being a collection of undated materials. . . . How completely amorphous this vast aggregate is, may be seen by an examination of the notes of place and time which it contains. . . . They practically amount,

---

tradition preserved in *Clem. Alex. Strom.*, vi, 15, *Origen, In Jos. Hom.*, ii, 1, and elsewhere, of the appearance to Joshua and Caleb of a double Moses, the one in company with the angels and the other a dead body being buried in the mountains, is due to the two conceptions, death and assumption, standing side by side.

* Burkitt, *Jewish and Christian Apocalypses*, p. 39, seems to regard the lost book as having been a single work from the beginning. Cf. also M. R. James, *The Lost Apocrypha of the Old Testament*, pp. 49 ff.

† So Jackson and Lake, *Beginnings of Christianity*, vol. iv, pp. 77–8.

‡ With Ass. Moys., i, 4, cf. Lk. 9[31]; with i, 7, cf. Acts 2[22]; with i, 11, cf. Acts 10[36]; with i, 15, cf. Lk. 9[51]; with i, 18, cf. Lk. 19[44]; with viii–ix, cf. Lk. 21[5 ff].

as Tischendorf saw, to the admission that in this part of his work St. Luke had no guide to arrangement, as indeed he had none when he left St. Mark, but had (sic) little real knowledge of topography and chronology except for occasional help from living spectators"* The problem is admirably stated by Streeter: 'The section 9^{51}–18^{14} is the centre and core of the Third Gospel. . . . The only safe name by which one can call it is the "Central Section"—a title which states a fact but begs no questions'.†

The material of the section is undoubtedly heterogeneous. The evangelist will probably have obtained it from various sources, and he has to exercise all his editorial ingenuity to make a connected sequence out of originally independent *pericopae*. Thus in 14$^{1-24}$ there is a cure of a man with dropsy, a parable about taking the lower place, a charge to invite the poor to feasts, and the parable of the Great Supper. Luke has linked them together by having the cure performed during a meal with a Pharisee, the first parable addressed to the guests (τοὺς κεκλημένους), the charge delivered to the host (τῷ κεκληκότι), and the second parable spoken in reply to a remark from one of his fellow diners (τις τῶν συνανακειμένων). Again, in 17^{5}–18^{8} the request of the apostles for their faith to be increased, the healing of the ten lepers, a little apocalypse, and the parable of the Importunate Widow are in some measure held together by the theme of faith in the Son of Man—'if ye have faith as a grain of mustard seed' (17^{6}), 'thy faith hath made thee whole' (17^{19}), 'ye shall desire to see one of the days of the Son of Man' (17^{22}), 'when the Son of Man cometh, will he find faith on the earth?' (18^{8}). But these provide only a tenuous and intermittent unity and there is something unsatisfactory in the view that so skilful a worker as Luke, after introducing his material with so weighty a sentence as 9$^{51-52}$, could do no better with it than this.‡ The question, therefore, arises whether this sentence was not intended by the evangelist to provide the main clue to the whole of this section of his Gospel.

Burkitt drew attention in his study of Jewish and Christian apocalypses to the resemblances between the expectations of the author of the Assumption of Moses and Christian expectations as preserved in the Synoptic Gospels. 'The Woes on the Pharisese

* *St. Luke's Gospel in Greek*, p. xix. † *The Four Gospels*, p. 203.

‡ A recent monograph, *L'Évangile des Voyages de Jésus*, by L. Girard, contains an exhaustive discussion of the chronological and philological problems of this section, and a full bibliography. The author's own solution is that Luke constructed a 'fourth Gospel' of the journeys of Jesus to Jerusalem, which is intended to be read alongside, and not subsequent to, the Galilean ministry. This seems an artificial way of saving the section for the purposes of chronological harmonization, and almost amounts to an admission that these chapters cannot be understood naturally in terms of chronology or of a Gospel harmony.

and Sadducees, the great Tribulation, the πειρασμός or trial
which lies before the faithful, the hopelessness of resisting evil,
the abomination of desolation in the holy place, the flight of the
Saints into the wilderness—all the eschatology of the Gospel
except the Central Figure—it is all implied in the Assumption of
Moses. And more than this: it is not only in the *mis-en-scène* that
we find the analogy. It is in the sacred drama also. The voluntary
death of the holy Taxo has a redeeming value, for it hastens the
End; it is effective, it acts like the death of the son of the Lord of
the Vineyard in the Parable of the Wicked Husbandmen'.* If a
Pharisaic Quietist of the first century A.D. could thus set out his
hopes and teaching in a book which professes to be a supplement
to Deuteronomy,† is it not possible that a Christian evangelist,
for whom the identification of Jesus with 'the prophet like unto
Moses' was axiomatic, and for whom also there was at one and the
same time both a correspondence and a contrast between the Gospel and the Law, has selected and ordered his material with a
view to presenting it as a Christian Deuteronomy? It was this
possibility which suggested a comparison between Lk. 9⁵¹–18¹⁴
and Deuteronomy in the manner set out in detail below.

Deut. 1. Israel journeys under Moses from Horeb ('you have dwelt long enough in this mountain') to the borders of the Promised Land beyond Jordan. The Lord has set the land πρὸ προσώπου ὑμῶν, you are not to fear. Moses chooses twelve men, and sends them, ἀποστείλωμεν προτέρους ἡμῶν to search the land, and bring word of τὴν ὁδὸν δι' ἧς ἀναβησόμεθα ἐν αὐτῇ, καὶ τὰς πόλεις εἰς ἃς εἰσπορευσόμεθα εἰς αὐτάς. The spies return with the fruit of the land, saying that it is a good land.

Lk. 10¹⁻³, ¹⁷⁻²⁰. Jesus and his disciples journey from the Mount of Transfiguration to Jerusalem via Samaria. He appoints Seventy in addition to the Twelve, and sends them πρὸ προσώπου αὐτοῦ εἰς πᾶσαν πόλιν καὶ τόπον οὗ ἤμελλεν αὐτὸς ἔρχεσθαι.

The harvest is plenteous but the labourers are few. They are sent as sheep in the midst of wolves. They return with news of their success.

Deut. 2–3²². Moses sends messengers to Sihon and Og with words of peace. 'Thou shalt sell me food for money, that I may eat; and give me water for money, that I may drink: only let me pass through on my feet' (2²⁸). But their hearts are hardened; they reject the embassy and are destroyed. 'There was not a city too high for us' (2³⁶, 3⁵). Let Israel see

Lk. 10⁴⁻¹⁶. The Seventy are sent with a message of peace. They are to eat and drink what is set before them. If rejected they are to wipe off from their feet the dust of that city. Destruction like that of Sodom, Tyre and Sidon for Chorazin, Bethsaida and lofty Capernaum in the day of judgement, because they did not repent and acknowledge the advent of

* *Jewish and Christian Apocalypses*, p. 40.
† 'The Testament of Moses which he commanded . . . in the prophecy that was made by Moses in the book Deuteronomy.' *Ass. Moys.*, i, 5. But there is doubt as to the original wording of the opening of the book—see Charles, *ad loc*.

what the Lord, who fights for them, has done to these two kings (3²¹).

God's kingdom when they saw the mighty works, but in rejecting his messengers rejected τὸν κύριον.

Deut. 3²³–4⁴⁰. Moses ἐν τῷ καιρῷ ἐκείνῳ, as the servant to whom the Lord has shown his power, prays to the Lord, who is the supreme God in heaven and in earth. Yet he is refused entry into the Promised land. As the Lord's authoritative teacher, and the mediator between him and the people, he urges them to keep the statutes which constitute ἡ σοφία ὑμῶν καὶ ἡ σύνεσις ἐναντίον πάντων ἐθνῶν, (4⁶), and which mark them as a nation to which God has drawn nigh. They are a people which has heard the voice of God and seen his fire (4³⁴⁻³⁶).

Lk. 10²¹⁻²⁴. Jesus ἐν αὐτῇ τῇ ὥρᾳ as the Son who is the unique mediator and revealer of God, gives thanks to the Father, κύριε τοῦ οὐρανοῦ καὶ τῆς γῆς, that he has concealed these things from σοφῶν καὶ συνετῶν and revealed them to babes (cf. Deut. 1³⁹: the babes go into the Promised Land with Joshua ('Ιησοῦς)). He blesses the disciples for what their eyes have seen and their ears heard.

Deut. 5–6. The Decalogue, summarized in the Shema (6⁵). Addressing Israel as a people with whom the Lord has spoken face to face, Moses rehearses the commandments so that they may observe to do them, and exhorts them to a complete devotion to God, ἵνα . . κληρονομήσῃς τὴν γῆν (6¹⁸), ἵνα ζῶμεν (6²⁴).

Lk. 10²⁵⁻²⁷. In reply to the lawyer's question τί ποιήσας ζωὴν αἰώνιον κηρονομήσω: Jesus asks 'What is written in the Law?' The Shema is combined with Lev. 19¹⁸. (Deut. also lays great stress on the love of ὁ πλησίον.)

Deut. 7. Destroy the foreigner and have no mercy on him (οὐδὲ μὴ ἐλεήσητε αὐτούς, 7²), lest he corrupt you from the true worship of the one God. If you do this the Lord will keep you from all evils, and will lay them on those who hate you (7¹⁵).

Lk. 10²⁹⁻³⁷. The Parable of the Good Samaritan. The foreigner who is corrupt in worship shows mercy (ὁ ποιήσας τὸ ἔλεος μετ' αὐτοῦ, 10³⁷) to a Jew who has fallen upon evil.

Deut. 8¹⁻³. Man does not live by bread only but ἐπὶ παντὶ ῥήματι τῷ ἐκπορευομένῳ διὰ στόματος θεοῦ.

Lk. 10³⁸⁻⁴². Mary and Martha. Mary who sits at the Lord's feet to hear his word (ἤκουεν τὸν λόγον αὐτοῦ, 10³⁹) has chosen the one thing needful, rather than Martha who is busied with food.

Deut. 8⁴ to end. On the way to the Promised Land the Lord has dealt with Israel as a father deals with a son, so that they might learn to walk in his ways and to fear him. They have not lacked, and are being led to a land ἐφ' ἧς οὐ μετὰ πτωχίας φάγῃ τὸν ἄρτον σου (8⁹). They are to beware lest they forget the Lord so as not to observe his commandments. It was he who humbled them ἵνα ἐκπειράσῃ σε, and brought them through the terrors of the wilderness to do them good at their latter end.

Lk. 11¹⁻¹³. The Paternoster. The prayer of sons to the Father for the hallowing of his name, the coming of his kingdom, the doing of his will, for sufficiency of bread, forgiveness of sins and preservation from πειρασμός The parable of the Importunate Friend who is supplied because of his need. Which of you that is a father shall his son ask a loaf, and he give him a stone? . . . If ye, being evil, know how to give good gifts to your children, how much more shall your heavenly Father . . .?

Deut. 9¹-10¹¹. An address to Israel which is about to go over Jordan to take possession of fierce nations ἰσχυρότερα μᾶλλον ἢ ὑμεῖς (9¹), the sons of Anak. This is only possible because the Lord goes before you. It is not for your righteousness that he does this, but for the impiety (ἀσέβειαν 9⁵) of these nations. You are a stiff-necked people which has provoked the Lord continuously from the deliverance out of Egypt until the present day by falling away into idolatry—at Horeb where the tables of stone were written ἐν τῷ δακτύλῳ τοῦ θεοῦ (9¹⁰), at Taberah, Massah, etc. (9²²⁻²³). Moses beseeches the Lord not to look upon the impieties (τὰ ἀσεβήματα, 9²⁷) of Israel, lest the nations say that he has led his people out of Egypt only to destroy them because he was not capable of bringing them into Canaan.

Deut. 10¹²-11. The Lord requires nothing of Israel but only to fear him, to serve him with the whole heart and to keep his commandments, because out of all nations he cherishes the seed of Israel.

Circumcise the foreskin of your heart and be not stiffnecked. God is no respector of persons and loves the stranger; do ye love the stranger and cleave to the Lord.

I am not speaking to those who have not seen the great wonders which he wrought in Egypt, or the chastisement with which he punished Dathan and Abiram. Your eyes have seen these things; therefore obey the Lord so that you may enter the land, for the 'eyes of the Lord are always upon it'. Lay these words up in your heart, let them be for frontlets before your eyes, teach them to your children, talking of them when thou sittest in thy house. . . . Then you shall possess nations.

I set before you a blessing and a curse, a blessing if you hearken, a curse if you do not.

Deut. 12¹⁻¹⁶. Clean and Unclean. These are the κρίσεις you must observe. You shall destroy every vestige of idolatrous worship, but you shall not destroy the true worship of the

Lk. 11¹⁴⁻²⁶. Jesus is casting out a demon. He is accused of doing this by the agency of Beelzebub. Others tempt him by asking for a sign.

If Jesus casts out demons ἐν δακτύλῳ θεοῦ then indeed the kingdom of God has come upon them.

The strong man armed keeps his goods until one ἰσχυρότερος αὐτοῦ comes, and makes him disgorge his prey. But deliverance from a demon is followed by a relapse into possession by seven devils, and the final state is worse than the first.

Lk. 11²⁷⁻³⁶. Blessed is Jesus' mother. Yea rather, blessed they that hear the word of God and keep it.

This is an evil generation of Israel which seeks after a sign, and no sign shall be given it. Aliens will condemn it in the judgement, for the queen of the south came to hear the wonderful wisdom of Solomon and the Ninevites repented at the preaching of Jonah, and now something greater than Solomon or Jonah is here.

One who possesses a light uses it so as to give light to others. The eye is the body's lamp. If the eye is single the whole body is light; if evil, the body is dark. Beware lest what is your light becomes your darkness. If your body has no darkness it is wholly enlightened.

Lk. 11³⁷-12¹². Clean and Unclean. Jesus is invited to dine with a Pharisee who objects because he does not wash before eating. The Pharisees fail to distinguish between inner and outer

The Central Section of St. Luke's Gospel

Lord. You shall resort to the Lord's sanctuary and in due order bring your sacrifices and your tithes (τὰ ἐπιδέκατα ὑμῶν 12¹¹), and rejoice before the Lord with your family and the Levite, etc.

Nevertheless, you may eat flesh in any of your cities after the desire of your soul, the unclean and the clean may eat thereof (ὁ ἀκάθαρτος ἐν σοὶ καὶ ὁ καθαρὸς ἐπὶ τὸ αὐτὸ φάγεται, 12¹⁵). But you may not eat the blood, for the blood is the life (cf. 12²³), you shall pour it out upon the earth (ἐπὶ τὴν γῆν ἐκχεεῖτε αὐτό, 12¹⁶).

Deut. 12¹⁷ to end. Rejoice with your wealth before the Lord. While you may eat flesh in any of your cities, you may not eat the tithes of your corn, wine, oil, flocks, etc., except before the Lord. There you shall rejoice (εὐφρανθήσῃ, 12¹⁸) in company with your family and the Levite. (You shall do this year by year for παντὸς γενήματος τοῦ σπέρματός σου, 14²¹.)

When the Lord increases your prosperity, and you say 'I will eat flesh', you may eat after the desire of your soul (ἐν πάσῃ ἐπιθυμίᾳ τῆς ψυχῆς σου, 12²⁰). When you go into the land of your inheritance, take care (πρόσεχε σεαυτῷ) that you are not ensnared to follow the example of the ἔθνη, and to enquire how they serve their gods. You shall observe to do (φυλάξῃ ποιεῖν) only what I command, when I have given you the inheritance (12²⁹⁻³²).

Deut. 13¹⁻¹¹. The judgement of death upon any who lead Israel to serve other gods. If a prophet induces you by signs to go after false gods, you must not hearken to him. God is testing you, to know whether you love him and will cleave to him. The prophet has spoken rebellion and must die. If any member of your family entice you, whether brother, son, daughter or wife, you shall not hearken to them, but put them to death.

Deut. 13¹² to end. Communal destruction for communal apostasy. If

cleanness. Give alms of what is within and all is clean.

Woe to the Pharisees who tithe (ἀποδεκατοῦτε) but neglect τὴν κρίσιν καὶ τὴν ἀγάπην τοῦ θεοῦ (cf. Deut. 11¹). It is they who, like whitened sepulchres, are inwardly unclean. Upon them comes all the blood shed (ἐκχυννόμενον) from the foundation of the world. Beware of the real leaven, which is their ungodliness (ὑπόκρισις). There is nothing hid that shall not come to light. Do not be afraid of their persecution; fear God alone.

Lk. 12¹³⁻³⁴. Rich towards God. Jesus is asked to adjudicate about an inheritance (κληρονομίαν). He warns: ὁρᾶτε καὶ φυλάσσεσθε ἀπὸ πάσης πλεονεξίας. The life is more than possessions. The parable of the Rich Fool who accumulated τὰ γενήματα καὶ τὰ ἀγαθά so as to supply him for many years when his land prospered, and who says to his ψυχή, φάγε, πίε, εὐφραίνου. Be not anxious about food and possessions; the ψυχή is more than food, and God will provide.

After all these things do the ἔθνη seek. Do ye seek the kingdom of God which it pleases God to give you. Sell what you have and give alms, and so gain eternal treasure.

Lk. 12³⁵⁻⁵³. Reward and punishment for faithfulness and unfaithfulness in the Lord's stewards. You must be true servants, ready and waiting for your lord. Woe to the servant who fails to survive the test of the Lord's delay and runs riot. He will be punished according to his offence, he who knew the truth more than he who did not. Jesus comes to bring the fire of judgement, not peace but division. A family will now be divided between believers and unbelievers, father against son, son against father, daughter against mother.

Lk. 12⁵⁴⁻13⁵. Communal judgement and repentance. This people

45

you hear that in one of your cities lawless men have enticed the inhabitants to follow other gods, and you find on enquiry that it is true, you shall completely destroy πάντας τοὺς κατοικοῦντας with the sword, and devote it utterly to the Lord; it shall remain uninhabited. So the Lord may turn from his anger and have mercy on you, when you shall do that which is good in his eyes.

knows how to discern the weather, why does it not discern this time of judgement, and judge what is right?

Make haste to be reconciled before the final judgement.

The Galileans whose blood Pilate mixed with their sacrifices were not sinners above all others—but you will all perish if you do not repent. Those on whom the tower fell were not sinners above πάντας τοὺς κατοικοῦντας 'Ιερουσαλήμ—but you shall all perish if you do not repent.

(Deut. 14¹⁻²¹ provides a list of which animals may or may not be eaten. 14²²⁻²⁷ repeats 12¹⁷⁻³¹.)

Deut. 14²⁸. Every third year (μετὰ τρία ἔτη) you shall bring forth the tithe of your increase, and deposit it in that year in your cities so that the poor may be satisfied, and the Lord bless you.*

Lk. 13⁶⁻⁹. A man has a vineyard, and it is τρία ἔτη ἀφ' οὗ ἔρχομαι ζητῶν καρπόν. Let it be this year also, and if it is still unfruitful, then cut it down.

Deut. 15¹⁻¹⁸. Release from debt and slavery.

Every seventh year shall be an ἄφεσις from debt for all who are fellow Hebrews. The Lord's release is proclaimed. If you observe this you will have no poor, for the Lord will bless you, and you will rule over many nations.

Beware lest when you see the year of release approaching your eye is evil and your heart sad, and you harden your heart against your brother, and you do not supply his need.

A Hebrew man or Hebrew woman who has served you as a slave for six years shall be sent away free in the seventh. It shall not seem hard to you to let them go.

Lk. 13¹⁰⁻²¹. The cure of the Bent Woman.

On the sabbath day Jesus releases (ἀπολέλυσαι) a woman from a spirit of infirmity which binds her down. The ruler of the synagogue is angry, and protests that there are six working days for such a cure. Jesus replies that the sabbath is the proper day on which to release a daughter of Abraham from the fetter with which Satan has bound her for eighteen years. The crowd rejoices.

Jesus announces the kingdom of God as already present as a seed bearing fruit, and as leaven at work.

Deut. 16¹⁻17⁷. The Three Feasts at Jerusalem.

You shall keep the Passover to the Lord, that you may remember your redemption from bondage all the days of your life. Sacrifice to the Lord in the place where the Lord ἐκλέξηται ἐπικληθῆναι τὸ ὄνομα αὐτοῦ ἐκεῖ (16⁶, ¹¹, ¹⁵, ¹⁶). Eat no leaven six days; on the seventh feast to the Lord. Keep

Lk. 13²²⁻³⁵. Jesus is journeying through cities and villages, πορείαν ποιούμενος εἰς 'Ιεροσόλυμα. He gives warning to enter through the narrow gate before it is closed. It will then be of no avail to protest:ἐφάγομεν ἐνώπιόν σου καὶ ἐπίομεν, καὶ ἐν ταῖς πλατείαις ἡμῶν ἐδίδαξας. They will be excluded from the feast of the Kingdom of God, and aliens will take their place

* In this and the following sections I am indebted to Dr. A. M. Farrer for valuable suggestions which he made available to me.

46

the Feast of Weeks, and rejoice before the Lord with your family and the stranger, etc.

Keep the Feast of Tabernacles. Three times a year shall all your males appear before the Lord in the place which he shall choose. (Thou shalt not sacrifice an offering in which is blemish.) You shall kill and stone those who do evil, who transgress the covenant and commit idolatry.

Deut. 17⁸–18 (cf. 16¹⁸ ᶠᶠ.). Appoint judges and γραμματοεισαγωγεῖς who will judge righteous judgement and who will not be perverted by respect of persons or bribe. To them shall ye go in matters too hard for you to decide. You shall do πάντα ὅσα ἐὰν νομοθετηθῇ σοι (17¹⁰). When you come into your inheritance you will wish to set an ἄρχων over you. He must be from among your brethren, and must not be set upon worldly magnificence. If he is to prolong his days he must learn from the law ἵνα μὴ ὑψωθῇ ἡ καρδία αὐτοῦ (17²⁰). (The priests, the Levites, have no inheritance among the brethren. They are to live on the sacrifices and your first fruits.) (Cf. 16¹¹ ᶠᶠ.: you shall feast before the Lord with the Levite, the stranger, etc.)

A prophet like Moses will be raised up; unto him shall ye hearken.

(Deut. 19 deals with cities of refuge for the manslayer, and with the treatment of false witnesses.)

Deut. 20. When you go into battle you must not be afraid, for it is the Lord's battle, but the γραμματεῖς may grant remission from service in the following cases. What man is there that has built a house and has not dedicated it, let him go and return to his house. What man has planted a vineyard? . . . what man has betrothed a wife? . . . let him return to his house. Further, anyone who is

in the company of the patriarchs at the table of God.

In reply to the warning that Herod is seeking to kill him, Jesus declares that he must continue his work and go on his way until he is perfected (in sacrifice? τελειοῦμαι). Only in Jerusalem, the city of God, can a prophet's blood be shed. Jerusalem is the apostate city which kills and stones the messengers of God. Its sanctuary is to be abandoned by God. You shall not see me until you utter the psalms which are sung at the Feast.

Lk. 14¹⁻¹⁴. Jesus dines on the sabbath at the house of τινος τῶν ἀρχόντων τῶν Φαρισαίων, and the νομικοί watch him.

He asks whether a man suffering from water sickness should be healed on the sabbath in the same way as a man or beast is pulled out of a water well on the sabbath. The νομικοί refuse to utter judgement, but cannot refute him.

Observing their love of chief places he exhorts to humility and the lowest place—then you will have glory from others. πᾶς ὁ ὑψῶν ἑαυτόν shall be humbled, and whoever humbles himself ὑψωθήσεται.

When you give a dinner do not invite your brethren and relations and the wealthy who can return your hospitality, but the poor who cannot requite you.

(The presupposition of Lk. 9⁵¹–18¹⁴ is the words at the Transfiguration (9³⁵: οὗτός ἐστιν ὁ υἱός μου ὁ ἐκλελεγμένος, αὐτοῦ ἀκούετε.)

Lk. 14¹⁵⁻³⁵. Blessed is he who eats at the feast of the kingdom of God. The parable of the Great Feast. The invited guests all ask to be excused. 'I have bought a field and must go and see it.' 'I have bought five yoke of oxen and must prove them; have me excused.' 'I have married a wife and cannot come.' The feast is thrown open to the multitude of the poor. To the many accompanying him Jesus

fainthearted, let him return to his house, lest he make his brother into a coward. When you approach one of the cities, which are μακράν σου, ἐκπολεμῆσαι αὐτούς, then ἐκκάλεσαι αὐτοὺς μετ' εἰρήνης, and all the inhabitants shall become tributary. If the offer is refused, then make war on it and destroy it utterly. The cities which are near, and which may entice you to idolatry, you shall destroy so that nothing living survives.

(Deut. 21¹⁻¹⁴ deals with the treatment of dead bodies and women captives.)

Deut. 21¹⁵⁻²²⁴. Father and Son. Restoration of what is lost. If a man have two wives, one beloved and the other hated, and the firstborn is the son of the hated, on the day that 'he causeth his sons to inherit that which he hath' he may not make the son of the beloved the firstborn, ὑπεριδὼν τὸν υἱὸν τῆς μισουμένης τὸν πρωτότοκον; he shall acknowledge the firstborn by giving him a double portion; the right of the firstborn is his.

If a man have a stubborn and rebellious son who will not hearken to his parents, they shall bring him before the elders, and say 'This our son (ὁ υἱὸς ἡμῶν οὗτος) is stubborn . . . he is a riotous liver and a drunkard', and he shall be stoned. You shall put away the evil from your midst.

When thou seest thy brother's ox or sheep go astray, μὴ ὑπερίδῃς αὐτά. Thou shalt return them to thy brother. If your brother μὴ ἐγγίζῃ you shall take it indoors and keep it until your brother seeks it. You shall do so with anything which your brother has lost and you find, ὅσα ἐὰν ἀπόληται παρ' αὐτοῦ καὶ εὕρῃς, οὐ δυνήσῃ ὑπεριδεῖν.

(Deut. 22⁵⁻23¹⁴ a collection of miscellaneous regulations.)

Deut. 23¹⁵⁻²⁴⁴. A slave who has escaped from his master shall not be handed over, but shall live in your midst (μετὰ σοῦ κατοικήσει, ἐν ὑμῖν), wherever he pleases. You shall not oppress him.

You shall not bring as a vow to the

gives warning that anyone who comes to him cannot be his disciple unless he hate the members of his family, even his own life, and unless he takes up his cross and marches behind him.

What man, wishing to build a tower, does not first count the cost? Otherwise men will jeer at him because he was not able to finish. A king πορευόμενος ἑτέρῳ βασιλεῖ συμβαλεῖν εἰς πόλεμον first reckons whether he can win. If he cannot he sends an embassy ἔτι πόρρω ὄντος, ἐρωτᾷ τὰ πρὸς εἰρήνην.

Lk.15. Three parables of Lost and Found. The Prodical Son.

Pharisees and scribes murmur because publicans and sinners draw near (ἐγγίζοντες) to Jesus, and because he receives them.

What man having an hundred sheep and losing one (ἀπολέσας), does not go after it? He gathers friends and neighbours to rejoice that the lost is found. What woman losing a drachma does not search (ζητεῖ) till she find it?

A man had two sons. He divides his inheritance between them. The younger leaves his father and wastes his means of livelihood as a spendthrift. He returns to his father in penitence and is given the chief honours. The firstborn son objects, but is told that all that is his father's is his, but that he should rejoice that 'this thy brother' ὁ ἀδελφός σου οὗτος (cf. ὁ υἱός σου οὗτος, 15³⁰) was ἀπολωλὼς καὶ εὑρέθη.

Lk. 16¹⁻¹⁸. The parable of the Unjust Steward.

The steward wastes his master's goods, but acts in such a way towards his master's debtors that when he is dismissed they will receive him εἰς τοὺς οἴκους ἑαυτῶν. The Lord approves

Lord money gained by religious prostitution—it is a βδέλυγμα to the Lord.

You shall not lend upon usury, usury of money or usury of anything that is lent upon usury.

When you vow a vow to the Lord you shall pay it; the Lord will require it. That which has gone out of thy lips thou shalt observe to do ... a freewill offering which thou hast promised.

If a wife fails to find favour in the eyes of her husband because of an unseemly thing, he shall write a bill of divorcement, and send her away, and she may become the wife of another (γένηται ἀνδρὶ ἑτέρῳ). If the second husband divorce her or die the first may not take her back to wife. It is a βδέλυγηα to the Lord.

τὸν οἰκονόμον τῆς ἀδικίας. Make friends through τοῦ μαμωνᾶ τῆς ἀδικίας that, when it fails, you may be received into the kingdom.

You cannot be the slave of God and mammon.

The Pharisees are lovers of money. You make yourselves appear δίκαιοι before men, but God knows the heart. What is lofty is a βδέλυγμα before him.

The law and prophets are till John; from now the kingdom is being forcibly entered. But the law abides and is completely binding.

Whoever puts away his wife and marries another commits adultery, and whoever marries a woman who has been put away from her husband commits adultery.

Deut. 24⁶–25³. Injunctions against oppressive treatment of the poor in Israel. Remember that you were delivered out of bondage in Egypt.

You may not take the millstone to pledge—it is a man's life (24⁶).

If any man is found stealing the life of any of his brethren from among the children of Israel, lording it over him and selling him into slavery, that thief shall die (24⁷).

Take heed of the plague of leprosy, that thou observe it diligently, and do according to all that the priests shall teach you. As I commanded them so shall ye observe to do it (24⁸⁻⁹).

Thou shalt not oppress (οὐκ ἀπαδικήσεις) the poor and needy in thy cities, whether of thy brethren or the alien. Give him his hire before sunset lest καταβοήσεται κατὰ σοῦ πρὸς κύριον and it be sin in thee (24¹⁰⁻¹⁵).

The fathers shall not be put to death for the children, nor the children for the fathers, but each for his own sin (24¹⁶).

When you reap your harvest and leave a sheaf ἐν τῷ ἀγρῷ σου, οὐκ ἀναστραφήσῃ λαβεῖν αὐτό. It shall be for the stranger, the fatherless and the widow. When you beat your olives οὐκ ἐπαναστρέψεις καλαμήσασθαι τὰ ὀπίσω σου. It shall be for the stranger, etc. (24¹⁷⁻²²).

If there be a controversy, and men come to judgement, the judges shall

Lk. 16¹⁹–18⁸. The vindication of the poor and oppressed by God in the judgement.

The parable of Dives and Lazarus. The rich man fares sumptuously; the poor man lies at the door wishing to be fed from the crumbs. The poor is rewarded as a true Hebrew in Abraham's bosom; the rich man dies and is with the wicked in Hades. He and his brethren should have heeded the law and prophets (cf. 16¹⁶⁻¹⁷); if they do not, they will not be convinced by the Gospel.

Better a millstone round the neck and death by drowning than to cause offence to one of the little ones. Forgive your brother when he sins as often as he repents. When you have done all that is required you are only unprofitable servants. Have faith as a grain of seed.

Ten lepers are told to show themselves to the priests, and only the alien returns to give thanks. 'Thy faith hath saved thee.'

The kingdom is ἐντὸς ὑμῶν; the future judgement and vindication are certain and sudden. When it comes upon men busy in their worldly occupations ὃς ἔσται ἐπὶ τοῦ δώματος καὶ τὰ σκεύη ἐν τῇ οἰκίᾳ, μὴ καταβάτω ἆραι αὐτά, καὶ ὁ ἐν ἀγρῷ ὁμοίως μὴ ἐπιστρεψάτω εἰς τὰ ὀπίσω. Whoever seeks to preserve his life shall lose it. One shall be taken and the other left. The parable of the Importunate

E

justify the righteous and condemn the wicked. (25¹).

(Deut. 25⁴ to end, deals with the refusal of Levirate marriage, false weights, etc.)

Deut. 26. When you come into the Promised Land you shall go to the Lord's sanctuary with a basket of firstfruits, and profess that the Lord heard your cries and delivered you out of affliction. You shall worship before the Lord and say: 'I have given the tithe to the Levite, the fatherless and the widow, and obeyed the commandment. I have not transgressed any of thy commandments, nor forgotten them; I have not eaten thereof in my mourning, nor made it unclean. . . . I have done according to all that thou hast commanded me'. Look down from thy holy habitation and bless thy people Israel . . . it is a peculiar and holy nation.

Here the law of Deuteronomy ends, the rest of the book consisting of the blessings and curses attached to it.

Widow who beseeches the κριτὴς τῆς ἀδικίας to vindicate her. Will not God vindicate his elect τῶν βοώντων αὐτῷ ἡμέρας καὶ νυκτός? Will the Son of Man find faith on the earth?

Lk. 18⁹⁻¹⁴. The Parable of the Pharisee and the Publican.

Both go to the Temple to pray. The Pharisee professes: 'I thank thee that I am not as the rest of men, extortioners, unjust, adulterers, or even as this publican. I fast twice in the week; I give tithes of all that I get'. The publican does not lift up his eyes to heaven, but asks for mercy on his sin. It is he who is righteous in God's sight.

The exalted shall be brought low and the humble exalted.

Here Luke rejoins Mark.

Some of the resemblances of subject matter and wording in these parallels may be fortuitous. Deuteronomy is a diffuse and very repetitive book, and Lk. 9⁵¹–18¹⁴ is heterogeneous. What is more striking, however, as generally in questions of this kind, is the coincidence of order. If, in addition to the general similarity of subject matter at so many points, the order of this subject matter in Lk. 9⁵¹–18¹⁴, an order which has perplexed the harmonists and has seemed to many to be no order at all, is the order of the subject matter in Deuteronomy and is explicable in terms of it, then the conclusion is difficult to resist that the evangelist has selected and arranged his material in such a way as to present it in a Deuteronomic sequence. His motive for doing so is not far to seek; it will have sprung from the conviction, of which there is more than one trace in the New Testament, and of which Acts 3²² is the clearest expression, that Jesus was the prophet like unto Moses. Both Matthew and Luke undertook the not inconsiderable task of incorporating a large quantity of teaching into the framework with which Mark had supplied them. Each has done it in his own way, but both have followed substantially the same course. Matthew has constructed five books of a Christian Pentateuch, in the first of which Jesus is depicted on a mount delivering a new Torah, which runs parallel with, but is antithetical to, the old; while Luke has cast that section of his Gospel which is made up of non-Marcan material into the form of a journey to the borders of the Promised Land, a journey which follows that of Deuteronomy by way of correspondence and contrast.

It may be further noted that Luke's principal source, Mark, not only provides a context for the insertion of such a section, but may well itself have suggested such a procedure. Even if the influence of the figure of Moses on the earlier chapters of Mark be left out of account, his importance in the story of the Transfiguration is clear enough. There Elijah is seen together with Moses in converse with Jesus, and the significant words ἀκούετε αὐτοῦ (cf. Deut. 18¹⁵: αὐτοῦ ἀκούσεσθε) are added to the words already spoken by the heavenly voice at the Baptism. These words supply an excellent introduction to a new Torah; indeed they almost demand it. The importance of this incident for Luke is evident from the way in which he has 'written it up'. He says that Moses and Elijah, here reversing the order of the names in Mark, were not only seen, but seen in glory, i.e. in the glory of their assumption; and in their converse with Jesus they were looking ahead in anticipation (as does the evangelist himself in 9⁵¹) to that which was to be accomplished in Jerusalem. What is to be accomplished there is described as Jesus' ἔξοδος, like ἀνάλημψις an ambiguous word, which could mean simply 'death', but which, to biblical ears, and especially as the object of the verb πληροῦν, might suggest a mighty act of redemption.* Bengel's comment is again worth quoting: Res magna: vocabulum valde grave, quo continetur Passio, Crux, Mors, Resurrectio, Ascensio.

On the basis of Mal. 4⁴ ⁵, Moses and Elijah, the two witnesses, had become closely connected and assimilated to one another in Jewish thought. Both had witnessed a theophany at Horeb, both had left behind a prophetic succession,† both had left the earth in mysterious fashion. The difference between them was that whereas Moses was a prophet mighty in both deed and word, Elijah was mighty in deed only. He had been filled with the spirit, but he had left behind no book of instruction, and so he did not lend himself as the prototype of the giver of a new law. Rabbinic thought had multiplied the tasks assigned to the heavenly Elijah, both his present succour of, and intercession for, Israel, and

---

* Where it is not used in the sense of 'fill', or of the completion of a period of time, or of the fulfilment of scriptural promises, πληροῦν in Luke-Acts has the sense of 'accomplish', 'carry through'—cf. Acts 12²⁵, 14²⁶.

† Ecclus. 46¹, 48⁸.

the part he was to play in her salvation in the last days, but he had almost disappeared from Apocalyptic, and his functions had there been distributed amongst others. But Luke does not neglect Elijah. Although he regards the Baptist as working in the spirit and power of Elijah (1¹⁷), he omits Mk. 1⁶ (if this verse is a genuine part of the text of Mark) which seems to identify the Baptist with Elijah, and he omits the conversation which follows the Transfiguration (Mk. 9⁹⁻¹³), where the identification is made explicit. His purpose is presumably to make way for the presentation of Jesus himself as the new Elijah.* Luke's editing in this latter passage would certainly suggest this, for although he greatly abbreviates Mark's account of the cure of the epileptic boy, which he has now brought into immediate proximity to the Transfiguration, he adds that the boy was μονογενής, and that Jesus ἀπέδωκεν αὐτὸν τῷ πατρὶ αὐτοῦ (cf. 7¹⁵ and III Bas. 17²³: ἔδωκεν αὐτὸν τῇ μητρὶ αὐτοῦ). Then follows the second prediction of the Passion, delivered to the disciples when 'all were amazed at all the things that he was doing', introduced by the emphatic words θέσθε ὑμεῖς εἰς τὰ ὦτα ὑμῶν, and concluded by the repeated affirmations that 'they understood not this saying', that 'it was concealed from them that they should not perceive it' and that 'they were afraid to ask him about this saying'. It is this paradoxical truth of glory through the Passion, and the consequent truth of the exaltation of the humble, (which is provided by the next Marcan *pericope*, the dispute over precedence, Mk. 9³³⁻³⁷, and which appears as a recurrent theme in Lk. 9⁵¹–18¹⁴), to which the disciples are to listen—'hear ye him', 'let these words sink into your ears'. The incident of the anonymous exorcist, also from Mark, Luke abbreviates in such a way as to make a distinction between following the disciples and following Jesus, and so to prepare for what Jesus says to would-be followers in 9⁵⁷⁻⁶². The omission of the Marcan sayings on Offences (Mk. 9⁴²⁻⁵⁰) brings Luke to Mk. 10¹, and so to the mention of a journey from Galilee to the borders of Judaea beyond Jordan, which he interprets as a journey through Samaria to Jerusalem via Jericho. This serves also to continue the theme of Elijah, for Elijah underwent an ἀνάλημψις, and on the way to it travelled with Elisha from Gilgal via Bethel to Jericho and Jordan (with Lk. 9⁵¹, cf. IV Bas. 2¹: καὶ ἐγένετο ἐν τῷ ἀνάγειν Κύριον τὸν Ἡλειοὺ ἐν συνσεισμῷ ὡς εἰς τὸν οὐρανόν, καὶ ἐπορεύθη Ἡλειοὺ καὶ Ἐλεισαῖε ἐκ Γαλγάλων (Swete'Ιερειχώ)); and the first two incidents on this journey are

---

* For a study of the place of Elijah in Luke's Gospel, see P. Dabeck, *Siehe es erschienen Moses und Elias*. Biblica, vol. xxiii (1942), pp. 175–89.

of Elijah. In contrast to Elijah who called down fire to destroy the messengers of the king of Samaria, James and John are forbidden to do the same upon the Samaritans who reject the messengers of Jesus. When Elisha, who is ploughing, receives his call, and begs 'Let me, I pray thee, kiss my father and mother, and then I will follow thee', he is sent back by Elijah (καὶ ἀνέστρεψεν ἐξόπισθεν αὐτοῦ). When the Son of Man who has not where to lay his head calls men to follow him, they are not allowed to bid farewell to their families, for 'no man having put his hand to the plough, and looking back, is fit for the kingdom of God'. Thus we are able to fill in the one gap left unoccupied in our consideration of Lk. 9^{51}–18^{14}. Luke has followed up the figure of Elijah before he turns to the figure of Moses, and he finds both figures in Mark's story of the Transfiguration.

Not only, however, does Mk. 9^2–10^1 provide Luke with a fitting prelude to his Deuteronomic section; Mk. 10^{13-34} furnishes an appropriate sequel to it. With the omission of the question on divorce* Luke was able, by following Mark, to return to the same themes with which he had begun, namely the necessity of receiving the kingdom as a little child, the insufficiency of the Law for salvation apart from being a disciple of Jesus and embracing his poverty, and a third prediction of the Passion (Lk. 18^{15-34}, cf. Mk. 10^{13-34}). That such a correspondence between prelude and sequel was in his mind is suggested by two things; he has edited the question of the rich man at 18^{18} so that it agrees verbally with the question of the lawyer at 10^{25}, and he has added to the third Passion-prediction the reiterated statements, 'they understood none of these things; and this saying was hid from them, and they perceived not the things that were said' (18^{34}) in such a way as to match his statement at 9^{45}.

* On the view taken here it will be unnecessary to have recourse to the hypothesis of a Proto-Luke to account for the omission by Luke of Mk. 10^{1-12}, 9^{42-50}, 12^{28-34}, 3^{22-27} in their Marcan order, since Luke will have desired to include them, or their equivalents, in their Deuteronomic sequence.

On Dispensing with Q

by

A. M. FARRER

(i)

WHY dig up solid foundations, why open questions long taken for settled? Much critical and expository work rests squarely on the Q hypothesis, and if the hypothesis loses credit, the nuisance will be great. The books we rely upon to guide our thought about the history of Christ will need to be read with painful and unrelaxing re-interpretation. Nor is it only the effect on past studies that disquiets us. We want an accepted foundation for our present studies, and it seems a grievous thing that we cannot proceed with them until we have re-investigated what was unanimously settled by a previous generation. Is there to be no progress in learning? Now that criticism is a science, are we not to hold any established positions as permanent conquests, from which a fresh generation can make a further advance? Have we always to fight the old battles over again? Minds of high ability and scrupulous integrity were brought to bear on the Q question in the great days of source-criticism. They sifted to the bottom, they counted every syllable, and they agreed in the substance of their findings. Is it likely that we, whose attention is distracted by the questions of our day, can profitably do their work again? And what reason have we to trust our judgement against theirs, if we find ourselves dissenting from their conclusions?

It would certainly be impertinence to suggest that the scholars who established the Q hypothesis reasoned falsely or misunderstood their own business; no less an impertinence than to talk of the great Scholastics so. St. Thomas understood the business of being an Aristotelizing Augustinian, and if I am not his disciple, it is not because I find him to have reasoned falsely. It is because I do not concede the premises from which he reasoned. And if we are not to be Streeterians, it will not be because Dr. Streeter reasoned falsely, but because the premises from which he reasoned are no longer ours.

I take the situation to be this. Since Dr. Streeter wrote, our conception of the way in which the Gospels were composed has gradually altered; so gradually, that we have not observed the extent of the alteration. Nevertheless the change that has taken place removes the ground on which the Q hypothesis stood. For the hypothesis wholly depends on the incredibility of St. Luke's having read St. Matthew's book. That incredibility depends in turn on the supposition that St. Luke was essentially an adapter and compiler. We do not now, or ought not now, so to regard him. And being once rid of such a supposition, we can conceive well enough how St. Luke could have both read St. Matthew's book as it stands, and written the gospel he has left us. Then at one stroke the question is erased to which the Q hypothesis supplied an answer. For the hypothesis answered the question, 'From what does the common non-Marcan material of Matthew and Luke derive, since neither had read the other?'

If there is no difficulty in supposing St. Luke to have read St. Matthew, then the question never arises at all. For if we find two documents containing much common material, some of it verbally identical, and if those two documents derive from the same literary region, our first supposition is not that both draw upon a lost document for which there is no independent evidence, but that one draws upon the other. It is only when the latter supposition has proved untenable that we have recourse to the postulation of a hypothetical source. Now St. Matthew and St. Luke both emanate from the same literary region—both are orthodox Gentile-Christian writings composed (let us say) between A.D. 75 and A.D. 90, in an area in which St. Mark's Gospel was known. Moreover, St. Luke's own preface informs us that he writes 'in view of the fact that several authors have tried their hands at composing an account of the things fulfilled among us'. He claims to know, and, one would naturally suppose, to profit by, more than one gospel-narrative other than his own. By all agreement he knew St. Mark's, but what other did he know? It would be natural for him to know St. Matthew's, supposing always that it had been in existence long enough.

The point we are making is that the hypothesis of St. Luke's using St. Matthew, and the hypothesis of their both drawing independently from a common source, do not compete on equal terms. The first hypothesis must be conclusively exploded before we obtain the right to consider the second at all. Such is the actual case. There are, of course, possible cases in which the hypothesis of a lost and unevidenced source might compete on equal terms with the hypothesis of simple borrowing. Suppose, for example, that the passages common to A and B have a strong distinctive flavour, unlike the remaining parts of either A or B. Suppose further that the common passages, once we have extracted them, cry aloud to be strung together in one order rather than in any other; and that being so strung together they make up a satisfyingly complete little book, with beginning, middle and end. Then indeed we might postulate the existence of a common source, without waiting to prove that B cannot derive directly from A, nor A from B.

But in the case before us neither supposition holds good. To begin with the second—it is notorious that Q cannot be convincingly reconstructed. No one reconstruction, to say the least of it, is overwhelmingly evident, and no proposed reconstruction is very firmly patterned. It is fair enough to object that Q may in fact have been a somewhat shapeless writing. It may indeed, but if it was, then no positive argument can be drawn from its shapeliness or cohesion to its existence as a single distinct work. Then to take the other supposition. Can we say that the Q sections of St. Matthew's Gospel have a strong distinctive flavour, marking them off from the rest of his writing? We cannot. They have a special character of a sort, but a character which can be plausibly enough described as Luke-pleasingness. It seems a sufficient account of them to say that they are those parts of St. Matthew's non-Marcan material which were likely to attract St. Luke, in view of what we know about the general character of his Gospel, or can conjecture about his aims in writing it. For example, St. Luke was not interested in the detail of the anti-Pharisaic controversy and neglects much teaching of Christ which attacks the Pharisees on their own ground. Must we therefore distinguish in Matthew two elements, M and Q, M rabbinic in tone, Q popular and non-rabbinic, of which St. Luke knew Q, but not M? Will it not do as well to say that St. Luke let alone what he did not care for, viz., the rabbinic parts of Matthew?

There is another supposition which, if we could make it, might raise the hypothesis of a lost and unevidenced common source to something like *a priori* equality with the hypothesis of direct borrowing by one of our documents from the other. And that would be, if the lost source we proposed to postulate were a sort of book known to have been plentiful at the time. For example, suppose we were struck by certain resemblances between two

Victorian novels, suggestive of actual literary affinity. Then there would be scarcely any *a priori* disparity between the two hypotheses (*a*) that one borrowed direct from the other (*b*) that both were indebted to some third novel unknown to us. For there were a great number of novels published at the time, and many of them have since sunk into oblivion.

But unhappily the postulation of Q is quite the opposite of such a case. We have no reason to suppose documents of the Q type to have been plentiful. It is vain to cite Streeter's M and L, for the M and L hypotheses are corollaries to the Q hypothesis and have no independent standing. No, in postulating Q we are postulating the unique, and that is to commit a *prima facie* offence against the principle of economy in explanation. St. Luke's preface is evidence that several authors earlier than himself had undertaken the composition of an account of the things fulfilled in the Christian dispensation. But Q does not answer to the description. The 'things fulfilled' are, in St. Luke's view, the death and resurrection of Jesus above all. Q is not supposed to have contained an account of them, and therefore Q is not covered by St. Luke's words. He was talking about gospels, about the sort of book he himself proposed to write. And Q was not a gospel.

There was a time when appeal was made from the silence of St. Luke to the supposed informativeness of the elder whom Papias cited. 'Matthew arranged the revelations (λόγια) in Jewish speech.' Had we not here, perhaps, a reference to the Aramaic original of Q? Our Gospel of St. Matthew was certainly not written by the Apostle whose name it bears, nor was it written in Aramaic. Perhaps, then, what St. Matthew really did compose was the Aramaic Q, and it was to this that the elder referred. Such was the suggestion. I do not propose to deal with it in this essay, partly because it has now been generally abandoned, and partly because I have written what I have to say about Papias's elder in the first chapter of my book called 'A Study in St. Mark'.

So there is no independent evidence for anything like Q. To postulate Q is to postulate the unevidenced and the unique. But there is worse yet to come. For it may seem tolerable to postulate even the unique and the unevidenced if the circumstances of the time were such as (in our judgement) to call for its production. 'We have no evidence that the primitive Christians ever put together a Q or anything like it. Never mind; we can see that a Q is just what they would have wanted to produce towards the year 60.' Can we indeed? I am afraid we cannot. But let us look once more at the familiar story. 'In the middle of the first century

58

men recited the saving Passion as a set piece. Its dramatic quality made it easily memorable and the need to commit it to writing was not early felt. But the teaching of Jesus Christ was another matter. It was miscellaneous and not easy to hold in one's head as a whole body of doctrine. Nor was there any occasion for the continuous recitation of the whole teaching, in the way in which we presume the whole Passion to have been recited. And so it was natural that the Christian teacher should be equipped with a written manual of the teaching, and no less natural that the narrative of the Passion should be omitted from it. And such a manual we take Q to have been'.

It is a well-sounding story, but unfortunately it does not square with the Q which the gospel facts require. For Q has to be allowed to possess a strongly narrative exordium, not to mention narrative incidents elsewhere interspersed. It is no simple manual of Christ's teaching. It tells us with considerable fulness how John Baptist preached before the public manifestation of Jesus, and how Jesus, appearing in fulfilment of John's prophecies—and, it would seem, undergoing baptism at his hands—endured a threefold temptation in the wilderness, after which he ascended a mountain, and was joined by disciples there. Having delivered beatitudes and precepts of life, he 'concluded his words' and presently made his way into Capernaum, where his aid was invoked by a centurion on behalf of his servant.

Not only is the narrative character of such an opening strongly marked; it further betrays a vigorous symbolical interest in the order of the events. It treats the Lord's temptations in the wilderness as the manifest antitypes to the temptations of Israel in the wilderness, three times citing the appropriate verses of Deuteronomy. Then it proceeds to bring Christ, as Israel was brought, to a mountain where divine teaching of special weight is delivered. If Q would have to be credited with a narrative of Christ's baptism immediately preceding his temptations (and it seems that it would), then another piece is added to the symbolical pattern. For, says St. Paul, it was after Israel had been 'baptized unto Moses in the cloud and in the sea' that the people underwent their several temptations, in trial of their steadfastness in the grace they had received (I Cor. 10^{1-11}). So Christ's baptism in Jordan and the descent upon him of the Spirit will answer to the passage of the Red Sea and the descent of the Shekinah.

This pattern of symbolism and narrative finds a natural place in St. Matthew's text, where, in our opinion, it indubitably originated. But what sort of place would it find in the imaginary

Q? After an exordium so full of dogmatic weight and historical destiny, is it credible that the book should peter out in miscellaneous oracles, and conclude without any account of those events which, to a Christian faith, are supremely significant? A primitive Christian writer might well string together the teaching of Christ and leave it at that. Or again, he might despair of the attempt to describe the ministry historically, and treat it as simply the field of a teaching activity, but provide it nevertheless with a historical exordium and a historical conclusion. What is hard to believe is that he should supply the exordium, while omitting the conclusion; that he should set in train the only story of unique importance, and break it off.

It can fairly be said that it took time for the whole body of Christian teaching to be brought into relation with Christ's redemptive acts. Men who knew themselves to be saved through Christ alone might make homilies on duties and virtues, citing the Old Testament, citing examples from common life, and making no mention of redemption through Christ. St. James's Epistle is not, perhaps, one of the earlier pieces in the New Testament, but it is arguable that it represents the survival of an early attitude. Such an attitude might find expression in the composition of a collection of Christ's sayings, without any narrative of his passion. But for an author to set about the narrative of Christ's life, and never conclude it with his death, is another thing.

Appeal has been made to the example of Old Testament prophecies. The call of an Isaiah, Jeremiah or Ezekiel is carefully narrated, and so are the acts in which the prophet begins to fulfil his calling. But the conclusion of the book is not the conclusion of his life, but (it may be) certain of his weightiest oracles. Isaiah was supposed to have suffered under Manasseh as Christ suffered under Pilate, but the book of Isaiah does not record his death. Why should not the author of Q follow the scriptural example, and write a 'prophetical biography' of Christ beginning with history, proceeding to discourse, and ending with eschatological oracles? Why should he not? Because Christ was no mere prophet. Isaiah was no more than a prophet, an instrument of the Lord's word. It concerns us to know the history of his call, and how it was obeyed, for therein his authentication lies. The story of his end might be edifying, but it would be irrelevant to his message. The divine act in Isaiah is his call, not his death. It is otherwise with Christ.

It has sometimes been supposed that there was a primitive Christianity—perhaps, indeed, the most primitive of all—which attached no positive value to Christ's death and resurrection, nor believed Christ to have attached any such value to these events beforehand. Christians of this school had only one concern about the Passion—to palliate with scriptural excuses a disconcerting interlude between the coming of Messiah and the Kingdom of God. I have yet to be convinced that there were such Christians, or that their existence in the first days was a psychological possibility. They were presumably Jews, and no Jew could hold a negative attitude to Messiah's suffering an accursed death. No Jew could apologize for the cross unless he could glory in it. Yet Jews of a kind (I take it) are credited with having composed Q, and passed it current upon the Gentile churches.

It is sometimes thought that a decent agnosticism about the shape and nature of Q is a safe and honourable position. Why not be content to say that our two evangelists drew from a common written source, or sources, may be, but that we are in no position to decide what sort of writing, or writings, they drew from? Very well; but if so, the Q hypothesis must be allowed to lose heavily in *a priori* probability. The postulation of unevidenced writing of an indeterminable sort is a hazardous proceeding. If we were dealing with a rich and various literature it might be tolerable. If, for example, we return to our imaginary case of the two Victorian novels. Then we might say, 'The common source may be another novel, or a magazine story, or a newspaper report of a law-court drama, or one or more of several other things'. But what did the primitive Christians write, beside letters and homilies and gospels? Q was neither a letter nor a homily, nor was it a gospel. 'Some writing or other, never mind what' will scarcely pass.

So far we have said nothing new. The difficulties of the Q hypothesis have been fully canvassed by its candid admirers, and subsidiary hypotheses have been introduced to meet them. A good deal of such hypothesis may be found in Dr. Streeter's 'Four Gospels', all of it developed with undeniable care and skill. But the palm should surely be awarded to his management of 'the agreements of Matthew and Luke against Mark'.

The difficulty Dr. Streeter has to face is that St. Luke, in a fairly large number of places, makes small alterations in the wording of his Marcan original which St. Matthew also makes. Now this is just what one would expect, on the supposition that St. Luke had read St. Matthew, but decided to work direct upon the more ancient narrative of St. Mark for himself. He does his own work of adaptation, but small Matthaean echoes keep appearing, because St. Luke is after all acquainted with St. Matthew. Such

61

is the apparent evidence against Dr. Streeter; such is the single hypothesis which springs immediately to our minds and covers all the facts.

What does Dr. Streeter do? He divides the evidence into several groups and finds a distinct hypothesis for each. In some cases he supposes that scribal error has assimilated St. Luke's text to St. Matthew's where no such similarity originally stood. In other cases it will be St. Matthew's text that has been assimilated to St. Luke's. In a third set of cases St. Matthew and St. Luke may really have coincided, but the original of their coincidence stood in St. Mark's text, from which scribal error has subsequently effaced it. In a fourth group of instances stylistic, and in a fifth doctrinal interests may have suggested the same emendation of St. Mark to St. Matthew and St. Luke independently. There remains a sixth group, where the coincidences are coincidences of substance, not amenable to any of the five methods hitherto advanced. In these cases it will be fair to suppose in Q itself a parallel to that Marcan paragraph upon which St. Matthew and St. Luke are both principally working. They both happen to incorporate the same Q features in their Marcan transcripts—that is all.

Thus the forces of evidence are divided by the advocate, and defeated in detail. His argument finds its strength in the fewness of the instances for which any one hypothesis needs to be invoked; but the opposing counsel will unkindly point out that the diminution of the instances for each hypothesis is in exact proportion to the multiplication of the hypotheses themselves. One cannot say that Dr. Streeter's plea is incapable of being sustained, but one must concede that it is a plea against apparent evidence, and that, other things being equal, we should accept the evidence and drop the plea. Of course, on Dr. Streeter's view, other things are by no means equal. There are solid grounds for denying that St. Luke can have known St. Matthew. Here is the heart of the matter. It is these grounds that we have to examine. But before we proceed to do so, let us sum up our preliminary survey.

The Q hypothesis is not, of itself, a probable hypothesis. It is simply the sole alternative to the supposition that St. Luke had read St. Matthew (or *vice versa*). It needs no refutation except the demonstration that its alternative is possible. It hangs on a single thread; cut that, and it falls by its own weight.

(ii)

Why is it said that St. Luke cannot have read St. Matthew? Five reasons may be considered.

1. There are texts in St. Matthew which St. Luke would not have omitted, had he been acquainted with them.

2. Where St. Matthew and St. Luke give the same saying of Christ, St. Luke's wording sometimes has the more primitive appearance.

3. Our indubitable evidence for St. Luke's manner of using a written source is his use of St. Mark, whom he follows in continuous order over considerable stretches. Whereas if he used St. Matthew we should have to suppose that he treated him in a quite different way, dividing his text into small pieces and making a fresh mosaic of them.

4. The order in which St. Luke places the material common to himself and to St. Matthew is mostly less appropriate and less coherent than the order it has in St. Matthew.

5. In St. Matthew much of the material common to him and to St. Luke alone is placed in the context of Marcan paragraphs. St. Luke, even when he reproduces the same Marcan paragraphs, does not place the material we are speaking of in them, but somewhere else.

I shall make immediate comments on these five considerations, and afterwards proceed to a more systematic argument.

1. No one has ever attached decisive importance to St. Luke's unexplained neglect of certain Matthaean texts, and whatever importance it ever had derived from an antiquated view of St. Luke's attitude to his work. If we regard him as essentially a collector of Christ's sayings, then the omission of some particularly striking blossom from his anthology may seem incompatible with his having known it. But if he was not making a collection but building an edifice, then he may have omitted what he omitted because it did not seem serviceable to his architecture nor come ready to his hand in the building of it.

2. The suggestion appears to be that we should take separate units of discourse in isolation and pronounce on their degree of nearness to the spoken words of Christ. And where we find greater primitivity of form in this sense we are to impute literary priority. If the more primitive form were always St. Matthew's, then we might suppose that St. Luke had used, and in using modified, him. But since (it is alleged) the more primitive form is sometimes St. Matthew's and sometimes St. Luke's, it is more

reasonable to suppose that they used a common source, which now the one modified, and now the other.

There is a deceptive simplicity about the proposed method of argument which evaporates as soon as we try to apply it. There is scarcely an instance in which we can determine priority of form without invoking questionable assumptions. 'If I by the Spirit of God cast out devils' writes St. Matthew, and St. Luke, 'If I by the finger of God'. St. Luke's version contains a forcible allusion which St. Matthew lacks (Exod. 8^{19}, Matt. 12^{28}, Lk. 11^{20}). Is such an allusion more likely to be original, and later effaced by a more commonplace substitute, or adventitious, and due to our evangelist's Bible learning? 'Until heaven and earth pass away, not one jot nor one tittle shall pass away from the law, until all be fulfilled'. So writes St. Matthew, and St. Luke, 'It is easier for heaven and earth to pass away, than for one tittle of the law to fall'. Who can say whether the rhetorical fulness of St. Matthew, or the pointed brevity of St. Luke is more likely to be original? Is the copiousness of St. Matthew that of the Galilean gospel, or that of (say) the Antiochene pulpit? If we look at the context, we observe that St. Matthew is developing a flowing discourse (5$^{17-48}$), whereas St. Luke is giving us one of those short paragraphs packed with gnomic sentences which are an occasional feature of his style (16$^{15-18}$, cf. 12$^{49-53}$, 16$^{8-13}$, 17$^{1-6}$). We are left in complete indecision. Either could be adapting the other's text to his own purpose.

Even the apparently plain cases turn out to be not plain at all. We all agree at first sight that Christ is more likely to have blessed the poor, than the poor in spirit. 'In spirit' looks like an editorial safeguard against misunderstanding: to be in lack of money is not enough. St. Luke's phrase, then, is the more primitive. But on the other hand St. Luke's eight beatitudes-and-woes with their carefully paired antitheses are not a more primitive affair than St. Matthew's eight beatitudes, but very much the reverse. And the phrase 'in spirit' cannot stand in St. Luke's beatitudes-and-woes without overthrowing the logic of the paragraph. The poor are opposed to the rich. The poor in spirit would challenge comparison with the rich in flesh, but that does not mean anything. Thus St. Luke may well have read 'in spirit' in St. Matthew, and dropped it in obedience to the logic of his own thought.

The case of the Lord's Prayer is equally inconclusive. Here we may hesitate to attribute the greater bareness of the Lucan version either to editorial economy or to the logical requirements of the context. For surely the words of the Lord's Prayer must be sacred to a Christian. But if they are sacred to him, it is because they are hallowed in usage, not because they happen to turn up in a book from over the sea. The presence of the Lord's Prayer in St. Matthew's Gospel may suggest to St. Luke the appropriateness of placing that prayer in his own, but he may nevertheless write it in the form familiar to those for whom he writes. Now it may be true that the prayer current in (let us say) Achaea towards the end of the first century was more primitive than the prayer current in Antioch at the same time and even a decade earlier. But that casts no light whatever on the literary relation between St. Luke and St. Matthew.

We must content ourselves with these few examples of an enquiry which yields no decisive results. To express my own opinion, I agree with the findings of Harnack and of Loisy, rather than with those of Dr. Streeter. For much the most part the Matthaean forms *look* the more original. But I would not base any argument on such grounds.

3. The suggestion that St. Luke might be expected to use St. Matthew as he uses St. Mark sounds reasonable on a first hearing, but it will not bear examination. To follow two sources with equal regularity is difficult. Anyone who holds that St. Luke knew St. Matthew is bound to say that he threw over St. Matthew's order (where it diverged) in favour of St. Mark's. He made a Marcan, not a Matthaean, skeleton for his book. But as to the clothing of the skeleton, was not St. Luke going to do that according to his own wisdom, or where was the peculiar inspiration God had given him to operate? Is it surprising that he should lay his plan on Marcan foundations, and quarry St. Matthew for materials to build up his house?

4. It may well be that we shall have to accuse St. Luke of pulling well-arranged Matthaean discourses to pieces and re-arranging them in an order less coherent or at least less perspicuous. St. Luke would not be either the first planner or the last to prefer a plan of his own to a plan of a predecessor's, and to make a less skilful thing of it. We are not bound to show that what St. Luke did to St. Matthew turned out to be a literary improvement on St. Matthew. All we have to show is that St. Luke's plan was capable of attracting St. Luke. You do not like what I have done to the garden my predecessor left me. You are welcome to your opinion, but I did what I did because I thought I should prefer the new arrangement. And if you want to enjoy whatever special merit my gardening has, you must forget my predecessor's ideas and try to appreciate mine.

F
65

5. It is largely true that St. Luke does not give non-Marcan material the same Marcan setting as St. Matthew gives it. But that is not to say that he transfers it to other Marcan settings. He does not incorporate it in Marcan episodes at all. What we have to explain is the single fact that St. Luke disencumbers the Marcan narrative of St. Matthew's additions to it, and puts them by themselves. The fact is striking enough, and certainly requires explanation. But it is capable of being explained, as we will proceed to show.

(iii)

The Q hypothesis is a hypothesis, that is its weakness. To be rid of it we have no need of a contrary hypothesis, we merely have to make St. Luke's use of St. Matthew intelligible; and to understand what St. Luke made of St. Matthew we need no more than to consider what St. Luke made of his own book. Now St. Luke's book is not a hypothetical entity. Here is a copy of it on my desk. Let me consider what kind of a book it is.

Dr. Streeter says that St. Luke wrote his book in alternate Marcan and non-Marcan strips. That is, roughly speaking, true, but it casts at the best an indirect light on what St. Luke was trying to do. 'Strip-formation' was not his formula for writing a gospel, especially as he was at pains to make the strips invisible. It is only by a tedious comparison of his text with St. Mark's that we establish the division into strips at all. The strip-formation is the by-product of something St. Luke really was trying to do, and it is this that we have to find out. Dr. Streeter's observation is exterior and diagrammatic, like the observation that my journeys to Paddington bunch together in certain months of the year, with wide gaps between the bunches. It is not my purpose to spend a good part of the months of March, May, July and October on the Oxford-Paddington line, while keeping off it in the intervening months. My doing so is incidental to the execution of more intelligible projects.

St. Luke's non-Marcan strips are very far from equal. One of them, in fact, is out of all proportion to the others (9^{51}–18^{14}) and it alone corresponds (very nearly) to a single striking and visible feature of this gospel. No one, reading St. Luke for his own sake, would notice the discrepancy between Marcan and non-Marcan strips in 4–9, but every attentive reader observes that 10^{25}–18^{30} constitutes a prolonged lull in the progress of the action, and that St. Luke uses it to set before us the greater part of the teaching of Christ.

Surely this part of St. Luke's plan is immediately intelligible. If you or I attempted an account of Christ's life, we might do worse than finish the history of the Galilean ministry, and then break off to give an account of our Lord's teaching, illustrated, perhaps, by anecdotes. Then we might resume the narrative style to describe the visitation of Jerusalem, the passion and the resurrection. And that is what St. Luke does, except that he does not formally abandon narrative style in his middle section. It would, of course, be quite alien from the ways of a primitive Christian evangelist to do that. What St. Luke does is to have a sort of narrative standstill. A period in which nothing of decisive historical importance happens provides a setting for the exposition of the teaching.

Such an arrangement is natural in itself, but more particularly it commends itself to a writer who has St. Mark's and St. Matthew's gospels both before him. He is struck by the special excellence of each and would be happy, if he could, to combine them. St. Mark has narrative vigour and rapidity of movement. St. Matthew has fullness of doctrine and exhortation. St. Mark is deficient in discourse, St. Matthew, by constantly exploiting the occasions for discourse which St. Mark supplies, somewhat muffles the action: the discourses run so long that we lose sight of the narrative situation altogether. An obvious way of keeping abundance of doctrine without allowing action to be muffled is to put doctrine in a place by itself. In nine and a half chapters of lively narrative St. Luke gives us the nativity and childhood, the relations with John Baptist, and the great events of the Galilean ministry: the works of power, the appointment and mission of the Twelve and the Seventy, the feeding of multitudes, the confession of Peter, the Transfiguration. In eight chapters more he gives us the teaching and in the remaining six and a half returns to unencumbered narrative for the events at Jerusalem.

The plan is a happy one, and in its narrative parts it is an undisputed success. It is only in respect of the teaching part that we can find a shadow of justification for Dr. Streeter's *boutade*, that if St. Luke did what he did after reading St. Matthew, he behaved like a madman. St. Luke's teaching section is not so complete a literary success as St. Matthew's great discourses. But then what St. Luke attempted was, on any showing, an awkward task. One great Sermon on the Mount covering eight chapters instead of three was not to be thought of, and three Sermons on the Mount, one after another, would be scarcely more thinkable. It is a paradoxical truth, but a truth nevertheless, that an evangelist who proposed to himself a long continuous teaching was bound to carve it up. The discourses of Christ in St. Luke's middle part are conceived in episodes of moderate length, one following another. And it must be difficult to employ such a method without seeming somewhat monotonous and somewhat miscellaneous. Fresh episodes arise, but nothing much happens; the teaching is the thing, but the teaching is unsystematic because episodic.

But even if St. Luke was going to give the teaching in episodes, not in great discourses, might he not have profited more from the preparatory work St. Matthew had done for him? Could not he have broken the Matthaean discourses as they stood into two or three parts each at the points of logical division, provided each part with a distinct narrative setting, and left it at that? Has he not given himself unnecessary trouble in his handling of Matthaean material, and trouble worse than vain, if the Matthaean paragraphs are better than St. Luke's mosaics?

To ask such a question is to misunderstand St. Luke's task in 10–18. He is not dividing and re-arranging existing material, he is presenting his vision of the gospel according to his inspiration. And inspiration works in such a field as this by novelty of combination. Every episode in these chapters puts together two texts at the least which had not been combined before, and the new combination reveals the point that St. Luke is specially inspired to make. To say that St. Luke's points are less natural or less well made than St. Matthew's is irrelevant. St. Luke was not re-writing, still less abolishing, St. Matthew: St. Matthew remained to teach the Church St. Matthew's lesson. St. Luke was bound to write what was committed to him, and he was not free to cross it out afterwards even if the excellent and candid Theophilus found it inferior to St. Matthew in literary skill.

Every one of the short episodes in Luke 10^{25}–18^{11} is composite. This fact, so far from being a scandal, so far from making St. Luke's handling of St. Matthew incomprehensible, is our best clue to what St. Luke was doing. It was the standing method of the Jewish preacher to seek his inspiration in the drawing together of old texts into fresh combinations: the striking of the flints brought forth the spiritual fire. The preacher would not merely juxtapose his texts, he would put in his own words what issued from their juxtaposition. St. Luke perhaps adds little of his own except by way of setting and suggestion. He puts the texts down side by side, and leaves them to speak for themselves, like the texts combined in the liturgy for a feast day.

But surely, it will be said, St. Luke was no Jew; it is not permissible to invoke the methods of the Jewish pulpit to explain him.

We must answer that the 'Jew or Greek?' issue is not so simple as that. No New Testament writer was all that Jewish, and none of them was all that Greek. Let St. Luke have been a Greek; that is to say, an uncircumcised man. That will not have prevented him from standing, year after year, among God-fearing gentiles in the local synagogue, storing his mind with the Septuagint (what primitive Christian knew it better?) and accustoming himself to the methods of the rabbinic expositor. And when he adhered to the Church he would find nothing different. There were the same Greek scriptures, as soon as the congregation had contrived to get a set; and there was the Christian preacher, using the same weapons to vindicate a fuller truth.

What strikes us about St. Luke is not his hellenism but his versatility. His history unfolds in the bosom of Jewish piety and works its way out into the hellenistic agora. The infancy of Christ is written in the spirit of Tobit, the tumult at Ephesus almost in that of Lucian. The appropriate manner comes ready to the matter. The preaching of Jesus Christ is Jewish preaching, and St. Luke becomes the Jewish preacher in delivering it. We must not first assign St. Luke the Grecian label and then argue to the contents of the parcel. We must study to unfold just how Greek and just how Jewish he was.

A few examples of St. Luke's method in 10–18 will have to suffice here.

In the Sermon on the Mount, St. Matthew attaches the Lord's Prayer somewhat loosely to the second paragraph on the unostentatious performance of the three good works, almsgiving, prayer and fasting (6^{7-15}). A couple of pages later, in what appears the most miscellaneous part of the Sermon, he has the paragraph 'Ask, and it shall be given you, seek and ye shall find' (7^{7-12}). The Lord's Prayer and the 'Ask' paragraph surely demand to be put together. At 11^{1-13} St. Luke in fact joins them in a single episode. There is no doubt about its singleness. It is marked off from what precedes by its own narrative introduction, 'And it came to pass that, as he was praying in a certain place'. It is similarly marked off from what follows by the introduction of the next paragraph 'And he was casting out a dumb demon, and it came to pass that . . .' Let us see how, in the area thus delimited, the new Lucan combination handles the old Matthaean material.

St. Matthew's paragraph on the Lord's Prayer ends with a comment: 'For if ye forgive men their trespasses, your heavenly Father will forgive you, but if ye forgive not men their trespasses, neither will your Father forgive you your trespasses'. The comment fixes our attention on one clause of the prayer particularly, 'Forgive us our debts, as we have forgiven our debtors'. But if we want to pass on from the prayer to the 'Ask and it shall be given you' paragraph, this is not the clause of the prayer to be kept specially in mind, but 'Give us this day tomorrow's bread'. For that paragraph continues 'What man is there of you, of whom his son shall ask bread, and he will give him a stone?' St. Luke smooths the transition by omitting the comment on 'Forgive us our debts'.

That omission once made, the transition from the one Matthaean paragraph to the other could perfectly well be immediate. But St. Luke prefers to embellish the transition with a parable from his own store, preached (as it might seem) on three phrases of the second Matthaean paragraph, 'Ask, and it shall be given you'—'Knock, and it shall be opened to you'—'If ye, being evil, know how to give good things'. . . . A man knocks up a friend at night to ask for the loan of three loaves. He is not a good friend; he yields to the other's importunity, not to his own good nature; but he yields. After the perfect introduction which such a parable affords, the second Matthaean parable follows with redoubled force. And who will hesitate to say that in the episode taken as a whole St. Luke has put an aspect of Christ's true teaching in a fresh and clear light, by means of the combination he has made?

St. Luke gives a twist to the last phrase of the discourse, when he particularizes the 'good thing' which above all we should ask of our Heavenly Father. It is 'Holy Spirit'. By means of this particularization the evangelist eases the transition to his next episode, in which Christ will cast out an unclean spirit 'by the finger of God', and give a warning against leaving the room vacated by the demon empty. It need not be empty, if the Heavenly Father only awaits our prayer to garrison it with Holy Spirit. But the special twist St. Luke gives to the termination of his episode not only opens the way to the next episode, it also echoes the termination of the episode preceding. It is not bread after all (the evangelist is telling us) that we should make most work about, but a diviner gift. And so, to go back a paragraph, Martha had been mistaken in being so preoccupied with the preparation of a meal. There was one thing needful and Mary had chosen the good part in seeking it at Jesus' feet.

To proceed with the next Lucan episode, the Beelzebul sayings (11^{14-28}). The divination on which St. Luke built that episode was a perception of the relation between two Matthaean parables, 'Who can enter into the strong man's house and spoil his goods, unless he first bind the strong, and then he will spoil his house'—

'When the unclean spirit goes out of a man he wanders through waterless places seeking rest, and finds none. Then he says, I will return to my house whence I came forth,' etc. (Matt. 12²⁹, and 12⁴³⁻⁴⁵). St. Luke perceives that it is actually the same house in the two parables, here despoiled of the gear of devilry, there found swept and garnished and re-occupied by the demon. Not content with juxtaposing the two parables, St. Luke equalizes them, writing up the first in the style and almost to the scale of the second. ' *When the strong man in armour guards his house,* his goods are in peace; but when the stronger than he comes upon him, he prevails over him, and takes his armour wherein he trusted, and divides his spoils. He that is not with me is against me, he that gathereth not with me scattereth. *When the unclean spirit goes out of a man,* he passes through waterless places, seeking rest; and finding none, he saith, I will return to my house whence I came forth. And coming, he finds it swept and garnished. Then he goes and takes seven other spirits more wicked than himself, and entering they dwell there, and the last state of that man is worse than the first.'

In Matthew the long discourse which ends in the parable of the house swept and garnished has for its pendant the visit of Christ's mother and brethren. That is a Marcan episode, and St. Luke has already reproduced it in a Marcan setting (Lk. 8¹⁹⁻²¹). He now writes an evident equivalent for it as a pendant to the episode of the disputed exorcism. Not the womb or the paps of Mary are so blessed as they who hear God's word and do it. Would St. Luke have taken the hint from St. Matthew and repeated his Marcan theme here unless it had served him to bring the conclusion of the exorcism episode into line with the conclusions of the two previous episodes? Not Martha, who prepares nourishment for Christ, is so blest as Mary, who listens to his word. It is good to ask daily nourishment from God, but above all it is good to ask for Holy Spirit. Not the womb that bore Christ or the paps that nourished him are so blest as they who hear the word of God and keep it.

In joining the house swept and garnished to the house defended in arms, St. Luke has omitted two intervening paragraphs, the blasphemy of the Holy Ghost and the sign of Jonah. He takes the sign of Jonah for the beginning of his next episode. But he links the new episode to the old in a peculiar way, which clearly betrays dependance on St. Matthew, or (if you will have it so) on a Q which was virtually identical with St. Matthew for a couple of pages.

St. Matthew has two connected episodes, each with its own

narrative occasion. (*a*) The accusation 'By Beelzebul' led Christ to give the Beelzebul parables and to add a warning against blaspheming the Holy Ghost. (*b*) The demand for a sign occasioned Christ to speak about the sign of Jonah and to give the parable of the house swept and garnished. As we have seen, St. Luke forms a single episode from the head of (*a*) and the tail of (*b*), the Beelzebul parables and the parable of the swept and garnished house. Then he begins a fresh episode with the head of (*b*), the sign of Jonah. But instead of giving each episode its own narrative occasion, he puts together both occasions into a joint occasion for the beginning of the first episode. '*Some of them* said, he casts out devils by Beelzebul the prince of devils, *and others* tempting him, asked of him a sign from heaven.' By the time we reach the end of the episode the malice of the *some* has been fully answered, but the temptation from the *others* has not been further alluded to. Christ addresses himself to it in the next episode (11 ^{29} ff.). 'And as the crowds gathered about him, he proceeded to say: This generation is an evil generation; it seeketh a sign, but there shall no sign be given it save the sign of Jonah.'

The sign of Jonah is only the beginning of the new episode. What makes the episode is the inspired juxtaposition of the sign of Jonah (Matt. 12 $^{38-42}$) and the lamp of the body (Matt. 6 $^{22-23}$). The lamp of the body is the eye; the body is enlightened if the eye is good. The 'good eye' signifies generosity, and St. Matthew is attacking miserliness in the Sermon on the Mount when he records how Jesus had declared that the good eye lets the light into our own person; it does not merely direct the beam of favour upon our neighbour. It is St. Luke's inspiration to see the connexion between the evil eye's exclusion of light, and the evil generation's blindness to a more than Solomon, a more than Jonah in their midst. In divining this connexion, St. Luke sees what is particularly characteristic of his own vision of the gospel. What shuts out the light of supernatural revelation is the refusal of a moral demand, and primarily the demand of generosity. Hearing Christ's teaching the Pharisees mocked him, because they were lovers of money (16 ^{14}).

The parable of the good and evil eye, if it is to have its full effect, must stand between matter explicitly concerned with failure to see divine signs on the one side and matter explicitly concerned with the denunciation of covetousness on the other. St. Luke makes a further divination no less brilliant than the last, when he passes on from the evil eye to the woes on the Pharisees. The evil eye darkens the whole man within, and Jesus had called the

Pharisees blind, because they cleansed the outside of the platter, when they should have taken thought lest what was inside it might be impoverishing the needy. He had proceeded to transfer the outside-inside antithesis from the platter to its owner, a sepulchre whitewashed without, but full of dead men's bones within. So in the episode of the Pharisaic lunch-party (11^{37-52}) St. Luke goes on to give a carefully arranged anthology of texts from the woes on the Pharisees (Matt. 23). He begins from the topic of miserliness and works round again to the rejection and suppression of divine truth. The Pharisaic brotherhoods are covetous and hypocritical (11^{39-44}), their scribal teachers are the enemies of God's word (11^{46-52}). They reject more than Jonah; their fathers killed the prophets, they complete their fathers' work and bring all the blood of God's messengers on their own generation.

We will turn back and pick up a couple of small points. (*a*) St. Luke simplifies the sign of Jonah by omitting the distracting allegory on the whale's belly and the Easter sepulchre (Matt. 12^{40}). Our attention is left free to concentrate on the perversity, more than that of Nineveh, which rejects a more than Jonah, and we are ready to be taught the cause of it in the parable of the evil eye. (*b*) The parable of the eye itself receives a convenient introduction in the form of a sentence culled from the beginning of the Sermon on the Mount: 'No man lighteth a lamp and putteth it in the closet or under the bushel, but on the lampstand, that those who come in may see the light'.

Nothing but a complete exposition of St. Luke's gospel could provide a complete refutation of the Q hypothesis, and, conversely, when such an exposition had been made, no further arguments in refutation of Q would be required. We have merely attempted a specimen of St. Luke's working from St. Matthew in 10–18. So far from his possession of St. Matthew making what he does a mystery, his possession of St. Matthew is the indispensable explanation of what he does. Let us follow St. Luke's eye and memory as they run up and down St. Matthew's pages under the direction of his own inspiration. To enter into the mind of St. Luke at work would be to dissolve the mystery, and, in the nature of the case, nothing else can possibly dissolve it.

(iv)

We have been discussing the teaching section (Lk. 10^{25}–18^{30}). This section, we have said, is roughly equivalent to the widest by

73

far of St. Luke's non-Marcan strips. But what are we to say about
the contents of the other strips? About those of them that consist
of incident we need say nothing at all. That St. Luke should
intersperse his Marcan narrative with non-Marcan incidents or
versions of incidents is the most natural thing in the world. So we
find him giving the Matthaean account of John Baptist's preaching and of the Lord's temptations; having his own views about the
migration from Nazareth to Capernaum, which St. Matthew has
mentioned in the same place (Lk. 4^{16-29}, Matt. 4^{13}) and about
the call of Simon Peter (5^{1-10}); paraphrasing the Matthaean story
of the centurion (7^{2-10}), and adding from his own store the widow
of Nain (7^{11-17}) and the sinful woman (7^{36-50}); adding Zacchaeus
to the story of Jericho and adding a parable to Zacchaeus (19^{1-27}).
There is nothing surprising about such embellishments of the Marcan story, nor is it at all surprising that they tend to come in
groups. St. Luke is following St. Mark as his main narrative guide,
and feels the spell. When he has once turned his eyes away from
the Marcan text he is open to think about his other stores of
knowledge. When at length he returns to St. Mark the spell
reasserts itself and he follows his written guide for some distance
before digressing again.

But since we have said that St. Luke's plan assembles the
Lord's sustained teaching in a single place (10–18), we may be
expected to show why the evangelist gives a Sermon on the Mount
(or under it, rather) in 6^{20-49}, and why Christ's sayings about
John Baptist are recorded in 7^{18-34}. The placing of the sayings
about John presents no difficulty on any showing. They are
inseparable from their Matthaean introduction, the message from
John in prison. By the time St. Luke's long teaching section
begins, John has been already reported dead (9^9). An incident
from his life in prison could scarcely come later than 7. But constant to his purpose of reserving the bulk of Christ's teaching for
the central section, St. Luke detaches all he can from the Lord's
discourse upon this occasion according to St. Matthew (Matt.
11^{12-15}, 11^{20-30}, cf. Lk. 16^{16}, 10^{12-25}).

St. Luke's sermon at the mountain is also vastly shortened from
the Matthaean form. It has the same beginning and the same end
as its original. But in the body of the sermon St. Luke, with a skill
from which no one can withhold the praise, extracts a single
essence from the wide range of the Matthaean sermon, renunciation seen as humility and generosity. Everything which does not
belong to the chosen theme is left for a more convenient occasion.
But why (it has still to be asked) should St. Luke give us even a

short sermon at the mountain, if he has resolved to keep Christ's teaching for the middle part of his book? If the sermon at the mountain is not a formal declaration of the teaching, then what is it?

Why St. Luke did what he did, rather than anything else, cannot be the question. He did what he was moved to do. It is enough if we can see what he did, and what he meant by it. At an earlier point in this essay we imagined St. Luke coolly resolving to put the mass of Christ's teaching where it would least impede the action. And that is what St. Luke did in effect resolve to do, and we may believe that he was not insensitive to the purely literary advantages of the choice he made. But it is not very likely that the choice would present itself to him as a mere point of literary craft. Let us endeavour to give a more plausible story of how a first-century evangelist arrived at such a decision.

We will suppose that St. Luke has St. Matthew before him. Now St. Matthew is a forerunner in the course which St. Luke is about to take: he first has written a new Mark with the Lord's teaching more fully embodied in it. What path has St. Matthew taken? How closely will St. Luke wish to follow it? St. Matthew has not been content simply to exploit such opportunities for the development of discourse as St. Mark happens to afford. He has so arranged his matter as five times to bring the teaching to a head in a set discourse, and in case we should fail to distinguish the five discourses from other passages of dialogue, he has concluded each discourse with an identical phrase: 'And it came to pass when Jesus had finished these sayings . . .'

It has been suggested that St. Matthew's five set pieces* have something to do with the five books of Moses, as though the evangelist were presenting his gospel as a new Pentateuch. The suggestion, in that form, remains sterile. We are disappointed to discover that the first set piece has nothing to do with Genesis nor the second with Exodus. We have made a mistake somewhere. Our mistake was to miss the first set piece of all, the genealogy, with which the Gospel opens. If that is not a set piece, what is? It cannot, of course, have the set conclusion 'When Jesus had finished these sayings', for it does not consist of his sayings but of his ancestors. In any case the set conclusion has not yet been set,

---

* It is sometimes assumed that the set pieces are each the conclusions of whole 'books' into which St. Matthew is divided. There is no obvious reason for that assumption. St. Matthew wrote his book in one continuous script, divided not by chapter headings, but by 'stripes' in the subject matter, the 'stripes' being these set pieces which carry the set terminations. The additional matter attaching to the 'stripe' may be on either side of it, or on both sides.

and the only reader who looked for it at 1^{17} would be the reader who read the book backwards. He who takes it as it comes is put on the right track from the very first moment by a different and far more explicit indication. 'Book of Genesis of Jesus Christ' is the title to the genealogy and the first line of the Gospel. The new 'Book of Genesis' derives the legal ancestry of Jesus from the hero of the old Genesis, Abraham. Having done with genealogy, St. Matthew resumes: 'Now the genesis of Jesus Christ was thus . . .' So much, then, for Genesis.

The Exodus set-piece is identified neither by heading nor by termination, but by context and character. That the Sermon on the Mount stands out as a formal unity scarcely needs to be said. It is a new law from the mountain, like the law of Sinai, and the setting is strikingly reminiscent. Jesus passes the waters and undergoes forty days' temptation in the wilderness after the pattern of Israel at the Red Sea and in the desert. Then he comes to the mountain of revelation. By using the formula 'When Jesus had finished these sayings' by way of conclusion to what is obviously an Exodus discourse in its own right, St. Matthew first gives it significance as the termination to a 'set scriptural piece'. When it recurs we shall know what to make of it.

St. Matthew's Leviticus is the mission-charge which is also, in his Gospel, the institution of the Twelve (10). The example 'Book of Genesis' in 1^1 (cf. 1^{18}) has already shown us that our author is sensitive to the *prima facie* meaning of a book-title. Now 'Leviticus' means 'The Book about Levites' and the Apostles are the corresponding ministry of the New Covenant. Similarly, if we are to go by titles, 'Numbers' is the muster of the host. St. Matthew's Leviticus (10) sends forth 'labourers into the harvest', the Parables which compose his Numbers (13) show how plenteous the human harvest is, how numerous the catch to which fishers of men were previously called (4^{19}); they deal with the criterion according to which some pass the muster and are admitted to the promised land, while others are rejected.

It remains that the next set piece (Matt. 18) should be a Deuteronomy. The Marcan original is already so Deuteronomic at this point that there is little left for St. Matthew to do. The Transfiguration has already brought Moses to witness the divine repetition of his Deuteronomic testimony about his great Successor, 'Hear ye him' (Deut. 18^{13}, Mk. 9^9, Matt. 17^5). In the discourse at Capernaum St. Mark, and St. Matthew following him, proceed to take up the next preceding paragraph of Deuteronomy, the Law of the Kingdom (Deut. 17^{14-20}, Mk. 9^{32-37}, Matt.

17^{25}–18). The princes in God's kingdom are not to exert privileges or make exactions like Gentile kings, but to humble themselves among their brethren. St. Matthew goes further than St. Mark by going one paragraph further back in Deuteronomy (Deut. 17^{2-13}, Matt. 18^{15-20}). The Israelite who has a grievance against his neighbour must be prepared first to call two or three witnesses, then to have recourse to a higher court: the decree of ultimate authority must be enforced. The sequel to the Matthaean set discourse rejoins St. Mark, and remains in step with Deuteronomy. It is the question of divorce (Deut. 24^{1-4}, Mk. 10^{1-12}, Matt. 19^{1-12}). The next paragraph, the embracing and blessing of the children, simply repeats the Deuteronomic theme of princely humility, while the paragraph after that carries us to the very heart of Deuteronomy (Deut. 5–6, Mk. 10^{17-31}, Matt. 19^{16-30}). For the episode of the rich man's question associates the keeping of the decalogue with the Oneness of God, the attainment of 'life', and 'inheritance'. The exhortation to make distribution and to shun the snare of riches is no less Deuteronomic.

We have had five Matthaean 'Books of Moses'. There remains one 'book' (24–25), the 'Book of Jesus' (Joshua) without a doubt. The new Jesus comes through Jericho, indeed, but it is Jerusalem he condemns to utter overthrow, so that not one stone shall remain upon another. The fall of the city is the sign and the condition of the gathering of Israel into the true land of promise under the leadership of Jesus (23^{37}–24^2, 24^{15-31}).

Such in outline is the structure of St. Matthew's hexateuch, and if we are allowed to reason *a priori* at all, we must suppose it to have been as evident to St. Luke as it is to us, for he was a next-door neighbour and we are visitors from a far country. Supposing then that St. Luke understood it, what did he do with it? Did he adopt it, or reject it? He did neither. He allowed the general pattern to stand, but he redistributed the weight of the teaching, placing as much of it as he could in the Deuteronomic position. Shall we allow the question 'Why?' to be asked once more? We have answered it already in terms of literary propriety and of respect for Marcan narrative. Must we answer it over again in terms of scriptural typology? Among all the books of Moses why should Deuteronomy appeal to St. Luke as specially typical of Christ's doctrine? We are not bound to find certain answers to such a question, probable answers will do. If there are still more probable answers than those we find, why, so much the better.

First, then, the primitive Christian saw the Law reasserted and yet transformed in the Gospel, and it would easily strike him that

77

a model for such a relationship was to be found within the Law itself. In his Deuteronomy Moses reasserted his Protonomy, that is, the Law from Exodus to Numbers, and in reasserting it illuminated it. Had not St. John this example in mind when he meditated on the commandment which in being new is also old (I Jn. 2⁷⁻⁸)? The very occasion upon which Moses gave his Deuteronomy enforces the same point to the Christian mind. For it was in his last hours and in connexion with his giving place to the *Jesus* who could alone fulfil his words, and who was the first to be designated by that promise on which we have already dwelt: 'The Lord will raise up unto you a prophet from among your brethren like unto me: to him hearken'.

Such considerations, being formal and typological, make less appeal to us, perhaps, than they did to the first-century mind. But there are more material considerations with which our sympathy will be as great as St. Luke's own. Deuteronomy is the book which adds the spirit to the observance, it is the law of love towards God and man, and especially of humility, generosity, and compassion. It is well indeed if these virtues are as dear to us as they were to St. Luke.

St. Luke might desire, therefore, on some such grounds as these to place the weight of Christ's teaching in what his predecessors had already marked out as the Deuteronomic position. But logic forbade him to gather the whole of it there. The Deuteronomy will not stand out as Deuteronomy unless there is some semblance of a Protonomy; without a first law the second law will be second to nothing. The recapitulation on the plains of Moab presupposes a first statement at the foot of Sinai. And so St. Luke gives us a short sermon beneath the Mountain in 6 as well as the long discourses of 10–18.

The Deuteronomic passage in which Moses most clearly draws a new command out of the old is to be found in Deut. 5–6. Here the Lawgiver first recapitulates the decalogue from Exodus and then adds the *Shema* as the heart of the matter. The Lord is One Lord, and is to be loved with entire devotion. Now we have already seen that the passage is commented upon by the paragraph of the Rich Man, in which St. Matthew's Deuteronomic section culminates. St. Luke allows his own Deuteronomy to run out into the same conclusion (18¹⁸⁻³⁰). But he is not content to conclude with the *Shema*, he must begin from it too (10²⁵⁻²⁸). His Deuteronomic exordium anticipates the explicit discussion of the *Shema* between Jesus and the Pharisaic scribe in the temple court, according to Matt. 22³⁵⁻⁴⁰. (That the Matthaean version rather than the Marcan is St. Luke's model is the natural conclusion to draw from a comparison of the texts. Streeter's plea to the contrary is a necessity forced upon him by his general position.)

The Scribe's Question and the Rich Man's Question are the twin pillars which mark out the extent of St. Luke's Deuteronomy, and the fact is made more evident by the evangelist's assimilation of the one to the other. A doctor of law is the questioner in 10, a ruler of synagogue in 18. Both ask the same question, the Deuteronomic question, 'What must I do to inherit eternal life?' Both are credited with a knowledge of the formal answer which the old law supplies. It is the new Deuteronomy, the life-giving exposition of the old precept, that is reserved for Christ.

It seems, then, that St. Luke consciously regarded what he wrote in 10^{25}–18^{30} as a Christian Deuteronomy. How far can we say that the contents of this Deuteronomy are Deuteronomic in order or in detail? They range over the field of human duty as Deuteronomy does, and in a Deuteronomic spirit. But do they follow the topics of the fifth Mosaic book with any particularity? Here is a complicated enquiry, and it is fortunate for us that Mr. Evans has undertaken it in this volume. We need only refer the reader to what he has written.

So much for St. Luke's Deuteronomy. But what, if anything, has he made of St. Matthew's Genesis, Exodus, Leviticus, Numbers and Joshua? He has denuded them of prolonged discourse; but has he entirely effaced them? Not entirely, but he has rubbed them faint.

As to the Genesis, St. Luke has his own infancy narratives, and their patriarchal, especially their Abrahamic, flavour is unmistakable. He has his own genealogy too, though he places it differently: after the end of his Genesis, not at the beginning. At first sight we are struck by the differences between the two evangelists in their opening chapters; their genealogies are not the same genealogy nor their narratives in any particular the same narrative. On second thoughts we observe the points of identity. The Matthaean genealogy has an artificial structure and an openly symbolical value: the Lucan genealogy develops the symbolical architecture of the Matthaean to a further pitch of elaboration, as the reader may see by referring to the note appended to this essay. The Matthaean narratives are made to revolve round two principal points: Jesus, by domicile a Nazarene, was a Bethlehemite by birth; Jesus, by family a descendant of David, was Son of God by supernatural generation. St. Luke's narratives present a story which a man who had it to tell might surely prefer to the Matthaean form, even if he knew it. But it is to be remarked that he so tells it as to cover the two principal Matthaean points. What shall we say? We used to say: 'His genealogy is a different genealogy, his infancy narratives are different narratives, he had not read St. Matthew'. But now we shall say: 'St. Matthew's early chapters define a task, which St. Luke takes up and deals with from his own resources and with his own improvements. It is most unlikely that he had not read St. Matthew's.' So much, then, for St. Luke's Genesis.

St. Luke's Exodus chapters preserve the most striking Matthaean feature, the temptations which Christ, after the example of ancient Israel, endured in the wilderness. They add two distinctively Lucan developments—the rejection at Nazareth, embodying the principal discourse of St. Luke's Exodus; and St. Peter's confrontation with the supernatural in the miraculous fishing. The Scriptural typology of these two episodes can be studied in St. Stephen's Speech, Acts 7^{23-35}. They are antitypical to Moses' rejection by his brethren on his first appearance, and to the vision at the Bush (Ex. 2^{11}–4^{17}).

After Exodus, Leviticus. St. Matthew's Leviticus is the institution, mission and mission-charge of the Twelve (10) with which the embassy from John Baptist is associated (11). St. Luke holds over the mission and mission-charge for the enrichment of his own 'Numbers', but he still is able to present the institution of the Twelve and the embassy from John in close succession ($6^{12 \text{ ff.}}$, $7^{18 \text{ ff.}}$). St. Matthew's Sermon on the Mount, i.e. his Exodus, becomes St. Luke's Sermon after the Mount, i.e. his Leviticus: it loses its character of being a comment on the Ten Commandments and becomes the ordination sermon of the new Levites ('Lifting up his eyes upon his disciples he began to say, Blessed are ye poor', etc.).

As the Leviticus begins with the institution of the Twelve, so the Numbers begins with their mission (9^{1-10}). The 'Numbers' typology of this section stands out clearly. When our evangelist is simply following a source (say St. Mark) it is unsafe to attribute to him a conscious interest in every symbolical feature already embedded in the text he reproduces. But where he introduces his own additions and modifications, as he does here, it is reasonable to make him responsible for their more evident symbolical bearings. We observe the following facts. St. Luke so abbreviates St. Mark as to bring a certain sequence of events into close proximity: the commission of the Twelve (9^{1-9}), Jesus' reception of them on their return from mission ($9^{10 \text{ ff.}}$), the disclosure of the

Divine Son to the Twelve and the leaders of the Twelve (9^{18-45}).
After a few short incidents, Marcan and non-Marcan (9^{46-62}), St.
Luke supplies a parallel cycle: the commission of the Seventy
(10^{1-16}), Jesus' reception of them on their return from mission
(10^{17-20}), and the disclosure of the Divine Son to his disciples
(10^{21-24}). Now that the Divine Son has been twice testified to as
the sole revealer (9^{35}, 10^{21-24}) his law, his new Deuteronomy,
most fitly follows ($10^{25\ ff.}$).

St. Luke is himself responsible for placing the commission of the
Seventy in striking and elaborate parallel with the commission
of the Twelve. But to do so is undisguisedly to invoke the example
of Moses, and of Moses in Numbers. For in Numbers the commission of the Twelve (1–2, cf. 7) is succeeded by that of the
Seventy (11), not immediately, but only after the solemn setting
forth of Moses and Israel for the promised land (10). St. Luke,
too, places Christ's solemn setting forth between the cycles of the
Twelve and of the Seventy (9^{51-62}). 'It came to pass, as the days
of his Assumption began to be fulfilled, he set his face to go to
Jerusalem'. 'Assumption' is a word commonly used of the ends of
Moses and Elijah. When we hear it, we still have those two
saints' voices ringing in our ears. We have just heard them con-
versing with Christ on the mount of Transfiguration about the
exodus he was to complete at Jerusalem (9^{31}).

In thus developing the theme of Numbers St. Luke lays the
appropriate foundation upon which to raise his great Deuteronomic superstructure. For Deuteronomy itself opens with a
recapitulation of precisely those incidents in Numbers to which
St. Luke has supplied the antitypes (Deut. 1^{6-8}, the setting forth
from Sinai; 1^{9-18}, appointment of ministers; $1^{19\ ff.}$, the sending of
men to prepare the way whither Israel was to come). The
Deuteronomic setting of Lk. $10^{25\ ff.}$, could, in fact, scarcely be
more strongly marked than it is. To ask for more would be blank
ingratitude. It is hardly necessary to say anything about St.
Luke's Joshua. For in any case the triumphant passion and
resurrection compose the 'Book of Jesus' *par excellence.* If the
birth is a Genesis and the ministry a Lawgiving, then the death
and resurrection are a Conquest. But we may anyhow observe
that St. Luke shows himself fully alive to the Jerusalem-Jericho
paradox. It is Jerusalem, not Jericho, that the new Jesus is called
upon to overthrow by the trumpet of his prophecy. Jericho, once
the city of the repentant harlot (Hebr. 11^{31}), is now the city of the
repentant publican, and Jerusalem that of the proud Pharisee.
That is the impression which we form, if we read the story of

Zacchaeus upon its Lucan background (19^{1-27} and 19^{41-48}, cf. 18^{9-30} and 10^{30}).

(v)

It is alleged by those who deny the credibility of St. Luke's having used St. Matthew, that St. Luke never places Matthaean material (in their language, Q material) in the Marcan place which St. Matthew assigns it; and that the fact is very surprising, if St. Luke knew St. Matthew's book. The allegation is not wholly true, to begin with; and what truth it has is no cause for surprise. Have we sufficiently considered the bewildering way in which Mk. 1–6 is used in Matt. 3–14? To find the 'Marcan place' of any one paragraph in these chapters may be a teasing puzzle. If St. Luke began with the best will in the world to use Matthew as a direct comment on Mark, is it surprising that he gave it up in the maze of Matt. 3–14, simply followed Mark through, and dealt with the Matthaean additions afterwards on a system of his own?

What, in fact, had St. Matthew done in these chapters? Four times he skipped selectively over the same Marcan ground, each time making a fresh selection until the material was exhausted. In 3–7 he covered Mk. $1–3^{13}$, recounting the teaching of John, the baptism and temptations of Jesus, Jesus' coming into Galilee and fixing upon Capernaum, his calling of the four; how a mission throughout Galilee (Mk. $1^{39\ ff.}$) led to the collection of a vast crowd from all the quarters of Palestine, which are named (Mk. 3^{8}) and how, in face of the crowds, Jesus ascended the mountain and his chosen disciples came up to him. So far St. Luke follows St. Matthew and refers all St. Matthew's special material to the corresponding Marcan places, *including the Sermon at the Mountain*. But when, in 8, St. Matthew jumps back to the scene in St. Peter's house, according to Mk. 1, St. Luke deserts him, and is he to be blamed? St. Matthew, unaccompanied by St. Luke, flies over Mk. $1^{29}–5^{21}$ in 8, leaps back to Mk. 2^{1} and flies forward as far as 6^{15} in 9–11, returns to Mk. 2^{23} and reaches as far as 6 again in 12–14, after which he goes on steadily forward. But we are not concerned to unravel St. Matthew's doings ourselves; we are merely excusing St. Luke for not making the attempt.

We will clear up an allied difficulty, and so make an end. It is common form to say: If St. Luke drew the so-called Q material from St. Matthew, and yet did not produce it in the Marcan settings St. Matthew had given it, we must suppose that he went carefully through his text of Matthew blocking out the Marcan parts, before he could see what was available for his own Q passages. And it is unlikely that St. Luke did this.

It is more than unlikely, but then there is no need to suppose it. Up to the point at which St. Luke makes his great desertion of St. Mark (9^{50} = Mk. 9^{40}) the issue does not arise at all. The Matthaean material in Lk. 3–6 has its Marcan place; in 7^1–9^{50} there are two Matthaean episodes, the centurion's message (7^{2-10}) and the Baptist's message (7^{18-34}). Each is already a distinct and self-contained episode in St. Matthew, wholly unconfused with its Marcan context, and St. Luke could be in no hesitation at all where to draw the boundaries round either. He shortens both, and makes internal rearrangements in the second, but that has no bearing on the point.

When, on the other hand, St. Luke laid St. Mark aside at 9^{40} and took up St. Matthew for the composition of his long teaching section, he had already made such use as he wished to make of the Marcan elements in Matt. 3–18. And so, when he set about quarrying these chapters, all he needed to do was to bear in mind what elements in them he had used already. St. Matthew's Marcan material was marked off for him by the mere fact that he had just been using it in its pristine Marcan form. Equally, of course, he had already used some of the Matthaean material, for example in the Sermon and in the reply to John's disciples. He had no difficulty in letting alone what he had used, and picking up what he had neglected. He has no strict rule against Marcan material in his teaching section, but only against used material. He is perfectly ready to transcribe unused Marcan sentences embedded in Matthaean discourses, for example, in the Beelzebul controversy (Lk. 11^{15-22} and 12^{10}) or in the sermon on the little ones (17^2).

There is no difficulty, then, about the selection of non-Marcan material from Matt. 3–18 for incorporation in Lk. 10–18. If there is a difficulty, it will concern the incorporation in these Lucan chapters of material from the Matthaean chapters which St. Luke has not yet skimmed of their Marcan elements, that is to say, from Matt. 19–25. For here we can no longer invoke the explanation we have given for the ready discrimination of Marcan from non-Marcan in St. Luke's use of Matt. 3–18.

The difficulty melts away on examination, because the anticipations of Matt. 19–25 which St. Luke does make in 10–18 are, with one exception, massively simple and not such as to lay up trouble for the future. There are six in all, and five of them are so whole and single, that they come away clean from their settings. Here is the list:

(a) The lawyer's question (Matt. 22^{35-40}, Lk. 10^{25-28}).

(b) Woes on scribes and Pharisees (Matt. 23^{1-36}, Lk. 11^{39-52}).

(c) Servants watching (Matt. $24^{42}-25^{12}$, Lk. 12^{35-46}).

(d) Jerusalem that slays the prophets (Matt. 23^{37-39}, Lk. 13^{34-35}).

(e) Invited guests (Matt. 22^{1-14}, Lk. 14^{16-24}).

The sixth, and exceptional, case is the apocalyptic cento in Lk. 17^{22-37}, put together from non-Marcan details of the augmented Marcan apocalypse in Matt. 24^{23-41}. Here, and here only, St. Luke must be credited with measuring the Marcan text against St. Matthew's augmented version of it, before he reaches the place. But there is no great difficulty in believing that St. Luke already knew that he meant to give the substance of the Marcan apocalypse in its Marcan place. Its Marcan place is also, of course, its Matthaean place: and if we are right in supposing that St. Luke was ranging forward through St. Matthew's text when he composed Lk. 17, we may reasonably suppose also that he saw the Marcan apocalypse through its Matthaean wrappings and realized that he would need it later in its own position. To suppose this is further to suppose that St. Luke had the Marcan apocalypse virtually by heart. But there is no text he is more likely to have had by heart than that.

So much for the six anticipations in Lk. 10–18. They are neatly made, but they do not in fact altogether avoid trenching on Marcan material. When in due course St. Luke arrives at Mk. 12, he discovers that he has already used up the good scribe's question in the lawyer's question (Lk. 10^{25-28}), so he allows the merest vestige of it to appear in its own place (20^{39-40}). Mk. 13^{21-23} is found to have been anticipated in the apocalyptic cento (Lk. 17^{22-23}) and so St. Luke omits it at $21^{24\ f.}$. Mk. 13^{33-37} has been anticipated in the parables of the watching servants (Lk. 12^{35-46}). St. Luke substitutes a generalizing paraphrase for it in 21^{34-36}.

Besides these anticipations in the Lucan Deuteronomy, there is one which falls outside it. In the story of Christ at Jericho, St. Luke anticipates a piece of the Matthaean apocalyptic discourse, the parable of money on trust (Matt. 25^{14-30}, Lk. 19^{11-27}). This anticipation creates no kind of difficulty. The parable is a single unit and manifestly non-Marcan; it has not the least tendency to bring Marcan masonry away with it when it is pulled out of its Matthaean setting.

Thus, when we come to look at the alleged mystery about St. Luke's wrenching of St. Matthew's non-Marcan material away from its Marcan contexts, it turns out to be no mystery at all. Everything that happens happens much as we might expect.

It is time that we concluded the whole discussion. Let us hope we have sufficiently stated the principles required for dispensing with the Q hypothesis, and done something besides to illustrate the application of those principles to the task. We have certainly not given a complete demonstration, for to do that would be nothing less than to write a complete exposition of St. Luke, beginning from the beginning and unfolding the movement of his thought as it comes. But, on the rash assumption that the fulfilment of such a labour would confirm our guesses, let us indulge ourselves a little here, and prophesy.

The literary history of the Gospels will turn out to be a simpler matter than we had supposed. St. Matthew will be seen to be an amplified version of St. Mark, based on a decade of habitual preaching, and incorporating oral material, but presupposing no other literary source beside St. Mark himself. St. Luke, in turn, will be found to presuppose St. Matthew and St. Mark, and St. John to presuppose the three others. The whole literary history of the canonical Gospel tradition will be found to be contained in the fourfold canon itself, except in so far as it lies in the Old Testament, the Pseudepigrapha, and the other New Testament writings.

The surrender of the Q hypothesis will not only clarify the exposition of St. Luke, it will free the interpretation of St. Matthew from the contradiction into which it has fallen. For on the one hand the exposition of St. Matthew sees that Gospel as a living growth, and on the other as an artificial mosaic, and the two pictures cannot be reconciled. If we compare St. Matthew with St. Mark alone, everything can be seen to happen as though St. Matthew, standing in the stream of a living oral tradition, were freely reshaping and enlarging his predecessor under those influences, practical, doctrinal and liturgical, which Dr. Kilpatrick has so admirably set before us in his book.* But then the supposed necessity of the Q hypothesis comes in to confuse us— these apparently free remodellings of St. Mark cannot after all be what they seem, nor are they the work of St. Matthew in his reflection on St. Mark, for they stood in Q before St. Matthew wrote. And that is not the end of the trouble, for if the so-called Q passages were in a written source, so, we must suppose, were other Matthaean paragraphs which have the same firmness of

---

* *The Origins of the Gospel according to St. Matthew.*

outline as the Q passages and are handled by the evangelist in the same way. They were not in Q, or St. Luke would have shown a knowledge of them, which he does not do. Never mind, we can pick another letter from the alphabet: if these are not Q passages, let them be M passages, or what you will. Once rid of Q, we are rid of a progeny of nameless chimaeras, and free to let St. Matthew write as he is moved.

NOTE: THE GENEALOGIES OF CHRIST

A

The Matthaean genealogy is commented on by its author. Three fourteens of generations correspond to three periods, before the kingdom, the kingdom, since the kingdom. The suggestion is, 'And now the kingdom again' (2^2, 3^2, 4^{17}). That *three* spans should bring us to the kingdom of Christ, seems inevitable to any one acquainted with the Gospel tradition, 'On the third day' or 'After three days' (12^{40}, 16^{21}, 17^{23}, 27^{63}). The three spans are of *fourteen* each, and a fourteen strikes the Jewish mind as a fortnight, a double seven. Three fortnights— otherwise put, six weeks, a working-week of weeks—and then, of course, the Sabbatical week, the Messianic kingdom, must follow. The total number of generations contained in the six weeks has the same significance—*forty*: 'After forty years of wandering and temptation, the Promised Land' (4^2).

The number forty is not obtained without art—$7 \times 6 = 42$, but St. Matthew makes it forty by making David and Jeconias each do double duty: they end one fortnight and begin another. Such a reckoning may suggest a similar function for the name of Jesus—he fulfils the working days and initiates the sabbath.

By noting the irregular marriages in the genealogy (Thamar, Rahab, Ruth, Bathsheba) St. Matthew shows that God can 'of the stones raise up children to Abraham' (3^9) and in particular graft his Son into Abraham's stock by a virginal conception.

This genealogy has two formal faults:

(1) The artificial doubling of two names, as indicated.
(2) The omission of several generations from the biblical list between David and Jeconias.

Both faults are eliminated in St. Luke's rewriting.

B

The Lucan genealogy was conceivably written out by its author in groups of seven names each, a division disregarded by his copyists. However that may be, the clue for counting in sevens remains embedded in the beginning of the list. Jesus is both the son of a Joseph, and the seventh descendant of another Joseph; and this remoter Joseph is himself both the son of a Mattathias and the seventh descendant of another Mattathias. For our present purpose it suffices to write down the beginnings and the ends of St. Luke's sets of sevens, leaving the middles blank.

1.	Jesus, Joseph	.	.	Jannai
2.	Joseph, Mattathias		.	Meath
3.	Mattathias .	.	.	Zerubbabel
4.	*Shealtiel*	.	.	*Er*
5.	Jesus .	.	.	Judah
6.	Joseph	.	.	Nathan
7.	David	.	.	Admin
8.	*Arni* .	.	.	*Abraham*
9.	Terah	.	.	Shelah
10.	Cainan	.	.	Enoch
11.	Jared .	.	.	God.

The genealogy is written backwards. The name of Joseph in (2) suggests the family background of Jesus, Mattathias in (3), being the name of the father of the Maccabees, suggests the second Jewish kingdom, Shealtiel father of Zerubbabel in (4) brings us to the exile. The rhythm is then repeated: it runs through an earlier Jesus and an earlier Joseph to David, the father of the former kingdom, as Mattathias was of the later. And so we arrive with (8) at the previous exile—Arni lived under Egyptian bondage, as did Shealtiel under Babylonish captivity.

By italicizing the exilic lines (4) and (8) as we have done, we reveal at a glance the meaning of the list. St. Matthew had a threefold division in his genealogy, of which Babylonish captivity marked the second period. St. Luke's system is likewise divided threefold, but now exile marks both the points of division. After a first captivity the Davidic kingdom arises, and in declining towards a second brings forth the name of Jesus, though not yet of *the* Jesus. After the second captivity the Maccabean state, declining towards a third captivity (the fall of Jerusalem, 21^{24}) brings forth Jesus Christ. But this coming of Jesus Christ closes no more than the *eleventh* 'week' of generations, and the eleven 'weeks' of St. Luke, like the six 'weeks' of St. Matthew, are an incomplete number (Acts 1^{13-26}). As the Matthaean six point forward to a seventh, so the Lucan eleven point forward to a twelfth, the week of the fall of Jerusalem in which St. Luke lives, a week destined to last until the times of the Gentiles are fulfilled (Lk. 21^{24}). And that is the end (21^9, ^{27}). The first advent occupies the seventy-seventh (11×7th) place, the eighty-fourth (12×7th) 'year' is that perfect period at which the Son of Man, returning, finds faith in the 'poor widow' who awaits him with constant prayer (2^{36-38}, cf. 18^{1-8}).

How does St. Luke obtain the liberty to construct so balanced a scheme as his genealogy? By deserting scriptural tradition from David to Jesus, he has the greater part of the list under his absolute control. He derives Jesus not from Solomon, but from his brother Nathan, whose descendants are nowhere listed in scripture.

A diagram of historical providence composed by the grouping of generations in 'weeks' or sevens could be found by our Evangelists already standing in I Enoch 93.

Paul and Mark*

by

J. C. FENTON

IT is generally assumed that the Gospels are easier to understand than the Epistles in the New Testament. For this reason Sunday School lesson-books and Agreed Syllabuses pay more attention to the life of Jesus and the stories in the Gospels than to the teaching of the apostles and the problems of the early Church as we know them from the Epistles. The Gospels (and here we may include Acts also) tell a story, and convey their meaning by means of a narrative; whereas the Epistles contain arguments for particular occasions and teaching for Christians in certain historical situations. Anyone can understand the Gospels; but you must be something of a scholar to understand the Epistles.

There is certainly a sense in which this is true. The pictorial medium of the evangelists will always have a wider appeal than the more abstract methods of the Epistle-writers. And no doubt the Gospels have always been more read than the Epistles; for example, a comparison of the number of extant ancient MSS. of the Gospels and Epistles suggests that this was so in the first centuries.

Nevertheless, from the point of view of one who wishes to interpret the New Testament, and to find out the authors' meaning, the Epistles are easier to understand than the Gospels. This is so, because in each Epistle the writer addresses one situation which can be more or less discovered; and his argument can be more or less expounded; whereas the Gospels, while they have a surface sense—a narrative—seem to have further and deeper senses which cannot be recovered with as much certainty. The

---

* This essay was almost complete before the publication of Dr. A. M. Farrer's *A Study in St. Mark* (1951), Dr. S. G. F. Brandon's *The Fall of Jerusalem and the Christian Church* (1951). It seemed better to leave it as it stood, rather than re-write it in the light of these books.

clarity of the narrative sense hides at first sight the obscurity of the deeper meaning; and the ease with which the Gospels can be understood is only a cloak covering the ease with which the Gospels may be misunderstood. It is not so in the Epistles. It was much easier, in the last century, to portray a 'liberal' Jesus than a 'liberal' Paul. Commentaries on the Gospels are superseded and become out of date more quickly than commentaries on the Epistles. Sanday and Headlam on Romans* is more helpful to the reader of Paul, than Swete on Mark† to the reader of the Gospels.

The Gospels, like the parables, have a sense which is deeper than that of the story which they tell. We might say that they are written in a code, and need a key before they can be understood. Or that their meaning is veiled from us, the veil lying on our minds. The fault lies in us, not in the Gospels: we approach them with our own presuppositions, and with our own interests. And so we ask the wrong questions, and they return no answer, or we mistake their silence and hearing the echo of our own voices we attribute it to them.

What is the key with which we may decode the evangelists' meaning? How can we remove the veil from our understanding? How can we school ourselves to ask the questions which the Gospels were designed to answer?

'The present form and setting of the contents of the Gospels has probably been partly determined by the experience and development of the Church in the period between the ministry of Our Lord and the time when they were written, that period which is chiefly represented for us by the Epistles of St. Paul.

'If we can train ourselves to regard the Gospels in this way, we shall be less likely to put questions to them which they were not designed to answer, and either to exaggerate or to underrate their great value, both historical and otherwise; we shall expect 'neither too much nor too little from them.'‡

That is to say, if we come to the Gospels from the Epistles, with our minds steeped in the teaching of the Epistles, we shall have entered into the world of the Gospels and their authors and first readers.

The faith of the evangelists is the faith of the writers of the Epistles; and since the latter is more or less clear, and cannot be so readily misunderstood, it will act as the key to unlock the meaning of the Gospels.

* W. Sanday and A. C. Headlam, *The Epistle to the Romans* (The International Critical Commentary) (first edition 1895).
† H. B. Swete, *The Gospel According to St. Mark* (first edition 1898).
‡ R. H. Lightfoot, in *The Interpretation of the Bible* (1944) (ed. Dugmore), p. 87.

For, as we are beginning to see more and more clearly, the New Testament and in fact the whole of the Bible, is a unity. 'The Scriptures are like an orchestra. The peculiarities of individual contributions are balanced by a higher unity pervading the whole. God himself has spoken, and his message is fundamentally one. Moreover notwithstanding all individual diversities, the dominant forms of biblical thought and expression transcend these divesrities and have a wider range.'* Because there is this unity in the Bible, one part can be used to throw light on the meaning of another part; and, in this essay, the Epistles of St. Paul will be used to expound the meaning of the Gospel according to St. Mark.

We are to examine here the relationship between Paul and Mark. Until recently, this relationship was usually approached by asking the question—is Mark a Pauline Gospel? That is to say— was the author of Mark influenced by the teaching of Paul? The answers ranged from one extreme to another. Some said that the earliest Gospel was written in order to defend the authority of Paul and the Pauline churches against the claims of the Church of Jerusalem (G. Volkmar, A. Loisy). Others would not go as far as this, and, while doubting the existence of a deliberate pro-Pauline motive in the composition of Mark, agreed nevertheless that a Paulinistic point of view could be detected (B. W. Bacon, J. Weiss, C. G. Montefiore). In the centre there was a party which denied even this: they found, in Mark, a type of Christianity independent of Paul; this was Gentile Christianity, the theology of Paul's predecessors (M. Werner, A. E. J. Rawlinson, F. C. Grant, A. M. Hunter). It was also suggested that Mark's point of view was the same as Peter's and reflected Peter's teaching (C. H. Turner). And, finally, that Mark was a plain, straightforward story, unadulterated by any theological *parti pris* (S. D. F. Salmond).

Thus the question in its older form ('Is Mark a Pauline Gospel?') was answered in various ways; and possibly the variety of answers arises out of the paucity of material upon which a decision can be reached. If Mark was written before A.D. 70, then it may be that only Mark and the Pauline Epistles have survived from the Christian literature of the period before the Fall of Jerusalem. Is it therefore to be expected that it will be possible to say with any degree of certainty what is Pauline, what is Paulinistic, what is typical of Gentile Christianity, or what is Peter's position?

Our aim here is not to make a diagram of the controversial positions in the early Church and locate Mark on it, but to enquire whether the Pauline Epistles help to bring out the mean-

* L. S. Thornton, *The Common Life in the Body of Christ* (1941), p. 3.

ing of Mark; whether they provide a key to his code; whether they help to remove the veil from our minds.

We shall take themes from the Epistles, and expound them; then read Mark with these themes in mind, in order to see whether the apostle helps us to go deeper than the narrative, surface sense of Mark, to his further meanings.

A. Fulfilment

Take first some of Paul's uses of the word 'fulfil'. The basic idea is that the time of fulfilment has come, one result of which is that the Scriptures have been fulfilled and God's promises have been made good. This will be illustrated by three examples: the new law, the new temple, and the new Israel.

The Time is Fulfilled. The Galatian Christians were considering the acceptance of circumcision. Paul tells them that to do so would be to turn back to the condition that they were in before the gospel came to them. Both for Jews and for Gentiles, life before the coming of the gospel was like childhood; that is, it was a form of slavery. The heir is not different from a slave, until the time appointed by the father; he is under guardians and stewards. And both Jews and Gentiles were under τὰ στοιχεῖα τοῦ κόσμου that is, the law of Moses and the worship of pagan deities. But the preaching of the gospel is the announcement of the fulfilment of the appointed time. 'When the fullness of the time (τὸ πλήρωμα τοῦ χρόνου) came, God sent forth his Son, born of a woman, made subject to the law' (Gal. 4[1-7]). God sent his Son at the right time, when the period of bondage was completed. Christ died for us κατὰ καιρὸν, 'in due season' (Rom. 5[6]).

To change the metaphor, those who receive the gospel are no longer in the darkness, but are in the light of the day. The day has not yet dawned for the whole world, but its light has already reached the believers through the preaching of the gospel. 'Ye are all sons of light, and sons of the day: we are not of the night, nor of darkness' (I Thess. 5[5]). Isaiah's prophesy has been fulfilled (Isa. 49[8]): 'Behold, now is the acceptable time; behold, now is the day of salvation' (II Cor. 6[2], cf. also Rom. 13[11-14]).

The Scriptures are Fulfilled. The coming of the time of fulfilment is also the coming of the fulfilment of God's promises in Scripture. Paul preaches the gospel of God 'which he promised before by his prophets in the holy Scriptures' (Rom. 1[2]); the gospel which Scripture preached beforehand to Abraham (Gal. 3[8]). Christ is the answer to all God's promises (II Cor. 1[20]), and the law and the prophets bear witness to him (Rom. 3[21]).

The Scriptures are fulfilled not only in Christ, but also in the Church. The account of the Israelites in the wilderness is full of lessons for the Church in Corinth. The former are types of the latter; and the story of the former was written as an admonition for the latter (I Cor. 10^{1-13}). 'Whatsoever things were written aforetime were written for our learning' (Rom. 15^4). Both the promises of God and his warnings, are being fulfilled in this new age of salvation.

The Fulfilment of the Law. The Scriptures are God's promises and warnings; the law is God's command, and it also has been fulfilled in Christ, in at least three senses. First, in the sense that what the law foreshadowed has been finally effected in the redemption which is in Christ Jesus. The law bears witness to this justifying act of God (Rom. 3^{21}); the demand in the law for an expiation of sin through the shedding of blood has now been met. Second, the law is fulfilled in the sense that it has now been superseded by the gospel: in Christ, God acted in a new way, apart from the law (Rom. 3^{21}); and the law, as a way of attaining righteousness, was replaced by faith. 'Christ is the end of the law unto righteousness to every one that believeth' (Rom. 10^4). The time of the law's dominion is ended. Third, the purpose of the law, the attainment of righteousness, is achieved by faith in Jesus Christ. We are justified by faith in him, and not by the works of the law. But we *are* justified; what the law aimed at, but failed to reach, has now been reached. 'The requirement of the law is fulfilled in us, who walk not after the flesh (the Mosaic Code), but after the Spirit' (Rom. 8^4). The Spirit teaches us to love, and love is the fulfilment of the law (Rom. 13^{10}, Gal. 5^{14}). Thus the law points forward to the work of Christ; it is superseded through the work of Christ; and its requirement is satisfied by the love of the Christian.

The New Temple. As the law has been superseded by the gospel, the temple, for which the law made regulations, has also been superseded. And just as the law is fulfilled in charity, so the temple has its antitype in the Church. Under the old covenant, the dwelling-place of God was the temple at Jerusalem; now, under the new covenant, God dwells in the Church. 'We are the temple of the living God.' Another promise has been fulfilled, 'I will dwell in them, and walk in them' (II Cor. 6^{16}). Christ's ministers are temple-workmen, building upon the foundation, Jesus Christ (I Cor. 3^{10-17}). And since, in this new order, each part is a microcosm of the whole, reproducing the characteristics of the whole, the body of each believer is the temple of the Holy Spirit (I Cor. 6^{19}).

The New Israel. Besides being the antitype of the temple, the Church is also the antitype of the temple-worshippers—the people of God. 'I will dwell in them and walk in them; and I will be their God, and they shall be my people' (II Cor. 6[16]). Before, there was a distinction between the house and those who entered the house; now the two coincide, and the church is both sanctuary and Israel. Moreover, there is no longer a distinction between worshipper and sacrifice: now the worshipper offers himself, a living sacrifice, holy, acceptable to God; this is his spiritual worship (Rom. 12[1]).

The Christians, whether of Israel after the flesh, or of the Gentiles, partake of the life of the olive (Rom. 11[17]). The Israelites in the wilderness are their fathers (I Cor. 10[1]). They are Abraham's seed, since they are Christ's (Gal. 3[29]). They are the circumsion (Phil. 3[3]).

Thus the gospel is fulfilment. It enters the world at the fulfilment of the time of waiting and promise; it fulfils Judaism: the scriptures, the law, the temple, the people of God. By fulfilment is meant the answer to promise through the coming of that which was spoken of beforehand; also the replacing and setting aside of the old by the new; and the satisfaction of the hunger of the old, by the fullness and richness of the new.

Turning to Mark with these themes in mind we ask whether the meaning of his narrative is unlocked by such considerations.

The Time is Fulfilled. The first words of Jesus in Mark are, 'The time is fulfilled' (πεπλήρωται ὁ καιρὸς) 1[15]. When we compare this with the statement of St. Paul in Gal. 4[4] (ὅτε δὲ ἦλθεν τὸ πλήρωμα τοῦ χρόνου) the only difference seems to be that Mark says the season of God's salvation has come, whereas Paul says that the time of preparation (before the season) has been filled up. In the former, the emphasis is on what is now present; in the latter, on what has gone before. Whichever way we look at it, the result is the same: the new fact is here. The coming of Jesus is God's last appeal. 'He had yet one, an only son: he sent him last (ἔσχατον) unto them, saying, They will reverence my son', 12[6]. The son comes last, after the servants of the lord of the vineyard; and of these servants the last was John the Baptist, whose coming terminated the time of preparation, and whose imprisonment marked the beginning of the gospel, the season of salvation (1[14]).

The Scriptures are Fulfilled. John the Baptist was the beginning of the gospel, because in him Scripture began to be fulfilled. He was the answer to God's promises made through Malachi and Isaiah

(Mk. $1^{2,\ 3}$). He was the Elijah returned of scribal teaching. Men did to him whatever they wished 'even as it is written of him' (9^{11-13}); he died at the hands of Herod and Herodias, a new Ahab and Jezebel. But he had already been the means of anointing the mightier one, the King in whom all God's promises were confirmed; the Son of Man who goes even as it is written of him; who is smitten as Zechariah had foretold; who is arrested and deserted that the Scriptures might be fulfilled ($14^{21,\ 27,\ 49}$). Moreover, this is he who sits at the right hand of power, and will come with the clouds of heaven, as David and Daniel had said (14^{62}). Paul and Mark, no less than the authors of Matthew and the Epistle to the Hebrews, believed that in Jesus the Scriptures were fulfilled.

The Fulfilment of the Law. The time of preparation is complete; the one who fulfils the will of God has come; therefore the law of Moses has been fulfilled. To Mark, as to Paul, this means three things; (*a*) the law bears witness (against itself) to Christ; (*b*) Christ is the end of the law—it has no more power; (*c*) the charity of the gospel sums up the commandments of the law.

(*a*) Before the series of stories which show the superiority of the gospel to the law and the conflict between the Church and the Synagogue (2^1–3^6), Mark places the cleansing of the leper. The cleansed man is commanded to show himself to the priest, and offer for his cleansing the things which Moses commanded, 'for a testimony unto them' (1^{44}). The meaning *may* be that the law, which the leper is to observe, bears witness to the purifying work of Christ. In a number of other passages however there is a clear appeal to the law of Moses in support of the action and teaching of Jesus. Thus he enquires whether it is lawful on the Sabbath day to do good, or to do harm; to save life or to kill (3^4). He contrasts the law of honouring parents with the tradition of the elders (7^{6-13}). His first words to the rich man are, 'Thou knowest the commandments' (10^{19}). Therefore, though in Christ God is acting apart from the law, his action is witnessed by the law.

(*b*) The law's function is confined to witnessing: it cannot restrain the grace of God in Christ. When it attempts to do so, it has transgressed its purpose, and it comes under the wrath of Christ (2^1–3^6. N.B., 3^5, μετ' ὀργῆς). The meaning of these five conflict stories is made clear in the central one: the new undressed cloth cannot be sewn into the surroundings of an old garment; the new unfermented wine of the gospel cannot be contained in the old bottles of the law, dry and stretched to the full. The gospel must therefore displace the law.

(*c*) Yet in another sense the gospel establishes the law (Rom.

3^{31}); it establishes it as *witness*, both to the gospel, and to the way of life which God commands. In the gospel, the law is kept, and in this sense fulfilled. There is no commandment greater than the love of God and the neighbour; and this is more than whole burnt offerings and sacrifices (12^{28-34}).

Furthermore, Paul had said that the law was imperfect: 'it was ordained through angels by the hand of a mediator' (Gal. 3^{19}). Mark similarly draws a distinction between the commandment, or word of God, and the tradition of men; and by means of this distinction declares the end of the law of clean and unclean meats (7^{1-23}, cf. I Cor. 6^{12} f., Rom. 14). And within the law itself, he finds a concession made for the hardness of Israel's heart, which was not in the will of God from the beginning of the creation (10^{1-12}, cf. I Cor. 7^{10}). Christ returns to the original intention of God; the gospel restores the true understanding of marriage which had been lost in the law as Israel had received it.

The New Temple. Charity is more than all whole burnt offerings and sacrifices (12^{33}) and as the law of sacrifice is fulfilled in charity, so the place of sacrifice is fulfilled in the Church. The old temple had become corrupt, a den of robbers; whereas the scripture had said that it should be a house of prayer for all the nations (11^{17}). What the old temple had failed to be, that the new will be. The old was like the fig tree which had leaves but no fruit—the appearance, but not the reality, of faith in God ($11^{12-14, \ 20-25}$). Jesus foretells the destruction of this building (13^2) and its replacement by another temple—for so perhaps Mark intended his readers to understand the evidence of the false witnesses (14^{57} f.) and the mocking at the crucifixion (15^{29}). Jesus is, in fact, what his enemies accuse him of being—the King of the Jews, the Christ, the Saviour, and the builder of the temple made without hands.* Moreover the words 'in three days' (14^{58}, 15^{29}) associate this work of Jesus with his death and resurrection. Thus the signs which follow his death are first the rending of the temple-veil; and second the confession of the centurion ($15^{38, \ 39}$), that is, the end of the old and the beginning of the new; already the promise that the house of prayer shall be for all the nations is beginning to be fulfilled in the case of the Gentile soldier.

The New Israel. The unfaithfulness (or unfruitfulness) of the Jews led to the destruction of the temple (11^{11-25}); and similarly, their withholding of the vineyard fruits led to their own destruction, and

* χειροποίητος probably means more than 'made by man'; it seems to carry some of the sense of 'idolatrous'; what man has made, as opposed to what God has commanded. See J. B. Lightfoot, *Saint Paul's Epistles to the Colossians and to Philemon* (1879), p. 181.

the giving of the vineyard to others (12^{1-12}). The Israelites according to the flesh are expelled from membership of the people of God,
and it is opened to the Gentiles. The patriarchs of this new Israel
were called and appointed in the mountain ($3^{13, 14}$); the covenant
was made in Christ's blood (14^{24}). The death and resurrection of
Christ took place at the passover season, when the Jews remembered the exodus from Egypt, but the Christians their ransoming
at the price of the life of the Son of Man (10^{45}).

B. *Hiding and Revealing*

Christ came to fulfil the promises made to Israel, and to bring
the old order to completion. But Israel did not recognize or
accept this new gift of God: they killed the Lord Jesus and drove
out Paul (I Thess. 2^{15}). This caused the apostle great sorrow and
unceasing pain (Rom. 9^2).

Why are there some both among the Jews and among the
Gentiles who reject the gospel of their salvation? Because for these
the gospel is veiled; veiled by the god of this age, who has blinded
the minds of the unbelieving (II Cor. $4^{3\ f.}$). Therefore they desire
the wrong things. The apostle preaches Christ crucified, setting
him forth to public view; but the Jews ask for signs, and the Greeks
seek after wisdom. So in their blindness to the truth of God, and
in their search for what they imagine to be the truth, the gospel is a
stumbling-block to the Jews, and foolishness to the Gentiles
(I Cor. $1^{22\ f.}$).

The wisdom of God in the gospel cannot be known except by
those who have the Spirit of God. God reveals it through the
Spirit; and the Spirit searches the deep things of God (I Cor. 2^{10}).
Others have not the Spirit; they have only the mind of the flesh.
The gospel is hidden from them, and from the rulers of this age
who hold them in bondage.

The man who believes is to learn humility from this mystery.
The fact of his faith is not to lead him to any boasting of himself,
but to the praise of God, who has had mercy upon him. God has
mercy on whom he will, and whom he will he hardens (Rom. 9^{18}).
All have sinned; all have been disobedient. Some are now called
to faith and some are still in unbelief; but in the end God will have
mercy upon all. 'For I would not, brethren, have you ignorant of
this mystery, lest ye be wise in your own conceits, that a hardening
in part (πώρωσις ἀπὸ μέρους) hath befallen Israel, until the fullness
of the Gentiles be come in; and so all Israel shall be saved' (Rom.
$11^{25\ f.}$).

Thus the rejection of the gospel leads the apostle to speak of folly and wisdom, hardening and mercy, hiding and revealing, offence and faith, flesh and spirit.

The evangelist was forced to face the same question—Why was the fulfilment of Israel rejected by Israel? Why was Jesus handed over by the Jews for crucifixion? Mark knew that Jesus was the Christ, the Son of God, the King of the Jews. The evil spirits had recognized him as the Holy One of God from the first; Peter's eyes had been opened, and he had confessed. But the leaders of the Jews did not receive him even when he answered I AM to the High Priest's question, Art thou the Christ, the Son of the Blessed? They accused him of blasphemy and condemned him to death (14^{61-64}). Why did the Jews reject their king? Why did Israel reject its fulfilment?

That Jesus is to be rejected by the Jews becomes clear to Mark's readers in the five stories which disclose the conflict between the two orders, the law and the gospel (2^1-3^6). In the first story, certain of the scribes reason in their hearts; in the second, scribes of the Pharisees raise objections with the disciples of Jesus; in the third and fourth the objection is brought to Jesus himself; and in the last, they are watching for grounds on which to accuse him. The series is rounded off with the plan of the Pharisees and Herodians to destroy Jesus. Thus from this point in the narrative, the reader knows that the new gift of God will be rejected. Moreover, Jesus, on his part, speaks also in this section of the day when the bridegroom will be taken away from the sons of the bridechamber and they will fast ($2^{19\ f.}$). Mark gives us one word to explain this mounting opposition, the end of which is the crucifixion; 'Jesus looked round about on them with anger, being grieved at the hardening of their heart'—ἐπὶ τῇ πωρώσει τῆς καρδίας αὐτῶν (3^5).

We meet the Jewish leaders next in the Beelzebub controversy (3^{22-30}). Scribes from Jerusalem say that the exorcisms of Jesus are done in the power of the prince of the demons; that is, they call the Holy Spirit, which came upon him at his baptism, and works the miracles, an unclean spirit; thus they blaspheme against the Holy Spirit and are guilty of an eternal sin. They have not the Spirit, 'who searches all things, yea, the deep things of God'; they are natural men, who know not the things of the Spirit of the God. The scribes from Jerusalem cannot receive the miracles, for such things are spiritually judged.

Before and after this section, and parallel to it, are the setting out and arrival of the relations of Jesus.* Like the scribes, his

---

* Assuming that οἱ παρ' αὐτοῦ in 3^{21} are the same as ἡ μήτηρ αὐτοῦ καὶ οἱ ἀδελφοὶ αὐτοῦ in 3^{31}.

family cannot understand and receive the gospel; it is foolishness to them; they say that he is beside himself and try to arrest him. They are fleshly relations, not spiritual; and it is not the children of flesh that are children of God (Rom. 9⁸). The true relations of Jesus are those who are sitting about him, and do the will of God; they hear the word which he speaks, and accept it, and bear fruit (4²⁰).

This is to look forward to the next section, the parables (4¹⁻³⁴), and Mark may have intended the reader to look forward. The theme of 3⁷⁻³⁵ (the scribes and the two families) is continued in 4¹⁻³⁴: some are like unfruitful ground, 'outside',* to whom the mystery is not given; others are like good soil, having ears to hear. From some the gospel is hidden, being proclaimed secretly in parables; to others, the gospel is revealed. But just as the apostle believed that the hardening of Israel was only temporary, so Mark also looks forward; 'There is nothing hidden, save that it should be manifested, neither was anything made secret, but that it should come to light' (4²²).

When Jesus comes to his own country, the distinction between flesh and spirit is made yet more clear. The synagogue congregation knows his relations—they know Jesus only according to the flesh; so they stumble in unbelief (6¹⁻⁶).

Finally, when we read that the Pharisees seek a sign from heaven of Jesus, tempting him, we remember that the Jews ask for signs; and that the gospel, which is the power and wisdom of God to those whom he has called, is therefore to them a stumbling-block (8¹¹⁻¹³).

Why did the Jews reject Jesus? The 'answer' which Mark gives is the same as the 'answer' of Paul; hardness of heart, unbelief, carnal, unspiritual; there is, in the last analysis, no answer beyond 'whom he will, he hardens'.

So much for the rejection of the gospel in Mark; there is also the other side, the acceptance of the gospel, the faith of the disciples; 'God has mercy on whom he will'. We shall see the mercy of God revealed in the faith of the twelve.

Although the twelve have been called and appointed, given the mystery of the kingdom and authority to preach and exorcize, nevertheless, like Christ's family and fellow-countrymen, like the scribes and the Sanhedrin, they cannot understand because they also are carnal.

The failure of the disciples is a notorious feature of this Gospel,

---

* Cf. 4¹¹ ἐκείνοις δὲ τοῖς ἔξω ἐν παραβολαῖς τὰ πάντα γίνεται with 3³¹ καὶ ἔξω ἐστῶτες, and 3³² ᾽Ιδού, ἡ μήτηρ σου καὶ οἱ ἀδελφοί σου ἔξω ζητοῦσί σε. See also ἔξω in I Cor. 5¹²,¹³ etc.

of which many explanations have been offered. These do not necessarily exclude one another. For example, it is possible to hold that this is how it happened; the disciples were afraid and did not understand; this is an historical reminiscence going back to Peter or another of the first disciples. Or, that Mark had to reconcile the clear claims and predictions of Jesus with the breakdown of the disciples after the arrest; and his method was to say that they did not understand the words of Jesus at the time when they were spoken. Again, it might be that the failure of the disciples is a dramatic device, useful for keeping the story moving, and acting as a foil to introduce further deeds and words of Jesus. Or, that Mark had to join together story-units each complete in itself, each manifesting Jesus as the Christ, into a connected narrative which ends in failure and fear. Another suggestion has been that the failure of Peter, Judas, the brethren of Christ and the others is stressed for polemic reasons; that it reflects the conflict between the Pauline and the Jewish Christian communities in the first century. Yet another interpretation is this: no man, as a man, can believe, unless it be given him from above. No one can say Jesus is Lord, except by the Holy Spirit. The disciple of Jesus is a disciple of Jesus because he has been made such by God and not only because he has chosen it for himself.

Jesus rebuked them that were about him with the twelve for not understanding the parables (4^{13}); for their fear and lack of faith in the storm (4^{40}); and for their fear when he walked on the sea, when Mark adds that they understood not concerning the loaves, but their heart was hardened (6^{50-52}). The first climax of the unbelief of the disciples comes in $8^{14ff.}$, when they reasoned because they had no bread: 'Do ye not yet perceive, neither understand? Have ye your heart hardened? Having eyes, see ye not? Having ears, hear ye not? And do ye not remember? . . . Do ye not yet understand?'

Jesus performs the miracle of the restoration of sight and the disciples see and understand and Peter says, 'Thou art the Christ'. But this is only part of the gospel. Jesus begins to teach them the suffering, rejection, death, and resurrection of the Son of Man and this they cannot yet accept. Mark tells us of their failure after each of the three main predictions: Peter rebuked him (8^{32}); they did not understand, and were afraid to ask, and reasoned who was greater ($9^{32 ff.}$); they were amazed and afraid, James and John asked for the places of honour in his glory, and the others were indignant ($10^{35 ff.}$). So they fulfil the scriptures and the words of Jesus: one betrays him; all are offended and scattered; one denies him three times. The Gospel ends on the same note of failure:* now that the men have deserted, the women are left, but they seek Jesus the Nazarene, the crucified; and when they are told of resurrection, trembling and astonishment come upon them, and they say nothing to anyone, because they are afraid. Flesh as flesh, man as man, cannot perceive and understand. Only the Spirit can search and make known the hidden things of God. The disciples' faith stands by the mercy of God and not by their works.

C. Defeat and Victory

The natural man does not receive the cross and resurrection which are the heart of the gospel, because they are foolishness to him; that is, they reverse the normal way of thinking. The gospel claims that victory was won in an apparent defeat, and that power was exercised in what seems to be weakness. This is the centre of the gospel; we shall consider it first in Paul, then in Mark.

It seems from the second epistle to the Corinthians that there was a party in Corinth which warred according to the flesh (10^3) and boasted according to the flesh. That is, they established their authority over the Church by means of this-worldly arguments: that they were Hebrews, Israelites, the seed of Abraham, ministers of Christ. Paul replies that, while he hates this kind of argument, he can out-bid such people: he has suffered more in the service of Christ than they. 'If I must needs boast, I will boast of the things that concern my weakness' (11^{30}, cf. 12^5). There are two ways in which Paul sees the force of his argument from weakness. First, when the minister of Christ is a weak and suffering man, then the power of Christ rests upon him and acts through him; the Lord had said to Paul, 'My power is made perfect in weakness' ($12^{9, 10}$). Second, the minister of Christ is an imitator of Christ; and Christ's work was done on the Cross, in weakness; therefore his minister must follow him in suffering; 'He was crucified through weakness, yet he liveth through the power of God' (13^4).

Moreover, weakness and power are not to be thought of as successive moments, one reversing the other. The power of God is exercised in the weakness of the flesh—whether it be Christ's death on the cross or Paul's sufferings in the ministry. When Christ was weakest, then he was strongest, and when Paul was weakest, then he was strongest (12^{10}). The deadness of Abraham's

---

* For the arguments in favour of 16^8 as the original conclusion of St. Mark's Gospel see for example R. H. Lightfoot, *The Gospel Message of St. Mark* (1950), pp. 80 ff.

body and Sarah's womb was the place where God's power acted, his promise was fulfilled, and faith and hope were centred (Rom. 4^{18-25}). The grave is the place of power; victory is won in defeat; death is the way to life. The triumph of Christ over the hostile powers was achieved on the cross (Col. 2^{15}).

The converse is also true. The apparent success of the hostile powers over Christ in the crucifixion was in fact their failure and defeat. The rulers of this world did not know what they were doing when they crucified Christ; they thought that they were destroying him, but in fact they were bringing upon themselves their own destruction (I Cor. 2^{6-8}). The law which declared the crucified Christ cursed, was at the same moment done away (Gal. $3^{13\ f.}$).

According to Paul, the gospel demands that we reverse the natural way of considering victory and defeat, power and weakness, glory and shame.

In the same way, Mark sees in the gospel God's act of reversal—turning defeat into victory and victory into defeat. This act is the fulfilment of Scripture:

> The stone which the builders rejected,
> The same was made the head of the corner:
> This was from the Lord,
> And it is marvellous in our eyes.
> (Ps. $118^{22,\ 23}$.)

The quotation is made at the end of the parable of the vineyard (12^{1-12}), and it summarizes the main point of the parable: Israel's rejection of the Only Son will be reversed by God into his rejection of Israel according to the flesh, and his giving the vineyard to others, that is, to the Gentiles. Israel's apparent success is in fact their failure, and Christ's apparent failure is in fact his success, for God makes him the king of the (new) Jews.*

Moreover, as the quotation from Ps. 118 summarizes the parable of the vineyard, so the parable summarizes the plot of the Gospel as a whole. There are two movements running through the Gospel, side by side, from the beginning to the end; they are the opposition of the Jews to Jesus, and the faith of the disciples; or, the casting off of the old Israel, and the covenanting of the new.

The former begins in the synagogue at Capernaum; develops in the conflict stories into the plot to destroy Jesus; continues in the

---

* Mark reserves the title βασιλεύς for the trial, mocking and crucifixion of Jesus, and then uses it six times: $15^{2,\ 9,\ 12,\ 18,\ 26,\ 32}$. He avoided it at the entry into Jerusalem, $11^{9\ f.}$. The royalty of Jesus is manifested in the giving of his life as a ransom, 10^{42-45}.

unforgivable sin of the Jerusalem scribes, and their blasphemy against the Holy Spirit; the rejection of Jesus in his own country; the hypocrisy of the Pharisees and scribes from Jerusalem; the request for a sign; the disputes with the Jewish leaders in Jerusalem; and finally in the Passion itself. This corresponds to the words of the husbandmen, 'This is the heir; come, let us kill him, and the inheritance shall be ours' (12⁷).

Side by side with this, Mark traces the other movement, namely, the calling of the new Israel and the faith of the disciples. This begins with the calling of the two pairs of brothers, and of Levi, continues in the appointment of the Twelve and their mission, and reaches its climax in the making of the new covenant in the Passion.

Thus the two movements, which have gone on side by side throughout the earlier part of the book, meet at the cross: the cross is both the husbandmen's act of rejection, and God's enthronement of the King of the Jews.*

Paul had said that the death of Jesus was the act of the rulers of this world (I Cor. 2⁶ ᶠᶠ·)—i.e. the demonic powers; they had used the Jews as their willing agents. Mark also shows the opposition of Jesus to the demons whom he has come to destroy; and it may be that Mark intended us to understand the conflict between Jesus and the Jews, and between Jesus and the demons, as one conflict.

Thus, in the first miracle story, Jesus is shown as the one who brings a new and authoritative teaching into the synagogue, and has authority to command the unclean spirits so that they obey him. That is to say, from the beginning Jesus is presented as one who is the fulfilment of Judaism, and the destroyer of Satan's power: he is preacher and healer. He manifests his setting-aside of Judaism, and his victory over the demonic forces; but this setting-aside and victory are achieved through his rejection by the Jews, and death at the hand of the demonic enemies who use the Jews as their agents. So his victory is won in an apparent defeat; and their apparent victory over him is in fact their undoing.† The new wine has burst the old skins, and the fulfilment has made a worse rent in the old garment (2²¹, ²²).

D. *Jesus is Lord*

Jesus died and was raised from the dead in order that he might be Lord. Death and resurrection were his way to Lordship. This

---

* See previous note.

† This is set out more fully in a note on 'Destruction and Salvation in St. Mark's Gospel', *J.T.S.* (April 1952).

is a spiritual fact which can only be perceived by those who are spiritual; that is to say, the primitive creed κύριος Ἰησοῦς can only be spoken by those who are in the Holy Spirit. The mouth says the words, but only the Spirit can move the heart to believe that God raised Jesus from the dead (Rom. 10⁹ ᶠ·, I Cor. 12³).

God has given to Jesus the name κύριος which is above every name, on account of his obedience and death. Unlike the first Adam, the second Adam humbled himself and kept the command-ment of God, and accepted death. All things will be put under his feet, as in the beginning all things were subjected to the first Adam. For Jesus is the second, heavenly man (I Cor. 15⁴⁵ ᶠᶠ·), whom the first man pre-figured (Rom. 5¹⁴) and who fulfils the words of Ps. 110¹ 'Sit thou at my right hand' (Col. 3¹, Rom. 8³⁴).

God 'has put all things in subjection under his feet' (Ps. 8⁶, quoted in I Cor. 15²⁷). Jesus is Lord. Lord over what? First, Lord over dead and living. 'To this end Christ died, and lived again, that he might be Lord of both the dead and the living' (Rom. 14⁹). That is to say, death has no power to separate us from Christ (Rom. 8³⁸ ᶠ·); those who die are still his. Second, he is Lord over the Jews and the Gentiles. 'There is no distinction between Jew and Greek; for the same Lord is Lord of all; and is rich unto all that call upon him; for Whosoever shall call upon the name of the Lord shall be saved' (Rom. 10¹², ¹³). He has abolished the ancient division, because he is the promised seed of Abraham, in whom all the Gentiles are blessed (Gal. 3¹⁶ ᶠᶠ·). That is, he is the true Isaac, the seed of Abraham to whom the promises were made.*

Third, Jesus is Lord over the spiritual powers. His name is above every other name (Phil. 2⁹). Angels and principalities cannot separate from him (Rom. 8³⁸, ³⁹). Amongst the spiritual powers Paul places also the law. As the Gentiles were under the στοιχεῖα, so the Jews were under the law, until the appointed time. Now that the heir has 'come of age', he has redeemed the Gentiles from the bondage of the στοιχεῖα, and the Jews from the bondage of the law (Gal. 4¹ ᶠᶠ·). He has cancelled the law, and triumphed over the principalities and powers by his death on the cross (Col. 2¹⁴ ᶠ·).

While the apostle expounds the faith of the Church in the Lordship of Jesus, the evangelist uses the Gospel stories to illus-trate the same faith.

* This fulfilment is present, not only in Galatians, but also in Romans 8³², ὅς γε τοῦ ἰδίου υἱοῦ οὐκ ἐφείσατο, Cf. Gen. 22¹⁶, LXX; see C. H. Turner's article, Ο ΥΙΟΣ ΜΟΥ Ο ΑΓΑΠΗΤΟΣ, *J.T.S.* (Jan. 1926), pp. 119 f.

Like Paul, he sees the fulfilment of Ps. 110[1] in the resurrection and exaltation of Jesus. The verse is quoted and commented on in Mk. 12[35-37] and is referred to again in the reply of Jesus to the High Priest: 'Ye shall see the Son of Man sitting at the right hand of power' (14[62]). The fact that this verse is quoted by both Paul and Mark is of less importance than the comment which is made on the verse in Mark. For the psalm is quoted to show that Jesus is only inadequately called the Son of David. 'David himself calleth him Lord' (12[37]). Unlike Matthew and Luke, Mark makes little use of the Son of David theme—the title is used by Bartimaeus, but during the period of his blindness (10[46-52]). Similarly, Paul has only few references to Christ as the Son of David; Rom. 1[3], 15[12], cf. Col. 1[13].* In this respect, Paul and Mark are together contrasted with Matthew and Luke, who use the title more frequently.

Jesus is Lord, seated at God's right hand, and he has entered into his glory by means of death and resurrection. The predictions of the Passion and Resurrection in Mk. 8, 9, 10, show the way of Jesus to his glory and Lordship. Nevertheless, the nature of a Gospel as a literary form is such that what Jesus became by his resurrection, must be shown to the reader before the Resurrection is recorded. That is to say, although Jesus became Lord through death and resurrection and exaltation, yet he is revealed as Lord during the ministry before his death.

First, as in Paul, Jesus is Lord of the dead as well as of the living. He raises the dead daughter of Jairus (5[22-43]), and the child with the spirit who became as one dead (9[14-29]). Second, Jesus is Lord over the Jews and over the Gentiles; there is now no distinction. The gospel must be preached to all the nations (13[10]): he has made all meats clean (7[19]) and so abolished the law's distinction between Israel after the flesh and the Gentiles. The words to the Syrophoenician woman contain a promise of the satisfaction of the Gentiles, when Israel after the flesh has had its opportunity; 'Let the children first be filled. . . . Yea, Lord, even the dogs under the table eat of the children's crumbs' (7[27 f.]). This story comes between the two feeding miracles, the Five Thousand and the Four Thousand; and if it is right to think of the former as Jews and the latter as Gentiles, as some commentators have suggested,† then in these two acts of feeding and filling we

---

* καὶ μετέστησεν εἰς τὴν βασιλείαν τοῦ υἱοῦ τῆς ἀγάπης αὐτοῦ, where τοῦ υἱοῦ τῆς ἀγάπης αὐτοῦ may be a reference to Christ as the Son of David, since David means Beloved; so W. J. Phythian-Adams, *The Way of At-one-ment* (1944), p. 23.

† E.g., A. Richardson, *The Miracle-Stories of the Gospels* (1941), pp. 97 f.; A. M. Farrer, *A Study in St. Mark* (1951), specially ch. XIII. Notice also the use of χορτάζειν in

have a further illustration of the Lordship of Jesus over the Jews and the Gentiles. In Mark, as in Paul, Jesus is the seed of Abraham, the true Isaac, the υἱός ἀγαπητός (cf. Gen. 22, Mk. 1¹¹, 9⁷, 12⁶); therefore he is the Lord of the new Israel, the king of the true Jews, enthroned on the cross. Third, Jesus is Lord over the spiritual powers; 'with authority he commandeth even the unclean spirits, and they obey him' (1²⁷). 'The unclean spirits, whensoever they beheld him, fell down before him, and cried saying, Thou art the Son of God' (3¹¹). 'Who is this, that even the wind and the sea obey him?' (4⁴¹), etc.

We found in Paul a link between the Lordship of Jesus, and the fulfilment of the Adam-type. Possibly Mark also intended his readers to understand that Jesus is the second Adam. Apart from the meaning of the title Son of Man, which Dr. Farrer thinks is another way of saying new Adam,* the Baptism story in Mark may have been intended to show Jesus as the new man, coming from the waters, receiving the Spirit, with the beasts, tempted by Satan, but not overcome by temptation (cf. Gen. 1–3). Paul had said that 'as through the one man's disobedience the many were made sinners, even so through the obedience of the one shall the many be made righteous' (Rom. 5¹⁹); that is, the saving act of the last Adam is an act of obedience to God. Perhaps this was how Mark understood the story of Jesus in Gethsemane (Mk. 14³²⁻⁴²): it revealed the obedience of Jesus to the will of the Father, an obedience which was the inner reality of the crucifixion, and which gave saving power to that act.

E. Faith and Discipleship

Jesus the Lord calls men to believe in him and to follow him. We must consider now the meaning of faith and discipleship, in Paul and in Mark, in so far as the Apostle illuminates the meaning of the Evangelist.

The gospel, Paul says, is the power of God unto salvation to everyone that believes. Faith is required, not descent from Abraham, or circumcision, or the other works of the law; therefore the gospel is powerful to save Jews and Greeks without distinction (although the Jew has a certain priority) (Rom. 1¹⁶). The gospel thus fulfils the words of Habakkuk: 'But the righteous shall

---

Mk. 6⁴², 7²⁷, 8⁴, ⁸; the five thousand are said to be 'as sheep not having a shepherd', which is a description of Israel in Num. 27¹⁷, I Kgs. 22¹⁷, Ezek. 34⁵ and Matt. 9³⁶ (cf. 10⁵, ⁶); of the four thousand it is said, τινὲς αὐτῶν ἀπὸ μακρόθεν ἥκασι, cf. Eph. 2¹³, ¹⁷ (quoting Isa. 57¹⁹), Acts 2³⁹, 22²¹, where the reference is to the Gentiles.

* *The Glass of Vision* (1948), p. 42; *A Rebirth of Images* (1949), p. 52; *A Study in St. Mark* (1951), pp. 247–89.

live by faith', and the words of the law concerning Abraham, that he believed God and it was reckoned unto him for righteousness. Abraham's faith is, in fact, faith of the same kind as Christian faith, because it is directed to God who raises the dead. In the case of Abraham, he believed in the promise of God to raise a living seed from himself and Sarah when they were both as good as dead. In the case of the Christian, he believes in God who raised Jesus the Lord (the second Isaac) from the dead. The birth of Isaac is therefore a type of the resurrection of Christ; Abraham's faith is of the same kind as Christian faith; and the law, which records this, is not annulled, but established, by the gospel (Rom. 3^{31}–4^{25}).

Abraham considered his own body as good as dead; and similarly the faith of the Christian unites him to Christ in death. The believer acknowledges his impotence, and is made one with Christ in death; he is buried with Christ, in order that he may be raised by God. Thus faith, like baptism, is an entering into the death and resurrection of Christ.

'I have been crucified with Christ. . . . Christ liveth in me' (Gal. 2^{20}). The believer is one in whom Christ dwells. When the faithful meet one another, they meet Christ. The Galatians had understood this, and had received Paul 'as Christ Jesus' (4^{14}). The Romans are to treat one another as Christ treated them; as he received them, so they are to receive the weaker brethren, and not to cause them to stumble. To offend a weaker brother is to destroy one for whom Christ died (Rom. 14^{15}).

In Mark, as in the Epistles of Paul, the response to the gospel is faith. 'Jesus came into Galilee, preaching the gospel of God, and saying, The time is fulfilled, and the kingdom of God is at hand; repent ye, and believe in the gospel' ($1^{14, 15}$). God offers salvation to those who believe, and the coming of salvation is symbolized in the healing of the sick. 'Jesus, seeing their faith, saith unto the sick of the palsy, Son, thy sins are forgiven' (2^5). 'Daughter, thy faith hath made thee whole; go in peace, and be whole of the plague' (5^{34}). 'All things are possible to him that believeth' (9^{23}). 'Go thy way, thy faith hath made thee whole' (10^{52}).

The opposite of faith is unbelief. The Jews sought to establish their own righteousness, by works of the law, and not by faith in Christ, and thus they failed to obtain the righteousness of God (Rom. 10^3). This is perhaps the meaning of the cursing of the fig tree in Mark, which is dovetailed into the first two visits to the Temple. 'Rabbi, behold, the fig tree which thou cursedst is withered away. And Jesus answering saith unto them, Have faith in God' ($11^{21, 22}$). Israel is fruitless, because of its lack of faith. Compare also the rejection in the homeland: 'And he could there do no mighty work, save that he laid his hands upon a few sick folk, and healed them. And he marvelled because of their unbelief' ($6^{5, 6}$).

But besides unbelief, there are other words for the opposite of faith in Mark, namely, fear and amazement. 'Why are ye fearful? Have ye not yet faith?' (4^{40}). 'Fear not, only believe' (5^{36}). This fear is not reverential awe in the presence of mighty and divine power, but terror caused by lack of trust and understanding. As we have seen above, the Gospel ends on the note of human failure, when the women flee in silence from the tomb 'for trembling and astonishment had come upon them; and they said nothing to anyone; for they were afraid' (16^8).

The last healing-miracle in Mark is the giving of sight to Bartimaeus. 'Go thy way; thy faith hath made thee whole. and straightway he received his sight and followed him in the way' (10^{52}). Faith issues in following Jesus in the way; and this way is the way to glory, through death and resurrection. The story of Bartimaeus is the climax and conclusion of the section which begins at 8^{27}. There Jesus declared his messiahship; and began to teach them the way in which he must come to his glory; and called the multitude with the disciples to follow him in his way. The Son of Man's victory in defeat is to be reproduced in those who are his; they save their lives by losing them for his sake and the gospel's.

Almost all the material in the section 8^{27}–10^{52} can be classed under one or more of these three questions; Who is Jesus? How does he come to his glory? How do men follow him? And it is made clear that the following is an imitation of his death, and a sharing in his glory. So the epileptic child becomes as one dead, and is raised up by Jesus ($9^{26, 27}$); the offending members are to be cut off and cast out, in order that life may be entered (9^{43-48}); James and John must drink the cup of Christ's suffering, and be baptized with him in death, in order to enter his glory (10^{35-40}).

The disciples have not yet faith in the way of the cross, and so they do not understand but fear. 'They wist not what to answer; for they became sore afraid' (9^6); 'They understood not the saying (concerning death and resurrection) and were afraid to ask him' (9^{32}). 'And they were in the way, going up to Jerusalem; and Jesus was going before them; and they were amazed; and they that followed were afraid' (10^{32}). In their unbelief and worldly spirit, they dispute who is the greater (9^{34}). Jesus, in reply, takes a little child and says 'Whosoever shall receive one of such little children in my name, receiveth me; and whosoever receiveth me, receiveth not me, but him who sent me' (9^{37}). Christ is present in the little ones that believe in him (9^{42}); to offend them is to offend against Christ; and to minister to them is to minister to Christ.*

F. The Future

The end of faith and discipleship is to share in Christ's glory, to enter the kingdom of God. But this is still in the future, and the object of hope. Before the believer can receive the spiritual body which is proper to that life, certain stages in the history of the world must be accomplished. For although the time of preparation and promise is fulfilled, the day of the Lord is not present (II Thess. 2^2); the end is not yet (Mk. 13^7).

In their understanding of the future, there is here, as elsewhere, an underlying agreement between Paul and Mark, which enables the reader of the Gospel to learn the Evangelist's meaning.

Paul had said that the gospel is to be preached to the Jew first, and also to the Greek (Rom. 1^{16}). Many of the Jews reject it, and through their rejection salvation comes to the Gentiles, in order to provoke the Jews to jealousy, so that they may return and be saved. Until the fullness of the Gentiles be come in, a hardening in part has befallen Israel; but when this fullness shall have come in, all Israel shall be saved (Rom. $11^{25, 26}$).

Meanwhile, the disciples share in the sufferings of Christ. Paul had told the Thessalonians when he visited them that they were to suffer afflictions (I Thess. 3^4). This persecution will increase as the end draws near; then there will be the falling away, the removal of the restraining power, and the revelation of the man of sin 'he that opposeth and exalteth himself against all that is called God or that is worshipped; so that he sitteth in the temple of God, setting himself forth as God' (II Thess. 2^4). This lawless one will use power and signs and lying wonders, to deceive those who are perishing (II Thess. $2^{9, 10}$). But the Lord will destroy him as Isaiah had said: 'He shall smite the earth with the rod of his mouth, and with the breath of his lips shall he slay the wicked' (Isa. 11^4, II Thess. 2^8). The Lord will come suddenly, as a thief in the night, as travail upon a woman with child. Therefore the disciples must not sleep but watch and be sober (I Thess. 5^{1-11}).

* Rom. 14, 15 is the best commentary on Mk. 9^{38} ff., 10^{13-16}; and notice the ideas common to both: offending and stumbling; the weak and children; Christ received us, 'he took them in his arms. . . .'

At the coming of Christ, those who have died shall rise, and those who are his shall be changed; corruption shall put on incorruption; mortality shall put on immortality; the image of the earthly shall be changed into the image of the heavenly (I Cor. 15).

In Mark too, the Jews have a certain priority; 'Let the children first be filled' (7²⁷). Yet the Jews reject Jesus, in the homeland and in Jerusalem. Therefore the gospel must be preached unto all the nations (13¹⁰). Possibly here again the two feeding miracles symbolize and pre-signify all Israel and the fullness of the Gentiles.

The sufferings of the disciples increase before the end: 'They shall deliver you up to councils: and in synagogues shall ye be beaten: and before governors and kings shall ye stand for my sake, for a testimony unto them' (13⁹).

Then there will be the manifestation of evil—the abomination of desolation standing where he ought not;* at that time there shall be false Christs and false prophets, leading astray all except the elect by their signs and wonders.

After this tribulation, there shall be the cosmic disasters, which herald the coming of the Son of Man, to gather together his elect. Mark says very little in chapter 13 about the coming of Christ, but he has already included material in the gospel which fills out the two verses 13²⁶, ²⁷. For example, in chapter 4 he had given us the parables of fruitfulness, full growth and harvest; in 8³⁸ he had spoken of the Son of Man being ashamed of those who were ashamed of him and his words, when he comes in the glory of his Father with the holy angels; in 9²⁻⁸ he had described the Transfiguration, which he may have intended to be a 'pre-view' of Jesus as he will come again; in 12²⁵ he had recorded the saying, 'When they shall rise from the dead, they neither marry, nor are given in marriage; but are as angels in heaven'.

The time of the end is not known, therefore the disciples must watch and not sleep. Though the day or the hour is not known, Mark, like Paul, expected the end during his lifetime: 'This generation shall not pass away, until all these things be accomplished' (13³⁰; cf. 9¹): 'Behold, I tell you a mystery; we shall not all sleep, but we shall all be changed' (I Cor. 15⁵¹).

Conclusion

We have tried to do two things simultaneously: to use the Pauline Epistles to find the meaning of the Gospel according to

* Presumably in the temple at Jerusalem, cf. Daniel, and reference to Judaea, 13¹⁴.

St. Mark; and to show the teaching common to Paul and Mark. No doubt there are other themes in Mark which are not present in Paul, just as there is certainly teaching in Paul which is not included in Mark. To understand Mark further, beyond that which can be found through the aid of the Pauline Epistles, one would need to use the two later editions of that Gospel—by Matthew and Luke—all the Johannine writings, and Hebrews and I Peter, at least. That is to say such is the unity and inter-connectedness of the New Testament, that in order to read one book we should have the contents of the other books in mind.

In conclusion, we may return to two points which were raised at the beginning of this essay.

First, it may be asked, if the relationship between Mark and Paul is such as has been suggested above, on what grounds is this relationship to be explained? Is it sufficient to appeal to the unity of the New Testament? Must we ask again whether Mark is a Pauline Gospel? Two considerations may be offered.

(*a*) The extant evidence points as much to Mark's companionship with Paul as to Mark's companionship with Peter; and if the pseudonymity of I Peter be accepted, the connexion between Paul and Mark is witnessed more strongly than the connexion between Mark and Peter: see Col. 4^{10} [II Tim. 4^{11}], Philem. 24, I Peter 5^{13}. If the Gospel according to St. Mark was written by a man called Mark, and if this Mark is the one mentioned by Paul, then we should have one reason for the complementary nature of their writings.

(*b*) Probably Mark and the Pauline Epistles are the only Christian writings which have survived from the period which ended with the fall of Jerusalem. Although there were great differences among the Christians at this time, as the Pauline Epistles show, yet the nearness in time of the two writers to one another may have contributed something to their similarity of outlook.

The other point is this. We saw at the beginning that the Gospels are, in a sense, difficult to understand, whereas the Epistles are not; because the purpose of the writers of the Epistles is in many cases clear, whereas the purpose of the writers of the Gospels is not so clear. In the light of what we have found in Mark, can we formulate some of the aims of the earliest evangelist?

He seems to have set out to do a number of things simultaneously.

(*a*) To give a connected account of the events from the baptism of Jesus Christ to the finding of the empty tomb.

(*b*) To expound, within this framework, the person and work of Jesus Christ.

(*c*) To explain the mission of the Church in the world.

(*d*) To include some teaching on the Christian life.

(*e*) To outline the future of the Church in the world, till the end.

Matthew and Luke have developed each of these. They have expanded the Marcan framework (*a*); for example, they have both added infancy narratives, and the stories of the temptation of Jesus, and they have thus developed the Christology (*b*). They have both added resurrection stories, partly to make more clear the mission of the Church to the world (*c*).* They have both added further material from the teaching of Jesus (*d*). And Luke has added another volume, Acts, in which the future of the Church until the end (*e*) is epitomized in the story of the expansion of the Church from Jerusalem to Rome.

If these were the intentions of the evangelists when they wrote, they should be before our minds as we read their Gospels. And thus the Epistles show us both the meaning of the stories in the Gospels, and the questions which we should ask when we read the Gospels. 'If we can train ourselves to regard the Gospels in this way, we shall be less likely to put questions to them which they were not designed to answer. . . .'†

* Cf. Matt. 28 [16-20], Lk. 24 [46-47].   † R. H. Lightfoot, see p. 90, n. ‡.

The Epistle to the Hebrews and the Lucan Writings

by

C. P. M. JONES

IT is no new thing to suggest a connection between the Epistle
to the Hebrews and the Lucan writings; this suggestion goes
back at least as far as the Christian scholar who first gave an
author to this Epistle. For Eusebius tells us that Clement of
Alexandria (as did all subsequent teachers in that city) stoutly
maintained that the Epistle was originally the work of St. Paul;
but he also believed that the apostle wrote it for the Hebrews in
the Hebrew language, and that Luke zealously translated it for a
Greek public, and so it is that both the Epistle and the Acts are
found to have the same complexion or style (χρῶτα).* Origen,
while reserving the secret of the authorship to the divine knowledge alone, passed on two current traditions, ascribing it to
Clement of Rome and St. Luke respectively; while Eusebius himself definitely opted for Clement of Rome. It is our purpose to go
over at length some of the points of similarity between Hebrews
and the Lucan writings which might have been apparent to
Clement of Alexandria, not, as he did, to solve questions of
authorship, but to suggest that they both share the same theological outlook and together represent a form of theological thought
that was current in the post-Pauline gentile church of the later
part of the first century.

It may perhaps be fairly said that this kinship has not been so
much unobserved as unlooked for by the majority of modern
scholars. There seem to be two reasons for this. In the first place,

---

* Eusebius, *H.E.*, vi, 14.

until comparatively recently, St. Luke has been regarded, according to his own evaluation (Lk. 1^{1-4}), as a pure historian, collecting and arranging his sources with little or no theological interest or purpose; whereas Hebrews has been regarded as the work of the theologian *par excellence*. More recently doubt has been cast on the value of St. Luke as a historian, and when, for instance, his narrative in Acts impinges upon the first-hand evidence of St. Paul's epistles, we can see either that his information was incomplete or that he has written up the story in a manner which is optimistic rather than accurate. But the destruction of Luke the historian has led to the discovery of Luke the theologian, or at any rate to the discovery that St. Luke has a distinctive and consistent religious outlook from which and towards which he writes, and which gives the clue to the unity and pattern of his writings. St. Luke is not St. Matthew, and it must not be assumed that his thought is clear-cut or simple. It is not the task of this essay to delineate St. Luke's theology in its fullness, we can only touch upon such features as are relevant to our purpose; but whatever sources he may have used (and he tells us he had many) come to us in the last instance through his mind and pen, and if only the possibility of a distinctive, unifying, theological outlook be allowed, one barrier which subconsciously separates St. Luke from Hebrews will be removed.

Secondly, there has been a widespread tendency to regard Luke-Acts as a work of solely gentile provenance and interests with an anti-Jewish bias, while Hebrews has been regarded as the work of one who had a deep knowledge of, and reverence for, Jewish institutions. Neither of these attitudes is entirely wrong, especially in the case of the Epistle, which has borne the title 'to the Hebrews' from a very early age: but it is our purpose to show that these attitudes unqualified do not do full justice to the facts, and that in any case they are not incompatible. St. Luke does indeed depict God's salvation in Christ as a 'light to lighten the gentiles', but it is equally 'the glory of thy people Israel' (Lk. 2^{32}). The latter St. Luke tries to make clear in many ways: by his description of the ideal law-loving piety from which the Lord arose in his opening chapters (1^5 to end of 2), which are deeply influenced by the language and associations of the Septuagint, as Dr. Creed has shown in his commentary;* by the thrice-repeated mourning of the Lord over Jerusalem ($13^{34, 35}$, 19^{41-44}, 23^{28-31}); by his desire to mitigate as far as possible the guilt of the Jews for the crucifixion (e.g., $23^{27, 28}$, 23^{34}, Acts 3^{17}); by his placing the Lord's resurrec-

---

* Pp. lxxviii–lxxx, 6–46, 303–7.

tion and ascension in or near Jerusalem, so that the holy city becomes not only the scene of the end of the Lord's work on earth but also the centre from which the new Church radiates (Acts 1 [4, 8]); by emphasizing the temple as the place of the disciples' praise at the end of the gospel (Lk. 24 [53]) and as one of the focal points of the Christian fellowship after Pentecost (Acts 2 [46], 3[1], 5[12], 6[7]); and by two passages (Lk. 24 [25-27, 44-47]) which teach more explicitly than any other gospel passage the complete fulfilment of the Jewish scriptures in the crucifixion and resurrection of the Christ, a theme illustrated *in extenso* in the speeches in Acts. St. Luke is a very biblically-minded writer, and his bible is the Septuagint.

Our estimate of the theological outlook of Hebrews has often been conditioned by our estimate of the religious predicament of the people to whom the epistle was addressed. Some have supposed that they were judaistic Christians in danger of relapsing into Judaism; others have supposed that they were on the verge of some gnostic aberration, like the recipients of St. Paul's letter to Colossae. Heb. 13[9], however, would seem to provide the only direct evidence that the letter is addressed to a dangerous situation of either kind, and that only when taken out of connection with the succeeding verses and the whole argument of the epistle, whose general tenor we may summarize as follows:

1. The recipients are accused of falling into spiritual torpor or slackness (Heb. 3[12], 5[11-14], 6[12]) which not only betrays their excellent beginning in the faith (6[9, 10], 10[32 ff.]), but even more impedes their progress towards the heavenly goal, or perfection, to which Christ has attained (6[20], 8[1], 12[2]), and to which he calls his people (4[10, 11], 6[1a], 10[19 ff.], 12[1]).

2. The author's key conception is that of the state of finality, completeness or perfection, which Christ has achieved and to which Christians are called, signified by the verb τελειόω and its nouns τελείωσις, τελειότης, τελειωτής, which dominate the whole course of the argument. But he can only show up this perfection of Christ by contrasting it with various Old Testament types, which manifest their own imperfection while pointing to him in whom they find their fulfilment.

3. Though perfection under various images is the end of his argument, its starting-point is always in the text of the Old Testament, i.e. the Septuagint. He is not contrasting with Christianity the Jewish system which was current in his day, and which might have offered a practical alternative to his readers. The argument concerns the Mosaic tabernacle of which he and his readers could learn in their bibles, not the concrete temple in

Jerusalem; in fact his argument could stand whether or not that temple was still standing, as it rests not on the temple, but on the text. Hence, we may note in passing, it is difficult to use the date of the destruction of the temple for dating the epistle: Heb. 8^{13b} seems to be the only point at which a contemporary reference emerges, and this passing allusion to the senescence of the old religion would be as appropriate after A.D. 70 as before it.

4. His attitude towards the Old Testament, which is for him as for St. Luke the text of the Septuagint, is as thorough as the Lord's key to the scriptures summarized in Lk. $24^{25-27, \, 44-47}$. Though the author undoubtedly has his favourite texts, in principle *all* scripture points to Christ, in him alone it coheres and its contradictions are resolved. For Hebrews scripture is explicitly the mouthpiece of the Holy Ghost (Heb. 3^7, which also covers $4^{3, \, 4, \, 7, \, 8}$; 9^8, 10^{15}), as it is also for the author of Acts (Acts 1^{16}, 4^{25}, 28^{25}). For this reason he can select the amazing catena of texts in his opening chapter which illustrate the pre-eminence of the Son and his superiority to the angels; for this reason each adornment of the sanctuary could be made to yield its message, though space or occasion forbid (Heb. 9^{5b}), as could also all the characters of Jewish history between Rahab the harlot and the time of the Maccabees (11^{32-40}).

Now to sum up what we are saying: both Luke-Acts and Hebrews share this common attitude towards the Septuagint, and presuppose it in their readers. This is not to say that either of the authors or their readers were necessarily Jews at any point in their lives, but that they and their readers both see the Septuagint as the necessary starting-point and root of Christianity. Nor does this merely reduce them to the common level of early Christian writers, for the attitude of both is, in its own way, more explicit, systematic and, one might suggest, self-conscious than that of any other family of Christian writers. One might also hazard the suggestion that neither had been Jews from the cradle, but that it was their Christian faith which had driven them to the study of the Jewish scriptures in the form most readily accessible to them: this study opened to them a world in which they did not move with ease, but they overcame its difficulties with meticulous thoroughness, and eventually dispensed their new-found riches with all the seriousness and calculation of a convert. And we may add that towards their readers they both share this common attitude: they do not write with the first-hand authority of the apostle or prophet, but with the authority of the man of the second generation, who has to support his position with appeals to the accounts of others

(Lk. 1¹⁻⁴, Heb. 2¹⁻⁴) or with weighty arguments based on scripture, accepted as authoritative in common with his readers.

Having so far pleaded for a hearing, we will go on to catalogue the points of correspondence. These may be conveniently set out in three sections: I. Similarity of language; II. Similarity of fact or interest, mainly in minor details; III. Similarity of doctrine.

I. Similarity of Language

Bishop Westcott in his commentary (p. xlviii) says that "no impartial student can fail to be struck by the frequent use (in Hebrews) of words characteristic of St. Luke among writers of the New Testament", and he gives the following instances: διαμαρτύρεσθαι, ἀρχηγός, ὅθεν, ἱλάσκεσθαι, μέτοχος, περικεῖσθαι with accusative, εὔθετος, καταφεύγειν, πατριάρχης, εἰς τὸ παντελές, σχεδόν, ἀνώτερον, παροξυσμός, ὕπαρξις, ἀναστάσεως τυγχάνειν, ἔντρομος, ἀσάλευτος, οἱ ἡγούμενοι, ἀναθεωρεῖν. We may concede that διαμαρτύρεσθαι and ὅθεν have no good reason to be there, and that in this list, as in all such lists, not all words are equally significant; yet even so it is a substantial list, and a good beginning, to which we may reasonably add: ἄγκυρα, ἀναδέχεσθαι, ἀνορθοῦν, ἀπαλλάσσειν, ἀπογράφεσθαι, ἀστεῖος, ἄστρον, βοηθεία, διαβαίνειν, διατιθέναι, εἰσίεναι, ἐκλείπειν, ἐνοχλεῖν, ἐπιστέλλειν, ἐσώτερος, ἦχος, ἱερατεία, καίτοι, κατάπαυσις, καταπαύειν, κεφάλαιον, λύτρωσις, ὀρθός, παλαιοῦν, παριέναι, παροικεῖν, πολίτης, πόρρωθεν, συναντᾶν, τάξις (of priestly order), τελείωσις, φύω, along with εὐλαβής and its derivatives εὐλάβεια and εὐλαβεῖσθαι. All the above occur only in Luke-Acts and Hebrews; to them we may add some dozen more words which are only rarely found outside these writings: ἀγαλλίασις (Jd. ²⁴), ἀξιοῦν (II Thess. 1¹¹, I Tim. 5¹⁷), ἔξοδος (II Pet. 1¹⁵), ἐπίθεσις χειρῶν (I Tim. 4¹⁴, II Tim. 1⁶), κατανοεῖν (Matt. 7³, Rom. 4¹⁹, Jas. 1²³, ²⁴), μεταλαμβάνειν (II Tim. 2⁶), μόσχος (Rev. 4⁷), ὁρίζειν (Rom. 1⁴), περιαιρεῖν (II Cor. 3¹⁶), περιέρχεσθαι (I Tim. 5¹³), σκληροῦν (Rom. 9¹⁸), στάσις (Mk. 15⁷), τεχνίτης (Rev. 18²²), ὑποστέλλειν (Gal. 2¹²).

We must not let ourselves be overpowered by the length of these lists. It is extremely difficult to assess their significance, and there are many factors for which allowance must be made. Luke-Acts and Hebrews are both writings of considerable length, in which there would be plenty of scope for casual overlapping, as may well be the case with many words (e.g. ἄγκυρα) which are used in different senses and contexts in the two writings; some words only occur in quotations from the Septuagint, and many of the words are compound verbs whose coining seems to be a common feature among later New Testament writers. Moreover, one can compile lists of words peculiar to Hebrews and the pastoral epistles, to Hebrews and I Peter and James, even to Hebrews and St. Paul, as well as those peculiar to Luke-Acts and the later non-Pauline epistles in general, which should be taken into account. But when all deductions have been made, the verbal correspondences are so numerous that a substantial area of common phraseology remains (including several significant words to which reference is made elsewhere), which may well be indicative of a closer kinship in the presence of other corroborating factors.

A consideration of two further sets of words will bring us to the fringe of a deeper common outlook.

1. Dr. H. J. Cadbury in his *Making of Luke-Acts* has pointed out the clear political and cosmopolitan interests of St. Luke; typical of this would be his use of the words οἰκουμένη and πόλις (with its derivatives). οἰκουμένη is used once by St. Matthew (Matt. 24¹⁴, 'this gospel of the kingdom shall be preached in all the inhabited world'), once by St. Paul (Rom. 10¹⁸, a verbatim quotation of the LXX of Ps. 19⁵) and three times in the Apocalypse; elsewhere it is found three times in St. Luke's gospel, five times in Acts and twice in Hebrews. Normally, in Luke-Acts, the word is used in its usual cosmopolitan, this-worldly sense; but in both instances in Hebrews it is introduced in a context in which one would expect a word with deeper theological overtones. In Heb. 1⁶, 'when he bringeth the first-born into the world', we would expect, and certainly St. John would have written, κοσμόν, but we find οἰκουμένην; and in 2⁵, 'for it is not to angels that he has subordinated the coming world', again we find this same word (unique in the New Testament for the 'world to come'), where we would expect such a word as αἰών, as actually occurs in 6⁵. He must have been a very 'oecumenically-minded' man who could spontaneously introduce this word in either of these theological contexts.

A similar consideration takes its starting point from the use of the word πόλις and its derivatives, so dear to St. Luke. We are apt to be so struck by the hieratic imagery of Hebrews, which dominates the centre of the epistle (2¹⁷, 3¹, 4¹⁴–10²⁵), that we may overlook his 'politic' imagery, and that implied by the word ἀρχηγός. This epistle has its own form of quasi-dramatic structure; just as it moves in the great rhetorical passages from warning through exhortation and invitation to assertion (let us fear, 4¹; let us draw near, 10²²; you have arrived, 12²²), so does its imagery move from the household (3¹⁻⁶), through the sanctuary (4¹⁴–10²⁵) to the city or fatherland. This last does not attain its fullest expression till 12^{22-24}, but it is prepared for by the saying about Abraham in 11^{10}, and the summarizing section, 11^{13-16}; while in the little section, 13^{10-14}, which recapitulates many of the preceding themes, it is the city (13^{14}) and not the altar which has the last word.

With regard to the military imagery implied by the word ἀρχηγός, prince or captain, we may note that the word only occurs elsewhere in the New Testament in Acts 3^{15}, 5^{31}, in both cases applied to Christ, who is described as 'prince of life' and 'captain and saviour' (cf. 'captain of their salvation', Heb. 2^{10}). In Hebrews the whole exposition of the work of Christ for us is flanked at either end by the use of this word (2^{10}, 12^{2}), whose imagery is sustained by the recurrent imagery of the fore-runner (6^{20}) and of Joshua the leader who heads the vanguard into the promised land. At two points the argument is only intelligible if we understand it to rest on an equivocal use of the word Ἰησοῦς = Joshua/Jesus. In 4^{8} Ἰησοῦς is clearly Joshua when the verse is construed with the verse before; but when taken with 4^{10} it is equally clearly Jesus, whose victorious rest alone is comparable to the divine sabbath. In $11^{1}-12^{2}$ we may wonder why the long list of worthies selected for individual treatment stops short with such a character as Rahab the harlot (11^{31}); up to that point the author has led us slowly through the patriarchs and the exodus, with Rahab the harlot he drops his leisurely pace and hurries through the rest of the Old Testament with rapid generalizations before summing up them all in Jesus, the ἀρχηγός and completer of the long tale of faith (12^{2}). Why should he start to hurry at such a point? Surely because after Rahab he is brought face to face with Joshua, who is however not merely Joshua, but the figure of a greater captain who must be last of the series.

The christological implications of this imagery and its relation to the christology of Luke-Acts will be considered later: here we are concerned with the words and their associations.

2. The second set of words consists of the two nouns μετάνοια and ἄφεσις, repentance and remission, words which at first sight one might consider part of a general Christian vocabulary; but an examination of their usage shows that they occur rarely outside the Lucan writings and Hebrews. μετάνοια is used in Mk. 1^{4} = Matt. $3^{8, 11}$ (all in connection with John the Baptist), three times by St. Paul, twice in the same context (Rom. 2^{4}, II Cor. $7^{9, 10}$), once each in II Tim. and II Pet.: but five times in Luke, six times in Acts, and three times in Hebrews, of which Heb. 6^{1} is important as it

heads a list which summarizes early Christian instruction, and so fits on to the usage of Acts, as will be shown later. ἄφεσις too, of remission of sin, is interesting. It is used in Mk. 1⁴ = Lk. 3³, Mk. 3²⁹, and Matt. 26²⁸ (= Mk. 1⁴, transposed from Matt. 3, where it is omitted), and once in Colossians and Ephesians (Col. 1¹⁴ = Eph. 1⁷): apart from this it occurs three times in Luke (though Lk. 4¹⁸ = Isa. 61¹), five times in Acts and twice in Hebrews. The significance of these last two references is perhaps greater than their number suggests, as in both contexts (9²², 10¹⁸) the author uses the word to clinch and conclude his argument. We may also note that καθαρίζειν is used for cleansing the heart or conscience only in Acts 15⁹ and Heb. 9¹⁴, 10²; while among 'common absences' we may note the non-use of such words as εὐαγγέλιον and παράπτωμα.

II. Similarity of Fact or Interest (mainly in minor details)

(a) It is very clear, says Hebrews (7¹⁴), that our Lord actually arose from the tribe of Judah; history has very clearly closed the controversy about the Judaic or Levitical origin of the Messiah traceable in the Jewish pseudepigrapha. The Judaic Messiah of history is identical with the high-priest after the order of Melchizedek of Ps. 110, and Levi has implicitly acknowledged his inferiority to Melchizedek, for he was already in the loins of Abraham, when Melchizedek met him, blessed him and received his tithes (7⁷⁻¹⁰). St. Luke also in his opening chapters reiterates our Lord's Judaic and Davidic descent (1²⁷, ³², ⁶⁹, 2⁴, ¹¹), even more strongly than does St. Matthew. He also tells us that John the Baptist arose from the tribe of Levi, through both his father and his mother. and records the odd incident in which the embryonic Baptist salutes the Saviour from his mother's womb (1⁴¹). There is no parallel to this incident in the New Testament, unless it be Heb. 7¹⁰. He also tells us that Zacharias was of the course of Abijah, the course which gives place to that of 'Jesus', in the succession of priestly duties as assigned in I Chron. 24¹⁰, ¹¹ (LXX).

Before we leave the infancy chapters we may note Heb. 1⁶, 'when he brings the first-born into the world, he says, And let all the angels of God worship him.' St. Luke alone tells of the chorus of worshipping angels at the nativity (Lk. 2¹³, ¹⁴). And the definition of the function of angels in Heb. 1¹⁴, 'ministering spirits sent forth for service for the sake of those who are to inherit salvation' is admirably illustrated in the stories of angelic activity in St. Luke's infancy narrative (1¹¹ ff., ²⁶ ff., 2⁹ ff.: also, if it be allowed, 22[43]), as also in Acts (Acts 1[10] (but see later), 5[19], 8[26], 10[3] etc., 12[7 ff.], 27[23]). Speaking generally, St. Luke records more instances of angelic activity than any other narrative writer of the New Testament, and Hebrews is the theological writer most interested in their status.

(*b*) In Hebrews there is a strong emphasis on the humanity of Christ, and in Heb. 5[7-10] we find a more vivid historical record of his earthly trial and suffering than in any other epistle. The reference is to his prayer with its crying and tears, no doubt in Gethsemane, and the author points out that through his suffering he learned obedience. This last point is implicit in the Marcan story, but is not dwelt on. If Lk. 22[43, 44] be considered part of the original text,* its similarity with Heb. 5[7, 8] is very striking: the general thesis of this essay may provide additional ground for holding these verses to be genuine. And we may note that it is St. Luke alone who records our Lord's subjection and obedience to his parents (Lk. 2[51]).

(*c*) Acts 13[39], 'and from all (the) things from which you could not be justified in the law of Moses, in this man (i.e. Christ) every believer is justified'.

This text, which occurs towards the end of St. Paul's speech at Antioch in Pisidia, has for long provided a difficulty for commentators,† who find themselves forced to hover between two meanings: (1) that Christ provides the only ground for complete justification ('from all things'), a thing which the law was powerless to provide, or (2) that Christ provides a ground for justification in all those matters ('from all the things') for which the law was inadequate. The first interpretation is required to bring this statement into line with the plain teaching of St. Paul in his own writings, where he consistently maintains that, though the law has many uses, as for instance in aggravating and making explicit our knowledge of sin and of divine condemnation, its observance is completely useless as the ground for justification before God; but it is the second interpretation which gives a more natural rendering of St. Luke's Greek. As J. H. Ropes has written of this verse: "This sounds well enough, and is evidently intended to embody Paul's characteristic doctrine of justification by faith, but, so soon as one tries to analyse it closely, it becomes apparent that the statement is by no means clear, and that, if taken strictly, it appears to present a formulation of Paul's central conception

---

* See J. M. Creed's commentary (p. 273), and C. S. C. Williams, *Alterations to the Text of the Synoptic Gospels and Acts*, pp. 6–8.

† E.g. Lake and Cadbury, *Beginnings of Christianity*, vol. IV, p. 157, n.

which does not touch his real doctrine and which he himself could never have accepted".* For St. Luke's attempted 'formulation of Paul's central conception' supposes that the law has a certain limited sphere of validity for justification, which Christ completes. And this is the plain teaching of the Epistle to the Hebrews. The ceremonial ordinances of the law, according to Hebrews, have a limited adequacy; they are 'carnal ordinances', valid for a certain time (9^{10}), and adequate for a limited purpose, 'for the purification of the flesh' (9^{13}), that is, for ritual purification: and as such they are quite inadequate to cleanse the conscience (9^9, 10^2). But this limited efficacy is assumed, and used as the basis for teaching that Christ, by his sacrifice, has provided that which they lacked, the power to cleanse from sin: 'for if the blood of goats etc. . . . sanctify unto the cleanness of the flesh, *by how much more* shall the blood of Christ . . . cleanse your conscience from dead works to serve the living God?' ($9^{13, 14}$).

And if this sounds an odd doctrine to liken to that of St. Luke, we should remind ourselves of the opening chapters of his gospel, where we find a selection of the 'ordinances of worship' (Heb. 9^1) of the old covenant being scrupulously observed. There are Zacharias and Elizabeth walking faultlessly in all the Lord's commandments and ordinances (δικαιώμασι, Lk. 1^6, cf. Heb. $9^{1, 10}$); there Zacharias correctly executes his priestly office, and it is during his ministration that the angelic visitation occurs; according to the prescription of Lev. 12, both John and Jesus are circumcised on the eighth day (cf. Acts 7^8), and on the fortieth Mary and Joseph bring their child to the temple with the offerings allowed in that chapter to those of lesser means, 'according to the law of the Lord' (Lk. $2^{22-24, 39}$), and later they take him to Jerusalem for the passover. It is a Matthaean phrase which most succinctly describes the ethos of these two chapters: 'for thus it becometh us to fulfil all righteousness' (Matt. 3^{15}). If the establishment of the second dispensation involves the removal of the first (Heb. 10^{9b}), at any rate the first was obligatory and in its measure effective until the greater and more perfect scheme was introduced.

(d) Acts 7: St. Stephen's Speech

In St. Stephen's speech in Acts 7 and the panegyric on 'faith' in Heb. 11 we find the two longest continuous expositions of Old Testament history within the pages of the New Testament. Their superficial differences are obvious: Heb. 11 covers the period from creation to Joshua, Acts 7 starts with Abraham and con-

---

* *The Synoptic Gospels* (Harvard University Press, 1934), pp. 77 f.

tinues as far as Solomon; Heb. 11 is directed towards Christians, drawing lessons of encouragement from the worthies of the Old Testament, St. Stephen's speech is directed against the Jews, and uses the Old Testament to show how that people have repeatedly disobeyed the divine call. Nevertheless there is a close correspondence between the doctrine attributed by St. Luke to St. Stephen and that of the Epistle to the Hebrews, particularly in its eleventh chapter. This has already attracted the attention of Professor W. Manson in his Baird Lecture of 1949,* where his aim was to show the continuity of the doctrine of Hebrews with the strand of early Christian teaching dominant in St. Stephen's speech. Our aim is less ambitious, to show the similarity of the thought of Hebrews to that of the Lucan writings, which include St. Stephen's speech, whether this be a record of primitive teaching or not. Professor Manson summarizes the points of correspondence under eight heads (*op. cit.*, p. 36), all of which have weight: to save merely repeating them here, we will tabulate the points of correspondence somewhat differently as follows:

1. St. Stephen significantly begins his speech with the phrase 'the God of glory' (Acts 7[2]), and his story ends with him gazing up to heaven, as the apostles had done at the ascension (1[10]), and seeing the glory of God and Jesus standing at the right hand of God. One cannot maintain that St. Luke and Hebrews have a monopoly of the glory of God or of Jesus at his right hand (cf. Mk. 14[62], Rom. 8[34], Col. 3[1], etc.); nevertheless the sense of the exalted majesty of the glorified Christ is very strong in Hebrews (Heb. 1[3]), and with the phrase 'looking unto Jesus' (12[2]) he encourages as a habit exactly that state of mind in which St. Stephen died.

2. Both writers pay much attention to Abraham (Acts 7[2-8], Heb. 11[8-19]), and their interest is of a different kind from that of St. Paul in Rom. 4 and Gal. 3[16-18]. Both stress Abraham's fidelity to God in going out from his native land, not knowing whither he went (Acts 7[3-6], Heb. 11[8, 9]). St. Stephen stresses the earthly insecurity of Abraham, Hebrews his heavenly aspiration: but they are both parts of a similar picture, Hebrews filling in what Acts leaves unsaid.

3. Both include sections on Moses (Acts 7[20-44], Heb. 11[23-29]), of which the former is considerably longer than the corresponding section about Abraham, and the latter shorter. But even so all the details used in Heb. 11 are found in Acts 7, notably references to Moses' childhood and upbringing. A peculiar feature of the account of Moses in Acts 7 is its division of the traditional 120

* *The Epistle to the Hebrews*, an historical and theological reconsideration, pp. 30-36, 73.

years of Moses' life (Deut. 31², 34⁷) into three equal spans of forty years (Acts 7²³, ³⁰, ⁴²), that is, forty years in Pharoah's household, forty years in exile, and the traditional forty years from the exodus through the wilderness. This span of forty years was also of special interest to the author of Hebrews, as is shown by his citation of Ps. 95 in the section Heb. 3⁷–4¹³.

4. Acts uses the phrase 'the Church in the wilderness' (Acts 7³⁸) of the wandering Israelites, which again recalls the comment on Ps. 95 in Heb. 3⁷–4¹³, and also Heb. 13¹¹⁻¹³, 'let us go unto him outside the camp'.

5. Acts 7³⁸ refers to the decalogue as 'living oracles' or living words, a phrase re-echoed in Heb. 4¹², 'the word of God is living and active'.

6. In Acts 7⁴⁴ and Heb. 8⁵, and there alone in the New Testament, we find Exod. 25⁴⁰ quoted of Moses' construction of the tabernacle according to the heavenly pattern revealed on the mount. In Acts 7 the argument is largely concerned with this tabernacle, which Solomon incidentally, we are told, turned into a stone building; in Hebrews the tabernacle is regarded as a witness to the truer type from which it is derived (cf. also Heb. 9²⁴); but in both the Mosaic tabernacle is the basis of the argument.*

7. In Acts 7⁴⁵ the record of the possession of the promised land under Joshua is shortly followed by a reference to God's rest (κατάπαυσις), just as we find in Heb. 4⁸⁻¹⁰ a similar collocation of the same ideas of Joshua's entrance into the promised land and of God's rest.

8. In St. Stephen's last words (Acts 7⁵³) we find a reference to the tradition that the law was mediated by angels, which also recurs in Heb. 2², though this tradition is referred to elsewhere in the New Testament (Gal. 3¹⁹).

(e) The Θεμέλιον, Heb. 6¹, ²

The last point in this section is no more than a suggestion, and concerns the θεμέλιον, or foundation principles of Christian faith as enumerated in Heb. 6¹, ². Here we find a summary of the first essentials of Christian faith, on which the author hopes to build, and which he assumes his readers to know, and to have known since the days of their first Christian instruction. It is an unusual list which corresponds exactly with no other such summary in the New Testament: we can only put forward the sug-

---

* One might ask whether the platonism, or philonism, of Hebrews, of which one hears so much, cannot be reduced to this text, Exod. 25⁴⁰, understood as our author understands it.

gestion that it is closer to the language and thought of Acts than to any other New Testament alternative.

This list can be elaborated by putting down the six items of Heb. $6^{1,2}$ alongside some of the parallels in Acts:

1. repentance from dead works (cf. Heb. 9^{14}): Acts 2^{38}, 3^{19}, 14^{15-17}, 17^{30}, 20^{21}, cf. Lk. 24^{47}.
2. faith in God: Acts 14^{15-17}, 15^9, 17^{24-28}, 20^{21}.
3. teaching about baptisms: Acts *passim*.
4. and the laying on of hands: Acts 8^{14-17}, 19^{1-7}.
5. of the resurrection of the dead: Acts $17^{18,31}$, 26^{23}.
6. and eternal judgment: Acts 17^{31}, 24^{25}.

It is especially noticeable that only here and in Acts do we find baptism and the laying on of hands specifically and distinctly mentioned in connection with the rite of Christian initiation.

The Hebrews summary does not contain all that we find in the evangelistic speeches of Acts: it is notably silent on all that concerns Christ: but the items it does contain are all characteristic of Acts.

III. *Similarity of Doctrine*

We now go on to consider a deeper kinship between St. Luke and the author of Hebrews in matters of doctrine and fundamental theological outlook. This we propose to do by a double approach, by way of christology and eschatology, though it will be readily seen that they are closely connected; while they also affect the doctrine of the church, or, more accurately, the conception of the relationship between Christ and his faithful. In either case one has to treat St. Luke at greater length in order to distil the doctrine that underlies his narrative: in Hebrews the doctrinal exposition is more direct, the task is to see through the imagery; which done, the doctrine is relatively clear.

(a) *Christology*

Someone has described St. Luke's story of Christ as 'the gospel of the ascension'. The whole narrative is so written as to lead, through successive phases in Galilee and Samaria, to a climax in Jerusalem which culminates in the ascension. 'Behoved it not the Christ to suffer these things, and *to enter into his glory*?', as the risen Christ explains to the two disciples on the way to Emmaus: to this conclusion all the scriptures point (Lk. 24^{25-27}). St. Luke may conceive the glorification of Christ being accomplished in two stages, resurrection and ascension, for these words are spoken by the risen Christ between his resurrection and his ascension, while in the parallel scene with the eleven in Jerusalem the resurrection on the third day replaces the phrase 'to enter into his glory' (24⁴⁴⁻⁴⁷). But this in no way diminishes the importance of the ascension in the narrative. As far back as 9⁵¹, at a critical point in the story,* our attention is directed to 'the days of his taking-up' (ἀνάλημψις), words which only find their echo and fulfilment in the ascension narrative (Acts 1², ¹¹, ²²),† in which Christ enters into his glory as a permanent, and almost static, condition. When Christ says to the high-priest 'from now on the Son of Man will be (ἔσται) seated at the right hand of the power of God', the emphasis is on the security of his own future position; his words do not confront his hearers with any hint of imminent eschatological activity (cf. Mk. 14⁶², 'and *you* will see the Son of Man seated at the right hand of the Power *and coming* with the clouds of heaven'). The single cloud which veils his departure (Acts 1⁹) will also accompany him at his ultimate return (Acts 1¹¹, Lk. 21²⁷, singular for the plural of Mk. 13²⁶).

The three manifestations of the glory of Christ, the transfiguration, the resurrection and the ascension, are also linked together by St. Luke in a subtle way, which may be set out as follows:

Lk. 9²⁹, ³⁰: ὁ ἱματισμὸς αὐτοῦ λευκὸς ἐξαστράπτων. καὶ ἰδού, ἄνδρες δύο συνελάλουν αὐτῷ....

Lk. 24⁴: καὶ ἰδού, δύο ἄνδρες ἐπέστησαν αὐταῖς ἐν ἐσθῆτι ἀστραπτούσῃ.

Acts 1¹⁰: καὶ ἰδού, ἄνδρες δύο παρειστήκεισαν αὐτοῖς ἐν ἐσθήσεσι λευκαῖς ...

At the transfiguration the Lord's raiment is described as lightning-white, and he is seen talking with two men, Moses and Elijah; this is re-echoed in the resurrection and ascension scenes. At the tomb, behold (καὶ ἰδού), two *men* stood by them in *lightning* vesture, and the description of these figures as men is remarkable, as later on they are referred to as angels (Lk. 24²³): and at the ascension, behold, again two *men*, this time in *white* clothes. The attributes of the Lord's glory are distributed between the messengers of his glorification. In view of this, it seems more likely that the 'exodus', which Christ was to fulfil in Jerusalem, and which was the subject of conversation with Moses and Elijah on the mount (9³¹), refers specifically to the Lord's depar-

* See C. F. Evans' essay in this volume, pp. 37 ff.
† See L. S. Thornton, *The Dominion of Christ*, pp. 190, 191.
126

ture by way of ascension or assumption, such as they, according to scripture or tradition, had already experienced, and for which they had already provided the model, rather than to Christ's victory over the powers of evil described in terms of the original exodus from Egypt.

It is highly significant that St. Luke alone of the evangelists records the mystery of the ascension in such a way as to suggest the departure of the Lord from his disciples. Leaving aside the question of the original ending of St. Mark, as is allowable in such a volume as this, St. Matthew and St. John make no reference in their closing verses to the Lord's departure. St. John may well have conceived the ascension as occurring at or immediately after Jn. 20[17], while St. Matthew makes Christ expressly conclude his final charge to his disciples with the words 'Lo, I am with you all the days until the completion of the age' (Matt. 28[20]). Even the longer conclusion appended to St. Mark, after stating naively that the Lord was received up into heaven and sat down at the right hand of God, goes on to add that the disciples went out and preached everywhere, 'the Lord working with them and confirming the word by the signs that followed' (Mk. 16[19, 20]). That St. Luke thought otherwise is borne out by the subsequent narrative of Acts: in the first chapter Christ is exalted to the heavenly sphere, then there is a distinct pause, a waiting for ten days, before Pentecost when, according to Christ's promise, but not, it would seem, as the result of his activity, the Holy Spirit descends on the disciples. Thereafter the church is run by the action of the Holy Spirit and of the disciples, either conjointly or independently, while Christ remains, and must remain, secure in the heavenlies, 'whom the heavens must receive until the times of the restoration of all things' (Acts 3[21]): if Christ wishes to appear or to act, it is necessary for the heavens to open to reveal him, as is pre-eminently the case with St. Stephen at his martyrdom (7[55, 56]) and Saul on the road to Damascus (9[3 f.]). Repentance and remission of sins are preached (Lk. 24[47]), and healing wrought (Acts 3[6, 16], 4[7-12]), in the power of his 'name': but we are left with no clear impression of Christ himself active in his apostles, uniting his faithful to himself by baptism, and living with them by virtue of his resurrection, or raising them to share his heavenly life, as we find throughout the epistles of St. Paul (e.g. II Cor. 5[17-20], Rom. 6[3-11], Gal. 2[20], 3[26-28], Phil. 3[10, 11], Col. 3[3]). Rather we are left with the impression that Christ is one thing and the church another, and that the church (and the Holy Spirit) carry on the work of an absentee Christ. This may be largely due to the fact that the author is trying to write church history, the history of what is visible and recordable of the church on earth; but the doctrine is consistent throughout, and is plainly different from that of St. Paul and St. John. In Acts, after the ascension, Christ's activity appears as an irruption, as in the christophanies already cited (cf. also Acts 23[11] and perhaps 16[7], 27[23,24]); though one must also add that the words addressed to Saul on the Damascus road, 'Saul, Saul, why persecutest thou *me*? . . . I am Jesus whom thou persecutest', definitely imply and presuppose the mystical identity of Christ with his persecuted disciples.

The epistle to the Hebrews begins with a panegyric on the exalted and glorified Son, who after effecting purification of sins 'has sat down on the right hand of the majesty on high' (Heb. 1[3]), a fact emphasized throughout the epistle (e.g. 8[1], 10[12], 12[2]). Christ by his sharing of our nature and sufferings has won through to glory; his session at the right hand is the figure of the thoroughness of his victory and the permanence of his possession. Of the actual heavenly life of Christ, Hebrews in effect tells us little more than St. Luke, except that he makes explicit the detail that 'he ever liveth to make intercession for us' (7[25]), a fact which may be implied in St. Stephen's vision of the Son of Man at the right hand of God in the priestly and intercessory posture of standing (Acts 7[55, 56]). Christ has entered once for all into the heavenly holy of holies, like the high-priest in the ritual of the day of atonement, 'to appear before the face of God for us' (Heb. 9[24]), and his faithful are left outside, like the Jewish congregation, to await his reappearing (9[28]). The conception of Christ as captain (ἀρχηγός) necessarily involves a complementary doctrine of the λαός, the people whom he leads. Christ has entered into his rest: the rest of the people of God hangs over us as a remainder (ἀπολείπεται), yet to be fulfilled, still in the balance (4[8-11], cf. Acts 3[19]).

It is not difficult to see the correspondence between these two doctrines: in both we find an emphasis on the completeness of Christ's past work and on his present glorified state, and a sharp distinction between the state of Christ and that of his faithful. If this correspondence be conceded, it may throw light on an enigmatic saying attributed to Christ by St. Luke (Lk. 13[32]). '. . . today and tomorrow, and the third day I am perfected (τελειοῦμαι)', where τελειοῦμαι is best taken in the sense common in Hebrews, of the attainment of heavenly perfection through suffering and death.

(b) *Eschatology*

To prove the existence of what we may call a family likeness, shared by St. Luke and Hebrews, it is not sufficient to point to general and specific correspondences alone: it is also necessary to show, as far as may be possible, that the two writings stand together in contrast to the other families of writings in the New Testament. And this we hope may be shown with regard to eschatology; but to show it a détour is necessary, to consider the other families with which St. Luke and Hebrews may be contrasted. These other families we may take to be three, St. Mark (which for this purpose may be held to include St. Matthew), St. Paul and the Johannine writings.

Let us start with St. Mark, who concentrates the bulk of his eschatological teaching in his thirteenth chapter. The discourse seems to be divided into two parts: (1) a 'programme' of the end, which is subdivided into three clearly marked stages, (a) a general or lesser tribulation (13^{5-13}), (b) the special tribulation under the desolating abomination (13^{14-23}), (c) the parousia (13^{24-27}); and (2) warnings of the suddenness of the end (13^{28-37}). In view of much that has been written on the subject we must first establish the congruity of Mk. 13 with the general teaching of the early church (and even possibly of Christ himself), and then show how this chapter coheres with the rest of St. Mark's gospel.

With regard to the first point, modern critics have been struck by the contrast between the two parts of the discourse, between the teaching about the programme and the teaching about the suddenness of the end.* And they have been led by this contrast to doubt the genuineness of the programme teaching, which, as they point out, only occurs in this section, and finds no counterpart in the non-Marcan eschatological teaching reproduced in Lk. 12 and 17; and they suggest that perhaps a small Jewish apocalypse has been somewhat carelessly incorporated alongside the genuine teaching of Christ. That may be, but the New Testament provides us with no evidence of this; for all the synoptic writers include both elements side by side and see no incoherence in so including them, and though St. Luke does not give as clear an outline of St. Mark's programme as St. Mark himself, he is not ashamed to follow its general pattern and to incorporate many of his details. This may suggest a failure to understand the primitive Christian mind rather than a fundamental inconsistency on the part of the evangelists: and this is more likely to be the truth when we see that St. Paul thought as they did.

* E.g. T. W. Manson, *The Teaching of Jesus*, pp. 260 ff.

For in I Thessalonians we find just the same juxtaposition of ideas: in I Thess. 4^{13-17} we have teaching related to one item of the programme, the Lord's parousia (1 (c) above), with special reference to the lot of those who have already died, and then in 5^{1-11} the emphasis is on the suddenness of the end (as in (2) above). And a great deal more of the programme can be reconstructed from the Thessalonian epistles. In II Thess. 2^{1} *ff.* St. Paul answers the possibility that the parousia may have already passed unnoticed, leaving the Thessalonian Christians ungathered; he says the parousia cannot happen unless it be preceded by the great apostasy and the revelation of the man of sin, the son of perdition, blasphemously taking God's place and sitting in God's temple (1 (b) above). And then he reminds them that he has already told them of this on his previous, and only, visit, that is to say when he originally preached to them: 'do you not remember that while I was still among you I used to tell you these things?' (2^{5}). This shows that items 1 (b) and (c) at any rate were part of St. Paul's initial instructions to his converts, and if our curiosity leads us to look for 1 (a) as well, we may find it by looking back to I Thess. 2^{14-16}, 3^{3-5}, where the present afflictions of the Thessalonian Christians are shown to be signs of their genuine Christian calling; thus they are true to type, for all this St. Paul had foretold them (3^{4}); they are at present at the stage of the general or lesser tribulation, and are already within the scope of the predestined scheme that as yet awaits completion. And so there is a close correspondence between St. Mark and St. Paul in his earliest letters; St. Mark corresponds exactly with what St. Paul said he taught. It would be hard to get closer to the primitive teaching in this matter, or even perhaps to the teaching of Christ himself.

To make the picture more complete, we should take a side-glance at the Johannine family of writings, which we will take to comprise the Apocalypse, the fourth gospel and the Johannine epistles, whether or not we regard these as all coming from the same pen.* The Apocalypse starts in the present and looks towards the future; the Apocalypse proper is released by the Lord's unsealing of the book of prophecy in chapter 5, and from chapter 6 onwards the general structure follows that of Mk. 13, as Dr. Farrer has shown:† in chapter 6 we have the signs of the lesser tribulation, chapters 12–18 cover the great tribulation and the reign of Antichrist, chapters 19 to end cover the parousia and its sequel. The fourth gospel looks back to the past, and sees in the

* See A. M. Farrer, *The Rebirth of Images*, pp. 22 ff.
† *The Rebirth of Images*, pp. 302, 303.

Incarnation itself the fulfilment of all Christian expectation; though some five references to the 'last day' persist, the evangelist tries to portray to his readers 'the glory of God in the face of Jesus Christ' (to borrow a phrase from St. Paul), and to show that all that Christians may desire or expect in present or future is already summed up in the accomplished work of Christ. But the same pattern persists: the passion is the glorification of the Son of Man and the gathering together of his elect (Jn. 11^{52}, 12^{32}), and the work of Antichrist is hinted at by the designation of Judas Iscariot as 'the son of perdition' (17^{12} = II Thess. 2^3). And in the first epistle, where the concern is pastoral and focused upon the writer's present, the same themes recur. So in the Johannine, as in the Pauline, family of writings we find reproduced the same pattern as in Mk. 13, to which we must now return.

We next need to show how this 'eschatological' chapter coheres with the rest of St. Mark's gospel; but this has already been done for us by Dr. Lightfoot and Dr. Farrer, who have shown how the pattern of the teaching concerning the last things is reflected in the subsequent narrative of the passion, and it is not necessary for us to repeat what they have written.* It is not possible, in fact, to separate the eschatological teaching of chapter 13 from the dramatic construction of the gospel as a whole: the eschatology underlies the narrative, and is itself part of the drama. We may note that, apart from hints in the introductory section on the baptist and the Lord's original proclamation in Galilee (Mk. $1^{1-8, 14, 15}$), in two enigmatic sayings concerning the Son of Man ($2^{10, 28}$) and in the parables of 4^{1-34}, eschatological references do not begin to abound until St. Peter has confessed Jesus as Messiah, and Jesus has begun to teach the necessity of his passion ($8^{27}-9^1$). Thereafter the two themes of the passion and the parousia are closely connected. Above all, in Mk. 13 the Lord gives a full-scale prophecy of the pattern of the future fulfilment, of the mystery of the divine purpose whereby after incomparable suffering the Son of Man will appear to gather his elect to himself. But this prophecy casts its shadow on to the passion itself, so that the sensitive reader can see that the mystery is already in operation in the person of the Lord himself. Mk. 13 has a wider reference than that alone; it covers all that intervenes between its enunciation and the consummation of all things, including the as yet incomplete passion of the faithful; but its first and greatest fulfilment is in the person of the Lord himself.

* R. H. Lightfoot, *The Gospel Message of St. Mark*, ch. IV, and A. M. Farrer, *A Study in St. Mark*, pp. 135–41.

Now if the tyranny of Antichrist is anticipated and recapitulated in the Lord's passion, to what does the parousia correspond? In various ways St. Mark hints that it is the resurrection, or, more accurately, the reunion of the Lord and his disciples, to which the physical resurrection is the necessary prelude. These hints we may find in (a) the recurrence of the words ὄψονται, ὄψεσθε in significant contexts (13^{26}, 14^{62}, 16^7), (b) the conjunction of 14^{28} and 16^7, and (c) the section Mk. 9^{9-13}, the discussion between the Lord and the three disciples on the descent after the transfiguration.* There the Lord enjoins them to disclose to no one what they had seen, until the Son of Man should have 'risen from the dead'. This phrase they do not understand, and ask a question about it which reveals the overtones which it calls to mind: 'the scribes say that first Elijah must come'. But before what is Elijah expected? Before the 'great and terrible day of Jahweh' (Mal. 4^5), which is described in Mal. 3^{1-6}, 4^{1-3}. The co-presence of Moses and Elijah with Jesus on the mount may well have brought this prophecy to mind (Mal. $4^{4, 5}$), but there is no reason for connecting Malachi's prophecy of the great and terrible day of divine visitation with a resurrection from the dead, unless there is some correspondence between them. This impression is confirmed by the flight, silence and terror of the women at the announcement of the imminent reunion of the Lord and his disciples, upon which note the gospel is supposed to conclude. More than a 'resurrection appearance' is expected; the women, and the reader, are left face to face with the parousia, or its equivalent.

We must not suppose that St. Mark naively identifies the resurrection of the Lord and his parousia, for that would stultify the prophecy of Mk. 13; and in any case, if the resurrection *was* the parousia, St. Mark would no longer be in a position to write about it. It is preferable to say that he sees the resurrection as the type of the parousia and a foretaste of it. With the sequel to the resurrection, the regathering of the disciples and their work in union with the risen Lord, he is not concerned, though fortunately for us others were; he chooses to end his gospel with the imminent advent of the risen Christ confronting his reader, who also realizes that the rest of the programme of Mk. 13 has yet to be fulfilled. Only those who have been through a passion comparable to Christ's, or indeed have allied themselves to him in his passion, can enter into the understanding of his risen glory. The gospel is preparatory to that end: one might paraphrase an ancient Roman offertory prayer and add that, as often as the Gospel of St. Mark is

* See R. H. Lightfoot, *Locality and Doctrine in the Gospels*, ch. II and pp. 52–64.

read with sympathy and insight, 'opus redemptionis nostrae exercetur'.*

St. Mark gives us a full-scale pattern of the divine plan and an account of its anticipation and recapitulation in Jesus Christ. But for the early Christians, not only does the prophecy cast the shadow of its pattern over the passion and resurrection of the Lord, but also the process works the other way round and the anticipation and recapitulation of the plan in the passion and resurrection of the Lord henceforth colour and determine the understanding of the general prophecy of suffering and deliverance. Christ, by his cruxifixion and resurrection, has given a definite and decisive shape to the Christian understanding of providence and redemption; the pattern of Antichrist and parousia reappears as the pattern of death and resurrection in the Christian life. We have seen that St. Paul in his earliest letters accepts and hands on the early tradition of the eschatological programme; that he does not refer to it so explicitly in his later letters, does not mean that he had dropped it as a childish superstition incompatible with mature faith (we have seen that it survives in the Johannine writings), but rather that he sees the programme, interpreted in the light of Christ's death and resurrection, reproducing its pattern in every aspect of the Christian life. The neophyte has to enter that life by a re-enaction of, and incorporation into, the Lord's death and resurrection in the baptismal sacrament (Rom. $6^{3\ ff.}$). And his knowledge of that life is brought to him by the apostle, who reproduces in his own life the pattern of the Lord's redeeming work, which transforms the downs and ups of his apostolic labours into a series of deaths and resurrections, by which God not only renews the life of his apostle (II Cor. $1^{9,\ 10}$, 7^6), but also allows the new life to pass on to his converts (II Cor. 1^{3-7}), for 'death worketh in us, but life in you' (II Cor. 4^{10-12}). St. Paul can even say that he rejoices in his sufferings on behalf of the Colossians, and fills up what is lacking in the sufferings of the Christ in his own flesh for the sake of his (Christ's) body, the church (Col. 1^{24}). Thus, in and after Christ, the sufferings of his apostle are taken into the divine mystery of redemption: they are marked with the authentic stamp of death and resurrection. And although this is pre-eminently true of the apostle, it is no exclusive prerogative, as this same transformation of suffering is open to ordinary Christians as well (Rom. 5^{1-5}, $8^{17\ ff.}$). Our present afflictions are working for us an exceeding weight of glory, though at the moment this is invisible (II Cor. $4^{17,\ 18}$). Though all this happens in the present, the

* Secret for the ninth Sunday after Pentecost.

future parousia is not rendered superfluous or overlooked; its function is to manifest to us, and with us to all creation, the glory which we already have in Christ (Rom. 8$^{19-21}$). 'If you were raised together with Christ, seek the things above, where Christ is at the right hand of God already seated. Set your minds on the things above, not on the things on the earth. For you died, and your life has been hidden with Christ in God. When Christ, who is our (your) life, shall be made manifest, then you too will be manifested *with* him in glory' (Col. 3$^{1-4}$). 'So shall we ever be *with* the Lord' (I Thess. 4^{17}).

It is extremely difficult for us to hold all these themes together, and it seems that it also became increasingly difficult to do so in the early church as time went on. St. Matthew, who follows St. Mark so closely in many ways, undoubtedly simplified, and probably spoilt, the subtlety of St. Mark's eschatology, particularly by his stress on the divisive function of the future judgment (cf. Matt. 13$^{24-30,\ 37-43,\ 47-50}$, 16^{27}, 25^{31} ff.): but with him we are not concerned here. We must return to St. Luke.

As we approach the eschatology of St. Luke's gospel, we may note at the outset the following points. First, as far as sheer bulk is concerned, there is not less eschatological teaching in St. Luke than in St. Mark, but more. In addition to Lk. 21, which covers the ground of Mk. 13, we find eschatological teaching in 12$^{35-\text{end}}$ and 17$^{20-\text{end}}$. Secondly, all this additional teaching is of the 'sudden', and not the 'programme', variety. Thirdly, as with other features of St. Luke's teaching, his eschatology is spread out more evenly over the gospel, and is not concentrated in one massive block immediately before the passion, as in the other two synoptic gospels. While it is impossible to escape 'the eschatological element' in the Lord's teaching according to St. Luke's account, it is reduced to the level of one element among many, and ceases to provide a significant back-cloth for the work of redemption; this has the effect of seriously reducing, or even of eliminating, the dramatic tension of the Gospel. Fourthly, there are certain indications that the end, though sudden when it occurs, is postponed into the remoter future. It is not with observation that the kingdom of God comes (17^{20}). The parable of the pounds is addressed particularly to those who should think that the kingdom of God should immediately appear and should have any connection with Jesus' arrival in Jerusalem (19^{11}), and in it the nobleman takes care to depart into a *far* country (19^{12}, cf. Mt. 25^{14}). And so we are not surprised to read later that 'the time has come near' is one of the cries of the false christs (21^{8}, cf. Mk. 13^{6}).

St. Luke's eschatological tendencies appear most clearly when we compare Mk. 13 with his own version in Lk. 21, particularly the sections which concern the 'programme' (Mk. 13⁵⁻²⁷, Lk. 21⁷⁻²⁸).

(*a*) The setting of the discourse is radically altered. In St. Mark the discourse is private, and has the nature of a secret but all-important revelation, marked off from the rest of the narrative by this secret character, by its setting over against the city on the Mount of Olives (cf. Zech. 14⁴), and by the definite date 'after two days' with which the narrative is resumed in Mk. 14¹. All these features disappear in Lk. 21. The scene of the discourse is the temple, and so far from being spoken to four chosen disciples, or even to all the disciples, it is directed to a general audience, and arises from some casual conversation about the temple. Finally, by the insertion of the important verses 21³⁷, ³⁸ between the discourse and the resumption of the passion narrative, St. Luke intends to make it clear beyond doubt that the eschatological discourse was a normal part of the Lord's ordinary public teaching in the temple, on the same level as all he had taught during those few days.

(*b*) Mk. 13⁴ ... ὅταν μέλλῃ ταῦτα συντελεῖσθαι πάντα.   Lk. 21⁷ ... ὅταν μέλλῃ ταῦτα γίνεσθαι.

The rephrasing of the question by St. Luke might not be significant in itself, but taken in context with the whole discourse it becomes a possible pointer to what is in store. St. Mark's συντελεῖσθαι may have the ordinary meaning of 'accomplish', but it has overtones which suggest the fulfilment of an eschatological plan. St. Luke's substitution of γίνεσθαι, however, has only one meaning; it does not suggest the fulfilment of a deep eschatological drama, but an ordinary sequence of events in time: 'when is all this going to happen'?

(*c*) Mk. 13⁶, Lk. 21⁸. St. Luke's addition of the words ὁ καιρὸς ἤγγικεν has been mentioned in the fourth point above in connection with the postponement of the end.

(*d*) Mk. 13⁷: δεῖ γενέσθαι, ἀλλ' οὔπω τὸ τέλος.   Lk. 21⁹: δεῖ γὰρ ταῦτα γενέσθαι πρῶτον, ἀλλ' οὐκ εὐθέως τὸ τέλος.

St. Luke's addition of πρῶτον and his substitution of οὐκ εὐθέως for οὔπω underline further the suggestion of a long-drawn-out time sequence before the end.

(*e*) Mk. 13⁸, Lk. 21¹⁰, ¹¹.

St. Mark touches but lightly on the earthquakes and famines;

St. Luke considerably magnifies these natural calamities, but by the words πρὸ δὲ τούτων πάντων (21¹²) admits that they are out of sequence in this context. In 21²⁵, ²⁶ we also find that St. Luke has magnified the celestial and terrestial calamities which usher in the parousia (cf. Mk. 13²⁴, ²⁵), and it is possible that St. Luke regarded 21¹⁰, ¹¹ and 21²⁵, ²⁶ as one series of events, indicating a radical disruption of St. Mark's 'programme'.

Mk. 13⁸ ἀρχὴ ὠδίνων ταῦτα finds no place at all in Lk. 21. St. Mark's phrase characterizes the sufferings of the 'lesser tribulation' he is describing; the birth-pangs proper are the 'great tribulation'. The image of the travail pains links together suffering and consolation in one causal and purposeful sequence (cf. Jn. 16²⁰, ²¹): no suffering, no glory (Rom. 8¹⁷). For St. Mark the travail pains are part of the deep eschatological mystery he is unfolding, and are in some sense productive of the final redemption. For St. Mark the maxim 'no suffering, no glory' is true, first of Christ and then of the faithful: but for St. Luke it is true of Christ alone; the faithful have to put up with suffering, but it is in no sense productive of their glorification. His omission of this clause is highly significant.

(*f*) Mk. 13¹², ¹³ .... καὶ θανα-
τώσουσιν αὐτούς. καὶ ἔσε-
σθε μισούμενοι ὑπὸ πάντων
διὰ τὸ ὄνομά μου.

ὁ δὲ ὑπομείνας εἰς τέλος
οὗτος σωθήσεται.

Lk. 21¹⁶⁻¹⁹ .'.. καὶ θανατώ-σο
υσιν ἐξ ὑμῶν, καὶ ἔσεσθε
μισούμενοι ὑπὸ πάντων διὰ τὸ
ὄνομά μου. καὶ θρὶξ ἐκ τῆς
κεφαλῆς ὑμῶν οὐ μὴ ἀπόληται.
ἐν τῇ ὑπομονῇ ὑμῶν κτήσεσθε
τὰς ψυχὰς ὑμῶν.

It is no doubt possible to effect a synthesis of these two statements on a theological level, Mark stressing human perseverance, and Luke asserting the divine protection; but it is quite clear that the tone of the two versions is very different. The subtle change from the second person to the third in Mk. 13¹³, coupled with the aorist participle ὑπομείνας, suggests the grim determination required, and the merely contingent possibility of success. Commentators have noted the incongruity of Lk. 21¹⁸ so close to Lk. 21¹⁶, a verse he might well have altered, had not the text of St. Mark been supported by actual instances of martyrdom. But the loss and the sacrifice is not complete, nothing will be lost; no hair will perish, as St. Paul assures his hearers later on the verge of shipwreck (Acts 27³⁴). The tone of Lk. 21¹⁸, ¹⁹ is identical with that of Lk. 12³², 'fear not, little flock; for the Father has been pleased to give you the kingdom'.

(*g*) Mk. 13¹⁴⁻²³, Lk. 21²⁰⁻⁴.

We now come to consider St. Luke's treatment of St. Mark's greater tribulation. St. Luke's section is considerably shorter than St. Mark's, as he has already used such verses as he could in chapter 17. This stage is ushered in by St. Mark's enigmatic 'abomination of desolation', and by St. Luke's reference to the siege and fall of Jerusalem. The significance of this change is usually limited to questions concerning the relative dates of the two gospels, but it goes somewhat deeper. St. Mark takes over a mysterious phrase from scripture (Dan. 12¹¹) and leaves it as he finds it, capable of diverse interpretation and fulfilment; St. Luke decodes the mystery and describes it in concrete historical terms.* It is no longer the apotheosis of evil, but one event along with others in the historical series. So too for St. Mark's prophecy of a tribulation without parallel between creation and the end of time (Mk. 13¹⁹, also taking over scriptural language, Dan. 12¹), we find a general state of confusion and anarchy (Lk. 21²³, ²⁴); and while St. Mark states that this tribulation would be literally intolerable were it not shortened under divine pressure (Mk. 13²⁰), St. Luke, by his reference to the 'times of the gentiles', suggests an indefinite postponement of relief (Lk. 21²⁴).

(*h*) Mk. 13²⁴, ²⁵, Lk. ²⁵, ²⁶: the immediate preface to the parousia.

Here we may note two points. First, St. Luke omits St. Mark's phrase μετὰ τὴν θλίψιν ἐκείνην (Mk. 13²⁴), thus further breaking down St. Mark's clear division of the programme. Secondly, he replaces St. Mark's description of the signs of the end, which is little more than a scriptural paraphrase (cf. Isa. 13¹⁰, 34⁴), with his own description of the failure of the powers of nature and the consequent human distress. These two points taken together reveal that there is nothing in St. Luke's account, except the failure of the heavenly bodies, that distinguishes the signs of the end from the other calamities already described (Lk. 21¹¹, ¹², ²³, ²⁴).

(*i*) Mk. 13²⁶, ²⁷, Lk. 21²⁷, ²⁸: the parousia.

Here we need only point to one thing: the complete omission by St. Luke of all reference to the gathering together of the elect (Mk. 13²⁷). He does also omit St. Mark's angels who are sent to do the gathering, but that is of little moment, as elsewhere he allows for them (Lk. 9²⁶, Mk. 8³⁸). But when we recollect that for St. Paul the parousia of Christ and the gathering together of his faithful were almost synonymous terms (cf. II Thess. 2¹), and that the purpose of the parousia was to manifest the union, hitherto

---

* 'St. Luke has replaced the mysterious phrases which are unquestionably original by interpretations of them suggested by the events themselves'. A. Wright, *Synopsis* (2nd edition), p. 131.

hidden, between Christ and his faithful (I Thess. 4^{17}, Col. 3^{1-4}), we can see that this is a very startling and significant omission indeed. So far from the parousia manifesting or effecting this union, so that the faithful may ever be *with* the Lord, they are exhorted to raise their heads towards him at the approach of their redemption (Lk. 21^{28}): and it is to be hoped that, by vigilance and avoidance of worldliness (Lk. 21^{34}), and by continued prayer that they may escape all the intervening troubles, they may eventually *stand before* the Son of Man (Lk. 21^{36}). One does not like to over-emphasize the significance of the verse just quoted, but it is the language of confrontation, not of union. Christ is one thing, the faithful another.

To sum up, St. Luke's eschatological doctrine is quite simple. Christ by his passion, resurrection and ascension enters into his glory (Lk. 22^{69}, $24^{25-27, \ 44-47}$) where he will remain; meanwhile the faithful will have many trials on earth, but in the end, quite suddenly he will return. This doctrine, though simple, is in fact a simplification of the complex nuances of the primitive eschatology which we have, with such difficulty, attempted to describe. In blurring over the older eschatological programme which colours alike the passion and the glorification both of the Christ and of his faithful, St. Luke in effect denies to Christians a union with their head in suffering and glory; there will be suffering indeed, but it has no redemptive significance. One hardly need add that the doctrine thus distilled from St. Luke's gospel is identical with that of Acts (cf. Acts 1^{11}, 2^{34-36}, 3^{19-21}, 10^{42}, 17^{31}), and, as St. Paul exhorted his converts, 'we must through many tribulations enter into the kingdom of God' (Acts 14^{22}): no less, no more.

We can hardly expect to find in the epistle to the Hebrews an eschatological doctrine as fully expressed as St. Luke's. In the first place he had not the responsibility of correcting the emphasis of a previous evangelist, and, secondly, his own concern is so largely with the perfection of Christ's past work and present state that we are lucky to find any eschatology at all. Christ, having like the high priest entered the holy of holies, will come out for the salvation of those who are waiting for him (9^{28}); 'he that cometh shall come, and shall not tarry', as he quotes from Habakkuk (10^{37}); a calamity is expected which will shake not only the earth but heaven as well ($12^{25, \ 26}$). He seems to regard the possibility of the end as near, perhaps nearer than would be suggested by Lk. 21, but not nearer than is suggested by Lk. $12^{35 \ \text{ff.}}$ and $17^{20 \ \text{ff.}}$; like St. Luke in those passages and in Acts, he uses the imminence of the end to add urgency to his exhortations. The end, here referred to as such, is simply the return of the Lord, to which the gathering together of the elect is not conjoined; rather the Lord, it is hoped, will return to find them already gathered together (10^{25}). As in St. Luke, no life and death struggle with the powers of evil is necessarily involved in the eschatological plan: the 'Hebrews' have suffered ($10^{32\text{ ff.}}$) and must suffer (12^{5-11}), but the suffering issues from God's paternal care, and is salutary, but not redemptive. Unlike St. Paul (Rom. 5^3, Col. 1^{24}), they cannot rejoice in their sufferings, though they will be glad of them afterwards (12^{11}). So far it is clear that it is quite easy to extract a Lucan doctrine from the epistle to the Hebrews: what is quoted above is there, and we hope that its evidence will be weighed.

But there is so much else in the epistle that to write thus briefly would suggest deceit. For the epistle tells its readers that they are 'partakers of Christ' (3^{14}), exhorts them to 'bear his reproach' (13^{13}), says they have 'tasted the heavenly gift . . . and the powers of the age to come' ($6^{4,\ 5}$), and have even arrived already at the heavenly Jerusalem (12^{22}) and so share in the heavenly life.

To deal with the last text first, the emphatic perfect tense, 'you have arrived', must be proleptic, designating the end at which the 'Hebrews' will arrive if they persevere. The author sees the fulfilment latent in the promise; the way had been laid open ($10^{19\text{ ff.}}$), the journey begun (10^{39}): they are, in a sense, already there.

The other texts involve a fuller examination of the soteriology of this epistle, or, more accurately, of its doctrine of the relation of Christ and the faithful. The foundation of this doctrine is securely laid in the great doctrinal statement at the outset of the epistle (1^{1-4}, $2^{5-\text{end}}$), which contains, in germ, the whole of the subsequent doctrinal elaboration of the next eight chapters. The eternal Son has established a union with humanity by assuming human, not angelic (2^5), or more specifically Judaic (2^{16}), nature, with its consequent suffering and death. By his patient bearing of his lot, and by his divine election, he qualifies to be the complete and perfect priest or representative of the human race before God (2^{17}, 5^{1-10}), for 'he that sanctifieth and they that are sanctified are all of one' (2^{11}), that is, by their common sharing of humanity. This point is not resumed until chapter $10^{10,\ 14}$: 'by the which will we are sanctified through the offering of the body of Jesus Christ once for all' . . . 'for by one offering he hath perfected for ever them that are sanctified'. These passages would seem to give us as full an identity of Christ with us as St. Paul could desire; but closer examination would suggest a considerable distance between the doctrine of Hebrews and that of St. Paul.

The difference is revealed by the word μετέχειν, and its derivative μέτοχος, which Hebrews uses to describe this union of Christ with human nature, and which also recurs when he describes Christians as 'partakers of Christ' (3¹⁴). Bishop Westcott pointed out in his commentary (p. 73): 'As distinguished from κοινωνός, which suggests the idea of personal fellowship, μέτοχος describes common participation in some common blessing or privilege. The bond of union lies in that which is shared and not in the persons themselves'. The idea is that of partnership or association in a common enterprise. Thus James and John were partners or associates with Simon and his brother in the joint enterprise of fishing (Lk. 5⁷): so also was Christ anointed with the oil of gladness above his associates (Heb. 1⁹ = LXX of Ps. 45⁷). This idea is illustrated more graphically in Lk. 22²⁸, ²⁹: 'you are those who have abided with me in my temptations. And I appoint to you a kingdom, as my Father has appointed me, that you may eat and drink at my table in my kingdom', that is, not here and now (Lk. 22¹⁶, ¹⁸), but in heaven, for the kingdom though it begins on solid Judaic foundations (Lk. 1³², ³³) is to be transferred with Christ to the heavenly places (Acts 1⁶). Seeing that the children of men had a common bond in blood and flesh (κεκοινώνηκεν), Christ also *took a share in* human nature (μετέσχεν, Heb. 2¹⁴), as one among many associated in the common enterprise of humanity, and in this and as this he qualified to be our representative before the face of God (9²⁴). He is there *for* us, qualified by his taking a share in our nature and by his obedience to the point of perfection. This notion is different from St. Paul's presentation of Christ as the all-inclusive head of a new humanity, parallel in the history of the new creation to that of Adam in the old (I Cor. 15²²). Christ for Hebrews is the accepted victim of the new covenant in virtue of his sinless offering (Heb. 7²⁶, ²⁷) and the perfection of his will (Heb. 10⁸, ⁹); Hebrews cannot go as far as St. Paul to say that the sinless Christ 'became sin for us' (II Cor. 5²¹, Rom. 8³), nor can he say that our 'old man (that is to say, the inheritance of Adam, in general and in each particular) was concrucified' with Christ (Rom. 6⁶); nor can he go on to say 'that we might be the righteousness of God in him' (II Cor. 5²¹, I Cor. 1³⁰).

For Hebrews Christ is our representative; he is also our model, in so far as we identify ourselves not so much with him as with his enterprise. In this sense we become 'partakers of Christ' (Heb. 3¹⁴), paraphrased elsewhere as 'partakers of the heavenly calling', sharers in the calling to look beyond this life to Christ and our heavenly goal (3¹). As he shared our lot, so must we share his, and participate in it by aiming towards the same end. In this sense we should understand 'the reproach of Christ'(13^{13}). Moses in his own day reckoned the 'reproach of Christ' of greater value than the treasures of Egypt (11^{26}), and bore with transitory inconveniences in his search for his heavenly destination. Christ also went outside the boundaries of the earthly Jerusalem on a greater enterprise: Christians must follow after him, bearing the same reproach ($13^{12, 13}$).

This point is illustrated dramatically by St. Luke, as we may see when we notice how closely features peculiar to his account of Christ's death are paralleled in his account of St. Stephen's martyrdom. Both Christ and St. Stephen forgive their executioners (Lk. 23^{34}, Acts 7^{60}) and commend their spirits to heavenly protection (Lk. 23^{46}, Acts 7^{59}); both have the assurance of bliss to come (Lk. 23^{43}, Acts 7^{56}). St. Stephen reproduces in himself features of the Lord's passion; but (*pace* Acts 9^{4}) the Lord is not suffering in his martyr, for he stands before him. There is no mystical identity between Christ and St. Stephen, but an identity through imitation: 'looking unto Jesus, the author and completer of our faith' (Heb. 12^{2}). Here Hebrews helps us in our understanding of St. Luke, by showing how the heavenly glory extolled by St. Luke may become practically relevant to ordinary Christians.

So far our understanding of Hebrews has been based, as his own argument is based, on the assumption of a share in our humanity by Christ and the reciprocal attitude demanded of the faithful. But we cannot fail to ask how our common fallen humanity departs from its normal fallen destiny and lays hold of its new heavenly inheritance in Christ. Acquaintance with St. Paul would suggest that this transfer is effected through apostolic preaching and sacramental initiation; in Hebrews we find both these features, but they are not emphasized (2^{1-4}, 6^{1-5}). The preaching is a call from God to look beyond this life to a heavenly goal, and the initiation is described as an enlightenment which enables this further vision, and as a foretaste of better things to come. We may note that Christian initiation is described by Hebrews in terms of enlightenment and not in terms of death and resurrection; nor does he go as far as to say that it consolidates us into Christ, so as to make us one man (εἷς, Gal. 3^{28}) in him. This enlightenment is a single irrepeatable act, just as Christ's sacrifice and procurance of forgiveness is an irrepeatable act, and there is no possibility of a second forgiveness (Heb. 6^{6}, $10^{26, 27}$). What Hebrews states didactically, St. Luke narrates dramatically in the story of Annas and Sapphira (Acts 5¹⁻¹¹). The Christian life is not a series of deaths and resurrections, but should be one of steady progress towards its other-worldly objective.

So far from extracting a Lucan doctrine from the epistle to the Hebrews, our further investigation suggests that the same basic attitude underlies them both, Hebrews stating more explicitly and systematically factors essential to the understanding of the writings of St. Luke.

Finally we may ask how far, if at all, there survive in St. Luke and Hebrews any traces of the eschatological 'pressure' which led the older writers to see the pattern of the last things reflected in the passion of Christ and in the life of the faithful. We may suggest that there are two points at which this pressure or tendency may be traced:

(1) We may connect St. Luke's interest in the part played by Pilate and Herod in the crucifixion with his reference to the 'times of the Gentiles' in the preceding eschatological discourse, and the failure of the sun at the crucifixion (23⁴⁴) with his own description of the failure of celestial bodies (21²⁵).

(2) Heb. 10²⁵: 'and *so much the more* as you see the day drawing near'. We have seen that Hebrews dissociates the parousia from the gathering together of the elect: and yet in this verse there is a relic of the old connection. For otherwise, how would the ἐπισυναγωγή of the faithful here and now specially prepare for the last day, if the gathering of the faithful were not implicitly connected with the return of Christ?

We do not know how many of these reflections were present in the mind of Clement of Alexandria when he made his suggestion that St. Luke was the immediate writer of the epistle; certainly not all of them, or he would not have maintained that St. Paul was its ultimate author. (It is noteworthy that the west, where we find the earliest traces of knowledge of this epistle, was latest and most reluctant to acknowledge its Pauline authorship.) Some may be led by these reflections to jump to the conclusion that St. Luke was the author of the epistle as well as of his gospel and of the Acts; so much we do not hope to have proved. All we have tried to establish is that there is between these writings a kinship of outlook, a common family likeness. This may be of value in two ways. First, it may be of value in classifying the writings of the New Testament: St. Luke and Hebrews stand together as forming a solid bloc in distinction from St. Mark and St. Matthew, from St. Paul, and from St. John. We hear so much nowadays of the 'theology of the New Testament', the 'New Testament eschatology', the New Testament doctrine of this and that, that it is wholesome to be reminded that the New Testament, like all other ages of the Christian church, presents us with a number of diverse presentations of the same and unique act of our redemption in Christ. In fact there is no 'New Testament doctrine' of this or that aspect of our redemption; but there are a number of doctrines within the New Testament, each of which throws light on some aspect of our redemption. It is the function of dogmatic theology, not of New Testament scholarship, to organize these elements into a coherent whole.

Secondly, if we can establish this family likeness between St. Luke and Hebrews, it may be valuable in interpretation to use one member of the family to illustrate and amplify the other. Some examples of this have occurred in this essay; and in general, we may find it possible to use the more systematic and thorough theology of Hebrews to amplify the rather jejune and nebulous theology of Acts.

We have suggested that St. Luke and Hebrews have introduced a simplification into the complex thought of the early church; let us remember that St. John did the same. This simplification may may have been fatal or it may have been inevitable, as the new revelation accommodated itself to the forms of life and thought of the world it was to permeate and convert. In this essay we may have had to stress the differences between the thought of St. Luke and Hebrews and that of their predecessors; but we have not intended to impeach St. Luke as the first of heretics, or to acclaim him as the first apostle of Christian enlightenment, especially when we realize that to this family we owe almost one-third of our whole New Testament. Among her sisters in the New Testament, the theology of Luke-Hebrews may seem to lack the enigmatic obscurity of St. Mark, or the mystical profundity of St. Paul and St. John, yet if her sisters will not show off her glory, the theological children of Luke-Hebrews have played a great part in Christian history, especially in the west; to this parentage we owe the conception of Christ as our vicarious representative and of the Christian life as an *imitatio Christi*, 'looking unto Jesus', following Jesus here on earth that we may be with him for ever in heaven.

The Gentile Mission in Mark and Mark 13 $^{9\text{-}11}$

by

G. D. KILPATRICK

I N any attempt to answer the question 'does Mark refer to a Gentile Mission?' we have to examine Mk. 13$^{9\text{-}11}$. This runs in the Revised Version, 'But take ye heed to yourselves: for they shall deliver you up to councils; and in synagogues shall ye be beaten; and before governors and kings shall ye stand for my sake, for a testimony unto them. And the gospel must first be preached unto all the nations. And when they lead you *to judgement*, and deliver you up, be not anxious beforehand what ye shall speak: but whatsoever shall be given you in that hour, that speak ye: for it is not ye that speak, but the Holy Ghost.' In this form the passage seems to provide a straightforward indication of the Gentile mission, but when we examine the exegesis of the passage we find it less straightforward than the English Version might suggest; in particular scholars have proposed various interpretations of verse 10.

Suggestions made by two British scholars, F. C. Burkitt and C. H. Turner, indicate the chief problems in the passage and seem to point to their solution. As Burkitt's 'Note on the Text and Interpretation of Mk. 13^{10}' may be a little earlier than Turner's work I shall take it first.* Burkitt quoted Matt. 10^{18} and the evidence of Greek manuscripts and versions to show that in antiquity Mk. 13^{10} εἰς πάντα τὰ ἔθνη was frequently taken with the preceding rather than with the succeeding sentence. He argued that this was correct and understood the resulting phrase εἰς μαρτύριον αὐτοῖς καὶ εἰς πάντα τὰ ἔθνη as equivalent to εἰς μαρτύριον αὐτοῖς καὶ πᾶσι τοῖς ἔθνεσιν.

C. H. Turner's suggestions were made only a little, if at all,

---

* F. C. Burkitt, *Christian Beginnings* (1924), pp. 145-7. These lectures were delivered in February, 1924.

later.* In the series of studies on Marcan usage he examined the evangelist's use of εἰς with the accusative and showed that Mark frequently used this construction instead of ἐν with the dative. He suggested that this was true of Mk. 13¹⁰ εἰς πάντα τὰ ἔθνη which would be equivalent to ἐν πᾶσι τοῖς ἔθνεσιν. Turner's next contribution on Marcan usage dealt with parenthetical clauses and he proposed that the whole of verse 10 should be treated as a parenthesis.† He contended that it broke the connection between verses 9 and 11.

From Burkitt's and Turner's suggestions we see clearly what our problems are: the meaning of εἰς πάντα τὰ ἔθνη and the punctuation of verse 10. These problems are inseparable and together they determine our understanding of the whole passage. When they have been solved we shall have to relate our conclusions to our enquiry into the Gentile mission in Mark.

Let us begin by investigating the meaning of εἰς πάντα τὰ ἔθνη on the punctuation of our printed editions, a full stop after verse 9 and another after verse 10. With this punctuation εἰς πάντα τα ἔθνη is usually translated 'unto all nations' or similarly. The phrase is taken to indicate the persons addressed in κηρυχθῆναι. But is this justified? We can say in New Testament Greek λέγειν πρὸς αὐτὸν or λέγειν αὐτῷ but we do not find λέγειν εἰς αὐτόν. for 'to say to him'. What do we find with κηρύσσειν?

How was the passage understood in antiquity? Matthew twice takes it as Burkitt suggested with εἰς μαρτύριον, Matt. 10¹⁸ εἰς μαρτύριον αὐτοῖς καὶ τοῖς ἔθνεσιν and 24¹⁴ εἰς μαρτύριον πᾶσιν τοῖς ἔθνεσιν. This information does not help us now but we shall recur to it. The Latin evidence at Mark 13¹⁰ varies. *b c d ff²* *i k r¹*, like Matthew and the Sinaitic Syriac, join the phrase to the preceding sentence. *a l n q aur* vg alone seem to follow the punctuation of the printed Greek Testaments. Of these *a n* render 'in omnibus gentibus' and the remainder 'in omnes gentes'. There is, alas, a further complication: after εὐαγγέλιον D adds ἐν πᾶσι τοῖς ἔθνεσιν and *d ff²* 'in omnibus gentibus'. This looks like an alternative interpretation of εἰς πάντα τὰ ἔθνη, but, however this may be, it is clear how the originators of the addition understood πάντα τὰ ἔθνη. They took it with κηρύσσειν and interpreted it, locally, 'among all nations'. The Peshitta and Harclean Syriac render with ܒ 'in'. Thus we see that in antiquity interpreters were divided. Many took the phrase with the previous clause. Of the remainder some understood the phrase as meaning

* *J.T.S.*, xxvi (October 1924), pp. 14–20.
† *J.T.S.*, xxvi, (January 1925), pp. 152 f.

146

'among all peoples', others 'unto all people'. In view of this divergence we must examine the usage of κηρύσσειν elsewhere.

Κηρύσσειν occurs some fifty-eight times in the New Testament. At Lk. 4¹⁸ (a quotation from LXX), Acts 8⁵, 10⁴², I Cor. 9²⁷, I Pet. 3¹⁹, we find it with the dative of the persons addressed, which is the construction we should expect. Do we find κηρύσσειν with εἰς and the accusative? Mk. 1⁴ κηρύσσων βάπτισμα μετανοίας εἰς ἄφεσιν ἁμαρτιῶν does not apply. At Mk. 1³⁹, as Turner suggested, we should read καὶ ἦν κηρύσσων εἰς τὰς συναγωγάς and translate 'and was preaching in the synagogues'. Mk. 14⁹ ὅπου ἐὰν κηρυχθῇ τὸ εὐαγγέλιον εἰς ὅλον τὸν κόσμον is ambiguous. If ὅλον τὸν κόσμον is strictly geographical, then this passage is comparable with 1³⁹ and the meaning is 'in the whole world'. If the phrase means immediately 'the people of the whole world', then we have the same difficulty as at 13¹⁰. Matt. 26¹³ took the expression in the first sense ὅπου ἐὰν κηρυχθῇ τὸ εὐαγγέλιον τοῦτο ἐν ὅλῳ τῷ κόσμῳ. The Latin witnesses are divided: in uniuerso mundo *a r¹ aur* vg, in totum orbem terrae *k*, in uniuersum mundum *d f i l q*, in totum mundum *ff*² in totum orbem *c*. Here 'in uniuersum mundum' or the like is the commonest rendering but *a* shows that 'in uniuerso mundo' is older than the Vulgate. The Sinaitic Syriac, the Peshitta and the Harclean all have ܒ 'in'. Thus our guides are divided, Matthew, the Syriac Versions, and some Latin witnesses favour treating εἰς ὅλον τὸν κόσμον as meaning 'in the whole world', the renderings of the majority of Latin witnesses favour 'unto the whole world'.*

What do we find elsewhere in the New Testament? Two passages in Luke require our attention, 4⁴⁴ and 24⁴⁷. Lk. 4⁴⁴ καὶ ἦν κηρύσσων εἰς τὰς συναγωγὰς τῆς Ἰουδαίας takes over Mk. 1³⁹ and shows that the evangelist understood and accepted this construction. At Lk. 24⁴⁷, καὶ κηρυχθῆναι ἐπὶ τῷ ὀνόματι αὐτοῦ μετάνοιαν εἰς ἄφεσιν ἁμαρτιῶν εἰς πάντα τὰ ἔθνη, we are back to our old problem, the meaning of κηρύσσειν εἰς πάντα τὰ ἔθνη. The Syriac Versions, Sinaitic Syriac, Peshitta and Harclean again render with ܒ. On the other hand, the Latin is divided. *f r¹* vg Cypr. Iren. 1/2 read 'in omnes gentes', *c e* have 'usque in omnes gentes', *d* 'super omnes gentes', Tert. 'uniuersis nationibus'. *b q ff*² give 'in omne gente', *a l* 'in omnibus gentibus', and Iren. 1/2 'in toto mundo'.

At I Thess. 2⁹, ἐκηρύξαμεν εἰς ὑμᾶς τὸ εὐαγγέλιον, the supporter

---

* I have assumed that *praedicare in* means 'to preach unto'. In classical Latin, however, *praedicare* takes the dative. If *praedicare in* means 'to preach among' then my argument is even stronger.

of the view that there is a construction κηρύσσειν εἰς, meaning 'to preach to', may feel that he has at last found an irrefutable example of this. He is confirmed by the evidence of the Peshitta which has ܠܟܘܢ 'to you'. Let us, however, look further. The Harclean has ܒܟܘܢ 'among you', which agrees with the Syriac renderings in the Gospels. Before we turn to the evidence of the Latin we must note that for εἰς ὑμᾶς ℵ* has ὑμῖν. Corresponding to this reading we find in Wordsworth and White 'uobis' *c dem* vg (AH*Θ*NR) Ambrst. εἰς ὑμᾶς is rendered by 'inter uos' *g* vg (D) Pel^B or 'in uobis' in the remainder. There is no trace of 'in uos'.

When we are in doubt about New Testament usage it is always advisable to examine the evidence of the Apostolic Fathers. We find that they use κηρύσσειν twenty times and in the same way as the New Testament. The dative of the persons addressed occurs at I Clem. 7⁷, 9⁴, Barn. 14⁹ (LXX), Hermas, *Sim.* IX, 16⁴, ⁵.

On the other hand in Hermas we have three examples of εἰς with the accusative. At *Sim.* VIII, 3², ὁ δὲ νόμος οὗτος υἱὸς θεοῦ ἐστι κηρυχθεὶς εἰς τὰ πέρατα τῆς γῆς, the Latin Vulgate is as follows: 'haec autem lex filius dei praedicatus est in omnibus finibus orbis terrae'. The Palatine Latin renders this: 'lex autem filius dei est praedicaturus (*read*, praedicatus) in uniuersis finibus orbis terrae'. The translators took the phrase in a local sense. Next we have *Sim.* IX, 17¹, ἐκηρύχθη οὖν εἰς ταύτας (*sc.* τὰς φυλὰς) ὁ υἱὸς τοῦ θεοῦ διὰ τῶν ἀποστόλων. Here the Vulgate has 'praedicatus est ergo in eis filius dei per eos quos ipse ad illos misit', and the Palatine Latin 'praedicatus est ergo in his per apostolos filius dei'. The translators again took the phrase in a local sense. Thirdly we have *Sim.* IX, 25², οἱ κηρύξαντες εἰς ὅλον τὸν κόσμον for which the Vulgate gives 'quos misit Dominus in totum orbem praedicare' apparently construing another Greek text than the one before us. The Palatine translator has 'qui praedicauerunt filium dei per totum orbem', here too understanding εἰς as having a local meaning.

Let us now sum up the arguments about the use of κηρύσσειν in the New Testament and the Apostolic Fathers. The regular construction for the persons addressed is the dative and of this there are ten examples.

On the other hand there are no clear examples of κηρύσσειν with εἰς and the accusative meaning 'preach to', but there are examples of this construction meaning 'preach in', Mk. 1³⁹, Lk. 4⁴⁴. At this point the evidence of the ancient versions is important and at every instance of κηρύσσειν εἰς in the New Testament we have found a tradition at least as strong for the meaning 'preach in' or 'among' as for the contrary. The Latin translators of Hermas understood the phrase in this sense only. The use of εἰς with the accusative where we should expect ἐν with the dative can be detected up and down the New Testament, but is particularly noticeable in Mark, as it is in Hermas. Finally the idea of preaching among all nations is no strange one in the New Testament, e.g., Col. 1[23] τοῦ εὐαγγελίου . . . . . . τοῦ κηρυχθέντος ἐν πάσῃ κτίσει τῇ ὑπὸ τὸν οὐρανόν. For κηρύσσειν with expressions of place in Mark we may compare 1[38,39], 5[20], 14[9]. These arguments taken together seem conclusive that if we follow the punctuation of the printed texts we ought to render 13[10], 'And the Gospel must first be preached among all nations'. Mk. 14[9] is rightly translated, 'Wheresoever the Gospel shall be preached throughout the whole world' (R.V.).

If this translation is accepted there is, strictly speaking, no mention of preaching the Gospel to all nations. If the Gospel were preached in all the synagogues of the Diaspora the hearers would probably regard the prophecy as adequately fulfilled. Nor need 14[9] mean more than this. With these two verses our clearest references to preaching to Gentiles disappear from Mark.

This interpretation of 13[10] is satisfactory only as long as we are satisfied with the punctuation that goes with it. But, as we have seen, Burkitt proposed to take the phrase εἰς πάντα τὰ ἔθνη with what goes before, putting a full stop after ἔθνη instead of after αὐτοῖς. Burkitt supported his proposal from the evidence of Matthew and the ancient versions, but he has not been followed by the modern commentators. Is he right or wrong?

There is one criterion which has not been employed in this connection and that is Marcan word order. Greek differs from Latin in that, apart from the arrangement of words within well-defined phrases, its order of words within the sentence is free. The verb, for example, can be put at the beginning, middle and end of its sentence as the writer thinks suitable. As a matter of fact in most authors the verb is to be found as often as not somewhere in the middle of the sentence, but there is no rule about this.

To this freedom in word order among Greek writers the Gospels constitute an exception. A German philologist, Kieckers,* investigating the practice of several Greek writers of different dates, obtained the following figures for the initial, medial and

* Kieckers, *Die Stellung des Verbs im Griechischen und in den verwandten Sprachen* (1911), Strassburg, particularly p. 5.

final position of the verb in their sentences on an examination of five pages of text from each evangelist, Matt. 37/51/20, Mk. 40/66/24, Lk. 63/55/31, Jn. 71/48/25. These figures seem probable for the First and Fourth Gospels. In Matthew, Luke and John, the number of instances of the verb in the medial position is less than the number of initial and final instances taken together. The Third and Fourth Gospels prefer the initial position and in John this position accounts for nearly fifty per cent of all instances. We should expect something similar in Mark whereas we find that the instances of the medial position are more than the other two taken together. Anyone who has read Mark with this detail of style in mind will at once feel that there is something wrong with the figures and the conclusion they suggest.

This is not the place for a detailed examination of Mark's word order and of Kiecker's figures,* but to illustrate our point let us consider the position of the verb in Mk. 13. In compiling the figures for this chapter I have used the Nestle text and have ignored some variants which affect the order of words and in particular the position of the verb. As the punctuation of verses 9–10 is disputed I omit them from consideration. Introductory particles and adverbs and negatives which come before the verb, e.g. καί, εὐθύς, τότε, have been ignored. While our enquiry recalls the dominant Semitic word order we must remember that we are concerned, for the present, with the position of the verb in Mk. 13, rather than with the relations of Semitic and Marcan word order. Verbs in clauses which contain only verb and particles have been excluded from the reckoning.

Working on this basis we get forty-eight initial, sixteen medial and nineteen final positions. We can increase the figure for the initial position if we take advantage of some textual variations, but such as it is, it is enough to show that at any rate for Mk. 13, the normal position for the verb is the initial one. We may infer from this that when punctuation is doubtful, the punctuation which gives the verb the initial position is, other things being equal, more likely to be right.

With this rule in mind let us examine verses 9–10. Βλέπετε introduces its clause which must end at ἑαυτούς. The following verb παραδώσουσιν stands at the beginning of its clause but where does the clause end? The next verb is δαρήσεσθε and, if according to the rule, we make it begin its clause then the previous clause must end with συναγωγάς. The next verb is σταθήσεσθε and, if it

---

* I plan to give a detailed examination of Mark's word order elsewhere as it affects the exegesis of several passages.

begins its clause, the previous clause ends with βασιλέων. Now we approach the crux. If we keep the punctuation of the printed text, then δεῖ, the main verb, is medial. We have seen that for sixteen examples of the medial position there are forty-eight examples of the initial position, so that the odds are three to one against a punctuation which gives the medial position. If we take the alternative punctuation, a full stop after ἔθνη, then we can read δεῖ πρῶτον with some manuscripts, or treat πρῶτον as an introductory adverb like εὐθὺς and τότε. In either case δεῖ has the initial position and conforms to Mark's dominant word order. Thus Burkitt's proposal has in its favour not merely the evidence of Matthew and some ancient manuscripts and versions, but also Marcan usage.

With this punctuation what is the meaning of εἰς πάντα τὰ ἔθνη? Burkitt treated the phrase as equivalent to πᾶσι τοῖς ἔθνεσιν and as parallel to αὐτοῖς 'for a testimony to them and to all nations'. He wrote, 'Here I feel inclined to accept the verdict of antiquity against that of grammar'.* We must admit that some witnesses from antiquity are in favour of Burkitt's suggestion, but not all. Matthew seems to support it. Alone of the Old Latin *c* has 'illis et gentibus' but all the other manuscripts which have this punctuation, *b d ff² i k r¹* have 'illis et in omnes gentes', conceivably 'against all nations'. The Sinaitic Syriac treats the expressions as parallel, 'to them and to all nations', using ॥ with both.

In this variety of opinions we must again resort to usage for the decision. μαρτυρεῖν and μαρτύριον are followed by the dative of the persons to whom witness is borne. There is no example apart from this passage of μαρτύριον εἰς, but there is one of μαρτυρεῖν εἰς, Acts 13¹¹ οὕτως σὲ δεῖ καὶ εἰς 'Ρώμην μαρτυρῆσαι. The Latin witnesses apparently all have 'Romae', except Cassiodorus who has 'in Romana urbe'. This evidence suggests that the constructions of μαρτυρεῖν and κηρύσσειν are parallel, that μαρτυρεῖν πᾶσι τοῖς ἔθνεσιν means 'to bear witness to all nations' and μαρτυρεῖν εἰς πάντα τὰ ἔθνη 'to bear witness among all nations'. This would be in keeping with the usage of the evangelist who uses εἰς freely where we should expect ἐν. If we feel that it is awkward to have εἰς used in two different ways in the same sentence, we have an example of this in verse 16 where the first εἰς is equivalent to ἐν and the second is not. We may conclude that we have a meaning as well as a punctuation for εἰς πάντα τὰ ἔθνη.

Let us now return to what is left of 13¹⁰. As Vincent Taylor

* *Op. cit.*, p. 146.

reminds us, 'This verse is widely regarded as an insertion made by Mark (or, less probably, a redactor) in his source'.* Turner suggested that the verse was a parenthesis and it certainly seems at first sight to break the connection between verses 9 and 11. As a parenthesis let us punctuate it: σταθήσεσθε ἕνεκεν ἐμοῦ εἰς μαρτύριον αὐτοῖς καὶ εἰς πάντα τὰ ἔθνη. (δεῖ πρῶτον κηρυχθῆναι τὸ εὐαγγέλιον.) καὶ ὅταν ἄγωσιν ὑμᾶς κτλ.

We now have to study the meaning of our proposed parenthesis. Let us begin with δεῖ πρῶτον or πρῶτον δεῖ. We can explain these words in several ways. In the first, πρῶτον is temporal in sense, as it is everywhere else in Mark, and means 'before some event' or 'events', namely before τὸ τέλος of verse 7. 'Before the end comes, the Gospel must be preached'. It is to be hoped that it will, but this is an odd point to mention here. There is no question of delaying the preaching the Gospel.

Lagrange took πρῶτον as temporal but has his own explanation. He wrote:

'Entendre πρῶτον comme Knab. *antequam veniat finis*, par allusion au v. 7, et entendre cette fin de la fin du monde, c'est créer du désordre, puisque nous n'en sommes pas encore a la profanation du Temple. One ne peu s'appuyer sur le sens de Mt. dont le contexte est différent. πρῶτον signifie donc 'avant tout, tout d'abord', puisqu'il est là absolument, sans aucun point de comparaison (Schanz, Loisy, Merx).'†

'Before everything else the Gospel must be preached.' We may doubt 'sans aucun point de comparaison'.

Are we to return to the first explanation despite its unsuitability? We need not. πρῶτον may refer not to τὸ τέλος of verse 7 but to the events of verses 9 and 10. 'Before you are arrested and beaten and appear before rulers, the Gospel must first be preached'. But, if that is the implication of πρῶτον, it may also point forward to the next clause, καὶ ὅταν ἄγωσιν ὑμᾶς παραδιδόντες. If this is right, what becomes of our parenthesis?

Let us reconsider our hypothesis about it. If our suggestion about the punctuation of verses 9 and 10 is sound, there is a real break after πάντα τὰ ἔθνη and so one end of our parenthesis is firm. But what of the other? Verse 11 begins with καὶ which should link it with what goes before and so with verse 10 in this instance. καὶ has not come at the beginning of a clause since verse 6, a noteworthy abstinence for Mark, and now that καὶ reappears it must be taken seriously. So perhaps our punctuation should be

* *The Gospel According to St. Mark*, p. 507.
† *L'evangile selon saint Marc*, p. 338.

δεῖ πρῶτον κηρυχθῆναι τὸ εὐαγγέλιον, καὶ ὅταν ἄγωσιν ὑμᾶς παραδιδόντες, κτλ. 'First the Gospel must be preached, and when they arrest you and bring you into court', etc. On this interpretation there is no need to assume a parenthesis. There is a clear break before δεῖ πρῶτον, verse 10 connects closely with what follows and πρῶτον has the temporal meaning, 'first', characteristic of it elsewhere in Mark.

It is now time to write out verses 9–11 as a whole with the proposed punctuation. They run:

Βλέπετε δε ὑμεῖς ἑαυτούς
παραδώσουσιν ὑμᾶς εἰς συνέδρια καὶ εἰς συναγωγάς,
δαρήσεσθε καὶ ἐπὶ ἡγεμόνων καὶ βασιλέων,
σταθήσεσθε ἕνεκεν ἐμοῦ εἰς μαρτύριον αὐτοῖς καὶ εἰς πάντα
τὰ ἔθνη.
δεῖ πρῶτον κηρυχθῆναι τὸ εὐαγγέλιον, καὶ ὅταν ἄγωσιν ὑμᾶς
παραδιδόντες κτλ.

In this passage a short introductory clause is followed by three clauses which have much the same structure. There is asyndeton, the verb comes first and is followed by two noun phrases which in the first two clauses balance each other. In the second clause the double καὶ has misled the commentators.* In the third clause the structure has not been maintained entire, ἕνεκεν ἐμοῦ stands outside it. This however need cause no difficulty. Sentences composed of four phrases can easily alternate with sentences composed of three. As the clauses stand they have a common structure sufficiently remarkable to distinguish them from what follows.†

The following sentences to the end of verse 11 seem to provide an explanation and development of the preceding three clauses. The first event is the preaching of the Gospel. Next (and presumably as a result of this) Christians are arrested and brought into court. When this happens they are not to premeditate their defence.

We may remark that a new structure is to be found in the clauses of verses 12–13a but commentary seems to return at the

---

* As Mark never uses τε this would be his only way of saying 'both . . . and'. He may however mean no more by the first καὶ in the clause than 'also' or 'even'. For another example of double καὶ in Mark misleading punctuators so as to ignore the evangelist's tendency to put his verbs well forward in their clauses we may instance 2¹⁵ f. This passage should probably be punctuated καὶ τοῖς μαθηταῖς αὐτοῦ, ἦσαν γὰρ πολλοί. καὶ ἠκολούθουν αὐτῷ καὶ οἱ γραμματεῖς κτλ. This is almost Swete's punctuation.

† Those who wish may relate the structure of these three clauses to the principles of Hebrew and Aramaic verse. According to these principles the first two clauses can represent lines with three beats and the third a line with four beats. For such variation in Hebrew compare Burney, *The Poetry of our Lord*, pp. 32 f., and for the same in Aramaic, *ibid.*, pp. 109 f.

last sentence of verse 13.* In fact verses 9–13 appear to consist of a series of clauses exhibiting recurrent structures interspersed with comments. This feature may run back as far as verse 6. One interpretation of the phenomenon would be that the structured clauses, if such I may call them, constitute lines of an oracle which have been broken up by larger or shorter comments and explanatory phrases. It is natural to attempt to relate such suggestions to historical research and to theories of a Semitic original, but we cannot look now at all the problems raised by these suggestions.

One problem however we must consider, as it leads on to the treatment of a major part of our subject. Among the reasons for treating verse 10 as it is punctuated in our printed texts as due to the evangelist was the fact that it clearly approved the Gentile mission. Has Jesus said anything so explicit, it is hard to see how any controversy could have arisen about preaching to the Gentiles. This is certainly an effective criticism of verse 10 as the editions print it; but from our point of view it is another ground for thinking that the traditional construe is wrong, because it is out of keeping with the tenor of the ministry as a whole.

Does this mean that all reference to preaching to the Gentiles disappears from this section? Let us look at it as a whole. The first step is to preach the Gospel. We are not told where or to whom it is to be preached. This leads to arrest, and, according to verse 12, the contrivers of arrest will sometimes be the relatives of the preachers, and so probably Jews. In verse 9 the prisoners are to be brought εἰς συνέδρια καὶ εἰς συναγωγάς. This expression at least leaves open the possibility that some of the courts will be Jewish. The faithful will be beaten before governors and kings. This suggests Palestine, the one area where we hear of Christians being brought before both governors and kings, though it was possible for them to suffer the same experience elsewhere.

There remains the last clause of verse 9 with the beginning of verse 10, 'ye shall stand for my sake for a testimony to them and among all nations'. 'To them' appears to mean, 'to governors and kings'. 'Among all nations' suggests that the events described in the neighbouring verses may happen anywhere and at any rate will not be confined to Palestine. But this clause does not say anything about a preaching to Gentiles, and, in view of the extent of the Jewish Diaspora, this is important. All that need be implied is the kind of event related in Acts. St. Paul, for example, preached in the synagogue, a practice which frequently led to dissension there, and his opponents in the synagogue hailed him

* Clauses with three phrases recur at verses 22, 25.

before the magistrate. Though Gentiles may have been present at St. Paul's preaching in the synagogue, it was primarily a preaching to Jews and we cannot at that stage speak of a Gentile mission. All our text need imply is a mission in the synagogues going far and wide beyond Palestine.

Let us now sum up our examination of Mk. 13⁹⁻¹¹. As we have seen, the interpretation which asserts a preaching to the Gentiles is the one which offends most of all against Marcan and New Testament usage. It depends on a conventional punctuation and an interpretation of English rather than Greek idiom. If we amend this fault, but retain the conventional punctuation, the preaching to the Gentiles disappears. If we let Marcan usage determine even the punctuation, the evangelist foretells a world-wide mission to Judaism but none to the Gentiles. The text, which, in an English version, appears the clearest evidence for a Gentile mission is an illusion.

Mk. 14⁹ on our interpretation says no more and no less than 13⁹⁻¹¹. It refers to the world-wide preaching of the Gospel but states nothing about a preaching to Gentiles.

The one important reference to Gentiles in 13⁹⁻¹¹ occurs in the two lines:

δαρήσεσθε καὶ ἐπὶ ἡγεμόνων καὶ βασιλέων
σταθήσεσθε ἕνεκεν ἐμοῦ εἰς μαρτύριον αὐτοῖς καὶ εἰς πάντα τὰ ἔθνη.

What does this mean? αὐτοῖς refers back to the governors and kings, most of whom will be Gentiles. But how are we to explain εἰς μαρτύριον αὐτοῖς? There are no grounds for thinking that αὐτοῖς means 'against them'. As we have seen, μαρτυρεῖν takes the dative, and this dative can be of two kinds. It can be used for the people to whose character, for example, witness is borne, in which case εἰς μαρτύριον αὐτοῖς will mean 'for a testimonial to them'; or, secondly, the dative can serve for those to whom the witness is given, like the judges in court. The second meaning seems the more probable here. We do not know how the evangelist would render 'for evidence against them' but we may suspect from analogy that he would write εἰς μαρτύριον πρὸς αὐτούς. Our analogy is from λέγειν. The evangelist writes λέγειν αὐτοῖς, not πρὸς αὐτούς, for 'speak to them', and he uses εἰς with the accusative with λέγειν in a local sense, but at 12¹² he has πρὸς αὐτοὺς τὴν παραβολὴν εἶπεν, 'he spoke the parable against them'.

If εἰς μαρτύριον αὐτοῖς means 'for a witness to them', the important question is what is the content of μαρτύριον. The word occurs thrice in Mk. 1⁴⁴, 6¹¹, 13⁹. The first is in connection with an act of healing, the second relates to the mission of the twelve, and the third to the sufferings of the disciples. These three events, healing, preaching and suffering, are characteristic of the time immediately before the end. In view of this we may suggest that the content of μαρτύριον at 13⁹ is eschatological, that the sufferings of the disciples are a part of the woes before the end and are a testimony to governors and kings that the end is near. This is not the same as preaching the Gospel to them. We may conjecture that this testimony is given to the governors and kings because the end involves them. This is, however, conjecture and Mk. 13 throws no light on the fate of Gentile rulers. One aspect of the end is clearly defined in 13²⁴⁻²⁷, but we do not know from these verses what happens to the world when the elect have been gathered.

This evidence for Jesus' teaching about preaching the Gospel and about the end coheres with what the evangelist relates elsewhere in his book. The one contact with the Gentile world occurs in 7²⁴⁻³¹. Here Jesus is in the marches of Israel, if we may so call the border lands of the north-east and north. The one act of healing a Gentile, the daughter of the Syrophoenician woman, is grudgingly performed and there is no record of any preaching on this journey.

Other references to the Gentiles in Mark are few. 10⁴² refers to the practice of Gentile rulers and is not to our purpose. 10³³ foretells the committal of Jesus into Gentile custody and again tells us nothing of a Gentile mission. It does, however, warn us to examine Mark's Passion story with our enquiry in mind.

In the Passion story the centurion's comment on Jesus' death is relevant. The centurion was presumably a Gentile. When he saw that Jesus was dead he said ἀληθῶς ὁ ἄνθρωπος οὗτος υἱὸς θεοῦ ἦν. This is a vexed passage. In particular there are many interpretations of the centurion's pronouncement, and it is only with hesitation that we offer another. In 13²⁴⁻²⁷ these abnormal phenomena immediately precede the coming of the Son of Man, the failure of the sun and moon, the falling of stars and the shaking of the heavenly powers. In 15³³⁻³⁹ abnormal phenomena immediately precede the death of Jesus. These events are, so to speak, a μαρτύριον to the centurion and he draws the right conclusion from the evidence. In giving his verdict he does not use the term 'Son of Man' but one corresponding, υἱὸς θεοῦ, which we may interpret with appropriate ambiguity 'no ordinary person' or even 'a supernatural being'. We are told the centurion's judgment of the evidence; we have no grounds for calling it his confession of faith and we have nothing to show that he became a disciple. The evangelist does not inform us in this context what happens to Gentiles who correctly read the signs of the times.

One important passage remains, 11¹⁷, ὁ οἶκός μου οἶκος προσευχῆς κληθήσεται πᾶσιν τοῖς ἔθνεσιν. πᾶσιν τοῖς ἔθνεσιν is usually taken with οἶκος προσευχῆς. This is then understood as a universalist phrase, 'a house of prayer for all nations'. There is nothing comparable to this in the whole Gospel and we may well wonder whether an interpretation so much out of harmony with the rest of the Gospel can be right.

Is another interpretation possible? πᾶσιν τοῖς ἔθνεσιν is nearer to κληθήσεται than to οἶκος προσευχῆς. Let us see if we can take the phrase with the verb. The Hebrew original of our quotation can be rendered, 'My house shall be called a house of prayer by all nations', but the dative of the agent is perhaps too uncommon a construction in the New Testament for us to invoke it here. πᾶσιν τοῖς ἔθνεσιν may however be a *datiuus iudicantis*.* If this is so we may paraphrase the quotation, 'My house will have the reputation of a house of prayer in the eyes of all nations.' With this interpretation universalism disappears from our passage which means 'You have turned my Temple, which is to have a world-wide reputation for sanctity, into a den of thieves.' We may, however, think that the common interpretation is right. If this is so, 11¹⁷ is the most explicit universalist pronouncement in the Gospels.

If the results of our examination are sound, universalism is absent from Mark. There is no preaching the Gospel to Gentiles in this world and there is no interest in their fate in the world to come. The Gospel is to be preached outside Palestine and the signs of the times are to be read by Gentiles as well as Jews, but that is as far as Mark goes.

Probably the most significant elements in the Gospel for the breakdown of particularism are sayings which do not mention the Gentiles at all. The attacks on the rigorist observation of the Sabbath and the dietary laws weakened some of the provisions that kept Jews and Gentiles apart and had their consequences in the Apostolic Church. Indeed the vision of Cornelius, Acts 10⁹⁻¹⁶, 11⁵⁻¹⁰, may be read as a kind of commentary on Mk. 7¹⁻²³. The author of Acts uses the story of Cornelius to introduce a new stage in the growth of the Gentile mission, a fact that makes Mk. 7 all the more significant.

---

* Cf. Gen. 34³⁰, μισητόν με πεποιήκατε ὥστε πονηρόν με εἶναι πᾶσιν τοῖς κατοικοῦσιν τὴν γῆν, ἔν τε τοῖς Χαναναίοις καὶ τοῖς Φερεζαίοις.

If, as seems probable, Mark was written about A.D. 65, this conservatism is striking, and even more so if the Gospel was produced at Rome. It shows that, at any rate in one important feature, the entry of the Gentiles and the controversies which this entailed had not materially affected the Gospel tradition by the time Mark was written. Further, the Gospel reveals the outlook of Jesus as entirely Jewish. In the story of the Syrophoenician woman he has to be over-persuaded to heal her daughter. His first reactions to the woman's plea are unforthcoming and his sympathy has to be awakened. The act of healing appears as the exception to the rule. If the common interpretation of 11^{17} is right, here alone in the Gospel we have unmitigated universalism, but, as we have seen, the interpretation is doubtful. The rest of the Gospel shows us a Jesus who worked and preached and thought within the limitations of his time and place. It is significant that, in these circumstances, his teaching contained elements which facilitated the developments of the Christian Church.

Before we close this enquiry we may allow it to point two morals for us. The first arises out of the appeal to New Testament usage and, in particular, to Marcan usage for the exegesis of the text. The conclusions drawn in this paper may be wrong, but often it is to usage that appeal must be made and by usage that the issue will be decided. Sometimes usage will not give us an answer, sometimes it cannot, nor will it always give us the answer we expect.* For making the appeal to usage we are today probably better equipped than any generation before us with synopses, concordances, lexicons and critical editions.

The second moral is that we must not ignore the most ancient versions of the New Testament. They come from the second and third centuries A.D. when a Greek little different from that of the New Testament was the living language. They often fail to agree among themselves and sometimes they are quite wrong, but usually one or other of them preserves at least a hint of the truth and they have a sense of idioms which we can otherwise only obscurely discern.†

---

* This paper is an illustration of how usage overrules preconceived ideas. When I began to write it I thought some such punctuation of 13$^{9f.}$ as follows was right: . . . . αὐτοῖς καὶ εἰς πάντα τὰ ἔθνη. (πρῶτον δεῖ κηρυχθῆναι τὸ εὐαγγέλιον.) καὶ ὅταν κτλ. It was solely a study of usage which led me to the punctuation and exegesis that I propose.

† When I had drafted this paper I received the *S.N.T.S. Bulletin*, III, with Professor Jeremias' article, 'The Gentile World in the Thought of Jesus', pp. 18–28. I thought it best to leave what I had written unmodified by Professor Jeremias' arguments, but I am glad to find that we are in a considerable measure of agreement, and wish to call attention to Professor Jeremias' suggestions about Mk. 14^9 and 11^{17}.

The Holy Spirit in the Writings of St. Luke

by

G. W. H. LAMPE

THE primary message of St. Luke's two-volume work is set before his readers in two great discourses. The first of these, the sermon of Jesus in the synagogue at Nazareth, declares the programme of the prophet-Messiah's saving work, foreshadows its rejection by his own people, and hints at its acceptance by the Gentile world, while the second, St. Peter's speech on the day of Pentecost, takes up the theme of the first, shows how the programme there set forth has been fulfilled, and, when it is read in its context of the gift of tongues and the apostles' preaching to the assembled peoples of the world, introduces the second part of St. Luke's story, the rejection of the gospel by the leaders of Judaism and its proclamation to the ends of the earth.

The connecting thread which runs through both parts of St. Luke's work is the theme of the operation of the Spirit of God. 'The Spirit of the Lord is upon me', Jesus declared, 'because he hath anointed me to preach the gospel to the poor: he hath sent me to proclaim release to the captives, and recovering of sight to the blind, to set at liberty them that are bruised, to proclaim the acceptable year of the Lord'. St. Peter tells the Pentecost crowd that this Jesus who was crucified and slain 'did God raise up. . . . Being therefore by the right hand of God exalted, and having received of the Father the promise of the Holy Spirit, he hath poured forth this which ye see and hear.' Through the death and exaltation of the Messiah, the Spirit which operated in him has come to be imparted to his followers, to be the bond of union between them and himself and the power by which the divine sovereignty into which he has entered is made effective among men through the preaching of the gospel in the Spirit's power and under its guidance.

Although the activity of the divine Spirit is the essential theme of his writings, St. Luke has little to say concerning the nature of that Spirit (apart from its vitally important relationship to the person and work of Jesus) that is not already found in the Old Testament. In the literature of Israel the Spirit of God is generally conceived of as an impersonal but divine force, deriving from its primary significance of 'breath' or 'wind' its two principal connotations of life-force and power. As the creative power of God the Spirit is closely associated with the divine word: 'By the word of the Lord were the heavens made, and all the host of them by the breath of his mouth (τῷ πνεύματι τοῦ στόματος αὐτοῦ).* It is also the mode of God's activity towards his people, so that we read of the 'Spirit of judgment',† and of the 'Spirit of salvation',‡ and as a divinely sent energy the Spirit possesses the heroes whom God raises up as saviours of the community of Israel from oppression at the hands of her enemies. The Spirit of the Lord 'clothed itself with Gideon', § enabling him to rally the tribes to deliver Israel; 'the Spirit of the Lord came upon Jephthah' ‖ as he began his victorious march against the Ammonites; and it endowed Samson with supernatural strength to rend a lion and to smite the Philistines.¶ The Spirit is always associated with power,[a] but not only with merely temporary and sudden accessions of physical strength or courage in battle. Leaders and rulers possess a more permanent endowment of the Spirit, giving them the qualities of wisdom and judgment which their office requires. Thus, the Spirit which was in Moses is imparted also to the seventy elders of Israel, manifesting its presence in their case in the form of prophesying;[b] Joshua possesses the Spirit, either, according to Num. 27[18], before he is commissioned by Moses as his successor through the sign of the laying-on of his hand, or, in the version of the story given by Deut. 34[9], as a consequence of that token of Joshua's spiritual kinship, or identification, with his Spirit-possessed predecessor; and, when Samuel had anointed David, 'the Spirit of the Lord came mightily upon David from that day forward'.[c] The distinctive characteristic of Isaiah's 'shoot out of the stock of Jesse' is that the 'Spirit of the Lord shall rest upon him', as the divine energy which will cause him to exhibit all the attributes of an ideal ruler.[d]

---

* Ps. 33[6]; cf. Gen. 1[2-3]; Judith 16[14].　　　† Isa. 4[4].
‡ Isa. 26[18] (LXX), a passage which, with its allusion to the 'falling' of the inhabitants of the land and the 'rising' of the dead, may perhaps have influenced Lk. 2[34].
§ Jd. 6[34].　　　‖ Jd. 11[29].　　　¶ Jd. 14[6, 19].
[a] Cf. Wisd. 5[23].　　　[b] Num. 11[17, 25].　　　[c] I Sam. 16[13].
[d] Isa. 11[2].

More especially, the Spirit is the prophetic energy which enables men to become the recipients and interpreters of divine revelation. Balaam and Saul are inspired by its power to prophesy;* Elisha, as Elijah's successor in the prophetic ministry, receives a double portion of the Spirit which was upon him;† the prophet is described as 'the Spirit-bearing man';‡ it is by the Lord and his Spirit that a prophet is sent;§ through the entering-in of the Spirit a prophet may receive the revelation of God;‖ and in the power of the Spirit he may be caught away from one place to another,¶ and, as in the case of Elijah and Elisha, work miracles that may include even the raising of the dead.[a] In relation to the prophetic inspiration the idea of the Spirit is closely akin to that of the 'hand' of God.[b] Its operation is also present in other modes of apprehending divine revelations, such as non-prophetical forms of divination and the interpretation of dreams.[c] It is also the Spirit of wisdom, understanding, and knowledge by which the artist Bezalel is enabled to reproduce the heavenly pattern in the construction and furnishing of the Tabernacle,[d] and it is the source of David's inspiration as a psalmist.[e] One instance of the Spirit's possession of an individual is especially important: for his office as a prophet and as the fulfiller of the divine purposes of redemption through suffering, the righteous servant of the Lord is one upon whom God has put his Spirit.[f]

The Spirit, inspiring the utterances of the prophets, is the means whereby God's ethical requirements and his judgments upon Israel are made known to his people;[g] it is the power through which his sovereign authority and his pastoral care are made effective in the life of the nation. Hence the Spirit comes to be thought of as something more than a divine energy. As the 'holy Spirit' it is the mode of God's self-manifestation, and it is virtually identical with the presence, the glory, or the angel of the Lord himself;[h] thus, the Spirit is said to have been set in the midst of Israel,[i] and by her rebellious conduct the Spirit is 'grieved'.[j] For the faithful, however, the Spirit is a guide and leader.[k] The Spirit's activity is thus an integral part of the covenant relation between God and the people. It is therefore not surprising that the thought of a renewal of this activity is closely bound up with

---

* Num. 24², 23⁶ (LXX); I Sam. 10⁶, ¹⁰, 11⁶, 19²⁰, ²³.
† II Kgs. 2¹⁵, etc.   ‡ Hos. 9⁷ (LXX).   § Isa. 48¹⁶.
‖ Ezek. 2².   ¶ I Kgs. 18¹²; II Kgs. 2¹⁶; Ezek. 3¹², 8³; 11²⁴; etc.
[a] II Kgs. 2¹⁴⁻¹⁵, etc.   [b] I Kgs. 18⁴⁶; II Kgs. 3¹⁵; Isa. 8¹¹; Ezek. 1³, 3¹⁴, ²², 8³.
[c] Gen. 41³⁸; Dan. 4⁸, ¹⁸.   [d] Ex. 31³,35³¹.   [e] II Sam. 23².
[f] Isa. 42¹, cf. 48¹⁶, 59²¹, 61¹.   [g] Ps. 106³³; Zech. 7¹²; Neh. 9³⁰.
[h] Ps. 51¹¹, 139⁷; Hag. 2⁵.
[i] Isa. 63¹¹.   [j] Isa. 63¹⁰.   [k] Ps. 143¹⁰ (LXX).

Israel's eschatological hope, and in particular with the expectation of a new Covenant. The faithful remnant, according to Isaiah, will be cleansed of moral defilement by 'the Spirit of judgment and the Spirit of burning',* a prophecy which may well have been in the Baptist's mind as he looked forward to a coming baptism of Spirit and of fire. In the future age of blessedness the Spirit will 'be poured upon us from on high', bringing an era of judgment and righteousness.† In those days God will pour his Spirit upon the seed of Jacob his servant,‡ and this outpouring of the Spirit will be directly connected with devotion to the Name of the Lord, so that a man will 'write on his hand, Unto the Lord'. Here we have a foreshadowing of the close connection between the outpouring of the Spirit and salvation by the Name (now the exalted name of Jesus as Lord and Messiah) which is so marked a feature of the thought of Acts. There is no explicit mention of the Spirit in Jeremiah's prediction of the new Covenant (though it is probably implied in the expectation of a law written in men's hearts) but the similar prophecies of Ezekiel§ express in strong terms the hope that in the age of the new Covenant the entire community of Israel may participate in the Spirit as the life-principle of a nation which truly knows the Lord and is inwardly his people. This expectation is reaffirmed in *Jubilees*, ‖ and as late as about A.D. 320 R. Acha cites Isa. 32[15], 61[1], and Lam. 3[49] ff. as proof that the bestowal of the Spirit of God is to be a primary characteristic of the age of final redemption.

Sometimes, as in the prophecy of Jl. 2[28] which is of such cardinal importance in the thought of St. Luke, this bestowal of the Spirit is conceived in terms of a universal outpouring of the prophetic gift; but, however it may be envisaged, it is associated with cleansing from ethical defilement and remission of sins, a thought which is also prominent in the many passages of the Old Testament in which the action of the Spirit is portrayed under the imagery of cleansing, healing and life-giving water, particularly the ὕδωρ ἀφέσεως flowing out from the ideal Temple of Ezekiel's vision.¶

All Israel will be possessed by the Spirit in the days of the renewed Covenant; but it is to be associated in a special measure with the community's leader. Isaiah's ideal ruler is to possess the fullest endowment of the Spirit,[a] and the Messianic hope is of one who will be truly anointed with the inward unction of the Spirit

---

* Isa. 4[4].   † Isa. 32[15–16].   ‡ Isa. 44[3, 5].
§ Ezek. 37[14], 39[29].   ‖ *Jub.* 1[21–5].
¶ Ezek. 47[3]; cf. Isa. 1[16–20]; Jer. 4[14]; Ezek. 36[25–27].   [a] Isa. 11[1–5].

of God. This hope of a Spirit-possessed Messiah is most explicitly stated in certain post-canonical writings.* It is, however, important to notice that in the Second Isaiah's figure of the Servant the ideas of Spirit-possession and Covenant relationship are already united in the person of an individual redeemer.† It is also clear, both from later Jewish literature and from the New Testament, that the notion of a Spirit-possessed Messiah was sometimes closely associated with the eschatological hope of a universal outpouring of the Spirit. The Messiah, in fact, was expected, at least in some quarters, to be the agent of God in the general bestowal of his Spirit in the age of fulfilment.‡

St. Luke follows the Old Testament in his conception of the nature of the divine Spirit. In his writings the Spirit is still, generally speaking, non-personal; it is the mode of God's activity in dealing with man and the power in which he is active among his people; and it is in terms of the Old Testament view of the Spirit, and as the historical fulfilment of the hopes which associated the Messiah with the Spirit, and a general outpouring of the Spirit of prophecy with the last days and the new Covenant, that St. Luke interprets the events which it is the purpose of his two books to record.

In the Infancy stories, which form a prologue to his narrative, Jesus is presented as the Messianic king, the son of the Most High, who is to receive the throne of his father David and reign over the house of David for ever. § Like the heroes of Hebrew antiquity, he is a saviour; he is Messiah and Lord, whose birth, itself due to the operation of the Spirit, is announced by the angels at Bethlehem as a gospel of great joy. In the synagogue at Nazareth Jesus describes himself as the fulfilment of the expectation of a Spirit-possessed prophet inaugurating the age of redemption and blessedness. ‖ During his ministry, he and his chosen Twelve and Seventy announce the advent of the Kingdom of God and demonstrate its power in word and deed. At the time of his death his followers regard him as a prophet, mighty in deed and word, whose mission, as they had hoped, was to be the redemption of Israel. At Pentecost St. Peter points to the fulfilment of the prophetic hope of the age to come. The Spirit of prophecy has been poured out by the exalted Christ whose Kingdom and Lordship, proleptically announced by angels in the Infancy stories, have now been realized. Jesus, who was slain in accordance with the counsel of

* En. 62², 49³, Pss. Sal. 17⁴², 18⁸. † Isa. 42¹, ⁶, 49⁸.
‡ *Test. Lev.* 18; *Gen. Rabbah* 2; Jn. 1²⁵, 7³⁸⁻⁴¹; cf. the obscure text in Lam. 4²⁰ (LXX).
§ Lk. 1³²⁻³³. ‖ Lk. 4¹⁸⁻²¹.

God by the hands of lawless men, has been raised from the dead according to prophecy and exalted to the right hand of God, so that all who are baptized in his name for remission of sins may receive the promised gift of the holy Spirit.*

In other speeches St. Peter develops the same theme. Jesus, who was denied and delivered over to death, has been glorified by God; his name is therefore powerful to do mighty works. Though the people and their rulers acted in ignorance, it was in accordance with prophecy that the Messiah should suffer. Salvation is in his name alone, for he has been exalted as a saviour at the right hand of God to give repentance and remission of sins. The reception of the gift of the Spirit through him by the apostles is the proof that these things are true. He has been exalted to heaven until the final *apocatastasis* of all things. The expectation of a prophet like Moses (Deut. 18¹⁵, ¹⁸) has been fulfilled, as also have the predictions of all the prophets, in accordance with which Jesus was raised up for Israel and sent to the ancient people of God who, so far as the leaders and the majority were concerned, rejected him.†

This rejection, which it is part of the object of Stephen's speech to compare with the previous rejection of Moses, is, like the Jews' disobedience to the Law and their obsession with the Temple made with hands, the proof that throughout their history they have resisted the Holy Spirit.‡

To Cornelius and his household, St. Peter expounds the gospel which began after John's baptism, the content of which is the message of peace proclaimed by Jesus who was anointed with the Holy Spirit and power and thus enabled to perform mighty works of healing and exorcism. He was slain and raised from the dead, as the apostles testify from their personal experience, and he has commissioned the apostles to bear witness that through his name those who believe on him receive remission of sins.§

St. Paul at Pisidian Antioch recalls the history of Israel's election and settlement in Canaan, laying special emphasis on the great Spirit-possessed leaders, the Judges, Samuel, Saul and David, from the last of whom the saviour is descended. John's baptism and preaching of repentance prepared the way for the coming of one greater than he. The rulers of the Jews and the people of Jerusalem had Jesus slain, being ignorant of the purport of the prophecies; but God raised him up, as the apostles testify, and the promises made of old to Israel are fulfilled to the Jews of the present time. His resurrection is the fulfilment of prophecy,

* Acts 2¹⁴⁻³⁸.
‡ Acts 7¹⁻⁵³.

† Acts 3¹²⁻²⁶, 4⁸⁻¹², 5²⁹⁻³².
§ Acts 10³⁴⁻⁴³.

and through him remission of sins is proclaimed, and justification which could not be obtained under the Mosaic Law.* Elsewhere, St. Paul lays stress on the necessity for the Messiah to suffer and to rise from the dead, and on the repentance and remission of sins which are available now that the prophecy of the suffering of the Christ has been fulfilled and, like the Servant of the Lord, he has brought light to Jew and to Gentile.† The preaching of this gospel is a proclamation of the kingdom of God,‡ and the triumphant conclusion of St. Luke's narrative leaves his readers with the picture of St. Paul preaching the Kingdom of God unhindered in the heart and centre of Caesar's empire.

Such, in a brief sketch, is the main outline of the gospel as St. Luke sums it up in his introduction to his work (the Infancy stories and the announcement by Jesus of his mission in the discourse at Nazareth), and in the speeches contained in Acts, which, whether or not they are derived from literary sources, have clearly been sufficiently worked over by the author and placed with enough care into their contexts to enable them to convey to us the authentic impress of St. Luke's thought. It is a gospel of the work of the Spirit, whose continuous activity before the birth of the Saviour, in him, and, then as the consequence of his death and exaltation, in and among his followers, runs as a unifying theme through these Lucan summaries. It is our present task to examine the distinctive features of this theme in fuller detail.

A most striking feature of the opening chapters of St. Luke's work is the outburst of the prophetic Spirit which forms the setting of the Forerunner's birth and mission and of the birth and infancy of Jesus. Prophetic inspiration had disappeared from the Hebrew scene since the days of the great canonical prophets, and Spirit-possession had apparently ceased in Israel.§ It suddenly reappears in full vigour at the beginning of the gospel story. Thus, in the theophany, so closely resembling the angel's appearance to Manoah, with which St. Luke's narrative opens, the birth of John is announced as the birth of a pre-eminently inspired prophet, which will bring joy and gladness—those characteristic features of the Spirit's activity as St. Luke conceives of it. || Holy Spirit and the power of the Most High (the terms are virtually synonymous) are to come upon and 'overshadow' Mary.¶ Elisabeth becomes a prophetess, filled with the Spirit, who blesses Mary under the

* Acts 13^{17-39}.　　　　† Acts 17^3, 26^{18-23}.　　　　‡ Acts 20^{25}.
§ Cf. Ps. 74^9; Zech. 13^4; Dan. 3^{38} (LXX); I Macc. 4^{46}.
|| Lk. 1^{15}, 1^{14}; cf. 1^{44, 47}, 10^{21}; Acts 2^{46}, 13^{52}, 16^{34}, and perhaps 8^{39}.
¶ Lk. 1^{35}.

165

Spirit's inspiration.* Zacharias prophesies in the Spirit when he utters his hymn of praise,† and Simeon and Anna are prophets like those of the Old Testament; the former receives a divine oracle in the Spirit, and his entry into the Temple is 'in the Spirit', that is, in a prophetic ecstasy.‡

It is, of course, part of the common Synoptic tradition that the Baptist was a prophet, resembling, but greater than, the Hebrew prophets of old. All the Synoptic writers, as opposed to the Fourth Evangelist, unite to portray him as Elijah *redivivus*. In some respects, however, John's character as Elijah is not brought out so clearly by St. Luke as by St. Mark. Thus, the Marcan description of John's personal appearance with its resemblance to Elijah's is omitted in this Gospel, as is also the discussion of Elijah's coming in the person of John.§ On the other hand, St. Luke emphasizes the fact that the office of the Baptist is to precede the Lord in the Spirit and power of Elijah, to turn the hearts of the fathers to the children. This is set out most plainly in the angelic annunciation to Zacharias, whose language recalls ben Sirach's description of the future work of Elijah‖ and also, but less clearly, the prophecy of Mal. 4⁵. His task as the preparer of the way is again foretold by Zacharias in words which are applied by Malachi to the office of Elijah as the forerunner of the Messiah.¶ St. Luke, moreover, emphasizes the prophetic character of John most strongly, and adds to the Synoptic picture of him as the new Elijah certain touches which serve to connect him with other prophets and Spirit-possessed leaders. If the appearance of the angel to Zacharias, and the announcement that John is to resemble the Nazirites in his abstention from wine and strong drink, recall the birth-story of Samson, the circumstances of his birth and to some extent also his Nazirite characteristics suggest a resemblance to Samuel, whom St. Luke regards, no doubt because he stands at the head of the prophetic line, as a pre-eminent prophet, superior, like Elijah and Elisha, to the generality of inspired men in the ancient prophetic succession. Like Samuel, he is the agent by whom, though in a very different manner, the Davidic and Messianic king is anointed; thus his action recalls the account of Samuel that is given in Ecclus. 46¹³. As one who is possessed by the Spirit from the womb he resembles Jeremiah,ª and the manner in which his prophetic ministry opens ('the word of God came to John') directly recalls the beginning of Jeremiah's prophesying ('the word of God which came to Jeremiah').

---

* Lk. 1⁴¹.   † Lk. 1⁶⁷.   ‡ Lk. 2²⁵⁻²⁷, ³⁶.   § Mk. 9¹¹⁻¹³.
‖ Ecclus. 48¹⁰.   ¶ Mal. 3¹.   ª Jer. 1⁵.

Jeremiah, we may infer from Matt. 16[14], occupied an important place in current eschatological expectations, and later rabbinical tradition referred to him the Deuteronomic prophecy of the raising up of a prophet like Moses.* We are also told by St. Luke that the 'hand of the Lord' (a concept closely related in the Old Testament to both the Spirit and the Word of God) was with John. In every respect the forerunner of the Christ is an outstanding prophet, reflecting the characteristics of the greatest inspired figures of the Old Testament. In this setting of the renewed activity in Israel of the long dormant energy of the Spirit, St. Luke places the birth and infancy of Jesus. It is a most appropriate circumstance for the Messiah's birth, for in St. Luke's view the Spirit is the instrument or power through which God's entire plan of salvation is carried out. In the Old Testament dispensation, God revealed his purposes through the prophetic Spirit; during the ministry of Jesus the Spirit works in him as the power in which the Kingdom of God is already operative among men; and after his death and exaltation the same power, as the Spirit poured out by the Lord Christ, is the guide and driving force of the apostolic mission to evangelize the whole world. The work of John forms the connecting link between the first two of these phases of the Spirit's activity, just as the narrative of the period between the Resurrection and Pentecost is the bridge that unites the second with the third.

John represents the old dispensation, as the last and greatest of the Hebrew prophets. In Jesus the Spirit is operative in a new way, for through the coming upon Mary of the Holy Spirit which is the power of the Highest (the language is Old Testament in character, but thoroughly typical of St. Luke's writing; indeed, it is likely that in the Infancy narratives, including perhaps even the canticles, he is writing freely and is bound by no written sources), her child is to be holy, that is, possessing the nature of the divine Spirit, and Son of God. His sonship is thus directly bound up with the operation of the Spirit, and this in turn is closely akin to the tabernacling of the glory of God. ἐπισκιάζειν (Lk. 1[35]) is used in the Old Testament to describe the tabernacling of the cloud among God's people† and the protection and shielding of men by the divine presence,‡ as well as, in one instance, the 'overshadowing' of merely human honour or reputation. § It is highly significant that St. Luke here employs the same word which is used in the common Synoptic narrative to describe the overshadowing

---

* Cf. Strack-Billerbeck, vol. 2, p. 626.
‡ Ps. 91[4], 139[8] (LXX).

† Ex. 40[35].
§ Prov. 18[11] (LXX).

of Jesus and the disciples by the cloud at the Transfiguration.* There, in the anticipatory glorification which precedes his journey to death and his entry into his glory,† Jesus is declared by the heavenly voice to be Son of God. It is no accident that St. Luke indicates by his use of this word the direct connection between the sonship possessed by our Lord through the working of the Spirit at his conception, and the reaffirmation of it before his death in anticipation of his entry into the full realization of Messianic sonship at the right hand of God. A link between these events may be discerned in the salutation of Jesus as Son of God at the Jordan, when his descent into the abyss of death and his ascension to receive the promise of the Holy Spirit‡ are foreshadowed in an act of prophetic symbolism. §

The narrative implies that the Spirit is fully present in Jesus from his conception. Although his growth and his advance in wisdom are described in terms somewhat similar to those which are applied to the child John,‖ it is significant that in the case of Jesus there is no mention of that 'growing strong in Spirit' which is related of the Baptist. At his baptism, however, there is a second coming of the Spirit of God. It descends, according to the Lucan narrative, in bodily form, that is to say in a manner wholly unlike the often transient inspiration of an ordinary prophet. Codex Bezae's reading of εἰς αὐτόν for ἐπ' αὐτόν in all the Synoptics, which falls into line with many patristic commentaries on the passage, is probably intended to indicate that the Spirit entered into Jesus and did not merely 'come upon him' externally. We may compare the indwelling of the martyr Polycarp by the Spirit in the form of a dove (see E. Nestle, *ZNTW*, 7 (1906), p. 359). The suggestion that there was thus a twofold activity of the Spirit in relation to Jesus may indicate that the descent of the dove at the baptism denotes a Messianic anointing with the particular divine power necessary for his mission, that is, with the same energy of the Spirit which his followers were to receive at Pentecost for the missionary task to which they had been appointed.

In his account of the baptism of Jesus, St. Luke adds comparatively little to the Marcan narrative.¶ He does, however, lay

---

* Mk. 9⁷ and parallels.   † Lk. 24²⁶.   ‡ Acts 2³³.

§ The symbolism of death and ascension is not so clearly brought out by St. Luke as by St. Mark, perhaps because the former is about to describe the actual Ascension in his second volume, possibly also in order to enhance the similarity between the Spirit-baptism of Jesus and that which his disciples received at Pentecost.

‖ Lk. 1⁸⁰, 2⁴⁰, ⁵².

¶ I consider it probable that Luke is following Mark in this narrative, that the Marcan σχιζομένους τοὺς οὐρανούς has been replaced by the weaker ἀνεῳχθῆναι under the influence of Isa. 64¹, Ezek. 1¹, and Isa. 24¹⁸, and that the Alexandrian reading is to be preferred in 3²².

a somewhat greater emphasis on the operation of the Spirit in this episode, both through his insertion of the phrase 'in bodily form', and through the fact that the Messianic unction of Jesus with the Spirit is a cardinal point in the speeches which are put into the mouth of the early apostolic preachers. He also calls attention to the fact that the descent of the Spirit took place while Jesus was praying. The mention of this circumstance serves to introduce one of the most characteristic features of St. Luke's teaching, namely, his insistence upon prayer as the means by which the dynamic energy of the Spirit is apprehended. Prayer is, in fact, complementary to the Spirit's activity since it is the point at which the communication of divine influence becomes effective for its recipients. According to St. Luke, alone of the Evangelists, Jesus is praying when the Spirit descends upon him, when the mighty works of his Galilaean ministry are being developed and are about to cause the first great clash with the scribes and Pharisees,* when he is about to appoint the twelve apostles,† at Caesarea Philippi and at the Transfiguration;‡ and although his prayer before his arrest is recorded by all the Synoptists, the agony and stress of that prayer is greatly heightened by the Lucan narrative.§ In the second volume of St. Luke's work we find that it is in prayer that the Church, like Jesus at his baptism, awaits the descent of the Pentecostal Spirit; ‖ 'the prayers' are one of the chief features of the Church's life in the Spirit;¶ the disciples are filled with the Spirit and enabled to speak the word boldly while they are engaged in prayer;[a] prayer is combined with the ministry of the word as the proper business of the Twelve;[b] prayer accompanies the ordination of ministers of the Church and the commissioning of its missionary preachers;[c] prayer, accompanied by an imposition of hands, is the means whereby the Samaritans receive the Pentecostal Spirit;[d] and prayer precedes the doing by the apostles of mighty works of healing and of raising the dead.[e] In all these instances there is a very close connection, either stated or implied, between prayer on the part of man and the communication from the side of God, in various forms and for different purposes, of the power, inspiration, or guidance of the Holy Spirit. Prayer is also intimately linked with the reception of revelations through dreams or angelic visitations,[f] both of which, in the Lucan writings, as in the Old Testament, are closely related to the activity of the

* Lk. 5[16].   † Lk. 6[12].   ‡ Lk. 9[18, 28].
§ Lk. 22[44].   ‖ Acts 1[14].   ¶ Acts 2[42].
[a] Acts 4[31].   [b] Acts 6[4].   [c] Acts 6[6], 13[3], 14[23].
[d] Acts 8[15, 17].   [e] Acts 9[40], 28[8].   [f] Acts 9[11], 10[4], 12[5].

Spirit.* Further, since prayer is the means by which men become subject to the Spirit's power and influence, it is natural for St. Luke to regard the gift of the Holy Spirit as God's principal answer to human prayer.† It is highly probable, in view of its agreement with the general Lucan teaching about the Spirit, that the Lucan form of the saying about the answer to prayer is due to the evangelist himself rather than to his source; and it also seems likely (though this is, of course, a much more controversial matter) that the petition, 'May thy holy Spirit come upon us and cleanse us' is part of St. Luke's own version of the Lord's Prayer. Although Marcion is the earliest witness to this reading,‡ the clause occurs in a different position in his version of the prayer from that in which it was known to Gregory of Nyssa, and the absence of any obvious doctrinal reason which might account for Marcion having altered the Lord's Prayer in this fashion strongly suggests, when taken in conjunction with the conformity of the petition to Lucan teaching, that the clause must be authentic. καθαρίζειν in the spiritual sense occurs again in close association with the gift of the Spirit in St. Peter's speech at the Jerusalem Council,§ and the idea expressed by this verb is parallel to the frequent Lucan insistence on remission of sins as a primary consequence of the Spirit's operation in men.

Filled with the Spirit with which he had been anointed at his baptism, Jesus is led by the Spirit (like St. Matthew, St. Luke avoids the more violent Marcan word ἐκβάλλει) into the desert for the Temptations. It is St. Luke alone who emphasizes the completeness of our Lord's Spirit-possession in connection with this event, and so brings the struggle with the devil within the scope of the Spirit's operation. To overcome the forces of evil, as well as to exercise wisdom and judgment, was part of the work of Spirit-possessed messianic leader prophesied by Isaiah, and the activity of the Spirit is often associated by St. Luke with the conflict against the adversary.‖

Jesus returns to Galilee, according to the Lucan account, 'in the power of the Spirit',¶ and in the synagogue at Nazareth he proclaims himself to be the Spirit-anointed prophet, foretold in Isa. 61[1], whose mission is to bring in the age of salvation. By this stress on the Spirit-unction of Jesus, St. Luke links this proclamation at Nazareth with the preceding narratives of the Temptations and the Baptism.

---

* The relationship of visions and dreams to the activity of the Spirit is strongly emphasized in St. Peter's citation of Jl. 2[28]. 'Angel' and 'Spirit' are almost synonymous in Acts 8[26, 29]. † Lk. 11[13]. ‡ Tert. *Marcion.* 4[26].
§ Acts 15[9]. ‖ Cf. Lk. 10[21] in its context in this Gospel. ¶ Lk. 4[14].

The reading of the prophecy and the announcement of its fulfilment in the mission of Jesus serve as a prologue to the whole of the rest of St. Luke's work. It was, no doubt, in order to use it for this purpose that St. Luke took the story of the Nazareth preaching out of its Marcan context and re-wrote it.

St. Luke does not say explicitly very much about the operation of the Spirit in and through Jesus during his ministry, apart from the introductory sentence which he prefixes to his account of Christ's thanksgiving to the Father:* 'He rejoiced in the Holy Spirit' (the variant readings do not materially affect the sense). The great age of the work of the Spirit has not yet dawned; it will begin after the death and exaltation of Jesus. We have, however, been told at the outset that the ministry began in the power of the Spirit, and the apostolic preaching declared that Jesus went about doing good and healing after he had been anointed with Holy Spirit and power. Power has also been associated with the Spirit in the Infancy narrative. We can therefore safely infer that the power which St. Luke, more frequently and emphatically than the other evangelists, ascribes to Jesus during his ministry is meant to be understood as the Spirit of God.

The power of Jesus is the translation into action, as it were, of the authority which he possesses, and it is therefore associated with his authority in the amazed comments of those who witnessed the exorcism of a man with an unclean spirit at Capernaum.† St. Mark speaks in this context only of ἐξουσία, such as was bestowed upon the Son of Man in Daniel's vision.‡ Similar power and authority are conferred by Jesus on the Twelve,§ a foretaste of their exercise of the power of the Spirit after Pentecost. This power is demonstrated chiefly in exorcisms and miracles of healing,‖ so that Jesus is described by his disciples on the Emmaus road as 'mighty (δυνατός) in deed and word'.¶ Usually it is described as the power of Jesus himself, but on one occasion it is spoken of as the power of the Lord which was with Jesus.[a] The same power of the Spirit works miracles after Pentecost at the hands of Peter and John, Stephen, and Philip,[b] and it characterizes the apostolic preaching just as it did that of Jesus himself. This power is, of course, the power of the Kingdom of God, already operative in Jesus. It is clear, therefore, that St. Luke brings the ideas of the power of the Kingdom and the working of the Spirit of God into a very close relationship with each other;

---

* Lk. 10²¹. † Lk. 4³⁶. ‡ Dan. 7¹⁴.
§ Lk. 9¹. ‖ Lk. 4³⁶, 6¹⁹. ¶ Lk. 24¹⁹.
* Lk. 5¹⁷. [a] Acts 4⁷, 6⁸, 8¹³.

they are in fact virtually identical. There is, indeed, one occasion
on which St. Luke appears to miss an excellent opportunity to
bring out this relationship. For the wording of the Matthaean
version of the famous saying of Jesus in answer to the accusation
of complicity with Beelzebub: 'If I by the Spirit of God cast out
demons, then no doubt the Kingdom . . . has come upon you', he
substitutes the form: 'If I by the finger of God . . .'* If the
Matthaean and Lucan accounts are derived from Q, St. Luke
must have either retained Q's original wording despite the
opportunity, which the context offered him, to introduce a reference
to the Spirit (a chance of which St. Matthew availed himself), or
actually substituted the allusion to the 'finger of God' for a
reference to the Spirit in his source. If St. Luke knew Matthew,
then of course he deliberately preferred 'finger' to the Matthaean
'Spirit'. The explanation for this apparent neglect of one of his
basic themes is, no doubt, that he is either retaining or introducing
an echo of Ex. 8¹⁹(LXX), where the magicians of Egypt, con-
fronted with the miracles of Moses, say of them, 'This is the finger
of God'. St. Luke is probably anxious to work this allusion into
his narrative in order to strengthen those elements in his portrait
of Jesus which are intended to recall Moses. In any case, the finger
and hand of God are practically identical in the Bible with the
Spirit of God, a fact which is especially true of the Lucan
writings.† The great emphasis which St. Luke lays on the δύναμις
of the Spirit in relation to our Lord's ministry is in complete
harmony with his broader treatment of the person and character
of Jesus. As one in whom the Spirit of God is so fully embodied
that his entire life and actions constitute a mode of the Spirit's
operation, Jesus is naturally presented to our view as a prophet-
like figure.

He is united with the Spirit in a far closer bond than any
prophet before him. The canonical prophets of Israel were
possessed by the Spirit in a relatively external and sometimes
spasmodic fashion, whereas, so far as his words and deeds are
concerned, Jesus is virtually identical with the Spirit itself. Not
even Moses, the faithful servant of God, who is contrasted with
the ordinary prophets as one to whom God spoke 'mouth to
mouth, even manifestly',‡ and who 'saw the glory of the Lord', §
stands in the same relation to the divine Spirit. Yet, although he
excels the ancient prophets, Jesus is nevertheless himself a prophet

* Matt. 12²⁸; Lk. 11²⁰.
† Passages in which the 'hand' of God fulfils the same functions as his Spirit include:
Acts 4²⁸, ³⁰, 7³⁵, 11²¹, 13¹¹.
‡ Num. 12⁷⁻⁸.   § Ibid. (LXX).

for whom they had prepared the way; his person and office, as described by St. Luke, recall many features of the character and work of the most outstanding figures among them; and he is presented to the readers of this Gospel and Acts as the fulfilment of the prophecy of Deut. 18[15]: 'The Lord thy God will raise up unto thee a prophet . . . like unto me (Moses): unto him shall ye hearken', a prediction which is of cardinal importance in St. Luke's understanding of the Scriptures and their fulfilment in the gospel events.*

St. Luke draws our attention, more often than the other evangelists, to the history of the ancient prophets as a foreshadowing of the work of Jesus. The mission to the Gentiles and the rejection of the gospel by the countrymen of Jesus are prefigured in the stories of Elijah and Elisha which St. Luke records in the Nazareth sermon. At the feast in the Kingdom of God, to which the Gentiles will be admitted but into which the unbelieving Jews cannot enter, 'all the prophets' as well as St. Matthew's 'Abraham, Isaac, and Jacob' have their share.† Jesus stands in the succession of prophets who were persecuted and martyred by the Jews of Jerusalem; like them, therefore, he must meet his death in the capital, for it cannot be that a prophet perish outside Jerusalem;‡ and it is in fulfilment of what the prophets had predicted of the Son of Man that he makes his journey thither, a journey whose ultimate significance is expounded on the way to Emmaus from 'all that the prophets have spoken', beginning from Moses and 'all the prophets'. § The slaying of Jesus was in keeping with the treatment meted out by the Jews to the prophets of old,|| but they all, from Samuel onwards, had announced the age of fulfilment which his death and exaltation inaugurated,¶ and had testified to the gospel of remission of sins through faith in him.[a] It was through ignorance of the prophecies that the people of Jerusalem and their rulers fulfilled them by their condemnation of Jesus.[b]

Jesus thus stands at the climax of the prophetic tradition, heralded by the last and greatest of the prophets of the old order. He is himself marked out from the latter as one greater than they;

---

* Cf. Acts 3[22–23], 7[37]. It is hard to say to what extent St. Luke's understanding of this text as a Messianic prophecy had been anticipated in Judaism. Rabbinic tradition did not usually identify the prophet like Moses with a single individual. See Str.-Bill. vol. 2, p. 626.

† Lk. 13[28]; Matt. 8[11].

‡ Lk. 13[33].   § Lk. 18[31], 24[25–27].

|| Acts 7[51], cf. Lk. 11[50], where St. Luke speaks of 'the blood of all the prophets' but St. Matthew only of 'all the righteous blood'.

¶ Acts 3[25].   [a] Acts 10[43].   [b] Acts 13[27].

so we find that St. Luke clarifies the sense of St. Mark's 'a prophet as one of the prophets' by re-writing the phrase in the form: προφήτης τις τῶν ἀρχαίων; Jesus is not merely a reincarnation of one of the prophets of old.

At Nazareth Jesus declares his mission in terms of a prophet's vocation; he is described as a prophet by the spectators of his miracle of raising the dead at Nain:* 'A great prophet has been raised up among us' (the use of the word ἠγέρθη recalls the raising up of the Judges as Spirit-possessed saviours and God's raising up of Cyrus to be his agent);† and Simon the Pharisee is inclined to regard him as a prophet, or even, if Codex Vaticanus is to be followed, as *the* prophet, that is, the prophet like unto Moses.‡ At the Transfiguration the heavenly voice echoed the words of the Deuteronomic prophecy; and it may be with the object of reproducing more exactly the wording of Deut. 18¹⁵ (αὐτοῦ ἀκούσεσθε) that St. Luke reverses the Marcan order (ἀκούετε αὐτοῦ) which St. Matthew is content to follow. § St. Luke certainly intends to show that the ancient prophetic line has given place to Jesus, now revealed in the glory into which he was to enter through his 'exodus' at Jerusalem. We can scarcely doubt that it is with this object that he tells us how Jesus 'was found alone', the great figures of the old dispensation having disappeared from the scene 'when the voice came'. ‖ In the speeches which St. Luke puts into the mouth of the early preachers and apologists, the Deuteronomic prophecy becomes a proof-text of great importance, a summary of the place of the person and work of Jesus in the plan of redemption,¶ and it is possible that an allusion to the claim that Jesus was the prophet, or at least a prophet, is contained in the use of the phrase ἀναστήσας 'Ιησοῦν in St. Paul's speech at Antioch. ἀνίστημι is similarly applied to the 'raising up' of the Prophet in Deut. 18¹⁵ and of Elijah in Ecclus. 48¹. It is not altogether clear in this passage whether St. Luke intends ἀναστήσας to refer to the raising up of Jesus as a prophet or to his raising up by God from the dead; but the proof-text that is cited in illustration of this 'raising up' is Ps. 2⁷, which is associated rather with the beginning of Jesus' ministry and his anointing than with his resurrection, and St. Luke appears to distinguish this ἀναστήσας from the ὅτι δὲ ἀνέστησεν αὐτὸν ἐκ νεκρῶν which follows in the next verse and seems to introduce a fresh line of thought.[a]

As the prophet of Deuteronomy, Jesus reproduces, according to

* Lk. 7¹⁶.   † Isa. 41²⁵, 45¹³.   ‡ Lk. 7³⁹.
§ Lk. 9³⁵; Mk. 9⁷; Matt. 17⁵.   ‖ Lk. 9³⁶.   ¶ Acts 3²²⁻²³, 7³⁷.
[a] Acts 13³³⁻³⁴.

St. Luke's portrayal, many characteristics of Moses and Elijah, the chief prophetic figures of the Old Testament and the witnesses of his own glory. Jesus' advance in wisdom and stature and favour with God and man* recalls ben Sirach's account of Moses: ἄνδρα... εὑρίσκοντα χάριν ἐν ὀφθαλμοῖς πάσης σαρκός, ἠγαπημένον ὑπὸ θεοῦ καὶ ἀνθρώπων,† as well as the description of the prophet Samuel's childhood,‡ with which it is probably more directly connected. As the Spirit came upon Moses' seventy elders after the Lord had descended in the cloud of glory and spoken with him, so Jesus commissions the Seventy after the Transfiguration to go out and exercise his own powers of the Spirit. § Like Moses, Jesus goes up into the mountain, ‖ but his purpose is not, as in St. Matthew, to give the new Law, but, as in the Marcan narrative, to appoint the twelve apostles, the future missionaries of the gospel. Moses was a man sent by God;¶ Jesus, according to St. Luke, lays emphasis on his own status as one sent by God.[a] We may notice in this connection St. Luke's alteration of the Marcan ἐξῆλθον to ἀπεστάλην at Lk. 4⁴³.

The language in which the Transfiguration is described is, of course, intended by all the Synoptists to recall Sinai and the glorification of the face of Moses; but this impression is heightened by the Lucan additions to the narrative, and, in particular, by the introduction of the reference to the 'exodus' which Jesus is to accomplish by his death. As we have already observed, the miracles of Jesus are made to resemble those of Moses, since they are said, like those of the latter, to have been effected by the 'finger of God'. The parallel between Jesus and Moses is, however, made most explicit in the speech of Stephen, much of which is devoted to a demonstration of how the action of the Jewish authorities in murdering the Messiah was foreshadowed in their ancestors' treatment of Moses. Like Jesus, Moses was mighty in words and deeds.[b] By the hand of Moses God gave salvation to his brethren. Like Jesus, Moses was denied by Israel[c] although he had been sent by God as a ruler and redeemer 'with the hand of the angel who appeared to him in the bush',[d] as Jesus had been sent with the power of the Spirit which came upon him at the Jordan. Just as Moses performed 'wonders and signs', so was Jesus 'a man attested by God by mighty works and wonders and signs'.[e]

With the notable exception of Stephen's speech, however, St.

* Lk. 2⁵².   † Ecclus. 44²⁷ (LXX).   ‡ I Sam. 2²⁶.
§ Num. 11²⁵; Lk. 10¹, cf. 10¹⁹.   ‖ Lk. 6¹².   ¶ Ex. 3¹⁰⁻¹⁵; Num. 16²⁸, etc.
[a] Cf. the citation at Nazareth of the prophet's claim to be sent from God.
[b] Lk. 24¹⁹; Acts 7²².   [c] Acts 3¹⁴, 7³⁵.   [d] Acts 7³⁵.   [e] Acts 7³⁶, 2²².

Luke nowhere presses the comparison of Jesus with Moses very far, and the reminiscence of the dispute of Moses with his Hebrew brethren, which appears at Lk. 12¹⁴, seems to point to a contrast rather than to a resemblance between them. St. Luke prefers to discern in Jesus the characteristic features of Elijah, the prophet who ascended into heaven, and of the Servant of the Lord, the Spirit-possessed sufferer and redeemer, rather than of Moses the Lawgiver. As we shall see, however, the character of the Servant is itself in some respects a reproduction, or reinterpretation, of that of Moses.

As we have already noticed, although St. Luke is well aware that the Baptist was the Messiah's forerunner 'in the Spirit and power of Elijah', he avoids copying the Marcan identification of him with Elijah *redivivus*. His picture of Jesus, on the other hand, includes a number of features drawn from Elijah, a fact which is not surprising in view of the analogy pointed out in the Nazareth sermon between the ministry of Jesus and that of Elijah and Elisha. Jesus chooses his disciples as Elijah chose Elisha, a fact which is brought out most conspicuously in the Lucan insertion of καταλιπὼν πάντα into the story of the call of Levi.* This phrase was perhaps suggested by I Kgs. 19²⁰ (καὶ κατέλιπεν Ἐλισαῖε τὰς βόας, καὶ κατέδραμεν ὀπίσω Ἠλείου). His great miracle at Nain, which causes the people to acclaim him as a great prophet, is full of echoes of Elijah's raising of the widow's son at Zarephath (through which Elijah also was acknowledged as a prophet),† particularly in the description of the dead man beginning to speak and of Jesus giving him to his mother.‡ The disciples of Jesus clearly regarded him as being in some way like Elijah at the time when they expected him to order them to call down fire from heaven on the Samaritan villagers, § but here, as the Western text insists with special vigour, the lesson is driven home that Jesus is one greater than Elijah, however plainly he may have shown that he possessed a prophetic character like his. On the other hand, the difficult saying of Jesus: 'I came to cast fire on the earth',‖ referring, no doubt, to the 'baptism of fire', that is, the process of sifting and judgment which he came to perform, may possibly owe something to the description of Elijah as one who ἀνέστη ὡς πῦρ, καὶ ὁ λόγος αὐτοῦ ὡς λαμπὰς ἐκαίετο.¶ The 'exodus' of which Elijah and Moses speak to Jesus at the Transfiguration may have symbolical affinities with the 'exodus' performed by Elijah and his disciple when they passed through the

---

* Lk. 5²⁸.   † Lk. 7¹⁶; cf. I Kgs. 17²⁴.   ‡ Lk. 7¹⁵; cf. I Kgs. 17²²⁻²³ (LXX).
§ Lk. 9⁵⁴.   ‖ Lk. 12⁴⁹.   ¶ Ecclus. 48¹.

divided waters before the former was taken up in the chariot of fire,* and the word used of Elijah's ascent (ἀναλαμβάνεσθαι) † is that which St. Luke employs to describe the ascension of Christ. Other parallels occur in the Ascension narrative. The repeated command of Elijah to Elisha (κάθου δὴ ὧδε) ‡ before his assumption and the transference of his Spirit to the latter resembles the emphatic order to Christ's disciples, ὑμεῖς δὲ καθίσατε ἐν τῇ πολεῖ, when they were to await the passing over to themselves of the Spirit and power of the ascended Christ; and the parallel which St. Luke draws between Elisha and the disciples of Jesus, corresponding to that between Jesus and Elijah, is enhanced by his insistence on the fact that the apostles actually saw the Lord ascending. Possibly he has in mind the promise given to Elisha that he would receive a double portion of Elijah's Spirit if he saw him being taken up. Because this did happen, and the Spirit of Elijah rested on him, Elisha was enabled to perform the same miracle of dividing the water which had previously been wrought by his master. § It is sufficiently obvious that this story might suggest a parallel with the Ascension, the gift of the Spirit to the apostles through the ascended Lord, and their subsequent ability to perform mighty works like those of Jesus himself. Finally, it may be observed that the ascension of Elijah, like that of Jesus, was a glorification. ||

More important, however, than this recognition of Jesus as an antitype of Elijah is the presentation of him as the Servant portrayed by the Second Isaiah, an identification which doubtless originated with Jesus himself. We must remember in this connection that the prophet of Isa. 61$^{1 ff.}$ was no doubt identified both by Jesus and by St. Luke and his readers with the figure of the Servant.

The Servant is pre-eminently a prophet, one in whom God had put his Spirit.¶ He is in some respects a new Moses. Like Moses, the Servant is commissioned for his task in the context of a declaration of the sovereign Name of God: 'I am Yahweh; that is my name'.[a] His office, like that of Moses, is to release men from bondage and darkness by the power of the Lord,[b] to lead them in a new exodus through the heat and the desert mountains by springs of waters to their own land[c], an exodus which Isa. 48^{21} shows very clearly to be an antitype or recapitulation of the journey out of Egypt. Moses himself was the Servant of Yahweh

* II Kgs. 2^8. † II Kgs. 2$^{9, 10, 11}$; Ecclus. 48^9. ‡ II Kgs. 2$^{2, 4, 6}$.
§ II Kgs. 2$^{9-15}$. || Ecclus. 48^4. ¶ Isa. 42^1.
[a] Isa. 42^8. [b] Isa. 42^7. [c] Isa. 49$^{9-11}$.

N 177

(Μωυσῆς ὁ παῖς κυρίου;* Μωυσῆς ὁ παῖς μου†) and, like him, the Servant comes to raise up the tribes of Jacob.‡ In this latter function the Servant also resembles Elijah who is to come to raise up the tribes of Jacob. §

Jesus, like the Servant, is named from the womb. ‖ He is to be a light to the Gentiles,¶ that the 'salvation' of God 'may be unto the end of the earth'.ᵃ In the Servant God declares that he will be glorified:ᵇ the glorification of God through the works of Jesus is a conspicuous feature of the Lucan narrative, although it is very rare in the other Synoptics.ᶜ By the Servant's mission, as by the work of Jesus, the deaf are to hear, and the blind to receive their sight.ᵈ This last point is, of course common to the First and Third Gospels, and it is the First alone which directly cites the first 'servant song' as a commentary on Christ's healing miracles. St. Luke, however, has provided an equivalent to this citation in his quotation of Isa. 61¹ as a preface to the entire ministry of Jesus.

The Servant 'sets his face' towards the endurance of suffering: ἔθηκα τὸ πρόσωπόν μου ὡς στερεὰν πέτραν,ᵉ a phrase which St. Luke echoes in his description of Jesus setting out on the road to Jerusalem: τὸ πρόσωπον ἐστήρισεν,ᶠ and in his death, as St. Luke alone of the Synoptists explicitly states, the prophecy is fulfilled of the righteous Servant who was to be 'numbered with the lawless'.ᵍ The fulfilment by Jesus of the prophecy of the Servant's sufferings is the theme of Philip's preaching to the Ethiopian, and probably underlies the description of Jesus in the early apostolic preaching as παῖς.ʰ The Servant, like Jesus, was to be exalted and glorified (ὑψωθήσεται καὶ δοξασθήσεται),ⁱ and a direct allusion to this prophecy is made in Acts 3¹³, with possible indirect references to it elsewhere.ʲ It must not, however, be assumed that all references to the exaltation and glorification of Jesus are intended to point to him as the Servant, for it was also said of the Davidic Messiah that he was exalted (ὑψωθείς);ᵏ nor do references to Jesus as ἐκλεκτός necessarily allude to the description of the Servant given by Isa. 42¹, for the Davidic king is also ἐκλεκτός,ˡ and so is Joshua the son of Nun.ᵐ On the other hand, it is quite probable that the Servant is in fact indicated in these cases, and the application to Jesus of the terms ὁ ἅγιος καὶ δίκαιος or ὁ

---

* Jos. 1¹³, 11¹², ¹⁵, 12⁶, 18⁷, 22².　　† Jos. 1⁷.　　‡ Isa. 49⁶.
§ Ecclus. 48¹⁰.　‖ Isa. 49¹; Lk. 1³¹, 2²¹.　¶ Isa. 42⁶, 49⁶; Lk. 2³²; Acts 13⁴⁷, 26²³.
ᵃ Isa. 49⁶; Acts 1⁸, 13⁴⁷.　　　　　　　　　　　　　　　ᵇ Isa. 49³.
ᶜ Lk. 2²⁰, 7¹⁶, 13¹³, 17¹⁵, 18⁴³, 23⁴⁷; Acts 4²¹, 13⁴⁸.
ᵈ Isa. 42¹⁸, 42⁷; Lk. 7²²; Matt. 11⁵.　　　　　　ᵉ Isa. 50⁷.
ᶠ Lk. 9⁵¹.　　　　ᵍ Lk. 22³⁷; Isa. 53¹².　　　　ʰ Acts 3¹³, ²⁶, 4²⁷, ³⁰.
ⁱ Isa. 52¹³.　　　ʲ Lk. 4¹⁵; Acts 2³³, 5³¹.　　　ᵏ Ps. 88 (89)¹⁹, ²⁴.
ˡ Ps. 88 (89)³, ¹⁹.　　　　　　ᵐ Num. 11²⁸.

δίκαιος* is in all probability intended to identify him with the Servant. This may also be true of St. Luke's version of the centurion's confession: 'truly this man was δίκαιος'.† If this be so, the centurion would represent the first-fruits of the believers who were to be enlightened by the light to the Gentiles.

Jesus is also described by the heavenly voice at the Baptism and the Transfiguration, and by St. Luke alone in the parable of the Wicked Husbandmen,‡ as ὁ ἀγαπητός. If St. Luke knew of the version of Isa. 42¹ given by St. Matthew (12¹⁸⁻²¹) ὁ παῖς μου ὅν ἡρέτισα, ὁ ἀγαπητός μου ὅν ηὐδόκησεν ἡ ψυχή μου, this term could also be understood as an allusion to the character of Jesus as the Servant; otherwise, since a direct connection between it and the ὁ ἠγαπημένος of Isa. 44² is unlikely, it is probably intended to link Jesus with the 'only' son of Abraham, the sacrificial victim, Isaac. The apostles also share in the character of the Servant through the transference to them of the Spirit that operated in Jesus. According to the promise of Acts 1⁸, when the Servant Jesus has been exalted and the Spirit has descended on the apostles, they will, in a sense, replace him as the Servant's continuing antitype. The Spirit will be put on them, as it was on the Servant, and, like him they will be witnesses 'unto the uttermost part of the earth'. §

Through the Servant's mission the salvation of God will be brought to the end of the earth, and his vocation is related to the coming of a 'day of salvation'. || Salvation (σωτηρία and τὸ σωτήριον), a term used with great frequency in the Old Testament to denote God's deliverance of Israel and his rescue and vindication of his covenant people from the hand of their oppressors, is also a cardinal theme in St. Luke's writings. Redemption and salvation are associated with the age of the fulfilment of God's covenant promises; to this age the Baptist's mission is the prelude.¶ The Second Isaiah's prophecy of the revelation of God's salvation to all flesh[a] is declared by Symeon, speaking in the Spirit, to have been fulfilled in the appearance of Jesus,[b] and it is in terms of the same prophecy that St. Luke interprets the work of John the Baptist, considering his whole task as one who prepared the way for the entire dispensation of the gospel, including its proclamation to the Gentiles.[c] Salvation is not now conceived in terms of deliverance from national enemies. It is intimately connected with remission of sins[d] and the gift of repentance,[e] so that when

---

* Acts 3¹⁴, 22¹⁴. † Lk. 23⁴⁷. ‡ Lk. 20¹³.
§ Cf. Isa. 49⁶. || Isa. 49⁶, ⁸.
¶ Lk. 1⁶⁹ (Ps. 17³, LXX), 1⁷¹ (Ps. 105¹⁰, LXX), 1⁷⁷. [a] Isa. 40⁵ (LXX).
[b] Lk. 2³⁰. [c] Lk. 3⁶. [d] Lk. 1⁷⁷. [e] Cf. Acts 5³¹.

Zacchaeus repents in the presence of Jesus he is told that salvation has come to his house.* After the exaltation of Jesus as Lord and Messiah, his name is the powerful instrument of salvation: 'In none other is there salvation; for neither is there any other name under heaven, that is given among men, wherein we must be saved'.† As the prophet like unto Moses, Jesus resembles the deliverer through whose hand God gave salvation to Israel.‡ The missionary preaching of the apostles is the 'word of this salvation', sent by God through their ministry; § thus the apostolic witness fulfils the predicted mission of the Servant of the Lord. ‖ The 'pythonic' spirit in the possessed girl at Philippi recognizes Paul and Silas as men who proclaim the way of salvation.¶ When, at the end of St. Luke's narrative, the Jews of Rome have received that proclamation with questionings and opposition, St. Paul denounces their blindness and grossness of heart in the words of God's commission to Isaiah (Isa. 6^{9-10}) which St. Matthew applies to the failure of the Galilaean hearers of Jesus to respond to the message of the Kingdom; as a consequence of their unwillingness to accept the word, they are to know that 'this salvation of God is sent to the Gentiles; they will even hear'.[a] Thus St. Luke's history of the gospel of salvation, which began with the words of the angel to a priest in the Jerusalem Temple, is brought to its conclusion in Rome with the offering of salvation to the Gentiles there and the hopeful promise of its acceptance, a promise of which the unhindered preaching of St. Paul in the capital is an earnest.

Salvation is not, indeed, associated directly by St. Luke with the death of Jesus. It is rather through his glorification that it is made available to the whole world. Yet the exaltation of Jesus is attained only through death, and in St. Luke, as in the Fourth Gospel, the death and glorification of Jesus are inseparably connected; the difference of emphasis between these writers lies only in that to the latter the death is itself a part of the glorification, whereas the former thinks of it as the necessary prelude, much as the crossing of the Red Sea in the exodus led by Moses was the gateway to the covenant of Sinai and the promised land. Salvation and the power of the Spirit stand in so close a relation to each other in St. Luke's thought, that the exaltation of Jesus and his reception of the Father's promise (to bestow it in turn upon his followers) must of necessity be the source of the salvation which can thenceforth be preached to the ends of the earth.[b] It must,

---

* Lk. 19^9.   † Acts 4^{12}.   ‡ Acts 7^{25}.   § Acts 13^{26}.
‖ Acts 13^{47}.   ¶ Acts 16^{17}.   a Acts 28^{28}.
b For the preaching of salvation (εὐαγγελίζεσθαι) cf. Ps. 95^2 (LXX); Isa. 60^6.

further, be remembered that it is the *suffering* Servant who is associated with the bringing of God's salvation to the end of the earth and the enlightenment of the Gentiles, so that it is as one whose mission embraced suffering that Jesus is exalted into heaven.

In view of the emphasis laid by St. Luke (alone among the evangelists) on the theme of salvation, it is not surprising to find that he applies the title σωτήρ to Jesus, in spite of its obvious pagan connotations in the Hellenistic world. Jesus is announced by the angel at Bethlehem as σωτήρ, ὅς ἐστιν χριστὸς κύριος, titles, which, having been thus revealed proleptically, are fully realized through his exaltation as ἀρχηγός and σωτήρ at the right hand of God. According to St. Paul's preaching at Antioch, God, according to his promise, has brought Jesus to Israel as a saviour, one whose coming fulfils the preparatory work carried out in the history of salvation by the great Spirit-possessed leaders of old, the Judges, Samuel, Saul, and David. Although the work of Jesus in the bestowal of salvation recalls the office of the Servant, the title 'saviour' does not belong to the latter; it is reserved by the Old Testament for God alone, apart from the Spirit-possessed heroes, Othniel, Ehud, and the Judges in general who are described as 'saviours who saved them out of the hand of their adversaries'.*

It was the task of the prophet whose mission Jesus fulfilled to give 'glory' to God's people.† As the Servant who is a light to the Gentiles, Jesus is also the glory of Israel.‡ His own glory belongs to his exalted state; the Son of Man will come in his glory (according to the Lucan version of this saying; its Marcan and Matthaean forms mention only his Father's glory) and the glory of his Father and the holy angels.§ The entry into that glory, however, is accomplished through suffering. ‖ His glory is therefore revealed only by anticipation during the earthly ministry, and then only at its decisive point when Jesus is about to begin his journey to death. At the Transfiguration there is a foreshadowing of the entry into glory which was to take place at the Ascension. The Lucan account of the former event is recalled to mind in the narrative of the latter in several ways. The word used to describe Christ's ascension (ἀναλαμβάνεσθαι) is reminiscent of the ἀνάλημψις which is the goal of the journey to Jerusalem on which he sets out

---

* Jd. 3⁹⁻¹⁰, 3¹⁵; Neh. 9²⁷. The word σωτηρία, not used by the other Synoptists and only once by St. John, in an entirely different context, is fairly frequent in the Pauline Epistles and frequent in Hebrews and I Peter; σωτήρ occurs in Phil. 3²⁰ and Eph. 5²³, in the Pastorals, I Jn. 4¹⁴, Jude, and II Peter.
. † Isa. 61³ (LXX).   ‡ Lk. 2³².   § Lk. 9²⁶.   ‖ Lk. 24²⁶.

shortly after the Transfiguration. At the Ascension, as at the Transfiguration, Jesus is received into the cloud of the divine presence. The two heavenly witnesses at the Transfiguration are parallel both to the two men who replace the Marcan 'young man' and St. Matthew's 'angel' in the Lucan account of the Resurrection, and to the two men who appear at the Ascension and attest its significance. The white apparel of the latter, the sign of angelic beings, recalls the shining whiteness of the garments of Jesus at the Transfiguration. The description of the Ascension, πορευομένου αὐτοῦ, πορευόμενον εἰς τὸν οὐρανόν, may be intended to bring to mind the journey to the Cross whose significance the Transfiguration was meant to illuminate; κατὰ τὸ ὡρισμένον πορεύεται,* ἐπορεύετο ἔμπροσθεν ἀναβαίνων.† The Transfiguration thus appears to be an anticipation of the glorification of Jesus through his death, while at the same time it looks back, in the words of the heavenly voice, to the symbolical foreshadowing of his death and resurrection which was enacted at his baptism, and, in the use of ἐπισκιάζειν, to the annunciation to Mary of his divine sonship through the operation of the Holy Spirit.

That the mission of Jesus to fulfil the prophecy of the 'light to the Gentiles' would involve his death is already hinted at in the words addressed to Mary by Symeon. It may possibly be the case that the story of the loss of the child Jesus and his discovery in the Temple also contains an indication of the time when he will enter the Father's sphere, be temporarily lost to his followers, and descend again to them in the presence and power of the Pentecostal Spirit. The episode occurs at the time of the Passover; it happens at Jerusalem, which, in this Gospel, is the scene only of the Passion with the events immediately leading up to it, of the Resurrection, the entry into glory, and the promise of the Spirit; his friends and family seek him sorrowfully (we may compare the μὴ εὑρόντες of Lk. 2⁴⁵ with the μὴ εὑροῦσαι of 24²³); it is after three days that he is found, having been ἐν τοῖς τοῦ πατρός; his parents, like the disciples at the second prediction of the Passion, fail to understand the word which he has spoken to them in explanation; and he goes down with them to Nazareth as the Spirit of the risen Christ was to descend to accompany the disciples into the Gentile world.

The Baptism of Jesus and his salutation as Servant-Messiah, prefigure his death and his exaltation both in St. Luke and in the

---

* Acts 1¹⁰⁻¹¹; Lk. 22²², where Mark, followed by Matthew, has ὑπάγει.
† Lk. 19²⁸.

other Synoptists, and in this gospel the connection between this symbolical action and his actual death is apparently indicated in the saying, 'I have a baptism to be baptized with, and how am I straitened until it be accomplished'.*

It may not be without significance that, in this Gospel, the feeding of the five thousand, which, from the language used to describe Christ's actions, appears to foreshadow the Last Supper, occurs immediately before the confession of St. Peter and the teaching on the Passion which it introduces.

At his entry into Jerusalem, the scene of his Passion and exaltation, the song of the angels at the announcement of the birth of the Messianic king is echoed by the crowds who greet Jesus, according to St. Luke, as the king who comes in the name of the Lord.† His kingship, proclaimed at his birth, is realized through the suffering and death which await him in the stronghold of his enemies. Shortly afterwards Jesus tells his disciples in the 'eschatological discourse' that men will see the Son of Man coming in a cloud with power and great glory.‡ This may allude to his future Ascension, when the Son of Man, as in the vision of Daniel, will be brought to the Ancient of Days. A similar significance seems to be attached by St. Luke to Christ's answer to the high priest: ἀπὸ τοῦ νῦν δὲ ἔσται (where Mark has ὄψεσθε and Matthew ἀπ' ἄρτι ὄψεσθε) ὁ υἱὸς τοῦ ἀνθρώπου καθήμενος ἐκ δεξιῶν τῆς δυνάμεως τοῦ θεοῦ (cf. Ps. 110¹), the further citation of Dan. 7¹³, given by St. Mark, being omitted. The consequence of the condemnation and death of Jesus will be his exaltation to the right hand of God, so that the penitent thief is right in his belief that Jesus on the Cross is about to enter his kingdom,§ and, later, St. Peter can point to the same text (Ps. 110¹) as having already been fulfilled. ‖ The Messiah was to suffer and to enter into his glory, and it is when he has ascended into heaven in the cloud of the divine glory that the Messianic sovereignty ascribed to him by Gabriel and the angel at Bethlehem is fully realized and he is made Lord and Christ.¶ His kingship is equivalent to his reception from the Father of the promise of the Holy Spirit, and as the result of his exaltation the kingdom which was operative in him on earth through the power of the Spirit becomes effective in the Spirit among his disciples and their converts.

The Kingdom is spoken of at the Annunciation as belonging to Jesus as the Messianic king, and the Last Supper prefigures his

* Lk. 12⁴⁹.   † Lk. 2¹⁴, 19³⁸.   ‡ Lk. 21²⁷.
§ Ac. 2³⁵.
‖ Lk. 23⁴², where B c e, al. read εἰς τὴν βασιλείαν, other MSS. ἐν τῇ βασιλείᾳ.
¶ Lk. 1³³, 2¹¹; Acts 2³⁶.

future eating and drinking with his disciples at his table in his own kingdom; but for the most part St. Luke means by the Kingdom the Kingdom of God, exercised through Jesus during his ministry and subsequently by his disciples in the power of the Spirit.

The first mention of the Kingdom of God in this Gospel is at 4^{43}, where Jesus explains that the preaching of the Kingdom is the task for which he has been sent. He has already declared the nature of his mission in terms of the work of the anointed prophet of Isa. 61^1. We may infer that the bringing of the gospel to the poor, the proclamation of release to captives, recovery of sight to the blind, the setting of the bruised at liberty, and the preaching of the acceptable year of the Lord, all performed in the power of the Spirit, are equivalent to the preaching of the gospel of the Kingdom of God. The connection between the Kingdom and the Spirit appears in the fact that the risen Lord's command to his disciples to await the promise of the Spirit-baptism seems to form part of a discourse about 'the things concerning the Kingdom of God', and that the apostles' reception of the power of the Spirit constitutes the answer to their question concerning the restoration of the kingdom to Israel. The Kingdom is defined in terms of the preaching of the gospel in the power of the Spirit instead of in terms of a nationalist restoration such as the disciples had hitherto expected. The second petition of the Lord's Prayer, assuming that the prayer for the Holy Spirit to come upon us and cleanse us represents St. Luke's own interpretation of the clause 'Thy Kingdom come', which he found in his source, supports the Lucan identification of the Kingdom of God with the operation of the Spirit. It may be noticed in this connection that St. Luke is fond of speaking of the Kingdom as 'coming upon' men, like the divine Spirit. Thus he describes the message of the Seventy as ἤγγικεν ἐφ' ὑμᾶς ἡ βασιλεία τοῦ θεοῦ whereas St. Matthew in his parallel passage relating to the mission of the Twelve, has only ἤγγικεν ἡ βασιλεία τῶν οὐρανῶν.

The proclamation by Jesus of the Kingdom takes the form of teaching with authority and the performance of works of power, healings and exorcisms. The link between teaching and healing receives special emphasis from St. Luke. We may compare his introduction to the story of the Paralytic with that which he found in Mark. The latter tells us merely that Jesus was speaking the word, but the Lucan version adds that the power of the Lord was with him to heal. Similarly, on the occasion of the feeding of the five thousand St. Luke says that Jesus spoke about the Kingdom of God and healed, whereas St. Mark states only that he taught many things and St. Matthew refers only to healing.

Other characteristics of the Lucan conception of the Kingdom, and its relation to the other evangelists' presentation of it, do not, for the most part, concern us here. We must, however, notice that in St. Paul's speech at Miletus the Kingdom is virtually identified with the gospel of the grace of God, repentance, and faith in Christ.* The Kingdom is the object of that favourite Lucan word, εὐαγγελίζεσθαι, which recalls the prophet's mission of Isa. 61¹, and also such passages as Isa. 40⁹, 52⁷, 60⁶, and Jl. 2³² (a text which follows immediately the prophecy of the out-pouring of the Spirit quoted by St. Peter in Acts 2¹⁷⁻²¹).

With this gospel of the Kingdom, St. Luke connects repentance and remission of sins. The words μετανοέω and μετάνοια, rare in the Old Testament outside the Wisdom literature (Isa. 46⁹ (LXX) being, however, an important instance), occur in the Third Gospel some eight times over and above the few instances where they are paralleled in Mark and Matthew; in Acts they are still more frequent. The purpose of Jesus' coming is to call sinners to repentance.† Repentance is the only means whereby the destruction of the Jewish system can be averted.‡ The climax of the Lucan version of the parable of the Lost Sheep is the joy in heaven over the repentant sinner and the contrast between him and the righteous who have no need of repentance.§ Dives believes that his brethren who are, no doubt, meant like himself to represent the official leaders of contemporary Judaism, would repent if one were to go to them from the dead,‖ a belief whose irony is revealed later in the Sadducee party's hostility to the preaching of Christ's Resurrection.

The divine forgiveness which meets man's repentance is to be reproduced in human relationships;¶ and, just as repentance had been the theme of the proclamation of the Kingdom by Jesus, so after his Ascension it is to be part of the fulfilment of the Scriptures that repentance leading to remission of sins shall be preached to all the nations.ᵃ The immediate answer, therefore, of St. Peter on the day of Pentecost to the question, 'What shall we do?' is to tell his hearers to repent.ᵇ It is the response demanded by the saving work of God in Christ, for the exaltation of Jesus as saviour had as its purpose the giving of repentance to Israel and remission of sins.ᶜ The Spirit's descent on the Gentile household of Cornelius is an

* Acts 20²¹⁻²⁵.   † Lk. 5³².   ‡ Lk. 13³.   § Lk. 15⁷.
‖ Lk. 16³⁰.   ¶ Lk. 17³⁻⁴.   ᵃ Lk. 24⁴⁷.   ᵇ Acts 3³⁸.
ᶜ Acts 3¹⁹.

185

irrefutable proof that God has given to the Gentiles also repentance leading to life.* Repentance is evidently regarded as the primary mode of the Spirit's operation in the converts, and it is natural to find that repentance, together with faith in Jesus as Messiah, is associated from the day of Pentecost onwards with baptism in his name and the reception of the gift of the Spirit. 'Repentance towards God' is combined with 'faith in our Lord Jesus Christ' as the substance of St. Paul's gospel, according to his speech to the Ephesian elders,† and in his defence before Agrippa St. Paul reaffirms that the object of his missionary task had been to announce repentance to Jews and Gentiles.‡ Thus the preaching of repentance and faith is equivalent, as the content of the Pauline gospel, with 'the things concerning the Kingdom of God', or simply 'the Kingdom of God'. §

These examples illustrate the fact that, although repentance had been proclaimed by Jesus during his ministry, it is far more strongly emphasized after Pentecost in the missionary preaching of the apostles. The time of repentance corresponds to the period of the Spirit's activity in the apostolic mission, and is determined by the coming judgment of the world through Christ. ‖ Its counterpart, remission of sins, is the object towards which the Baptist's work was directed. ἄφεσις is, of course, one of the blessings produced by the mission of the prophet foretold in Isa. 61[1]. Certain individuals receive remission of sins from Jesus during his ministry, namely the paralytic (the Lucan narrative here follows Mark) and the woman who was a sinner, and (assuming the authenticity of the passage) Jesus prayed for forgiveness for his executioners. These instances, however, like the call to repentance during the earthly ministry of Jesus, are, to some extent, proleptic in character. They are demonstrations of the power to remit sins which Jesus possessed; but that power is not generally exercised, and forgiveness is not made universally available, until the new dispensation of the Spirit has been inaugurated after his glorification. Until then remission of sins is to be an object of prayer,¶ but it is an eschatological gift, not yet fully realized. When, however, the risen Christ promises to send the gift of the Spirit upon his disciples, he declares that remission of sins, as a consequence upon repentance, is to be proclaimed to all nations.[a] In this, as in so many other departments of St. Luke's teaching, the fact is strongly emphasized that the coming of the Spirit and the gifts which result therefrom and which are aspects of the Kingdom of God waited upon the

---

* Acts 11[18].   † Acts 20[21].   ‡Acts 26[20].   § Acts 19[8], 28[31].
‖ Acts 17[30].   ¶ Lk. 11[4].   [a] Lk. 24[47].

death and exaltation of Christ. Once the Spirit has been poured out upon the disciples, remission of sins becomes a cardinal element in the apostolic message. It is obtained through the name of the ascended Lord and Christ, and it is directly associated with the reception of the Holy Spirit by those who believe in his name, so that it stands in the closest connection with baptism in the name of Jesus Christ.*

Repentance is a stage in the attainment of eternal life, the life of the age to come,† which is the consummation of the dispensation of the Spirit. In this Gospel the gaining of eternal life is linked with the observance of the essential moral and spiritual command-ments of the Law in the introduction to the parable of the Good Samaritan,‡ a passage which St. Luke composes out of the similar material in Mk. 10¹⁷⁻¹⁹, which he sets in a different context. The coming of the Spirit upon Cornelius and his house proves that God has given to Gentiles repentance εἰς ζωήν,§ and whereas the Jews, by their rejection of the Gospel, judge themselves unworthy of eternal life, the Gentile hearers of St. Paul are 'disposed' to it.‖ Life, in this sense, is very closely related to the Kingdom of God in Mk. 10¹⁷, ²³, followed by Lk. 18¹⁸, ²⁴, and it is possibly also directly connected with the Holy Spirit if we may assume that it is as the recipient of the promise of the Father and as the leader and inaugurator of the new era of the Spirit's activity that Jesus is the ἀρχηγὸς τῆς ζωῆς.¶

Peace is another characteristic of the Kingdom of God, or of the operation of the Spirit, to which St. Luke draws special attention. In the Old Testament peace is a mode of the divine activity, or a fgit of God, which plays an important part in the eschatological hope. It is especially associated with God's demonstration of his righteousness in saving and vindicating his people.ᵃ In the Third Gospel it is part of the Baptist's mission to guide God's people into the way of peace;ᵇ peace on earth and glory to God are the theme of the angelic hymn of praise for the birth of the Messianic king,ᶜ and 'peace in heaven and glory in the highest' is the cry which, in the Lucan version of the entry to Jerusalem, greets Jesus when he is saluted as king on his arrival at Jerusalem to die and so to enter upon his royal glory.ᵈ Later, in his address to Cornelius, St. Peter summarizes the gospel, in terms which echo Isa. 52⁷, as 'the word which God sent to Israel preaching a gospel of peace through Jesus Christ who is Lord of all'.ᵉ In this passage peace is

---

* Acts 2³⁸, 5³¹, 10⁴³, cf. 13³⁸, 26¹⁸.   † Lk. 18³⁰ (Mk. 10³⁰).
‡ Lk. 10²⁵⁻²⁷, Mk. 10¹⁷⁻¹⁹.   § Acts 11¹⁸.   ‖ Acts 13⁴⁶, ⁴⁸.   ¶ Acts 3¹⁵.
ᵃ Ps. 85¹⁰, 125⁵, 128⁶; Isa. 9⁷, 39⁸, 52⁷; Ezek. 34²⁵, 37²⁶; Hag. 2¹⁰; Mal. 2⁵.
ᵇ Lk. 1⁷⁹; cf. Isa. 59⁸.   ᶜ Lk. 2¹⁴.   ᵈ Lk. 19³⁸.   ᵉ Acts 10³⁶.

obviously closely related to the Kingdom of God and the Spirit.

Such are some of the effects of the power of the Spirit as St. Luke presents it. They are aspects of the Kingdom of God whose approach was proclaimed in word and deed by Jesus and which became his own sovereignty through his death, resurrection, and ascension. They become fully operative when the Lord has ascended into his heavenly glory and the Spirit given through him has brought about the new era of fulfilment.

The dawn of this age of the Spirit is the climax of St. Luke's narrative. When Jesus is exalted, the disciples are empowered by the Spirit with which he had been anointed to act as the agents and stewards of his kingdom throughout the world. The Spirit mediates his sovereignty to all men who believe on his name, and by its power the gospel is preached by his apostles and mighty works, such as he had performed, are wrought by their hands. St. Luke's theme is powerfully illustrated by the Johannine text: 'He that believeth on me, the works that I do shall he do also; and greater works than these shall he do, because I go unto the Father'.*

For their vocation as instruments of the Spirit and stewards of the Kingdom Christ's disciples are trained during the earthly ministry, especially during the journey of Jesus to his death and his bodily departure from them. The nature of their task is indicated from the moment of the choice and appointment of the Twelve. They are 'apostles', for it is to be a missionary task, partaking of the same character as that of Jesus who was himself 'sent out' to preach the gospel of the Kingdom of God.† St. Luke, thinking of the Twelve in relation to their missionary function, habitually alludes to them as 'apostles'. They were not, of course, the only disciples; indeed St. Luke, alone of the Synoptists, explains that they were chosen out of a company of disciples large enough to be described as a 'great crowd';‡ and it is not always possible to decide whether teaching addressed to 'the disciples' is confined to the apostles or extended to a wider circle, though it is likely that the Twelve are intended in most cases. The question of the relation of the Twelve to other apostles, such as Paul and Barnabas,§ does not here concern us. Their appointment and training are directly related to the approaching death of Jesus. They are to be agents of the Spirit and missionaries of the Kingdom after his departure, and in St. Luke's narrative they are chosen and named apostles immediately after his enemies, scandalized by his claim to forgive sins and by his attitude to the

* Jn. 14¹².   † Lk. 4⁴³.   ‡ Lk.6 ¹³, ¹⁷.   § Acts 14⁴, ¹⁴.

Law and the Sabbath, have discussed what they might do to him.*
Their work is to reflect the character of their Master's mission. It
is to involve suffering, and it is remarkable that in this Gospel all
the Beatitudes, with their commendation of suffering and sorrow,
are addressed directly to the disciples in the second person, and
that, although the Matthaean version similarly addresses the
blessings pronounced on the persecuted to the disciples, St. Luke
adds a more emphatic prediction of hatred and excommunication.
In the Lucan version the disciples so addressed are the Twelve, no
doubt along with others, but in St. Matthew's account the Twelve
have not yet been appointed. The Woes are perhaps to be understood as a warning of the condemnation that the disciples would
incur should they prove unfaithful to their mission and refuse to
accept its painful consequences. It is possible that the whole of the
teaching contained in Lk. 6²⁷⁻⁴⁹ is intended for the disciples; it is
then a series of illustrations of the nature of their task and the
qualities and conduct required for its execution. Certainly the
two sayings recorded in 6³⁹⁻⁴⁰ seem to be intended for the apostolic
missionaries. The former of these, on the blind leading the blind,
occurs in a wholly different context in St. Matthew, where it
alludes to the Pharisees.† Here, however, it seems to present a
warning to the Church's future leaders against spiritual blindness.
The second saying, 'A disciple is not above his master' is explicitly
addressed to the Twelve in the Matthaean 'mission charge',‡
where it reminds them of their vocation and its implications.

The sending out of the Twelve is a foretaste of their commissioning after the Resurrection, and as at Pentecost they receive the
power of the Spirit so now they are given power for exorcism and
healing.§ They are also sent to preach the Kingdom of God, as we
see St. Paul doing at Rome in the closing scene of the history. The
other Synoptists say nothing in this context of a preaching of the
Kingdom, nor do they mention the gift of δύναμις; but St. Luke
intends to show that they were to act in Christ's stead and to be,
like him, 'mighty in word and deed'. The instruction given to
them about the approaching death of Jesus, its necessity, and its
implications for the cost of discipleship, at least in so far as the
first and second predictions of the Passion are concerned, contains
few peculiarly Lucan touches, and need not concern us to any
extent; but it is possible that the Lucan addition of 'daily'‖ to the
Marcan 'let him take up his cross' may be meant to allude to the
continual trials and persecutions which the missionary representatives of Christ will have to endure. It is more likely that this

* Lk. 6¹¹⁻¹³. † Matt. 15¹⁴. ‡ Matt. 10²⁴⁻²⁵. § Lk. 9¹. ‖ Lk. 9²³.

saying bears something of the meaning of the Pauline 'dying daily' rather than that it represents a reduction of the uncompromising Marcan demand into a pious precept for ordinary Christian living.

When we turn to the narrative of the journey to Jerusalem we are struck by the immense amount of the teaching addressed to 'the disciples' or 'the apostles' which it contains. St. Luke is, of course, limited to some extent by his sources in his disposition of his material, and the 'travel narrative' has to comprise a good deal of other matter as well as this teaching, but, after allowing for this fact, we may regard this section of his gospel as his equivalent for the discourses delivered after the Last Supper in St. John. On the way to his ἀνάλημψις, Jesus prepares his disciples for his death and resurrection, for their reception of the Spirit, and for their future role as his deputies in his Kingdom and preachers of it to the world.

Jesus' sending out of messengers to prepare the way, and his despatch of the Seventy, foreshadow the Church's future mission. The setting in this context of the teaching on the hardness of discipleship* and the saying on putting the hand to the plough† implies that these are intended as instruction for missionary disciples; 'fit for the Kingdom of God' may then be meant to signify 'fit for the exercise of the Kingdom of God in the preaching mission'. The saying, 'He who hears you, hears me . . .' etc.,‡ again emphasizes the preacher's function as Christ's representative, while the success of the mission of the Seventy prefigures the triumphs of the apostles' later labours. The episode of Martha and Mary may perhaps be seen by St. Luke as possessing some relevance to the conflict that was to arise between the administrative and preaching functions of the apostles.§ In 11$^{37\,ff.}$ and 12$^{1-12}$, St. Luke so arranges his material as to draw a contrast between the Pharisees and lawyers as leaders of the old Israel and his own disciples as leaders of the missionary Church. The latter are specially warned in this teaching to expect persecution.

What is most distinctive in St. Luke's treatment of this topic is that he inserts into this context the saying on blasphemy against the Holy Spirit. It is thus brought into immediate relationship with the promise that the 'confessor' who maintains his faith before synagogues and before secular courts will be directly inspired by the Spirit in what he says. This remarkable fact suggests strongly that St. Luke understands the blasphemy against the Holy Spirit to be rejection of the Spirit's inspiration

* Lk. 9$^{57-60}$; cf. Matt. 8$^{19-22}$.   †Lk. 9^{62}.   ‡ Lk. 10^{16}.   § Acts 6$^{2,\,4}$.

when one is required to testify before persecutors, and (in direct opposition to the Spirit's influence) the denial of Christ. Confession of Jesus as the Christ accompanies the baptismal reception of the Spirit; correspondingly, denial of Christ means the expulsion, as it were, of the Spirit, so that apostasy by those who have received the Spirit is the unforgiveable sin, worse in every respect than blasphemy against the Son of Man committed by unbelievers. Conversely the 'confessor' who, like Stephen, is full of the Holy Spirit and makes his defence in the Spirit's power is enabled to reproduce in his death the Passion of Jesus and to see the exalted Son of Man.

The teaching on watchfulness and on faithful stewardship;* much of which appears in the 'eschatological discourse' in the First Gospel,† is made by St. Luke to apply to the disciples as stewards of the Lord in the time between his removal from them and his future return, and a warning is added against disloyalty to this trust.‡ The same teaching is driven home by the parable of the Unjust Steward and by the Lucan setting of the sayings on faith, on offences, and on the servant's wages, the last of which is addressed specifically to the apostles.§

The disciples failed, however, to understand the significance of the situation in which they were receiving this teaching, and St. Luke lays great stress on their total inability to comprehend the third prediction of the Passion, delivered on the Jerusalem road. It is significant that he proceeds immediately from his description of their mental blindness to the narrative of the blind man at Jericho and his physical enlightenment. The disciples were ignorant of the approaching death of Jesus and so could not understand the implications of his sayings about their own future task. Not until his death, resurrection, and exaltation had brought about the coming of the Spirit could they enter, with understanding, on the work for which they had been trained. The parable of the Pounds, however, was evidently intended to make the situation plainer to them. It was delivered, says St. Luke, because they were near Jerusalem and they thought that the Kingdom of God was to appear immediately. He was, in fact, about to go from them to receive his kingdom, and they were to be entrusted as his stewards with the work of multiplying the treasure committed to them until his return, that is, with the missionary enterprise of the Church. The nature of that task, and the persecutions which it would bring upon them, were further revealed in the 'eschatological discourse', where a renewed promise is given of immediate

* Lk. 12³⁵⁻⁴⁶.　† Matt. 24⁴³⁻⁵¹.　‡ Lk. 12⁴⁷⁻⁴⁸.　§ Lk. 17¹⁻², ⁵⁻⁶ ⁷⁻¹⁰.

inspiration for 'confessors'. On this occasion the promise is not of the Spirit, but of the gift by Jesus of 'a mouth and wisdom'.* This is a reminiscence of Ex. $4^{12,\ 15}$, and suggests that the disciples as confessors will reproduce something of the character of Moses. The promise is fulfilled at Stephen's trial.

Finally, at the Last Supper, a kingdom is 'appointed by testament' to the apostles as the Father had appointed it to Jesus, with the promise that they will sit on thrones judging the twelve tribes of Israel. Here is the culminating point of the apostles' training to act as the agents and representatives of Jesus; but the promise of the kingdom cannot become effective until after the Spirit has been given. It may be that for St. Luke the primary significance of the Last Supper lies in this 'testamentary disposition' and that that this pre-eminently, was the covenant brought about by Christ's death.†

What the nature of that kingdom was to be they began to discover after the Resurrection. It turned out to be, not a restoration of the kingdom to Israel, but a mission to the world. The testamentary promise was reinterpreted to them as: 'You shall receive power when the Holy Spirit comes upon you, and you shall be witnesses . . . to the ends of the earth'.‡ In Acts, therefore, the phrase 'the Kingdom of God' appears but seldom, and when it is mentioned it is identified with the content of the apostolic gospel. This reinterpretation was not a departure from the previous teaching of Jesus. The Twelve had been designated as 'apostles' and sent out to preach; indeed, the call of Peter, James, and John is represented by St. Luke in such a way as to prefigure their future role as missionaries with Peter as their leader, occupying the position in which we encounter him in the first part of Acts.§

The concluding verses of the Gospel prepare us for Pentecost as the great turning-point in the story, the hinge, as it were, of the two-volume narrative. The fruits of the suffering and resurrection of the Messiah were now to be the preaching in his name of repentance for remission of sins to all nations, and the apostles were to be the witnesses by whom the preaching would be carried out, beginning, like the origin of the gospel in the episode of Zacharias, at Jerusalem. They have only to await the ascended Lord's sending of the Spirit to empower them for their mission. The repetition of this promise at Acts 1^5, and its echo at Acts 11^{16},

---

* Lk. 21^{15}.
† I am indebted to the Rev. R. C. Leaney for this observation.
‡ Acts 1^8.   § Lk. 5^{1-11}.

look back to John's prophecy of a baptism with Holy Spirit. The last days have now dawned, and the ancient hope of the gift of the Spirit is to be fulfilled through the crucified and exalted Messiah. The Spirit's previous activity in Jesus is to be reproduced on a wider scale in the apostles and their converts until its operation reaches the heart of the Gentile world. Thus the promise of the Spirit recorded in Lk. 24[49] corresponds in some degree to the Annunciation. Like Mary, the apostles are to be endued with 'power from on high'. At Pentecost they actually receive the power of the Spirit in which Jesus had preached, healed, and exorcized.

The mode of the Spirit's bestowal corresponds to their missionary vocation. It is the Spirit of prophecy, foretold by Joel, and its coming is symbolized by the gift of tongues for the inspired proclamation of the gospel to the different nations of the world.* This baptism of the Spirit corresponds to the anointing of Jesus at the Jordan. It 'clothes' them† with power for the preaching mission and for the mighty works which are to be performed by them as they were by Jesus during his earthly life and which will attest the preaching by visible 'signs'.‡ Its bestowal inaugurates an intermediate period in the history of God's redemptive purposes, for it is at once the fulfilment of the prophetic expectation of an outpouring of the Spirit in the last days and the ground of a new hope that Jesus will come again in like manner as the disciples have seen him go into heaven. His return will be the *apocatastasis* which the disciples had expected to occur in a quite different form before the Ascension. The promise of the heavenly witnesses at the Ascension is in fact the answer to the apostles' question recorded in Acts 1[6].

St. Luke's conception of the Spirit is differentiated from that of St. Paul, and to a lesser extent from that of St. John, by his predominant interest in it as the power of the gospel preaching, the Spirit of prophecy, 'tongues' and 'signs'; but he is at one with the New Testament writers as a whole in his understanding that it is the Spirit of Christ. As the words of Jesus in Lk. 24[49] make clear, it is the same Spirit with which he had been anointed, and it is by virtue of his own possession (as the Servant) of the divine Spirit that he now gives his followers power 'to speak the word with

---

* If Weinstock (*JRS*. 38, pp. 43–6) is right in connecting the list of peoples in Acts 2[9–10] with a conventional list of the nations used in pagan astrology, the crowd at Pentecost, like the phenomenon of fiery tongues, is symbolical; the Pentecost narrative is a proleptic summary of the missionary story which is to be unfolded in the whole of the subsequent record in Acts.

† Lk. 24[49].   ‡ Acts 4[16, 22], 8[6, 13].

παρρησία᾽ (one of the chief effects of the Spirit's operation in the missionary preaching),* 'with the stretching out of the hand' of God 'for healing and for signs and wonders to be done through the name of Jesus'.† It is the bond which unites the ascended Lord to his people, for it was received at Pentecost by those who had been instructed by the risen Lord through the Spirit,‡ and it is those who repent and are baptized into his name, that is, 'entered up in his name' as his property, who are promised participation in the same gift. In one passage the Spirit is explicitly called the Spirit of Jesus.§

The fact that the same Spirit which worked in Jesus is now given by him as the exalted Messiah to his followers renders the subsequent history of his Church and its mission parallel, in certain respects, to that of his own life and work. After the Spirit-baptism at Pentecost which corresponds to Christ's own baptism, the disciples' progress in the Spirit is described in language which recalls St. Luke's earlier description of the advance of the child Jesus in favour with God and man.‖ The ministry of the apostles and of other disciples resembles that of Jesus at many points. They perform numerous signs and wonders; Jesus, too, was attested by signs and wonders.¶ As Jesus fulfilled the prophecy of Isa. 35⁶ by making the lame to walk, so Peter and John fulfil it even more literally by causing a lame man to 'leap' and walk.ᵃ This miracle, the first recorded in Acts and the incident which gives rise to the first clash between the apostles and the Jewish authorities, resembles the healing by Jesus of the paralytic, the first miracle which brought him into a similar conflict. Among the points of similarity we notice the command, 'arise and walk', the reaction of the healed man, the ἔκστασις of the spectators, and the glorifying of God. The general healings at Jerusalem, when the shadow of St. Peter is said, like the Spirit itself, to 'overshadow' the sick,ᵇ are somewhat similar to the general healings by Jesus at Capernaum.ᶜ St. Peter's cure of Aeneas recalls, once again, the healing of the paralytic by Jesus, and the raising of Dorcas very clearly resembles that of Jairus' daughter, both in its circumstances and in the method of its accomplishment. Both these raisings of the dead have some affinities with Elisha's miracle at Shunem.ᵈ It is remarkable that the raising of Jairus' daughter immediately precedes the sending out of the Twelve with power to preach and to heal, and that the similar episode of Dorcas is the immediate

* Acts 2²⁹, 4¹³, ²⁹, ³¹, 9²⁷, 13⁴⁶, 14³, 18²⁶, 19⁸, 28³¹.
† Acts 4²⁹, ³⁰.   ‡ Acts 1⁵.   § Acts 16⁷.   ‖ Acts 2⁴⁷; Lk. 2⁵².
¶ Acts 2²², ⁴³.   ᵃ Lk. 7²²; Acts 3⁸.   ᵇ Acts 5¹²⁻¹⁶.   ᶜ Lk. 4⁴⁰⁻⁴¹.
ᵈ II Kgs. 4³²⁻³⁷.

prelude to the first preaching of the gospel to Gentiles. The latter event is marked by a 'Gentile Pentecost', an unmediated bestowal of the Spirit on Cornelius and his household. Thereafter a second series of mighty works begins, in many respects parallel to the former. These constitute the signs of the Spirit's operation through St. Paul in the mission to the Gentiles, as the earlier series had comprised the signs of its operation through St. Peter and others towards Jews and Samaritans. St. Paul, filled with the Holy Spirit, deals with Barjesus as St. Peter treated Simon Magus, though in a more drastic fashion; the lame man at Lystra corresponds to the lame man at the gate of the Temple; the δυνάμεις οὐχ αἱ τυχοῦσαι performed by St. Paul at Ephesus resemble the general healings by St. Peter at Jerusalem and by Jesus at Capernaum; and the raising of Eutychus matches the miracles of Dorcas and the daughter of Jairus. St. Paul's immunity to the bite of the serpent on Melita recalls the language in which Jesus spoke of the authority given to his missionaries,* and his healing of Publius' father is reminiscent of the cure of Simon's mother-in-law (in common with which it is followed by general healings), and, in the method that is adopted, the healing of the woman in the synagogue, described in Lk. 13^{12-13}.

The power of the Spirit thus operates in mighty works through the disciples as it formerly worked through Jesus. Confession of the gospel message in the face of persecutors, and especially martyrdom, also exhibit, in a very marked degree, the activity of the Spirit that was in Jesus. The 'boldness' of Peter and John before the Sanhedrim fulfils Jesus' promise of an immediate inspiration by the Spirit in such circumstances. The charge brought against Stephen is similar to that which, according to St. Mark, was preferred against Jesus in his trial before the high priest. St. Luke omits that section of the Marcan narrative, but reproduces its substance in this context, perhaps because he believed that the supersession of the Temple by one made without hands did not come about until the dispensation of the Spirit had begun and the Temple authorities had finally rejected the gospel after its proclamation to them in the power of the Spirit by Peter and John and by Stephen himself. It is probably for the same reason that the full Marcan account of the Cleansing of the Temple is greatly shortened by St. Luke; a more drastic conception of the entire supersession of the Temple is reserved by him for the speech put into the mouth of Stephen.

The reaction of Stephen's hearers and their 'casting' of him

* Acts 28^{5-6}; Lk. 10^{19}.

'out of the city' recall the effect of Jesus' initial sermon at Nazareth, which foreshadowed his rejection at the hands of the Jews, and it is reminiscent of the 'casting out of the vineyard and killing' of the Son in the parable of the Wicked Husbandmen. The vision of Stephen, when, full of the Holy Spirit, he 'looks up steadfastly into heaven' and sees the exalted Christ, recalls the 'looking up steadfastly' of the disciples at the Ascension and the revelation of Christ in glory to the three disciples at the Transfiguration,* as well as the 'opening' of the heavens at Christ's baptism.† This would seem to imply that his martyrdom is a participation in the death and exaltation of Jesus, which were foreshadowed at the Baptism and the Transfiguration and completed at the Ascension. Stephen's dying words are identical in substance with the prayer of Jesus for his executioners (on the assumption that this was in fact recorded by St. Luke). Thus we may infer that the death of a martyr, filled with the Spirit in accordance with the promise of the immediate inspiration of confessors, is shown to reproduce, in its own degree, the death and glorification of Christ. The later theory that martyrs and confessors are to be classed with prophets as men pre-eminently possessed by the Holy Spirit is easily understandable in view of the teaching implied in St. Luke's treatment of this episode.

Like Stephen and Jesus himself, Paul and Barnabas are 'cast out' of the city at Antioch. The journey of St. Paul to Jerusalem in the face of Agabus' warning is reminiscent of the deliberate 'going up' thither of Jesus; the charge brought against him by the Jews of Asia of defiling the Temple is akin to the charge against Stephen and, according to St. Mark, against Jesus; like Jesus he is tried before the high priest, the procurator, and one of the Herods; and his acquittal by the Pharisees in the council, Festus and Herod recalls the verdict of acquittal pronounced by Pilate and recorded by St. Luke alone. By such similarities St. Luke wishes to show how, as the result of the gift of the Spirit, the disciples who once could not understand that the Messiah must die, are now able to enter into his trials and death through the Spirit's power, and to reproduce them in their own persons.

Above all, the Spirit operates in the Church's mission, the content of whose preaching it supplies and of which it is both the driving force, so that the preaching of the gospel in the Spirit cannot be withstood,‡ and the guide that appoints missionaries and directs their course. § It is through the express guidance of

---

* Acts 7[55].   † Acts 7[56].   ‡ Acts 4[20], 5[39, 42], 6[13], 7[51, 55], 9[17].
§ Acts 13[2], 8[29, 39], 10[19], 11[12], 13[4], 16[6, 7], 19[21], 20[22], 21[11].

the Spirit, with the closely related method of divine revelation through visions and angelic appearances, that St. Peter is led to understand that the sphere of the Kingdom, and so of the Spirit's activity, must embrace Gentile as well as Jew.

In the Third Gospel we are told at the outset that Jesus has come to be a light to the Gentiles, and this fact is implied in the Nazareth sermon and again in the parable of the Great Supper, but the allusions in St. Luke's sources to work carried out by Jesus himself among Gentiles are omitted or much reduced. This no doubt, accounts for the 'Great Omission' from Mark, and for the differences between the Lucan and Matthaean handling of the story of the Centurion's servant, in which, according to St. Luke's version, the Gentile centurion never comes face to face with Jesus. The Gentile mission belongs to the era of the Spirit, the age of fulfilment, and awaits the death and ascension of the Servant who was to be the light to the Gentiles.

Within the Church the Spirit endows the leaders of the community with such authority that the apostles can execute the divine judgment against offenders such as Ananias and Sapphira, and the Jerusalem Council can preface its decisions with the astonishing claim, 'it seemed good to the Holy Spirit and to us'.* The visible fruit of the Spirit's activity is the κοινωνία, the unity and harmony of the Christian body, marked by the institution of the common fund, and the mutual sharing in that joy which is so prominent a feature of the Lucan conception of the Spirit's working.† Into this life in the Spirit the convert enters by baptism.‡ St. Peter's command to his hearers at Pentecost to be baptized is identical in form with John's announcement of his baptism, save for the vital difference that the old rite, no doubt derived directly from the Johannine baptism by the followers of Jesus, has now become baptism in the name of Jesus Christ. The meaning of the rite has been transformed by the Messianic anointing which Jesus received when he participated in the baptism of John. The Johannine rite was preparatory, symbolizing an eschatological expectation. Jesus, however, when he underwent that baptism received the fulfilment of this expectation, the descent of the Spirit. To be baptized in his name involves the reception of the same baptism of fulfilment, the Spirit-baptism to which John had looked forward. Baptism is thus a re-presentation of Christ's own bap-

---

* Acts 15[23].   † Acts 13[52], etc.

‡ The case of Cornelius is unique. The first Gentile convert receives the Spirit exactly as the apostles did at Pentecost (cf. Acts 11[15]). The immensely important event of a Gentile Pentecost is not to be treated as though it were a sample of the way in which ordinary converts joined the Church and received the Spirit.

tism, and it necessarily carries with it the gift of the Spirit for those who repent and acknowledge him as Messiah. So much is implied in Acts 2[38]. Some other Lucan accounts of baptism fail to mention that the converts received the Spirit; such are the stories of Lydia, the jailer at Philippi, Crispus and others at Corinth. It is fairly clear, in view of Acts 2[38] and the prophecy of Joel, that St. Luke believes the gift to be conferred on all Christians, and it is very probable that he deems it unnecessary to mention in every case of baptism that the baptized person received the Spirit. It could safely be left to his readers to infer so much. In the case, however, of the Philippian jailer we are told that he 'rejoiced' when he was converted,* a fact which, when we remember St. Luke's close association of joy with Spirit-possession, we may perhaps believe to have been mentioned in order to imply his reception of the Spirit. The same interpretation should perhaps be given to the story of the Ethiopian eunuch. We are not told that he received the Spirit when he was baptized; at the point where we should expect this to be mentioned we learn instead that the Spirit caught away Philip, like a prophet of old. The Western reading which asserts that the Spirit fell upon the eunuch and an angel caught away Philip† probably represents an attempt to remove the obvious difficulty. It is, however, stated that the eunuch 'went on his way rejoicing', and this may be intended to indicate Spirit-possession. The case of Apollos is more difficult. He knew only the baptism of John, that is, in all probability, the Johannine baptism of expectation as it was administered by the Lord's disciples before Pentecost; but he is not said to have received any other baptism; he was merely given further instruction by Priscilla and Aquila. Yet even before he received this instruction he was already 'fervent in the Spirit', which can scarcely mean anything other than that as a missionary preacher he was inspired by the Holy Spirit. Possibly, since he was a high-ranking apostle, equal in the eyes of many Corinthians to Peter and Paul, he had received the Spirit from the Lord in person in some post-resurrection appearance, but this is unlikely if, as is most probable, the Ephesian disciples mentioned below were his converts, for they were not aware that the age of the Spirit had begun. A satisfactory explanation of this problem is perhaps unattainable.

In three cases, those of Philip's Samaritan converts, Saul of Tarsus, and the disciples whom St. Paul found at Ephesus, the Spirit is imparted through the sign of the laying-on of hands either after baptism, as in the first and last of these instances, or, as in the

* Acts 16[34].   † Acts 8[39].

case of Saul, before it. This sign is given by apostles in the instances of the Samaritans and the Ephesians, and in the case of Saul by a senior disciple, Ananias of Damascus. In the last-mentioned case the purpose of the action was partly the restoration of sight, and the imposition of hands is commonly met with as a means of healing. It is very difficult to substantiate the view that St. Luke believes that the laying-on of hands was regularly attached to baptism as the special mode of the bestowal of the Spirit. The reception of the Spirit is involved in the very notion of baptism if the rite represents Christ's baptismal anointing at the Jordan (and if it does not it is hard to account for the adoption of baptism in the Church). The Ethiopian was given no such sign and apparently had no opportunity of obtaining it subsequently. The theory that Philip was unable to administer the laying-on of hands because it was an apostolic prerogative to do so runs into difficulties in the case of Ananias and Saul. Indeed, the view that there was a regular rite of 'Confirmation' in the apostolic Church, especially if it is held that its administration was confined to apostles, is full of contradictions.

In the case of the Samaritans, racial prejudice may have prevented the converts from entering into the full fellowship of the Spirit until the two chief apostles had come from Jerusalem and assured them, by this token of personal identification and solidarity, that they had really been incorporated into the community of the Spirit, but although such reasons may have been present also in the case of Saul, the former arch-enemy, they were not apparently operative in the instance of the disciples at Ephesus.

In all three cases the gift is a special one. It is the conferment of the particular endowment of the missionary power, expressing itself at Samaria in such visible and spectacular signs of the Spirit that Simon Magus wished to buy the ability to produce such wonderful phenomena, in the case of Saul the power (ἐνεδυναμοῦτο)* to preach mightily and confound the opponents of the gospel, and at Ephesus in the Pentecostal gifts of tongues and prophesyings. It may well be that in all three instances a special transference of the missionary power is given to converts of special importance in the development of the missionary enterprise, and that it is made by the sign of personal fellowship received from members of the original apostolate, from an old believer who had received a special apostolic commission for the purpose in a vision from God,† and from St. Paul who had received it in the same manner himself. If this is a correct interpretation of a difficult problem, we

* Acts 9²².   † Acts 9¹⁰⁻¹⁵.

may suppose that at three major turning-points in the history of the mission to the world new centres or foci of the Spirit are inaugurated by means of a transference of special endowments of the Spirit, such as Joshua received from Moses. These episodes will then have little bearing on the baptism and the reception of the Spirit experienced by the generality of Christian believers, not all of whom were endowed with the special *charismata* of prophecy and tongues. This whole matter is, however, complicated by the obscure allusion to layings-on of hands which occurs in Heb. 6² in close conjunction with 'teaching of βαπτισμοί', a passage which lies beyond our present scope.

Since baptism is the effective sign of the reception of the Spirit, it results in remission of sins, as St. Peter indicated at Pentecost. It is therefore the means by which sins are 'washed away' when the convert enters the fellowship of the Spirit.*

St. Luke cannot always make his theology entirely clear. He is bound to some extent by his sources and committed to follow certain written and oral traditions whose form and content were already determined, and he can bend these to the service of his doctrinal purposes only by modifying their content in small and subtle details or by setting them in a new arrangement of his own choice. Unlike the Fourth Evangelist, he does not re-write history in order to bring out its deeper significance. His theological teaching has often to be conveyed by hints and by subtleties of order or language. Yet his theme of the activity of the Spirit in relation to the birth, life, death, and exaltation of the 'prophet like unto Moses' and in the origin, life and mission of the apostolic Church is impressive and ably worked out.

Certain passages from the Fourth Gospel serve to make explicit some of the fundamental truths which had been set forth by implication in the Third Gospel and Acts: 'I have beheld the Spirit descending as a dove out of heaven; and it abode upon him';† 'But this spake he of the Spirit, which they that believed on him were to receive; for Spirit was not yet, because Jesus was not yet glorified';‡ 'And I, if I be lifted up from the earth, will draw all men unto myself'; § 'Jesus therefore said to them again, Peace be unto you: as the Father hath sent me, even so send I you. And when he had said this, he breathed on them, and saith unto them, Receive ye the Holy Ghost: whose soever sins ye forgive, they are forgiven unto them'.||

* Acts 22¹⁶.   † Jn. 1³².   ‡ Jn. 7³⁹.   § Jn. 12³². || Jn. 20²¹⁻²³.

Sacrament and Common Meal

by

D. M. MACKINNON

RECENT years have seen a remarkable outpouring of books and articles on matters related to the Eucharist, written both from the angle of scholarship and from that of theology. In the present essay all that is offered is a few suggestions based on a study of part of the literature.

It seems clear that in the Synoptic Gospels the various references to Jesus' table-fellowship with the outcasts of society are pregnant with a very deep significance indeed.

For instance, in the episode recorded in Mk. 2¹⁵ ᶠᶠ· the question is put to Jesus' disciples by the Pharisees ὅτι μετὰ τῶν τελωνῶν καὶ ἁμαρτωλῶν ἐσθίει; Jesus himself gives the answer that the strong have no need of a doctor, only the sick. It was not to call righteous persons, he adds, but sinners that I came. Luke, in his version of the episode (5³⁰ ᶠᶠ·) shows the disciples' behaviour as the object of the Pharisees' displeasure. But it is Jesus who retorts on behalf of the disciples insisting that it is the sick, not the healthy, that require medical care: οὐκ ἐλήλυθα καλέσαι δικαίους ἀλλ ἁμαρτωλοὺς εἰς μετάνοιαν. The addition of the last two words subtly alters the Marcan sense; for surely in Mark the suggestion is that the sinners' call is to sit at table with Jesus. For though these meals have superficially nothing of a ritual or sacramental character, the invitation to join in them, although perhaps almost casually given, is a sign of the kingdom of God, a type of the call to the Messianic banquet.

The suggestion is familiar that the feedings of the 5,000 and of the 4,000 have a Eucharistic import. However we understand the factual basis of the narratives, the feedings are almost naturally regarded as 'signs' in the Johannine sense, and we do not find it altogether difficult to associate what they signify with the action of

Jesus in the upper room.* But to some at least the realization
that the common meal, even the everyday social fact, is one of the
great New Testament images comes as something strange and
almost exciting. Yet we can hardly escape the recognition that it
is so; and the occurrence of the image in parabolic description of
the kingdom has its background in the simple day-to-day courtesy
of the Lord.

No one has worked out the implications of this series of types
more thoroughly than the late Ernst Lohmeyer in his *Kultus und
Evangelium.*† He may have turned his insight to the service of
his own peculiar theories of Christian origins, but he has nevertheless worked out the significance of the table-fellowship of Jesus
in the pattern of his ministry. The readiness of the Lord to eat and
drink with tax gatherers and prostitutes is seen by Lohmeyer as
something quite fundamental to the Lord's ministry. In it is
focused that same challenge to the whole apparatus of the temple-
cult which on Lohmeyer's view is present in the narratives of the
cleansing of the temple and finds climactic expression in the rending of the temple-veil, recorded as an eschatological portent
accompanying the death of Jesus. But *in a way* it would seem to
Lohmeyer that the stern action in the courts of the temple as well
as the rending of the veil were less fundamentally revealing of the
ways of Jesus than his free association with the ragtag and bobtail
of his society.

Granted that the circumstances of his last years made it
impossible for Lohmeyer to revise his book, the reader can still
hardly escape the sense that he would have liked to use his
exegesis to expel from the Christian gospel any endorsement of the
sacrificial, cultic or ritual aspects of religion. He succeeds in fusing
together all the elements in the ministry of Jesus which constituted
a challenge to the vast fabric of the temple-cult. Thus the Johannine identification of the risen body of Jesus with the new temple
of God (Jn. 2²¹) is quite alien to Lohmeyer's theology. What he
succeeds in bringing out with a relentless clarity is the judgment of
the way of Jerusalem by the way of Jesus. The rending of the
temple-veil is the mark that that judgment reaches its final point
in the passion of the Lord. But what is declared finally in the
passion is present all along in the movement of his ministry of
awful mercy, as the harlots eat with him and the righteous remain
apart, assured and content.

Yet has ritual action no place in the work of Jesus? Were not
his words over bread and wine at the last supper in some sense

---

* Cf. the structure of Jn. 6.   † Vandenhoek und Ruprecht.

ritual words? That the last supper stands in the series of the meals of Jesus is undeniable. It is their climax, where he so solemnly says: ἀμὴν λέγω ὑμῖν ὅτι οὐ μὴ πίω ἐκ τοῦ γεννήματος τῆς ἀμπέλου ἕως τῆς ἡμέρας ἐκείνης ὅταν αὐτὸ πίνω καινὸν ἐν τῇ βασιλείᾳ τοῦ θεοῦ (Mk. 14²⁵). Dare we say, as, if I understand him, Professor Joachim Jeremias implies, that the days of the 'gluttonous man and wine-bibber' are now over, that the 'taking away of the bridegroom' puts an end to the feast, that the moment of renunciation and departure is now come? The meal in the upper room is the last table-fellowship that Jesus enjoyed with his own. But it is also ritual action and religious performance.

Was it a Passover meal? Jeremias makes out a remarkably strong case for saying it was. But whether we are prepared to go the whole way with him or not, there is, I think, absolutely no doubt that the meal Jesus ate with his friends was saturated with the profound traditions of the Passover. The language he used derived some at least of its force from the living memory of that first deliverance of Israel and of the pledges made and received at Sinai. It is clear, too, that whatever exegesis we offer of the words and actions of Jesus on that night, they were stamped with a tremendous significance for those who heard and saw them. It is no accident that Luke, before the Fourth Evangelist, has begun to crowd tracts of Jesus' esoteric teaching into the intercourse of those last hours. The upper room is a place of revelation. Of that revelation the action upon the bread and wine is the focus. However we relate it to the pattern of Jewish meals, whether Paschal or not, it was a ritual act, and, in a most pregnant way, one that designated the Messiah (expected to arrive in the night when the first deliverance of Israel was rehearsed by the people of God).

Here, I think, we can learn something from those who, like Sir Will Spens and the late Père de la Taille approach the question of Christ's actions in the upper room from the standpoint of traditional Eucharistic theology. When de la Taille speaks of that action as *oblatio hostiae immolandae* we seem a very long way from the idiom with which, for example, Jeremias in *Die Abend-mahlsworte Jesu* seeks to characterize the behaviour of the Lord. This sudden invocation of scholastic distinction between oblation and immolation seems foreign to the temper of the Gospel. Yet what de la Taille seems to me to do is to offer a condensed and generalized interpretation of action whose precise historical detail may always elude us. By this I mean that we may never be able finally to decide whether the Synoptic or the Johannine chronology of the last days of Jesus is the right one. We must always try to make up our minds: and certainly in the effort we are bound to come on much that is profoundly relevant to an understanding of the Eucharist, as Jeremias, for example, certainly does. Yet the ambiguity may remain; and we may have to say simply that, by his blessing of the bread and thanksgiving over the cup, Christ throws over the things that are coming upon him an overwhelming, in fact a final, significance. By words at once conveying the burden of a most mighty religious tradition and bright with an awful novelty, he reveals the meaning of his death to his own. More than this: as de la Taille's use of the word 'oblation' suggests he makes himself over to God.

To my mind (following here Hoskyns rather than Dodd) the inwardness of Christ's action over the bread and wine is declared in the 'high-priestly prayer'—Jn. 17, cf. e.g. 19, καὶ ὑπὲρ αὐτῶν ἀγιάζω ἐμαυτόν, ἵνα ὦσι καὶ αὐτοὶ ἡγιασμένοι ἐν ἀληθείᾳ. Hoskyns insists that the whole shall be called 'the prayer of consecration'. In it Jesus consecrates himself on behalf of his own. And that is, in effect, what he does by his words and actions upon the bread and wine, at the same time drawing his disciples into the very depths of his redeeming work by bidding them eat and drink.

Behind the upper room lie the many meals of Jesus, among them, if we allow historical weight to John, the wedding-feast at Cana, when his hour was not yet come. Yet he gave the guests good wine. Other feasts we remember too, as when, for instance, he gave hope to Zacchaeus by eating at his house. But in the upper room it is a last, climactic supper, and to it only his intimates are bidden. For now his hour has come, and what men have seen in part will now be revealed in whole. The meals with publican and sinner have spoken reconciliation; but the ground of that reconciliation is in the action to which he now wholly abandons himself. As his Father gives him commandment, so he does. No man takes his life from him; he lays it down of himself. At the supper table he lays his consecrating hand upon the life now drawing to its close, at once bestowing its fulness upon his disciples and setting it upon the altar of his Father's will.

The hour of Jesus in the upper room is presented by John as an hour of glory. Dodd sees it suffused with a kind of resurrection splendour; and indeed, if there is anything in my interpretation, it can be seen as the hour of Jesus' absolute self-giving to which the resurrection is the crown. What immediately follows, betrayal, mockery, trial and death, is in the upper room embraced and taken by Christ into the very substance of his being. What follows has however most really to happen, to be *done*.

What I am suggesting is that in the Last Supper we find our-selves in the presence of that which fuses religion and life, prayer and endurance, eternity and time. It is inescapably ritual per-formance. Yet it is a meal. We may perhaps suggest that the meals with publicans and sinners were 'prophetic signs' (in the full sense of the word) of the birth of the Messianic Age. In the upper room the woe (the πειρασμός) which is to usher in that age is about to break upon the disciples of Jesus: indeed in that room he offers himself to endure the full impact of its onslaught, and declares himself ready to endure the ultimate contradiction of human existence. In that hour Jesus' disciples eat again; enjoy a fellowship more intimate, more deeply pregnant with the finalities of redemption, than the crowds of earlier, happier days. At that supper (Passover, or anticipated Passover, still full of Paschal significance) Messiah is himself the Paschal lamb; and by what he says and does he makes it clear that this is indeed the Messianic banquet. 'Is'—yet the fulfilment lies beyond, fulfilment which is yet contained in the action and the gift.

Under the symbolism of a meal Jesus conveys to his Father and to his own the ultimate burden of his mission. By action upon bread and wine he conveys himself to God; and at the same time he transforms the whole sense of the Messianic banquet by setting it forth as a participation in his passion. The Messianic banquet remained for the Jews of Hitler's Europe a symbol of promise; according to Arthur Koestler, in the death-trains to Auschwitz they sang of the meal where Leviathan would be given them for food. But the last Passover of Jesus fuses that hope with the presence of sinful men to the mysteries of his rejection and desola-tion, of his victory and glory.

As Père Daniélou has well written: 'The Last Supper comes to us rich with the whole complex symbolism which the meal-typology of the Gospels forces us to see there. It is first a meal of Jesus with his own, and as such it is of course a realization of the Messianic banquet where men are bidden to eat with the Son of Man. Thus it is presented as a fulfilment of the banquet typology of the Old Testament. It is, at the same time, a figure of the eschatological meal where Christ will drink in his kingdom the fruit of the vine and will receive his own at his table. It is a Paschal meal, and in this sense it is presented as both the fulfilment of the lamb by whose blood the doorposts of the faithful were sprinkled and as an augury of the Lamb, the light of the city of God. Yet it is much more than that. For it is not a prefiguration, but the institution of the Eucharist. And therefore it stands at a kind of watershed, belonging to the visible biography of Jesus, yet at the same time to his sacramental continuance with his own. So it seems to gather up into itself various levels of meaning and to be the focus of the whole rich biblical typology of the meal'.*

The Last Supper, then, is a supreme moment of interpretation. In Luke, as I have said, and of course supremely in John, it gathers to itself, as it was bound to do, more and more of the esoteric teaching of Jesus. But this moment of interpretation points beyond itself to the ultimate interpretation which the Jew saw also under the form of a banquet. Even in the Middle Ages when the eschatological sense of the Eucharist was partly obliterated, St. Thomas Aquinas could end his hymn *Lauda Sion* with a rich vision of the heavenly banquet. At first it may seem odd to speak of the Messianic banquet as interpretation. But when in the Apocalypse it is suggested that to the Lamb alone is it given to open the seals of the book of life it is surely implied that to him it falls to disclose the sense of human history. Where his own history was concerned he gave it its sense in the upper room; for to him alone among men in his absolute transparency to God was the ordering of his coming and going plain. We know not what we are made of; we receive our sense from him and in him.†

It is thus, I think, that we should approach the Church's Eucharistic observance. Anglican theology has wisely tried to correlate the Church's performance of the Eucharistic action with the heavenly intercession of the Lord. But often there has been a failure to conceive that intercession eschatologically in relation to judgment at once past, present and to come. The incorporation of the Church's prayer into the prayer of Christ, perhaps the ultimate meaning of the *praesentia realis*, has been seen indeed as an incorporation into his prayer of consecration. But that that prayer is an eschatological mystery has been too easily forgotten. For it is that whose full burden will only be made plain in the end of time, when the fullness of Christ's sacrifice is disclosed.

When the Eucharist is celebrated it is the last supper which is most obviously recalled. The style is that of the upper room, not of Emmaus. For although the Church looks back to Christ's death, in the sense in which Jesus looked forward to it, she looks backward from within history; she still has Christ's death to pass

---

* La Maison Dieu 18 (Editions du Cerf).

† But all this was done in utter obedience to the Father, from whom the Son of Man received his hour. As within the abyss of the godhead, the Father is the Utterer and the Word Utterance, so in the visible ministry of Jesus it is a reality of dependency which is expressed. If the Father is revealed in the Son, it is because the Son's dependence is unconditioned, without shadow of reserve. To Christ what He is remains plain, because he is substantially incarnate dependence upon the Father.

through. The liturgy does capture the triumphant accents of the heavenly liturgy, yet the men who perform it belong to time and history. What they bring to the altar comes out of the stuff of changing human existence. They give to their being the shape of prayer and ask that that should be stamped with the seal of the prayer of Christ. For they know that in him is the ultimate sense of their endurance as well as the forgiveness of their sin. Adoration, thanksgiving, impetration, propitiation, the four traditional ends of sacrifice, have to find their counterparts in the activities of human life. But such counterparts are only lasting and stable if they are marked with the seal of Christ's fulfilment of those ends in his own being. For in him the impulses those words call up were expressed ultimately in the nakedness of his Cross—their one final and definitive expression. He gave us the common meal of the Eucharist that we might see the Cross in it. Thus for the Christian it is the theology of the Eucharist which raises most sharply the issue of his understanding of the relation of time to eternity. For here it is that the stuff of his everyday existence is brought to the place where sense is given it; but hidden sense, glimpsed only now and then. Yet sense is given; for that which there lays hold of his life and bends its present moment into worship is the One with whom the last word as well as the first rests, the Alpha and Omega.

Realized Eschatology and the Messianic Secret

by

T. W. MANSON

JUST over fifty years ago, in 1901, Schweitzer's sketch of the life of Jesus on the basis of 'thorough-going eschatology' and Wrede's work on the Messianic Secret, a standing challenge to any attempt to make sense of the Gospel record on any basis, eschatological or other, were published. Five years later in his *Von Reimarus zu Wrede*, Schweitzer presented the whole history of research on the life of Jesus as a kind of evolution leading inevitably to the point reached in 1901, and demanding a definite decision for one or other of the only alternatives left: thorough-going scepticism or thorough-going eschatology. In 1910 Burkitt, writing a preface to the English translation of Schweitzer's book, remarked, 'We treat the Life of our Lord too much as it is treated in the Liturgical "Gospels", as a simple series of disconnected anecdotes'. Within a decade the practice which Burkitt criticized became a principle of criticism. K. L. Schmidt published *Der Rahmen der Geschichte Jesu* and Martin Dibelius the first edition of his *Formgeschichte des Evangeliums* in 1919; and Bultmann's *Geschichte der Synoptischen Tradition* followed shortly after in 1921. Bultmann recognized that Wrede, so far from having said the last word in 1901, had only begun a process which was destined to come to fruition in the new discipline of Form-criticism. Thorough-going scepticism could be carried beyond Wrede.

At the same time thorough-going eschatology was not allowed to stand still. Rudolf Otto's *Reich Gottes und Menschensohn* (1934) and C. H. Dodd's *Parables of the Kingdom* (1935) presented the idea of realized eschatology as the key to the understanding of what is given in the Synoptic accounts of the Ministry. It is, I think, important that we should make clear to ourselves what is involved in speaking of '*realized* eschatology' in contrast to '*thorough-going* eschatology'. Schweitzer's interpretation of the gospel story seems to be reducible to a few simple propositions. First, Jesus shared the expectations of his contemporaries regarding the coming of the Kingdom of God. Second, he thought it imminent, bound up with his own Ministry, and later, when early expectations had been disappointed, with his sacrificial death. Third, neither the Ministry nor the death of Jesus availed to bring about the expected consummation. But, fourth, the practice of Jesus was better than his theory, and the spiritual power that flowed from him is something far greater than the consummation that did not come. He still commands his disciples and makes himself known to them in their obedience.

The weak point in this construction is the fact that the practice of Jesus is better, so much better, than the apocalyptic hope to which he is assumed to be committed. The practice, that is the Ministry, must be supposed to be based upon his deepest convictions. Could those convictions be brought into agreement with the hopes of the current Jewish eschatology? Could the Jesus, who held the ideals embodied in the Ministry, have swallowed uncritically the contents of the Jewish Messianic hope? His independent attitude towards the other great branch of Jewish doctrine, the scribal exposition of the Law, at least suggests that he may have had a mind of his own on the subject of the Kingdom of God and the Messiah.

Realized eschatology is, I think, committed to the view that the attitude of Jesus towards the Messianic hope, no less than his attitude towards the Jewish Law and its scribal interpretation, is to be gauged from the words and deeds of the Ministry as a whole. But that is not all. The mind of Jesus concerning the Law and the Kingdom is not just formulated in general propositions: it is embodied in living words and deeds that belong to actual situations and concern real people. The Law of God is promulgated, and his Kingdom comes, in the Ministry itself. In the last resort it can be said that Jesus himself is the New Law, is the Kingdom, in present reality; or, to paraphrase St. Paul (I Cor. 1^{24}), Christ crucified is the fulfilment in power of the wise purpose of God.

I propose to discuss in this paper the question whether the interpretation of the Gospels offered by Realized Eschatology is an adequate answer to the searching questions asked by Wrede half a century ago. We may begin by reminding ourselves of the main lines of the argument in *Das Messiasgeheimnis in den Evangelien.*

That argument is worked out most clearly and fully in the first main section of the book (pp. 9–149). The central hypothesis is that our earliest evangelist, Mark, had at his disposal a collection of historical or quasi-historical data. The tale they told was this.*

Jesus was a Galilean teacher, who went about giving his instructions accompanied by a group of disciples. Within this group was an inner circle, who enjoyed the Master's special confidence; on the fringe of the group was the crowd. Jesus had a liking for the parabolic method in his teaching. Besides his teaching there was his miracle-working. All this aroused great interest and drew great multitudes to him. He had much to do with demoniacs. In his contacts with the general public he did not disdain the society of publicans and sinners. His attitude to the Jewish Law showed independence of mind. He fell foul of the Pharisees and the Jewish authorities, who set about compassing his downfall. They succeeded when he ventured into Judaea and Jerusalem. There, with the collaboration of the Roman government, he was put to death.

In Mark's thinking, and consequently in his Gospel, this simple story is crossed by a set of dogmatic convictions. In these Jesus is a supernatural Being possessed of supernatural powers and engaged upon a divine mission. This mission involves him in suffering and death, and finds its completion and consummation in the Resurrection. This means that during the Ministry the Messiahship is hidden. It must remain a secret until the Resurrection, which thus becomes the official proclamation of the Messiah. Those who have an inkling of the truth before the Resurrection must be made to keep it to themselves. The key to the problem is given in Mk. 9^9: 'And as they were coming down from the mountain he gave them distinct instructions not to describe what they had seen to anyone until after the Son of man had risen from the dead'. This injunction to secrecy is the explanation of all the others in Mark.

The evidences of messianic secrecy are well distributed through the Gospel. Whether Mark invented them or inherited them is of small moment, since in any event they are unhistorical. They comprise such things as the silencing of the demons (Mk. $1^{25, 34}$, 3^{12}); the commands to keep silence about certain miracles ($1^{43\ ff.}$, 5^{43}, 7^{36}, 8^{26}); the instructions to the disciples to say nothing after Peter's confession (8^{30}) and the Transfiguration (9^9); the attempts of Jesus to travel incognito (7^{24}, $9^{30\ f.}$); and, somewhat unexpectedly, even the crowd's injunction to Bartimaeus to

* *Messiasgeheimnis*, p. 130.

keep quiet (10^{48}). All these phenomena must be explained in the same way; and any explanation of one group that fails to explain all the others must be rejected. This principle is an essential article of Wrede's dogmatic scheme; and, in one form or another, it is frequently asserted, though never proved. It has been rightly questioned* more than once. No voice from Heaven has declared that all the injunctions to secrecy in Mark spring from the same motive, and there is no reason on earth why we should suppose that they do. Indeed when they are examined on their merits, without presuppositions, other motives or reasons than the messaianic secret readily suggest themselves.

As an example we may consider the commands of silence after the performance of miracles. In Mk. 5^{43}, after the account of the raising of Jairus' daughter, we are informed that Jesus 'gave them definite and emphatic orders that no one was to know this. He also told them to give her something to eat'. If 'this' means the fact that the girl is cured, the absurdity of the prohibition is at once obvious. The moment the door of the room was opened the truth would be out. Dibelius† took the right line when he distinguished between the cure itself and the means by which it was effected. The latter could be kept secret, the former not. This is the case also in the cure of the deaf-mute (7^{32-37}) and the blind man at Bethsaida (8^{22-26}). In all three stories the cure is performed away from the crowd—this seems to be true also of the cure of the epileptic boy (9^{25}). Only a few picked persons are allowed into the room where Jairus' daughter is lying; the deaf-mute is dealt with κατ' ἰδίαν; the blind man is taken out of the village. Dibelius aptly compares the procedure of Peter in Acts 9^{40} where it may be remarked there is no question of a messianic secret. Further, in Mk 1^{44} the leper is enjoined in the same breath, both to keep the secret and to take the proper steps to make the fact of his cure known to the authorities, and so to the general public. It seems reasonable to conclude that it is the method of the cure rather than the cure itself that is to be kept secret.

On the supposition that these stories are fictitious, we may well ask what motive there can have been for bringing in this peculiar feature. Wrede's explanation of the messianic secret will not do; for it is concerned with the fact of the cure as evidence of the Messiahship. The explanation that lies nearest to hand is that suggested by Mk. 9^{38-41}, where John voices the anxiety of the

---

* Most recently by Professor H. J. Cadbury in a very interesting paper, 'Mixed Motives in the Gospels', *Proceedings of the American Philosophical Society*, 95 (1951), pp. 117-124.

† *Die Formgeschichte des Evangeliums*[2], pp. 69 f.

disciples that those who are not members of the circle should not be allowed to use its methods: 'Master, we saw a man who is not a member of our group, making use of your name to drive out demons; so we tried to stop him'. With this we may compare the narratives in Acts 8^{9-25} and 19^{11-20}, as well as Peter's action in Acts 9^{40}. Here we have a clear indication that the disciples who, according to Mk. 3^{15}, 6^7, ^{13}; Matt. 10^8, had been given certain powers by Jesus, wished to keep these powers in their own hands. This, incidentally, has a bearing on the question of the historicity of the healing miracles themselves. Is this wish to keep the methods secret explicable, if there is nothing in the stories at all? If there were no cures and no means of effecting cures, there would be nothing to hide. The evidence goes to show that the disciples themselves believed in the miracles and in the power to perform them. Unless, of course, they were a set of quacks and impostors.

We may go a step farther. If the stories are not fictitious, the injuctions to secrecy would still be a welcome feature to disciples keen to maintain their exclusive rights. But we know from Mk. 9^{38-41} that Jesus did not support their policy of a 'closed shop'. If, then, these prohibitions have any historical basis in fact, Jesus' reasons for making them must be of another kind. Here it is important to recall that there are a number of cures recorded in which there is no secrecy and no injunction to keep silence; further, that in two of these cases the cure is explicitly said to be the result of the patient's faith (Mk. 5^{34}, 10^{52}, cf. 9^{23} $^{f.}$, 6^5 $^{f.}$). It would seem that the normal picture of a healing miracle presents it as an act of co-operation between Jesus and the patient, a confluence of love and faith. Where the faith was weak it might be helped by words or acts appropriate to the particular case; but the patient must not be allowed to suppose that the secret of the cure lay in some magical formula or technique, still less to broadcast the news that, say, 'Effatha' was an infallible charm for curing deafness, or that a blind man might recover his sight if you got the right person to spit in his eyes.

Whether this is the true explanation of the injunctions to silence in connexion with healing miracles I cannot claim to know; but I do venture to suggest that it is a more reasonable reason for the injunctions than Wrede's messianic secret.

But miracles of healing were not the only things on the messianic secret list. Wrede's catalogue includes:

(*a*) The Messiahship or divine Sonship of Jesus.

(*b*) Miracles as evidence for (*a*).

(c) The teaching of Jesus as a whole. Its real meaning is beyond the ken of the mass of the people.

(d) The meaning of the parables.

(e) The inevitability of the Passion.

The last of these has a special importance for our enquiry. Wrede starts from the three formal predictions of the Passion of the Son of man in Mk. 8, 9 and 10. To these he adds as supporting testimony Mk. $9^{9,\ 12}$; $10^{38\ f.,\ 45}$; 12^{6-11}; $14^{7f.,\ 18,\ 21,\ 24,\ 27\ f.,\ 30,\ 41}$. He points out the difficulty—and it is a real difficulty—of reconciling these definite predictions of the Passion with the complete bewilderment of the disciples when the predictions were fulfilled, and draws the conclusion that the predictions are *vaticinia ex eventu*. He points out—what is undeniably a fact—that there is a tendency for sayings that have no reference to the Passion to be given a twist in that direction and appeals to Lk. 11^{30} as compared with Matt. 12^{40}; Lk. $9^{30\ f.}$ as compared with Mk. 9^4; Lk. $17^{24\ f.}$, as compared with Matt. 24^{27}; Lk. $24^{6\ f.}$, as compared with Mk. 16^7; and Jn. $2^{19ff.}$, as compared with Mk. 14^{58}. But the conclusion which Wrede draws from these data,* that these passages are 'die genaueste Formulierung des Gedankens, dass Jesus die Leidensgeschichte, wie sie wirklich geschehen war, pünktlich vorausgewusst habe'; and that 'sie gehören demnach in das Kapitel von der altchristlichen Apologetik' is altogether too drastic. For a tendency to reinterpret existing sayings in the light of the Passion is one thing, and a very natural thing. The creation of such sayings *ex nihilo* is quite another. Moreover, as Dr. Lightfoot has pointed out,† 'neither the substantive cross nor the verb to crucify occurs in Mark, except the noun used metaphorically in the phrase 'to take up the cross' at 8^{34}, until chapter 15, which describes the actual crucifixion; in it the words occur ten times. It is odd that where there is so much alleged prophecy after the event the only prophecy of crucifixion in the mouth of Jesus should be of the possible crucifixion of potential followers.

But this is not the only peculiarity of the Passion predictions. Not only do these sayings contain no specific reference to the crucifixion; they have no specific mention of the Crucified. They speak in increasingly detailed terms of the sufferings, death, and resurrection of the Son of man, but not of the crucified Messiah Jesus, who is the subject of the primitive *kerygma*. In Mk. 8^{31-33} Jesus announces the hard lot of the Son of man. Peter protests, in what terms we are not told. Jesus, with his eye on his disciples, sternly rebukes Peter and accuses him of caring more for an

---

* *Op. cit.*, p. 90.　　　　　　　† *The Gospel Message of St. Mark*, p. 36.

earthly empire than for the Kingdom of God. It is Matthew who interprets 'Son of man' as meaning Jesus himself and provides Peter with a speech in keeping with this identification. The second prediction (Mk. 9^{30-32}) is equally general in its terms. Mark tells us that the disciples did not understand the purport of the saying and that they were afraid to ask him. Matthew tells us not that they did not understand, but that they were vexed*— presumably by what they took it to mean. The third prediction (Mk. $10^{33\,f.}$) gives a much more detailed picture of the fate of the Son of man, one moreover that has many points of contact with Mark's narrative of the Passion. But again crucifixion is not specifically mentioned; and while the sufferings are this time referred to Jesus, in verse 32, this is Mark's own *enarratio ex eventu* and no part of the text of the saying. Here again Matthew makes things more definite by substituting 'crucify' (20^{19}) for Mark's colourless 'kill'.

Wrede insisted that what Mark portrays in these three passages is a complete failure of the disciples to understand the sayings and a complete absence of any attempt by Jesus to help them to an understanding.† I suggest that this is a completely wrong interpretation of the Markan account; and that the time has come for a thorough reconsideration of the evidence.

The starting point must be the fact that the subject of the predictions as they stand is not 'the Messiah' or 'I' but 'the Son of man'. The 'Son of man' appears a good many times in Jewish literature, canonical and extra-canonical; but we have a clear indication in Mk. 14^{62} which of these Jesus had in mind. It is the Son of man of Dan. 7, the representation in the seer's vision of 'the people of the saints of the Most High'.‡ Now it must be admitted that the term Son of man has a certain flexibility of denotation. In this it resembles other well-known expressions in the Bible, the 'Servant of the Lord', for example. In Mark it is possible to trace a gradual narrowing of the denotation until at the last the term has become a name for Jesus alone. The point in the Marcan narrative at which this takes place is significant: it is at the Last Supper. There Jesus says (14^{18}), 'One of you will

---

* For this meaning for ἐλυπήθησαν cf. LXX, Neh. 5^6; Jon. $4^{4,\,9}$ where the verb is used to translate the Hebrew *hārāh*. The verb seems to be used in a like sense in Matt. 18^{31} and possibly Jn. 21^{17}.

† *Op. cit.*, p. 93.

‡ I have discussed the interpretation of 'Son of man' in *The Teaching of Jesus*, pp. 211–34 and in an article on 'The Son of man in Daniel, Enoch, and the Gospels', in the *Bulletin of the John Rylands Library*, 32 (1950), pp.171–93. I may refer also to my note on Mk. $2^{27\,f.}$ in *Coniectanea Neotestamentica* XI (*in honorem* A. Fridrichsen), pp. 138–46.

betray *me*'; in verse 21, 'Alas for that man by whom *the Son of man* is betrayed'.* Here for the first time in Mark the title and the first personal pronoun are interchangeable terms in the mouth of Jesus. And here for the first time we have the announcement by Jesus of the impending desertion of the whole body of his followers (Mk. 14$^{26-31}$). It is a strange coincidence—I venture to think that it is more than a coincidence—that our Lord's certainty that he would be left to face his destiny alone and his assumption of the name 'Son of man' as a personal designation come at the same point in the story.

These considerations suggest that we may be justified in entertaining the hypothesis that in the earlier predictions of the sufferings of the Son of man, Son of man still has its collective sense of 'the people of the saints of the Most High' and that what is pictured in these sayings is the realization of the ideals represented by the Servant of the Lord through the service and sacrifice of the Son of man, who comes upon the stage of history in the corporate body formed by Jesus and his disciples. If this is what Jesus meant by these sayings, then this is what the disciples failed to understand; and one must ask how and why they failed. In our search for an answer we are not left without clues.

In the first place it is an important fact that each of the three Passion predictions has in its immediate context a piece of evidence about the hopes cherished by the disciples. In Mk. 8 the first prediction evokes an immediate and indignant protest from Peter, who cannot tolerate the idea that the destiny of the Son of man should be anything but swift and certain triumph. The second prediction is accompanied by the record that there had been a lively discussion among the disciples about their rank and precedence—doubtless in the coming kingdom (Mk. 9$^{33-35}$). The third has as its pendant the request of the sons of Zebedee for leading positions in the new order (Mk. 10$^{35-45}$). The way in which Jesus deals with these situations makes it increasingly evident that there is a deep-seated difference between his conception of the Kingdom of God and the Messiahship and that of his followers. The difference is stated unequivocally in Mk. 10$^{42-45}$, which is the best commentary on Mk. 8^{33}. The difficulty of the disciples in understanding the predictions of the sufferings of the Son of man arise in the first instance from the fact that their minds are already occupied by a very different conception of what the Son of man is to be and do.

* 'The Son of man' is omitted in this clause by D 700 *a*; but this is of no consequence; for even if the omission were right, which it most probably is not, the verb would still look back to 'the Son of man' in the first half of the verse.

And here it must be granted that the disciples had the support both of scripture and the apocalyptic tradition. For in Dan. 7 what happens is that by a Divine decree the Son of man has everlasting and universal dominion, glory, and empire handed to him. Once the Almighty takes action the triumph of the Son of man is immediate, complete, and irreversible. That programme is endorsed in the *Psalms of Solomon*, particularly 17 and 18, in the *Assumption of Moses*,* in *Philo*,† and in the *Magnificat* and the *Benedictus*. To men who had grown up in this atmosphere the Passion predictions could not but be a major problem.

I have suggested elsewhere‡ that the disciples found a working solution for themselves. I think that that suggestion can now be worked out in greater detail than was possible in the earlier paper. In Mk. 8 we are presented simply with the first violent reaction of the spokesman of the Twelve against the idea of a suffering Son of man. In chapter 9 we are taken a stage farther. In verses [9-10] we learn that during the descent from the Mount of Transfiguration Jesus told the Three not to report what they had seen until such time as the Son of man had risen from the dead. The Three then began to discuss among themselves what Jesus meant by 'rising from the dead'. Obviously they were not discussing the meaning of the term: the meaning was well enough known already. They can only have been asking what the term could mean in connexion with the Son of man. Later in the same chapter (verses [30-32]) we have the second Passion prediction and the report that the disciples did not understand it and were afraid to ask. Again we may suspect that their unspoken question was, 'What have suffering, death, and resurrection to do with the Son of man?'

It seems to me that they found an answer to this question by taking the predictions of suffering, death, and resurrection to mean that the triumph of the Son of man would not be a walk-over, but would come only as the result of a hard fought battle. They, as belonging to the people of the saints of the Most High, must steel themselves along with their master to endure hardships and privations, hatred and contempt, wounds and death, in the cause. Victory would not come quickly or easily; but come it must. Jesus himself acknowledged this by adding resurrection as the last chapter in the story of the Son of man. We may ask ourselves what the mention of resurrection would be likely to suggest to Palestinian Jews *before the first Easter Sunday*. Surely the first

---

* Chap. X.   † *De praem. et. poen.*, §§ 15–20; *De execr.* §§ 8–9.
‡ *Journ. of Eccl. Hist.*, 1 (1950), pp. 1–11.

thing that would spring to mind would be the passage in Daniel,* where, after describing in considerable detail the career of Antiochus Epiphanes, with all the suffering that it involved for loyal Jews, Daniel's celestial informant goes on to picture for him the final deliverance and vindication of the righteous in Israel.

'And at that time Michael will arise, the Great Prince who stands by the sons of your people. And it will be a time of distress such as had never happened in all the existence of the nation up to that time. But at that time your people will be delivered, every one found written in the book. And many of those who sleep in the dusty earth will awake, some to everlasting life, and some to reproach, to everlasting abhorrence.'

The people who are to rise to everlasting life in Dan. 12 are in fact no other than 'the people of the saints of the Most High' in Dan. 7, that is, the people who are represented by the figure of the Son of man.

Again the thought of the Son of man rising again after three days might well suggest the famous passage in Hos. 6[1-3], with its picture of the restoration to life of the community. A third passage of Scripture that might be recalled is the vision in Ezek. 37. And here again it is a community that is brought back to life. In this connexion it is relevant that Professor Martin Buber† maintains that the normal way for the Jew to think of the resurrection was as the resurrection of a great community as a whole. The individual rises as a member of that community; and the Jew found it extremely difficult to accept the idea of the rising again of an individual as a single event in history, detached from this corporate resurrection.

Once the idea that Passion predictions were concerned with a corporate body, to which they themselves belonged, had established itself as a working theory in the minds of the disciples, there were a good many sayings of Jesus that would tend to confirm it. The Son of man is delivered up (Mk. 9[31]): so are the disciples (13[9, 11]). He is brought before the authorities (8[31], 10[33]); so are they (Mk. 13[9], cf. Lk. 12[11]). He is treated with hatred and contempt (8[31], 9[12]): the disciples may expect the same treatment (Mk. 13[13], Lk. 10[16], cf. Matt. 5[11], Lk. 6[22]). He is scourged (Mk. 10[34]): so are the disciples (13[9], cf. Matt. 10[17]). He is put to death

---

* Dan. 12[1-3].

† *Two Types of Faith*, pp. 100 f. It may be added that if Buber is right, we have the explanation of the incredulity of the disciples at the first reports of the resurrection of Jesus.

Also the words of Martha in Jn. 11[24] will reflect the typical Palestinian Jewish way of thinking about the resurrection.

(8^{31}, 9^{31}, 10^{34}): the disciples are repeatedly warned that they must be prepared for the same fate ($8^{34\,f\cdot}$, cf. Matt. $10^{38\,f\cdot}$, Lk. 14^{27}, 17^{33}), though not all of them may be called upon to suffer it (Mk. 9^1). We may also compare the saying about the Son of man in Mk. 10^{45} with that to the disciples in Mk. 8^{35}.

All this the disciples contrived to accept: I think they could do so because they were able to construe all these predicted sufferings and sacrifices as the price of victory. The nature of the triumph that was to follow on the sacrifices and sufferings remained for them unchanged. The pattern of it was still that shown in the *Psalms of Solomon* and kindred pictures of the coming Golden Age. This comes out clearly if we consider the request of the sons of Zebedee, which Mark places immediately after the third prediction of the sufferings of the Son of man. What James and John ask is that they may sit in state on either hand of the Messiah when the time comes. This is countered by the question, 'Can you drink the cup that I drink or be baptized with the baptism with which I am baptized?' In other words, 'Are you prepared to share my lot, whatever it may be? Are you as completely committed to the service of God's Kingdom as I am?'* Jesus is here in effect saying, 'Whatever else the term Son of man may denote, it denotes Jesus of Nazareth: does it also denote James and John, sons of Zebedee?' To the confident 'Yes' of the two brothers, Jesus says 'So be it. But what you asked for in the first instance is something different, which is not at my disposal'. James and John are prepared to accept hardships now as a prelude to better things to follow—and to follow quickly. They are willing to postpone the glory and humble themselves to the role of the servant in the meantime. They are not ready or willing to find the supreme glory in the role of the servant.

I suggest that it is here that we meet the real messianic secret, and that it is an open secret, given in the words of Mk. 10^{42-45}. Here we have stated in a nutshell the true nature of the Kingdom of God as opposed to the Israelite world-empire that the disciples

* To share in one cup is to have the same fortune, good or evil. See the abundant evidence collected by Billerbeck, *Komm.*, i, 836 ff. Baptism, at the time when these words (and those in Lk. 12^{50}) were spoken meant one thing above all else—self-committal. The proselyte to Judaism consents to share the lot of God's people in all respects and to take upon himself the yoke of the Kingdom, i.e. the Law. This is symbolized in the ritual of proselyte baptism in that during the rite two scholars stand by the proselyte and recite to him some of the lighter and some of the weightier commandments. As G. F. Moore says (*Judaism*, i, 334), 'In the whole ritual there is no suggestion that baptism was a real or symbolical purification; the assistants rehearse select commandments of both kinds as an appropriate accompaniment to the proselyte's assumption of all and sundry the obligations of the law, the "yoke of the commandment". It is essentially an initiatory rite, with a forward and not a backward look'.

have in mind. Here we have the messianic task clearly and simply defined. It is and remains a secret until after the Crucifixion and Resurrection, simply because no secret is ever so well kept as that which no one is willing to discover.

This, of course, is a very different messianic secret from Wrede's. For him the grand secret is the fact that Jesus is the Messiah; and the idea of the secret is part, and an essential part, of the structure of Mark's gospel. Having adopted this idea, Mark, according to Wrede, is inevitably landed in the hopeless contradiction that he must record acts and words of Jesus that demand publicity and recognition of him as the Messiah within a framework that demands secrecy and non-recognition. Obviously there is something wrong somewhere. For Wrede it could not be the framework which he had fathered on Mark: therefore it must be the record. 'Es muss offen gesagt werden: *Markus hat keine wirkliche Anschauung mehr vom geschichtlichen Leben Jesu.*'* When it comes to explaining how Mark came to be possessed by a dogmatic notion which compelled him to write historical nonsense, Wrede moves less confidently. The evangelist cannot be given the credit of having invented the lunatic structure by himself; and so we fall back on that ever-present help in critical difficulties, the anonymous group.† They concocted the bulk of the farrago of nonsense, which Mark, with a few embellishments of his own, eventually put into writing.

It is generally easier to pull down than to build; and when Wrede's task is finished we are left, if we think the work well done, with the debris of Mark as a permanent rubbish-heap, which might contain some sound building material, if only we knew how to sort it out, and how to put it together when we had got it.

Against all this we have to place the simple fact that the messianic secret, which undoubtedly exists in the Gospels, is not concerned with the identity of the Messiah but with the nature of his task. On this subject the contemporaries of Jesus had clear and definite ideas. We know what they were, partly from literary documents, that can be dated with more or less certainty in the period between the capture of Jerusalem by Pompey and its

---

* *Op. cit.*, p. 129. Italics Wrede's. He states his case clearly and bluntly on pp. 130 f., and again on p. 135: 'Geschichtlich verstanden enthält Markus eine ganze Anzahl schlimmer Sinnlosigkeiten. Nimmt man als Idee, was Idee ist, so befreit man ihn davon, d.h. man wird auf sie kein Gewicht legen. Man würdigt sie als wohl begreifliche Begleiterscheinungen einer Schriftstellerei, die etwas unbeholfen aus Gedanken Geschichte zu formen sucht'.

† *Op. cit.*, p. 145: 'Es handelt sich also um eine Anschauung, die grössere Kreise, wenn auch nicht notwendig grosse Kreise, beherrscht haben muss'. How, on Wrede's theory, these groups came into existence and formulated their strange notions; these are questions to which we should perhaps not expect an answer.

capture by Titus; and partly from the nature of the abortive attempts made during this period to usher in the Messianic Age. It is a political, economic, and social revolution which is to issue in a new order where the one true God will be worshipped and his worshippers will enjoy peace, prosperity, and happiness under the administration of the legitimate heir of the Davidic dynasty.

That programme was left unaltered by John the Baptist. His concern was not with the nature of the new order but with the qualifications necessary to secure a place in it.

The programme *was* challenged by Jesus. While all others were asking 'Who is the Messiah?', he asked 'What is the Messiah?' and he found the answer by fusing the two Old Testament conceptions of the Son of man and the Servant of the Lord. The inevitable result of this fusion appears in our Lord's statements about the Son of man, and in his public career, which we rightly call the Ministry, and in everything that we are told about his own thoughts and desires from the temptations in the wilderness to the agony in the Garden and the last cry from the Cross. The essence of the matter is that the Ministry *is* the kingdom and the power and the glory. That is the messianic secret; and it is an open secret—παρρησίᾳ τὸν λόγον ἐλάλει.

Right up to the arrest of Jesus the disciples were prepared to make a working compromise with as much of this as they were able to accept. They were willing to share hardships, losses, sacrifices, even to face the risk of death; they were, in fact, willing to take a full part in the ministry of the Son of man, so long as it was not regarded as an end in itself, but only as an interim dispensation leading on to something bigger and better. Their point of view is put quite simply and openly by Peter in the conversation which follows the story of the rich man in search of eternal life. The man has gone away dissatisfied at the stringency of the conditions; and, after some talk about the difficulty of giving up great possessions for the sake of the Kingdom of God, Peter points out that he and his colleagues have sacrificed all they had for the cause (Mk. 10[28]). The reply of Jesus is addressed not so much to his spoken statement as to his unspoken question, 'What may we expect as a result?' That this reply was not entirely satisfactory may perhaps be surmised from the fact that the next approach to Jesus, by James and John, ignores the spacious generalities about abundance of fathers, mothers, other relatives, houses, lands— and, for good measure, persecutions—and makes a specific request for places of rank and power. But Jesus is equally evasive on this question. The only thing he will promise definitely is a share in his cup and his baptism.

From the day when Peter blurted out what seemed to him and to the other disciples to be the messianic secret, Jesus did his best to tell them the real messianic secret. But his most persevering efforts could make little or no headway against their stubborn hopes of something that to them, as to most of the godly and patriotic Jews of the time, seemed better than his best. So the messianic secret remained a secret; and the Messiah was cheered into Jerusalem, and later crucified, as the latest claimant to the throne of David and Solomon.

If the argument advanced in the preceding pages is sound, the conclusion follows at once that the messianic secret and the essential meaning of realized eschatology are one and the same and can be expressed in a single sentence: the Ministry of Jesus *is* the kingdom and the power and the glory for ever and ever.

The Order of Events in St. Mark's Gospel— an examination of Dr. Dodd's Hypothesis

by

D. E. NINEHAM

IN the *Expository Times* for June 1932 Professor C. H. Dodd published an article entitled 'The Framework of the Gospel Narrative'.* The purpose of the following essay is to examine in detail the argument of that article; if this should appear a rather narrowly conceived subject for an essay such as this, the defence must be the great intrinsic importance of Professor Dodd's article and also the wide influence it has exerted since its publication.

The central subject of the article is the question on what principle St. Mark arranged the order of events in his Gospel. That the question is a live and important one does not need emphasizing; scholars have concerned themselves for several generations with it, and even now fresh answers to it are still being propounded. But in the last twenty years or so one particular answer, or type of answer, has been winning increasing acceptance, at any rate among English students of the New Testament. This answer is what might be called a modified 'form-critical' answer. It stands within the 'form-critical' tradition inasmuch as it accepts the thesis that the Gospels can fairly be analysed into separate sections, or *pericopae*, which originally circulated independently of one another before their incorporation into the Gospels. But it is a modification of the earlier 'form-critical' view in so far as it rejects the opinion of such scholars as Karl Ludwig Schmidt, Rudolf Bultmann and Martin Dibelius that the order in which the evangelist arranged these isolated *pericopae* was dictated solely by topical and theological considerations. This view holds rather that, along with the independent *pericopae*, the Church preserved

---

* It has now been republished together with a number of Professor Dodd's other essays in a book entitled; *New Testament Studies* (Manchester University Press).

an outline account of the Lord's ministry and that this provided the evangelist with a historical framework into which he could fit the independent *pericopae* he found at his disposal.

It would appear that this view owes its origin to Professor Dodd, and in particular to the article in the *Expository Times* referred to above. Many subsequent writers who propound a view of this kind refer explicitly to the article,* and others, though they make no explicit reference to it, seem also to be indebted to its argument.† Since 1932 Professor Dodd has himself restated and extended the scope of the general argument in his two books, *The Apostolic Preaching and Its Development* and *History and the Gospel*, but on the particular point in question it does not appear that his treatment has anywhere been so full as it was in the article in the *Expository Times*, and indeed in his *Apostolic Preaching and Its Development* he himself refers his readers back to the article for a fuller treatment of the subject.‡

In his book *A Study in St. Mark*, Dr. Farrer has subjected the whole position to hostile criticism from the point of view of his own argument. The aim of this essay is much more modest; it does not seek to advance any alternative hypothesis in the light of which Professor Dodd's view can be criticized, but simply to examine the argument as he presents it to see if it can be accepted as it stands and if it will bear the great weight of reliance that subsequent writers have placed upon it.

I

To begin with, it may be well to point out that Professor Dodd's conclusions, as he himself formulates them, are both more tentative and less far-reaching than those advanced by some more recent writers who champion a view similar to his. In particular he does not, like Professor Vincent Taylor, for example, argue to the substantial historical accuracy of St. Mark's order on the grounds that St. Peter and other eye-witnesses survived the Lord's death and must have remembered and spread abroad in the early church the knowledge of the exact order in which the events in fact occurred. Of this widely used argument there is no hint in

* For example, Professor Vincent Taylor in his book, *The Formation of the Gospel Tradition*, Dr. A. S. Duncan in his book, *Jesus, Son of Man*, and Professor A. M. Hunter in his book, *The Words and Work of Jesus*.

† Here, of course, it is not possible to speak so confidently, but examples would appear to be: Professor E. F. Scott, in *The Validity of the Gospel Record*, Professor Harvie Branscombe, *St. Mark* (Moffatt commentaries) and perhaps Professor D. M. Baillie his book, *God was in Christ*.

‡ P. 104, n. 1.

the article;* Professor Dodd's own conclusions, as he himself expounds them in the last paragraph of his paper, are modest enough in their scope. He thinks of the evangelist as having had at his disposal:

(*a*) A skeleton outline of the Lord's earthly career. This was in some detail—longer and more detailed, for example, than the account of the Lord's ministry given in Acts 10^{37-41}, but still no more than a skeleton outline.

(*b*) A considerable quantity of *pericopae* relating to the Lord's ministry, some in isolation, others gathered into larger or smaller groups, usually according to similarity of subject matter, but none of them explicitly related to any particular place in the skeleton outline.

The task of the evangelist, on this view, was confined to fitting these *pericopae*, or groups of *pericopae*, into their proper place in the outline as best he could. The procedure he adopted for this purpose resulted, to use Professor Dodd's own words, in 'a compromise between a chronological and a topical order'. That is, where a *pericope* contained some indication of time or place which seemed to rivet it to a particular point in the outline, St. Mark put it there. For example, a *pericope* which implied the use of a boat must belong to the point, or at any rate *some* point, in the outline where Our Lord was at the seaside, and so on. Where *pericopae* were already grouped on a topical basis the evangelist did not normally break up the grouping, but fitted the first *pericope* of the group into the skeleton outline by the method just described and allowed the remaining *pericopae* of the group to follow it in accordance with the topical principle on which they were already grouped. Where a *pericope*, or group of *pericopae*, contained no direct internal evidence as to where it should go in the outline, St. Mark found a place for it as best he could, being sometimes guided by topical considerations and sometimes by a sense of the chronological stage to which a particular episode seemed most naturally to belong.

Before going further it may be well to ask what exactly has been shown about St. Mark's order, if these conclusions are sound. If they are correct, St. Mark's order is, as Professor Dodd himself says, 'in large measure the result of the evangelist's own work rather than directly traditional', and 'we shall not', therefore, 'place in it the implicit confidence it once enjoyed'. But he also says that St. Mark did not do his work 'arbitrarily or irresponsibly, but under such guidance as he could find in tradition', and

---

* It would be interesting to know why Professor Dodd felt precluded from using it.

'thus we need not be as scornful of the Marcan order as has recently become the fashion'. By 'placing confidence' in Mark's order and 'being scornful' of it, is presumably meant believing or not believing that Mark's order faithfully reflects the order in which the events he describes did, as a matter of historical fact, occur. Assuming that that is what is meant we shall proceed to examine how far Professor Dodd's arguments bear out his conclusion.

In the first place, the suggested outline, however accurate it may have been, must, in the nature of the case, have been very brief; it cannot have contained more than a minute fraction of all the things that the Lord must have said and done, even if we assume a ministry of only one year's duration. This is important, for it means, to take only one example, that the Lord may well have paid visits to the seaside on ten or twenty occasions not mentioned in the outline; and if, therefore, the evangelist dated a given *pericope* to a particular point in the outline simply on the basis of a reference in it to the sea or shipping, he may very well have put it in the wrong place, even perhaps at the wrong end of the ministry.

The next point we must notice is that very few *pericopae* contain internal evidence exact enough to tie them firmly to one particular place in the outline; more often it must have been, as Professor Dodd himself hints, a matter of 'suitability', that is, of where a particular *pericope* would fit into the outline most 'suitably'. But 'suitability' is a highly subjective category. For instance, Professor Dodd suggests that the first conflict story (2^{1-12}) was placed where it is because that seemed to the evangelist the most 'suitable' position for it in the outline. We may agree that it does fit very suitably in that position, but many people might feel that it would fit equally suitably, or even more suitably, elsewhere. What in fact this line of argument suggests is not that St. Mark *knew* where the various events fitted into the outline, but that he fitted them in where he thought, on grounds of general probability, they were most likely to have occurred; and that is a very different thing. At the best this will have been inspired guesswork on the evangelist's part, and, unless we take the word 'inspired' in that phrase very seriously, we may be tempted to feel that our guess is sometimes as good as, or even better than, St. Mark's.

Thirdly, we have to remind ourselves that, on Professor Dodd's own submission, a good half of St. Mark's account of the ministry consists of *pericopae* which had been grouped together on a topical basis before ever they reached the evangelist, and have been left by him in the order in which he found them. In these cases, we may presume, St. Mark cannot be held to guarantee any historical basis for the grouping. This last presumption, however, cannot be allowed to pass without further discussion, in view of an argument advanced earlier in Professor Dodd's paper. It runs as follows: the fact that a group of incidents as related in the gospel is dominated by a common *motif* does not by itself prove that these incidents have been artificially or arbitrarily put together; they may have occurred together in historical fact. The point is developed with special reference to two groups of *pericopae*, those in Mk. 8^{27}–10^{45}, which are dominated by the thought of the approaching Passion, and those in 3^7–6^{13} which, according at least to Karl Ludwig Schmidt, are dominated by the idea of the hardening of Israel's heart. About the first group, that concerned with the Passion, Professor Dodd writes as follows: 'Was there, or was there not, a point in the life of Jesus at which he summoned his followers to accompany him to Jerusalem with the prospect of suffering and death? Is it or is it not likely that, from that point on, his thought and his speech dwelt with especial emphasis upon the theme of this approaching Passion? Surely it is on every account likely. Thus, if one particular section of the gospel is dominated by that theme, it is not because Mark has arbitrarily assembled from all quarters isolated *pericopae* referring to the approaching Passion, but because these *pericopae* originally and intrinsically belong to this particular phase of the ministry'. Similarly with the other group, that concerned with the hardening of hearts, Professor Dodd takes as his starting-point the well-attested saying in Matt. 11^{21} (cf. Lk. 10^{13}) 'Woe unto thee Chorazin! Woe unto thee Bethsaida! for if the mighty works had been done in Tyre and Sidon which were done in you, they would have repented long ago in sackcloth and ashes'. This, he says, strongly suggests some particular incident as the occasion of its utterance and looks back to a period of unfruitful work in Galilee, now regarded as closed. What more natural, then, than that in this period and mood the Lord should have uttered a number of sayings about the hardening of men's hearts?

As a corrective to exaggerated scepticism about the general picture of the Lord presented in the gospels, the value of this contention may be conceded at once; but if it is used as an argument to support the historical accuracy of the order of events in St. Mark's gospel, it seems to have serious weaknesses and limitations. They may be briefly set out as follows.

What the argument shows is that we know of two occasions in the life of the Lord which might well have given rise to such sayings and incidents as those described respectively in these two groups of *pericopae*; and therefore the attribution of those *pericopae* to those occasions is, from the historian's point of view, entirely plausible. But it must be emphasized again: it is one thing to claim that an account of the past is historically plausible and quite another to know it to be historically accurate. As far as the present case is concerned, must there not certainly in the course of the ministry— even if it lasted only for one year—have been numerous other occasions such as will also have given rise to sayings about the approaching passion and about the hardening of men's hearts? And may not sayings which were originally uttered on some of these occasions have been grouped together by the evangelist and attributed *en bloc* to the two occasions under discussion because he elected to treat these two as typical, and either could not, or did not care to, tell us about any of the others? Given the known habits of ancient writers, such a procedure seems highly probable; by ancient standards it would certainly not have seemed 'arbitrary' or 'irresponsible'. Indeed, if Professor Dodd's account of the matter were right, would it not be very odd that so much of what the Lord said on *these two* occasions about his coming passion and the hardening of hearts should have been preserved, while almost everything he said about these subjects on *other* occasions should have been lost?

It may seem then that the hypothesis of a traditional skeleton outline of the Lord's career preserved by the early Church will do even less to guarantee the historical accuracy of St. Mark's order than Professor Dodd's very modest claims might suggest. We must now pass to an examination of the hypothesis itself.

II

Professor Dodd recognizes right at the beginning of his article that many scholars before him had rejected the idea of such an outline on the ground of its 'intrinsic improbability'. His reply to this is to point to evidence that, however 'intrinsically improbable' it may seem to us now, such an outline did in fact exist. He points first to two passages in Acts, 10^{37-41}, part of St. Peter's speech to Cornelius, and 13^{23-31}, part of St. Paul's speech in the synagogue at Pisidian Antioch. He then shows that these passages, and especially the former, give, in brief compass, an account of the Lord's earthly career which tallies more or less exactly with the account underlying St. Mark's gospel.* But does not this line of argument prove either too little or too much? On the one hand, if the speeches in the early part of Acts reflect genuine historical reminiscence of what was said by the Apostles, then they can afford no evidence for the existence of a formal outline account of the ministry; for it can hardly be supposed that the original Apostles were dependent on any such traditional outline; they had their own memories. If, on the other hand (and this seems more probable to many scholars), these speeches were produced by the author of Acts as a general summary of the sort of thing *likely* to have been said, after the Thucydidean model, then the outline of the ministry contained in them can have no independent evidential value; for it may have been derived by St. Luke from St. Mark's gospel, which we know him to have had before him. And this point is not affected if it be conceded that St. Luke used sources in the compilation of these speeches, for it still remains true that, *in the form in which we have them*, these speeches have passed through the medium of St. Luke's mind, and St. Luke intended Acts to be read as a complement to the gospel he had just finished writing. To put the matter on the lowest plane: is it likely that St. Luke, having just completed a detailed account of the Lord's ministry in the gospel, would then, in his second volume, ascribe to the original Apostles accounts of that ministry inconsistent with the one he had just given? Whatever sources he may have possessed, this does not seem a very plausible suggestion.

We may conclude then that, whatever be the origin and status of the early speeches in Acts, they afford no clear evidence for the currency in the early Church of a formal outline account of the progress of the Lord's earthly ministry. And we may add that, even if the two passages quoted from Acts could be taken as providing such evidence, they are so slight in content that they could afford only the most limited support to the historicity of Mark's order. It is true that, so far as they go, they are in agreement with St. Mark's, or rather, significantly, with St. Luke's account of the ministry, but even if their evidence is combined, it refers only to the lineage and baptism of Our Lord, and in general to a healing ministry in Galilee and a journey to Jerusalem; so that by far the greater part of St. Mark's detailed account is unaffected by this agreement.

Two further passages from the New Testament are adduced

---

* This argument Professor Dodd subsequently stated in much greater detail, notably in *The Apostolic Preaching and its Development*.

as evidence for the currency of a traditional outline, namely I Cor. 11$^{23-25}$, St. Paul's account of the institution of the Eucharist, and I Cor. 15$^{3-7}$, his account of the crucifixion, resurrection, and post-resurrection appearances. It is true that in both cases St. Paul seems to ascribe his account to Church tradition,* but it must be pointed out that both these passages refer to events included in what is generally called the 'Passion Narrative'.† For it is generally agreed by students of the New Testament that, in respect of the matter under discussion, the *pericopae* which form the Passion Narrative stand on a different footing from the narratives recounted earlier in the gospel. There is general agreement that, for obvious reasons which have often been stated, the Church early drew up an agreed, and more or less fixed, account of the events from the plotting of the chief priests and scribes to the resurrection of the Lord. The question at issue is precisely whether there was any such agreement about the events *preceding* the Passion Narrative, and to the settlement of that issue it will conduce nothing to cite examples taken from the Passion Narrative itself. These two passages cited from I Cor. are not, therefore, relevant to the issue under discussion, and cannot be quoted as evidence for the existence in the early Church of a skeleton outline of the Lord's ministry.

None of the evidence so far cited by Professor Dodd can be held to have weakened the contention that the existence of such an outline is 'intrinsically improbable'.

For the sake of completeness it may be well to emphasize just how strong this argument from intrinsic improbability in fact is. If the form-critics have shown anything, they have shown the essential importance of the factor they call *Sitz-im-Leben* in the preservation of the material included in our gospels; that is to say, no such material is likely to have survived for long unless it was relevant to *something* in the life, worship, beliefs and interests of the earliest communities. The question then is: what *Sitz-im-Leben* can plausibly be posited to account for the preservation of a skeleton outline of Our Lord's ministry which, on Professor Dodd's own admission, contained nothing of any hortatory or edificatory value? For it should be noted that the suggested outline was simply a bare chronicle of Our Lord's movements and activities, containing no material sufficiently detailed to be of any religious or practical value. Its only value could have lain in the satisfaction of historical curiosity, and all our evidence seems to suggest

---

* Though this is, of course, notoriously uncertain in the case of I Cor. 11^{23}.
† That is, in the case of Mark's gospel 14^1 to end.

that historical curiosity, as such, was something in which the early Church was conspicuously lacking.

The point may be put in the form of a question. What sort of people can be envisaged as having drawn up, memorized and preserved the suggested outline and in what circumstances and for what purpose are they conceived as having done it? If it were a question of the individual *pericopae*, no one who has heard the reading of the Liturgical Gospel at the Holy Communion need have much difficulty in answering these questions; but with the suggested outline it is a much more difficult matter. It is certainly hard to accept the suggestion that 'the simplest of the simple-minded early Christians' will have kept this outline in their minds, ready to fit any stories they might hear about the Lord into their appropriate place in it. Apart from this, the only answer to these questions suggested by Professor Dodd is contained in the following words: 'The outline which we have recognized as existing in fragmentary form in the framework of Mark may well have belonged to a form of the primitive *kerygma*'. But if *kerygma* means the preaching, or proclamation, of salvation, it is hard to see why, at any rate on ancient presuppositions, such a skeleton outline of events should have formed part of it. If we are to judge from the way St. Matthew and St. Luke felt free to alter and interpolate St. Mark's order of events and the way the author of the Fourth Gospel treated the synoptic tradition, it does not appear that the precise order in which the saving events occurred seemed to the early Christian mind a very vital element in the saving proclamation or *kerygma*.

At this point it may be well to anticipate a possible objection. It may be asked: 'If it is generally agreed that the Church from a very early period preserved a memory of the order in which the events of the Passion Narrative occurred, why should it be thought unlikely that a little later it should have taken the trouble to discover and preserve the order of events of the earlier period of the ministry?'

In reply three things may be said. First, the Passion Narrative is, on any showing, different from the rest of the gospels. It deals with a small and readily compassable number of events, and claims to give a more or less exhaustive account of them. The order of events is largely determined by the logic of the matter, arrest before trial, trial before crucifixion, crucifixion before resurrection, and so on, and is in any case easily memorable when the events are so few. To the earlier ministry none of these considerations applies.

Secondly, the reason for holding this view of the Passion Narrative is that the four gospels here display a closeness of approximation not found in their accounts of the earlier ministry. Thus the very evidence which suggests that the Early Church did preserve an account of the order of the events of the Passion, suggests that it did not do so for the events of the preceding ministry.

Finally, the Passion Narrative does not really provide any parallels to the suggested outline. For what is claimed about the Passion Narrative is that the *pericopae* which make it up were themselves arranged in a fixed order; but the suggested skeleton outline is not a set of *pericopae* in a fixed order but a general historical outline of events with no *pericopae* attached to it, into which each man could fit such unattached *pericopae* as he could discover. Clearly the two cases are very different and no argument lies from the one to the other.

We seem driven, therefore, to agree with the scholars mentioned above that the existence of such an outline as Professor Dodd posits is intrinsically very improbable. What we know of the life and habits of the early Church strongly supports their contention and, as we have seen, the passages adduced by Professor Dodd hardly appear to weaken it. We must now go on to ask what positive evidence there is to set against that improbability.

III

Professor Dodd throws the earlier part of his paper into the form of a discussion of a book published in 1919 by Professor Karl Ludwig Schmidt and entitled *Der Rahmen der Geschichte Jesu* ('The Framework of the Story of Jesus'). This book was one of the pioneer works of what is called the Form Critical School and its* 'thesis is that the gospel according to Mark is compiled out of separate *pericopae*, each transmitted as an independent unit in the folk tradition of the Church. The arrangement of these *pericopae* is the work of the evangelist, who in arranging them has had little regard for chronology or topography, but groups them in the main according to the topics with which they deal, or the features of the ministry which they illustrate.

Apart from the arrangement, and the insertion of such insignificant connecting words as εὐθύς and πάλιν the work of the evangelist himself is to be recognized in the composition of short, generalizing summaries (*Sammelberichte*), which punctuate the narrative,

---

* The quotation is from Professor Dodd's own masterly résumé of the book.

help the transition from one *pericope* to another, and remind the reader that the particular incidents narrated in detail are episodes in a widely extended ministry. These summaries can be recognized by their contrast in manner and content to the traditional narrative units. They lack the concreteness and particularity of the *pericopae*. They relate nothing which belongs to one point of space and time to the exclusion of all other times and places.' Their verbs, we may note, are usually in the imperfect, the tense of continuous or habitual action. While the *pericopae* possess a high historical value, these *Sammelberichte* are mere 'framework' and not to be taken seriously as a contribution to our knowledge of the course of the ministry.

With the main outlines of this view, the reducibility of the gospel to short narrative units and the imposition of a framework upon these units, Professor Dodd professes himself in substantial agreement; 'Professor Schmidt', he says, 'seems to have made out his case'. It is not within the scope of this essay to discuss the general question whether he is right in accepting so much of the form-critical position; we turn at once to the points on which he diverges from Schmidt's account. He doubts first whether the order in which the *pericopae* are arranged is entirely arbitrary— the work of St. Mark—and he also declines to believe that the framework is nothing more than the artificial construction of the evangelist. He thinks that in arranging the *pericopae* Mark was controlled by the traditional skeleton outline and that the so-called *Sammelberichte* are, frequently at least, parts of that outline.

He opens his case by emphasizing Schmidt's own conclusion that several of the collections of *pericopae* in the gospel were grouped as we have them before they reached St. Mark. Examples quoted are the groups of *pericopae* which make up 1^{23-38}*, $4^{35}-5^{43}$† and 6^{34-53}‡. But no significant conclusion can be drawn from this until the further question has been settled on what principle these pre-Marcan groups of *pericopae* were collected together in the pre-Marcan stage. Professor Dodd does not explicitly raise this question, but a little later, when he is dealing with 2^1-3^6, which he regards as a pre-Marcan collection, he says that it was clearly put together on a topical basis. But if these pre-Marcan collections were themselves put together on a topical

* The Man with an Unclean Spirit, Simon's Wife's Mother, General Healing in the Evening and the Lord's Departure to a Desert Place. The third of these approximates to the character of a *Sammelbericht*.

† The Storm, the Gadarene Swine, Jairus's Daughter and the Woman with the Issue of Blood.

‡ The Feeding of the Multitude, the Voyage and the Landing (cf. also 8^{1-10}).

basis, they afford no evidence for the existence of any such *non-topical* basis of arrangement as the traditional outline. One contrary argument is indeed adduced on the basis of such verses as 7²⁴, 9³⁰, and 10¹ where a *pericope* begins with the words ἐκεῖθεν δὲ ἀναστάς or some similar phrase.* This, it is argued, implies the question πόθεν; and suggests a geographical and historical, rather than a topical, basis of connection. But if this line of argument is to have any cogency it must be assumed that these phrases had been an integral part of their *pericopae* from the beginning, and that must remain at best conjectural. Is it not more likely that St. Mark, or some pre-Marcan compiler, added these notes of place as part of a plan to present his collection of *pericopae* in the guise of a peripatetic ministry such as he knew the career of Jesus to have been? After all, if Mark was to present the Lord's ministry as having been exercised in a number of different centres at all, he was bound sometimes to insert between one *pericope* and the next some indication that Jesus left one place and went to another. What better phrases for the purpose than 'ἐκεῖθεν ἀναστάς' or 'κἀκεῖθεν ἐξελθόντες' or the like?

Professor Dodd's next main argument against Schmidt's position is very weighty and must be considered in detail, especially as it is repeated in a slightly different form later in the article. It comes in effect to this. If Schmidt is right in claiming that Mark's order is exclusively topical, then it should be comparatively easy for him to expose the precise topical basis on which Mark worked, and to show, in the case of every *pericope*, its topical relevance to the position assigned to it in the gospel. This, on his own admission, Schmidt can by no means always do; he is often forced to admit the apparent irrelevance of a *pericope* to the subject matter of the part of the gospel in which it occurs. To quote just one example, Schmidt places the *pericopae* in 8²⁷–10⁴⁵ under the topical rubric 'The Thought of the Approaching Passion', but he is then forced to admit that he cannot see the relevance to this subject of the *pericope* 10²⁻¹², the discussion of divorce. His own explanation of this awkward phenomenon is that sometimes when Mark found material joined together in his sources he did not bother to disjoin it in the interests of complete topical consistency. Thus, finding the *pericope* on divorce joined in some source to other *pericopae* concerned with the forthcoming Passion, he put it, *with them*, into the section of his gospel to which they, but not it, were relevant. To this Professor Dodd replies: why was the *pericope* on divorce conjoined with the other *pericopae* in Mark's source? Was it not

---

* E.g., καὶ ἐκεῖθεν ἐξελθόντες, 9³⁰. κἀκεῖθεν ἀναστάς, 10¹.

because the compiler of the source knew that historically the two belonged together, and was it not for that reason that Mark respected the conjunction when he incorporated this material into his gospel? At least, it is argued, we have evidence here of non-topical grouping, and if not topical, then presumably historical.

On this argument two comments of quite different kinds may be offered. First, it must not too readily be assumed that because two *pericopae* seem to have no topical connection as we have them in St. Mark, their juxtaposition in Mark's source was due to purely historical considerations. It is always possible that in their context in the source some topical connection was apparent between them,* or even that the source used by Mark at this point was simply a collection of disconnected sayings units. And if then it be asked why Mark did not disjoin them and fit each one into a topically suitable context, it may well be replied that such complete topical consistency did not seem to him of sufficient importance to merit all the labour involved† or even that he had no other context in the gospel which seemed to him to be appreciably more suitable for the *pericope* in question. He might, for example, have felt inclined to leave the divorce *pericope* with its surrounding material because there was no other point in the gospel where a discussion of divorce was self-evidently in place.

The second comment is of a completely different kind. Professor Dodd's argument at this point is correlative to the particular account of the matter offered by Schmidt. That is to say, the argument rests on the failure of one particular scholar to furnish an exhaustive explanation of St. Mark's order on a purely topical basis. But Schmidt was a pioneer in this attempt; since 1919 other scholars have attempted to improve on his appraisal of Mark's order, and perhaps some of them have succeeded. They may have shown that the lack of topical consistency lay not in Mark's order, but in Schmidt's *incomplete understanding* of that order. It may be that, in the light of a further understanding of Mark's mind and purpose, *pericopae* which seemed to Schmidt and Professor Dodd irrelevant to their context can be seen in fact to be

---

* This point may be clearer if set out as follows: Let a, b, c, d, e, f, g, ... be a series of *pericopae* in St. Mark's gospel as we have it, and suppose that d seems topically irrelevant in its present position. Mark may have drawn it and c together from a source in which they appeared in company with a quite different set of *pericopae*, thus: u, v, w, c, d, x, y, z. In *that* context they may have had topical relevance to each other and to the surrounding *pericopae*. There is thus no evidence that the basis of conection in the source was historical rather than topical. It is not difficult to think of a context, for example, in which Mk. 10^{2-12} was grouped on a topical basis with 10^{13-16}, and possibly with 10^{17} ff. as well.

† Parallels could be quoted from ancient authors.

highly relevant to it.* And even if as yet no attempt to explain Mark's order on a purely topical basis has proved wholly success- ful, it is always in principle possible that one may, and so Pro- fessor Dodd's argument, from incompleteness of topical connection to the probability of historical connection, remains, in the last resort, as inconclusive as *ad hominem* arguments must always be. To some it may seem absurd to suggest that St. Mark's gospel is based on a single topical arrangement which has yet succeeded in eluding readers for nearly 2,000 years. To deal fully with that objection would take us far afield; here let it be said that critical scholarship has so far taken little account of typological and liturgical and other theological factors which were undoubtedly very important in the production of the gospels, and also, in general, that the more fully we realize the complexities and the richness of the minds of the Biblical writers, the more ready we shall be to believe that no one as yet has plumbed the full depths of this particular writer's mind, purpose and order.

There is one further line of argument in Professor Dodd's article. For the purposes of this the *Sammelberichte* or 'connecting summaries' which Schmidt believes to be the creations of the evangelist, are isolated from the rest of the text. Professor Dodd then writes them out as a continuous narrative, omitting the detailed *pericopae* which separate them in the gospel. He then comments: 'The striking thing here is the way in which the sum- maries fall naturally into something very like a continuous narrative. We have in fact obtained merely by putting them together, a perspicuous outline of the Galilean ministry, forming a frame into which the separate pictures are set. So continuous a structure scarcely arose out of casual links supplied here and there where the narrative seemed to demand it.' We must first com- ment on the last sentence of this quotation; for it is far from clear how the conclusion it states follows from the preceding statements. If St. Mark sought, as we know he did, to represent the Lord's career as a peripatetic ministry exercised in Galilee and its environs, and culminating in a journey to Jerusalem, then, surely, on any reckoning, if we put together all his statements about the Lord's movements, we shall be bound to get a continuous narra- tive which conveys that impression. But this seems to be a truism;

---

* As it happens, Professor Lightfoot himself provides a good example of the sort of thing envisaged in connection with the very *pericope* we have been discussing (Mk. 10^{2-12} on divorce). In his book, *The Gospel Message of St. Mark* he suggests reasons why Mark may deliberately have put this *pericope* in its present position *out of purely topical considerations* (p. 114 text and note).

it surely cannot prove anything either for or against the historicity of the impression Mark sought to convey.

But the argument is developed further by Professor Dodd. Having isolated the *Sammelberichte* and set them down one after another, he goes on to analyse the outline thus arrived at into three stages:

A. Synagogue preaching and exorcism in Capernaum and elsewhere.

B. Teaching, healing and exorcism by the seashore.

C. Retirement in the hill-country with a small circle of disciples, who are sent on preaching and healing tours.

He then has no difficulty in showing that, if this is the framework into which Mark sought to fit his material, he has done it very badly. For example, although stage A is entitled: 'Synagogue preaching and exorcism', at least a third of the Marcan material which deals with synagogue episodes falls outside it; and likewise with stage B. The question therefore arises: if Mark had constructed his framework on a purely topical basis would he not have taken care to devise one into which all his material would have fitted neatly without remainder?

Whatever exactly the implications of this argument may be, they seem to be very damaging to the hypothesis of a traditional outline account of the ministry based on historical reminiscence. Professor Dodd's contention is that Mark had such an historical outline and that he tried conscientiously to fit all his detailed material into it at the appropriate place. The first stage indicated by this outline was a period of activity centred on the synagogue at Capernaum and other synagogues. Yet Mark has, on Professor Dodd's showing, deliberately refrained from inserting no less than one-third of his synagogue *pericopae* into their proper place in the outline; and the same sort of thing has happened with the second stage in the supposed outline—the period of activity by the seashore. But if so, can Mark really have taken this outline as seriously as Professor Dodd suggests? Can he, as Professor Dodd would have us believe, have regarded it as the controlling factor in the arrangement of his material? Can he in fact have had any such historical outline at all?

In conclusion it may be well to do two things. First to emphasize again the very strict limits of the scope of this essay. The aim has been simply to examine the validity of Professor Dodd's argument.

Accordingly, even if the arguments advanced in this essay should find any acceptance, they could do no more than throw doubt on the validity of Professor Dodd's argument. They cannot possibly *disprove* that Mark's order was historical, for there may be arguments quite different from Professor Dodd's for believing that it was. They cannot even disprove that Mark had a skeleton historical outline of the Lord's ministry if fresh reasons can be advanced for believing that he had.

And then it may be well to anticipate the possible objection that the whole discussion is 'much ado about nothing' by pointing to some of the reasons for thinking the subject of considerable theological importance. Professor Dodd himself emphasizes the importance of the subject at the beginning of his article and he hints at the grounds of this importance when he says that many modern 'Lives' of Jesus are based on the assumption that Mark's order preserves—or can be made to yield—an historically and chronologically accurate summary of the days of the Lord's flesh. The point may be considerably extended—not only are certain modern 'Lives' of Jesus based on this assumption; any possible life of Jesus *must* be based upon it, if, by a 'Life', we mean a biographical study which seeks, as it were, to penetrate inside the *psyche* of the subject and to trace his inner and outer development. Such a study can be written only if the writer has exact information about the order in which the various episodes in the subject's career occurred and a sufficiently detailed knowledge of them to be able to show for what reasons he felt and acted and developed as he did. Our subject therefore is closely linked with the question of the possibility of producing a 'Life' of Jesus in the biographical sense.

In many theological circles nowadays it is a commonplace that the gospels are not biographies, but it may be doubted whether even now the implications of that statement are fully appreciated and faced. To be sure it is no longer fashionable to regard Christianity as consisting *primarily* in a relation of reverence and imitation to the earthly Jesus. But many who would firmly reject any such view seem often to handle the gospels in their meditating, writing and preaching as if the order of events at least could be regarded as accurate in the modern historical and biographical sense. It is of practical importance, therefore, to discover whether or not this assumption is well founded and, if it is not, to address ourselves to the further questions: what considerations did control Mark in the ordering of his material and what sort of conclusions were meant to be drawn in detail from the way in which he has arranged it?

If the gospels are not biographies and not to be regarded or approached as such, then what are the assumptions with which to approach them in seeking to define the life of the believer and his relationship to his Lord? These are clearly questions of vital importance, but their very asking presupposes an answer to the question discussed in this essay.

The Doctrine of the Divine Fatherhood in the Gospels

by

H. F. D. SPARKS

I

NEARLY all Englishmen to-day are prepared to pay at least lip-service to Democracy as a political ideal, to the advancement of understanding and co-operation between the nations, and to the improvement of social conditions at home. But, being Englishmen, few are prepared to justify their position intellectually. In so far, however, as they are so prepared, any justification is likely to be based on a firmly-held, if ill-defined, sense that mankind is somehow a unity; and in many cases this sense is coupled with an equally firmly-held idea that caring for other people is 'real Christianity', or, maybe, 'the religion of Jesus', and therefore, in some vague way, good and desirable.

There are, of course, those who are not only able, but willing, to think more deeply. And they will be more specific. The Humanist, if challenged, will in all probability reply with an up-to-date version of the tag from Terence—that he himself is a human being and for this reason, and for this alone, he can regard nothing that concerns human welfare and progress as outside his concern and interests:* in other words, the Humanist takes his stand four-square on a Doctrine of the Brotherhood of Man and nothing else. But if the Theist is challenged he will reply 'As children of God men are members of one family, and life should be ordered as far as possible with a view to the promotion of brotherly fellowship among all men':† the Theist, that is, while accepting the Doctrine of the Brotherhood of Man, bases it firmly, just because he is a Theist, on a Doctrine of the Fatherhood of God, in whose image Man is made. And if the Theist is also a professing

---

* Ter., *Heaut.*, I, i, 25.
† W. Temple, *The Hope of a New World* (1940), p. 92.

Christian he will inevitably sooner or later go on to explain his own particular conception of how life should be ordered within the 'family' by reference to the gospels; for in the gospels, he will say, is to be found both the classical expression of the Christian point of view, and also the authority for it which derives from Jesus himself.

Clearly, then, there is not a little shared in common on this matter by the man-in-the-street, the Humanist, the Theist, and the professing Christian. Yet the distinction between them is apt to be blurred. And it is blurred not least by the circumstance that the professing Christian is so frequently ill-informed about what the gospel teaching actually is. Without realizing what he is doing, and with the best will in the world, he will accept and propagate, either a watered-down version of the gospel teaching, or even a complete travesty of it, as if they were genuine. And the result is only to make confusion worse confounded. The Christian, for his part, remains blissfully unconscious of the richness of his own heritage, and (what is more important) totally unaware of many of the obligations which his profession as a Christian entails; while the world at large, under the delusion that it has safely in its keeping the distilled essence of Christianity, unashamedly turns its back on the Church, convinced that the Church has outlived its usefulness.

To begin an academic essay with such a general preamble may be thought by some improper. If so, I make no apology. The purpose of the essay is indeed academic—namely, to examine the gospel teaching about the Fatherhood of God as a whole, and, in passing, to draw some conclusions about how much of it may legitimately be attributed to the Central Figure. But I have deliberately chosen to set what I have to say in a modern 'frame' because, on the one hand, I believe that for the reasons already given the subject is by its very nature of much more than purely academic importance; and because, on the other hand, of the further consideration that we are always, to a greater extent than we often realize, the children of our age, and consequently cannot escape, however much we may try, from seeing any problem in relation to our own contemporary situation and treating it in the light of our own contemporary assumptions. And nothing is to be gained by refusing to recognize, or by attempting to obscure, either of these facts.

In what follows, however, the non-academic and contemporary aspects of the subject will be kept to the minimum. We shall start with an examination of Mark—by almost universal consent the earliest gospel. Then will follow an examination of the evidence of the material found both in Matthew and Luke but not in Mark —i.e. what is commonly called 'Q'. From this we shall pass to Luke, from Luke to Matthew, and, finally, from Matthew to John. And then, in the concluding section, an attempt will be made to draw the threads together and to display the resultant picture 'framed'.

II

Mark

The first thing that must strike the student who has been brought up to believe that 'Father' is the most characteristic Christian epithet to apply to God, when he examines Mark, is the small number of passages that come up for consideration. There are in fact only five explicit references to God as Father in Mark* (two of which occur in the same context) † and one implicit (in the Parable of the Wicked Husbandman). ‡ And all of them are found in Words of Jesus.

The first and last two explicit references and the single implicit reference are best taken together. At 8^{38} Jesus says 'For whosoever shall be ashamed of me and my words in this adulterous and sinful generation, the Son of man also shall be ashamed of him when he cometh in the glory of his Father with the holy angels': here, clearly, God is spoken of as 'Father' in relation to His Messianic 'Son'—a conception which has a respectable Old Testament ancestry.§ Similarly, at 13^{32}, when asked 'When shall these things be?', Jesus replies 'Of that day or that hour knoweth no one, not even the angels in heaven, neither the Son, but the Father'. At 14^{36} Jesus, himself the Messianic Son, addresses God directly as 'Abba, Father'. And in the Parable of the Wicked Husbandmen, although the word 'Father' does not actually appear, there can be no doubt that the 'lord of the vineyard' is to be understood as God, and the 'beloved son', whom he sent, as a thinly veiled allusion to Jesus as 'Son of God'. In all these passages, therefore, the aspect of the Divine Fatherhood presented is severely, indeed exclusively, Messianic.

But it is otherwise with the passage $11^{25, 26}$, in which the two remaining references in Mark to God as Father are found. The sight of the withered fig-tree—cursed the day before—has pro-

---

* Mk. 8^{38}, $11^{25, 26}$, 13^{32}, 14^{36}.   † Mk. $11^{25, 26}$.   ‡ Mk. 12^{6}.
§ E.g. II Sam. 7^{14}; Ps. 2^{7}.

voked a comment from St. Peter. Jesus has replied with some words on the need for faith, and has told the Twelve that 'All things whatsoever ye pray and ask for, believe that ye have received them, and ye shall have them'. And then he adds immediately:

> 'And whensoever ye stand praying, forgive, if ye have aught against anyone; that your Father also which is in heaven may forgive you your trespasses. But if ye do not forgive, neither will your Father which is in heaven forgive your trespasses'.

Here, indubitably, the reference is to God as Father, not of the Messianic Son, but of the Twelve, since He is spoken of as 'your Father' and it is the Twelve who are being addressed.

However, the question must be faced whether we are entitled to regard either of these two verses as belonging to Mark at all.

So far as the second verse ('But if ye do not forgive . . . trespasses') is concerned there can hardly be any doubt about its not belonging. It is omitted by an impressive combination of important Greek uncials, Greek cursives, and versions. The Revised Version relegates it to the margin. And nearly all moderns are at one in thinking it an interpolation from Matt. 6¹⁵: thus, T. W. Manson, in his very full and searching analysis of the Synoptic evidence in the chapter on 'God as Father' in his *The Teaching of Jesus*, is content to state categorically 'Mk. 11²⁶ is rejected on textual grounds'* and pass on without further comment.

But Mk. 11²⁵ is more difficult. *Prima facie* the case for its genuineness is unassailable. No textual authorities omit it. Hence to doubt it might seem hypercritical. Yet on closer examination there are several points which converge to make it every bit as questionable as 11²⁶. These points may be summarized as follows:

1. Both verses obviously belong together. They are about the same subject—Forgiveness: they use the same phrases; and they both find their Matthaean parallels in adjacent verses of the Sermon on the Mount.† Consequently, if any suspicion is raised about the genuineness of one of them, that suspicion is bound in some measure to be communicated to the other.

2. A comparison of Mark with Matthew shows that the suspicion is well-founded. At Matt. 21²⁰⁻²⁷ the whole of the material in Mk. 11²⁰⁻³³ is reproduced verse by verse, with only minor alterations, except for the two verses Mk. 11²⁵, ²⁶. This suggests that both verses, and not one only, were lacking in St. Matthew's

---

* T. W. Manson, *The Teaching of Jesus* (2nd edit., 1935), p. 94.
† Matt. 6¹⁴, ¹⁵.

copy of Mark—i.e. it suggests that 11^{25}, no less than 11^{26}, is a later addition to the text of Mark.

3. This suggestion is confirmed by a consideration of the internal evidence of the section Mk. $11^{20-25}(^{26})$ itself. As remarked by a number of commentators the transition between verses 24 and 25 is decidedly abrupt.* The subject under discussion up to the end of verse 24 has been Faith. In verse 25, however, it is Forgiveness. The sequence of thought is thus broken. We are, in fact, left with the impression that the end of verse 24 is the natural end of the section, to which something else has been added as an afterthought.

4. Finally, the style of verse 25 is very definitely Matthaean and not Markan. 'Your Father which is in heaven' is, as we shall see, a favourite phrase of St. Matthew's,† but it never appears in Mark apart from this passage. The word used for 'trespasses' (παραπτώματα) is not found elsewhere in the gospels except in two passages in Matthew.‡ The expression 'to have aught against anyone' (ἔχειν τι κατά τινος) occurs again at Matt. 5^{23} and nowhere else.§ And the Jewish custom of 'standing' for prayer is mentioned otherwise only once by St. Luke (in the Parable of the Pharisee and the Publican)‖ and once by St. Matthew (in the strictures on the prayers of the 'hypocrites' in the Sermon on the Mount).¶

These points taken together lead to the conclusion that Mk. 11^{25} is no more part of the true text of Mark than is 11^{26}. Both verses, it seems, are spurious. But the fact that the latter has an exact parallel at Matt. 6^{15} while the former is no more than an echo of Matt. 6^{14}, coupled with the fact that there is textual evidence for the omission of the one while there is no textual evidence for the omission of the other, forbids us to think of a single interpolation made at one and the same time. We must think rather of a process in two stages. First, a scribe with the Sermon on the Mount running in his mind, and with 'prayer' as a stitch-word, added verse 25, concluding with words almost identical with Matt. 6^{14}: then later, another scribe, recognizing the allusion, rounded the section off with the verse which in Matthew immediately follows, either because it came naturally to him, or because he thought it essential in order to complete the sense.

If the above argument be sound, and if we are right in rejecting

---

* Thus, E. P. Gould, *A Critical and Exegetical Commentary on the Gospel according to St. Mark* (I.C.C., 1897), p. 216, stigmatizes verse 25 as 'inapposite and diverting'.

† See below, pp. 254, 255.   ‡ Matt. $6^{14, 15}$, 18^{35}(?).

§ Cf. also the similar Matthaean expression εἰπεῖν ῥῆμα (λόγον) κατά τινος at 5^{11} and 12^{32}.

‖ Lk. 18^{11}.   ¶ Matt. 6^5.

both these verses, two considerations follow which are of the utmost consequence to the present study. In the first place, the already small number of explicit Markan references to God as Father is reduced by two—from five to three; and in the second place, St. Mark's Doctrine of the Fatherhood of God appears as Messianic and nothing else. God, according to St. Mark, is Father of Jesus only; and He is Father of Jesus because Jesus is Messiah.

III

The material found both in Matthew and Luke but not in Mark

Without embarking on a lengthy discussion about how and in precisely what form this material came to St. Matthew and St. Luke, we may say that there are certainly five passages in it which must of necessity be considered (and one of them contains no less than five references to God as Father—the well-known Prayer of Thanksgiving at Matt. 11^{25-27} ‖ Lk. $10^{21, 22}$), while there are seven others which might well be.

We may start from the Prayer of Thanksgiving. According to St. Matthew after the departure of the Baptist's emissaries, according to St. Luke after the return of the Seventy, Jesus gave thanks as follows:

> 'I thank thee, O Father, lord of heaven and earth, that thou didst hide these things from the wise and understanding, and didst reveal them unto babes: yea, Father, for so it was well-pleasing in thy sight. All things have been delivered unto me of my Father: and no one knoweth the Son, save the Father; neither doth any know the Father, save the Son, and he to whomsoever the Son willeth to reveal him.'

The passage is here quoted in St. Matthew's version; but the differences between his version and St. Luke's are so slight as to make it immaterial which of the two is used. As at Mk. 14^{36} Jesus addresses God directly as 'Father': he then refers to Him as 'my Father'—presumably to the disciples who are in attendance*; and he goes on to draw attention to the intimate and unique relationship which exists between the Father and himself. This is, of course, consonant with what we have already discovered in Mark. It is no more than another, though more detailed, exposition of the

---

* Many manuscripts of Luke attempt to set this beyond doubt by inserting before the words 'All things have been delivered. . . .' the stage-direction 'And turning to his disciples he said'.

Messianic Father-Son relationship which we have seen to be characteristic of Mark. What is new, however, is the idea contained in the last clause, namely that it is possible, at the expressed desire and through the agency of the Messianic Son himself, for that intimate and unique relationship in which he stands to God to be extended so as to include certain selected human beings as well— i.e. that it is possible for those whom the Son chooses as the recipients of his revelation to know God even as he does, and hence to stand to God, through him, in the same relationship as he does himself.

In the light of this assertion the four other passages that must of necessity be considered fall naturally into place. All of them, it should be noted, are in Words of Jesus which are recorded by both evangelists as having been uttered, not to the crowds or to the Jewish authorities, but to 'disciples'. This is important because Jesus is, in consequence, represented as speaking, not to 'them that are without', but to the chosen few to whom is given 'the mystery of the kingdom'. They are accordingly enjoined to be 'perfect' (or 'merciful') as their Father is 'perfect' (or 'merciful'):* they are taught to address God in prayer directly as 'Father':† they are assured that He knows their needs;‡ and they are assured, too, that He will shower upon them from heaven the best of all possible gifts.§

The remaining seven passages which might well be considered in this section of the essay are those where one evangelist has 'Father', but the other, in the parallel, has something else. For example, St. Matthew writes 'that ye may be sons of your Father',‖ St. Luke 'and ye shall be sons of the Most High': ¶St. Matthew says of the birds 'your heavenly Father feedeth them',[a] but St. Luke 'God feedeth them';[b] and where St. Matthew refers to 'the Spirit of your Father'[c] St. Luke has 'the Holy Spirit'.[d] We can, of course, in theory argue for or against the originality of either version, or neither, in every instance. In practice, however, it would be unprofitable to do so. We need now only observe (1) that in each instance it is St. Matthew who has 'Father' against St. Luke and that St. Luke never has it against St. Matthew, and (2) that St. Matthew, as we shall see later, has a special interest in the

---

* Matt. 5^{48} ‖ Lk. 6^{36}.   † Matt. 6^9 ‖ Lk. 11^2.   ‡ Matt. 6^{32} ‖ Lk. 12^{30}.

§ Matt. 7^{11} ‖ Lk. 11^{13}. I assume here, not only that the Lukan version of the saying is the more original, but also that those manuscripts which omit the 'ὁ' before 'ἐξ οὐρανοῦ' preserve the true Lukan text. The saying will then run '. . . how much more shall your Father give from heaven. . . .' It is probable that the very awkward 'ὁ πατὴρ ὁ ἐξ οὐρανοῦ' of the Received Text in Luke is the result of partial assimiliation to Matthew's 'ὁ πατὴρ ὑμῶν ὁ ἐν τοῖς οὐρανοῖς'.

‖ Matt. 5^{45}.   ¶ Lk. 6^{35}.   [a] Matt. 6^{26}.   [b] Lk. 12^{24}.   [c] Matt. 10^{20}.

[d] Lk. 12^{12}: cf. also Matt. 7^{21} ‖ Lk. 6^{46}; Matt. 10^{29} ‖ Lk. 12^6; Matt. $10^{32, 33}$ ‖ Lk. $12^{8, 9}$; Matt. 18^{14} ‖ Lk. 15^7.

Divine Fatherhood. It is, therefore, more probable on general grounds that St. Matthew has added rather than that St. Luke has omitted.* But even so, if each one of these instances be counted as genuine—i.e. if the Matthaean version be preferred every time—there is no substantial gain for our present enquiry. The references to 'my Father' at Matt. 7²¹ and 10³², ³³, are plainly Messianic,† while all the other references to 'your Father' are in Words addressed to 'disciples'. This is exactly the situation as it was before—Jesus can call God his Father because he is himself the Messianic Son, and he can call God the Father of his disciples because to them, as Messianic Son, he has 'willed' to reveal Him.

IV

Luke

Of the Markan references to God as Father St. Luke reproduces two: the reference at Mk. 8³⁸ to the Son of Man coming 'in the glory of his Father' is reproduced without significant alteration at Lk. 9²⁶; and the address in prayer, 'Abba, Father', at Mk. 14³⁶ is reproduced at Lk. 22⁴², although the Aramaic 'Abba' is omitted—presumably because St. Luke thought it unsuitable for his readers.‡

That he does not reproduce Mk. 11²⁵, ²⁶ should occasion no surprise: in the first place, it is unlikely that he found either of these verses in his copy of Mark; § and further, he passes over entirely the incident of the Fig Tree, to which they have been attached. And similarly, the omission of Mk. 13³² is for our purposes without significance: it may be that St. Luke boggled at even seeming to attribute ignorance to the Son; yet it is to be observed that there is no exact parallel in Luke to what immediately follows in Mark either, ‖ so that it looks rather as if the omission of this particular verse is no more than part of St. Luke's rewriting of St. Mark's End-time Discourse as a whole. In any case, the fact that St. Luke has reproduced two of the Markan references makes it quite clear both that he accepted, and that he was prepared to re-

---

* This is not to suggest that St. Luke is in any of these instances necessarily 'more original' than St. Matthew. He may very well have altered independently what came to him, although in a different way from St. Matthew. Thus, I would see very evident traces of St. Luke's editorial hand in 'the Most High' at 6³⁵ and in 'the Holy Spirit' at 12¹². In such cases we have to face the fact that in all probability no 'original' is recoverable.

† The reading 'my Father' for 'your Father' at Matt. 18¹⁴ has very strong textual support and may well be right.

‡ Compare the similar omissions of *talitha cumi* from Mk. 5⁴¹ at Lk. 8⁵⁴ and of *Golgotha* from Mk. 15²² at Lk. 23³³.

§ For the reasons given above, pp. 244, 245.   ‖ i.e. Mk. 13³³⁻³⁷.

affirm, St. Mark's doctrine of God as the Messianic Father of Jesus the Messianic Son.

About his use of the material which he shared in common with St. Matthew there is little to add to what has been said already when we were dealing with the material itself. Obviously his inclusion, not only of the Prayer of Thanksgiving where Jesus addresses God as 'Father' and speaks of Him as 'my Father', but also of passages where Jesus teaches his disciples to address God as 'Father' and speaks of Him to them as 'your Father', shows that for St. Luke, as well as for his sources, the concept of the Messianic Fatherhood was capable of extension. Once again, he has accepted and re-affirmed on this point the doctrine which he found in the common material as it came to him.

We turn accordingly to the material peculiar to St. Luke in order to discover what, if any, aspect of the Divine Fatherhood appealed to him especially.

At 2^{49} the boy Jesus in the Temple replies to his parents' question with the words 'Wist ye not that I must be in my Father's house?'—a clear case of the use of Father in relation to Jesus as the Messianic Son. Later on, Jesus tells the 'apostles' at the Last Supper 'I appoint unto you a kingdom even as my Father appointed unto me'*—again the reference is Messianic. Twice on the Cross Jesus addresses God as 'Father' in prayer.† And then, in the Upper Room at Jerusalem after the Resurrection, he commissions the Eleven as his witnesses, and 'sends forth' upon them 'the promise of my Father'.‡

There can be no question that these references are all of a piece in representing God as the Father of Jesus. How far we should think of all, or any, of the passages in which they occur as derived by the evangelist from a written source or sources, or from oral tradition, it is impossible to say. Nor can we say with certainty what modifications he himself may have introduced into whatever sources or tradition he relied upon. What we can say, however, is that whatever his sources, and whatever modifications he may have introduced into them, he was certainly not averse from the Messianic aspect of God's Fatherhood.

To complete the picture, however, there is one further passage which should be mentioned.

It is Lk. 12^{32}. After the injunction 'Seek ye his kingdom and these things shall be added unto you' follows the saying 'Fear not, little flock; for it is your Father's good pleasure to give you the kingdom'. Many regard this saying as a verse of the material

* Lk. 22^{29}. † Lk. $23^{34, 46}$. ‡ Lk. 24^{49}.

shared in common by St. Matthew and St. Luke, which St. Matthew has omitted, but which St. Luke has retained.* Personally, I cannot accept this view. Rather does the verse seem to me to be a comment of St. Luke's own,† which, in reproducing his source, he has put into the mouth of Jesus in order to reassure his readers, many of whom, as he well knew, were seriously disturbed about the delay in the Second Coming. This delay was a standing problem in the early Church;‡ and we can see St. Luke attempting to deal with it in other ways elsewhere. § Here he simply warns his readers not to desist in their search for the Kingdom merely because its advent is delayed: there is no need to fear, he explains, because the Kingdom will come in 'your Father's' good time. And he moulds the language of the saying appropriately to fit the context.

If this explanation be rejected, and the verse be assigned to the common material, we are left in the position that all the references to God as Father in the material peculiar to St. Luke are Messianic. If, on the other hand, the explanation be accepted, and we think of St. Luke as having created the saying, then we must allow that, although he may have been concerned primarily to stress the Messianic aspect of the Divine Fatherhood in his gospel, he could nevertheless permit another aspect to peep out, as it were, in passing. For, as well as being the Father of the Messiah, Jesus, God was also the Father of the 'little flock' of faithful Christians who acknowledged that Messiahship. The former aspect, for St. Luke, might be the more important, but it was clearly not the only one there was.‖

---

* E.g., B. H. Streeter, *The Four Gospels* (1924), pp. 284, 291.

† Compare in this connection the 'ecclesiastical' use of the word ποίμνιον ('flock'), which occurs elsewhere in the New Testament only in St. Paul's speech to the Ephesian elders at Acts 20[28, 29] and at I Pet. 5[2, 3].

‡ E.g., II Thess. 2[1, 2]; II Pet. 3[3, 4].

§ E.g., Lk. 17[20, 21], 19[11].

‖ In the above discussion I have passed over altogether the Parable of the Lost Son (Lk. 15[11-32]) for the following two reasons:

1. It is generally agreed that in interpreting any of the longer Lukan parables it is impossible to press the details. The teaching of these parables is conveyed by presenting different types of character rather than by strict analogy. To argue, therefore, that the father in the Parable of the Lost Son 'stands for God' is to show oneself ignorant of the teaching method of the class of parable to which the Lost Son belongs.

2. In Luke the Lost Son forms the third parable in a triad, the other two being the Lost Sheep and the Lost Coin—compare especially the refrain in verses 6, 9 and 32. Consequently, if we are going to insist on an analogy between the human father of the parable and the Divine Father, and to maintain that the Lost Son must of necessity be taken into account in any treatment of the Doctrine of God as Father, we ought logically to insist on analogies in the other two cases also, and so involve ourselves in the absurdity of maintaining that the Lost Sheep must of necessity be taken into account in any treatment of the Doctrine of God as Shepherd and the Lost Coin in any treatment of the Doctrine of God as Housewife.

V

Matthew

Whereas Mark (in what would appear to be the true text) has only three references to God as Father, the material shared in common by St. Matthew and St. Luke nine, and Luke seventeen, Matthew has no less than forty-four references. Since Matthew is only about half as long again as Mark, and is not quite as long as Luke, these figures indicate that the author had a special interest in the Divine Fatherhood.

An examination of the actual references in terms of sources confirms this view.

The three Markan references are reproduced intact—at least, so far as the use of the word 'Father' is concerned.* Furthermore, on four other occasions when St. Matthew is reproducing Mark he either alters the wording, or else makes a deliberate addition, with the result that 'Father' appears in the Matthaean version where it does not in the Marcan. At Mk. 3³⁵ Jesus says 'Whoever shall do the will of God . . .': at Matt. 12⁵⁰ he says 'whosoever shall do the will of my Father . . .'. At Mk. 10⁴⁰ a place on the right or left hand of Jesus will only be given to those 'for whom it hath been prepared': at Matt. 20²³ it will be given to those 'for whom it hath been prepared of my Father'. At Mk. 14²⁵, in the Words of Institution, Jesus affirms 'I will no more drink of the fruit of the vine until I drink it new in the kingdom of God': at Matt. 26²⁹ 'the kingdom of God' has become 'my Father's kingdom'. And at Mk. 14³⁹, in the Garden, Jesus 'again went away and prayed, saying the same words': at Matt. 26⁴² the words are supplied— 'O my Father, if this cannot pass away . . .' In each of these instances St. Matthew has altered Mark in that he has altered St. Mark's *ipsissima verba*. But he has not altered his sense. For just as St. Mark's own three references to God as Father are all Messianic, so also are St. Matthew's four additions. In other words, in reproducing Mark, St. Matthew has underlined, but no more than underlined, what he found in his source.

And we reach the same conclusion from St. Matthew's treatment of the material which he shared in common with St. Luke. As we saw, there are indubitably nine references to God as Father

---

* Matt. 16²⁷, 24³⁶, 26³⁹. If 16²⁷ be compared with the Markan original it will be seen that, although St. Matthew has made considerable alterations in the wording of the passage as a whole, he has retained the essential word 'Father'. Similarly, at 26³⁹, although St. Mark's Aramaic '*Abba*' is omitted, as it also is in the parallel passage in Luke, 'Father' again remains.

in this material: five of them are references to God as Father of the Messianic Son (all in a single passage), and four are references to God as Father of the Christian disciple. St. Matthew has reproduced all these faithfully; and, if we are prepared to agree that in those cases where Matthew and Luke differ it is more probable on general grounds that St. Matthew has added 'Father' rather than that St. Luke has omitted it,* he will himself have been responsible for some eight more references. Three of these Matthaean additions are Messianic (two of them are in a single passage),† while the other five are references to 'your Father' and are all addressed to disciples.‡ As with his treatment of Mark, then, St. Matthew has underlined, but no more than underlined, what he found in the material as it came to him.

What the evangelist found in Mark and the common material, together with what he added to both of them, thus accounts for more than half of the references to the Divine Fatherhood in Matthew. The remaining twenty references occur in material peculiar to this gospel.

No less than ten of these are in the Sermon on the Mount—addressed, of course, to 'disciples'. The disciples are to 'let their light shine before men', so that men may recognize the true source of that light and come to 'glorify', not them, but their 'Father'.§ Again, they are urged when giving alms, or praying, or fasting, not to be misled by any ideas of impressing their neighbours: their 'Father which seeth in secret' knows well what they are doing and will duly recompense them. ‖ And if they desire forgiveness from God, they, in their turn, must forgive their fellow-men, for 'if ye forgive not men their trespasses, neither will your Father forgive your trespasses'.¶

It will be appreciated that all these Sermon on the Mount references are references to God as Father of the Christian disciple. There are two references of this kind outside the Sermon: at 13⁴³ Jesus, at the end of the explanation of the Parable of the Tares, says 'Then shall the righteous shine forth as the sun in the kingdom of their Father'; and at 23⁹ he utters the warning, 'Call no man your father on earth; for one is your Father, which is in heaven'.

The first of these calls for no special comment. The saying is said to have been uttered in the presence of disciples when Jesus

---

* See above, p. 248.
† Matt. 7²¹, 10³², ³³. To these two must be added 18¹⁴ if we read 'my Father' for the more usual 'your Father'.
‡ Matt. 5⁴⁵, 6²⁶, 10²⁰, ²⁹, 18¹⁴.   § Matt. 5¹⁶.
‖ Matt. 6¹, ⁴, ⁶ *bis*, ⁸, ¹⁸ *bis*.   ¶ Matt. 6¹⁴, ¹⁵.

had 'left the multitudes' and had gone 'into the house': in any case, God is said to be the Father of the 'righteous', who are manifestly not all and sundry.

But the second is more interesting. It is said to have been uttered 'to the multitudes and to his disciples'. It is, therefore, the only example we have met so far of God being spoken of by Jesus as 'your Father' to anyone else but disciples. Superficially the mention of 'multitudes' might be set down as the exception which proves the rule. However, a closer inspection raises a doubt whether it really is an exception. Whatever we may say about 'the multitudes', it still remains true that the discourse of which the saying forms a part is addressed to 'his disciples' as well. And it further seems as if 'disciples' were what the evangelist had particularly in mind when he pictured the scene to himself.

The Markan framework, into which he has fitted this block of his peculiar material, represents Jesus as 'teaching in the temple'* and speaks of 'the great multitude hearing him gladly'.† St. Mark then continues 'And in his teaching he said, Beware of the scribes . . .'.‡ If the sequence here be pressed, the warning 'Beware of the scribes . . .' is addressed to 'the great multitude'. But St. Mark does not explicitly say so; and it is questionable whether the sequence ought to be pressed. St. Matthew, however, seems to have accepted the implication in what he had before him, and in consequence represents the entire discourse as addressed to 'the multitudes'. Yet he significantly adds 'and to his disciples'— because, of course, he instinctively realized that 'disciples' were a much more appropriate audience.§ If left to himself to reproduce his peculiar material here apart from Mark, he would doubtless have represented it as addressed to 'disciples' only. But as it was, he decided to fit it into the framework of Mark. From Mark he derived the idea of 'multitudes', and then conflated it with his own picture of 'disciples' to form the doublet in the text. The mention of 'multitudes' alongside 'disciples' at Matt. 23¹ is thus no more than an editorial accident. It is certainly interesting, but hardly important.

The other eight references in St. Matthew's peculiar material which yet remain to be considered are all Messianic. Seven times in discourse, from chapter 15 onwards, Jesus refers to 'my

---

* Mk. 12³⁵.   † Mk. 12³⁷.   ‡ Mk. 12³⁸.

§ It is worth noticing that St. Luke apparently felt the same too, since, although he inserts no additional matter into Mark at this point, as does St. Matthew, he nevertheless rewrites St. Mark's 'And the great multitude heard him gladly. And in his teaching he said . . .' as 'And in the hearing of all the people he said unto his disciples . . .'—Lk. 20⁴⁵.

Father';* and then in the Baptismal Formula at the end of the gospel he instructed his followers to baptize 'into the name of the Father and of the Son and of the Holy Ghost'.† Nothing fresh emerges here. We merely note that the Messianic aspect of the Divine Fatherhood is in no way lacking in the peculiar material.

But the question arises—In discussing the references to God as Father in this material, how far is its present form to be trusted? If St. Matthew has interpolated additional references to God as Father into Mark and also into the material which he shared in common with St. Luke, is he not likely to have treated his peculiar material in the same way, and to have interpolated additional references there as well?

For obvious reasons no direct answer can be given to this question. All we can say is that St. Matthew's treatment of his other sources suggests forcibly that the Divine Fatherhood was something that meant to him personally a very great deal. It is probable, therefore, by analogy, that in editing his peculiar material he was influenced by his interest in the Fatherhood to the same extent as he was in editing the other sources—i.e. if his peculiar material had been preserved as it came to him, we should probably find that to the references to God as Father already there he had added several more. Yet, also by analogy, it is probable that these additions would be of no special significance. In our examination of his additions to Mark and the common material we saw that he had underlined, but no more than underlined, what was there previously. There is no reason to think that the result would be otherwise if we were able to examine in detail his treatment of his peculiar material—i.e. we should probably find that the peculiar material, as it came to St. Matthew, contained a number of references to God as Father, both as Father of the Messianic Son and as Father of the Christian believer, although, no doubt, in less profusion than might now appear.

Before we leave Matthew there is one final point which demands attention, namely, the phrase 'which is in heaven', or 'heavenly', which is so often attached to 'Father' in this gospel. Altogether it is found in one form or the other no less than twenty times. An analysis of the instances, however, sheds no light either on the problem of its immediate origin, or on any possible special significance it may have had for the evangelist. The phrase is, of course, characteristically Rabbinic.‡ It is found in no other gospel except Matthew. But in Matthew it is found scattered in either

---

* Matt. 15^{13}, 16^{17}, $18^{10, 19, 35}$, 25^{34}, 26^{53}.　　　　　　　† Matt. 28^{19}.
‡ See G. F. Moore, *Judaism* (1932), vol. ii, pp. 201-11.

form, with roughly equal frequency, throughout the gospel, in material derived from all the recognizable sources, and attached to references to God as Father of the Messianic Son as well as references to God as Father of the Christian believer.* There is thus no clearly recognizable principle at work, either in its use, or in its disuse. All that seems certain is that it is one of those Rabbinic phrases which made a particular appeal to St. Matthew, and, as such, bears witness to his essentially Jewish background and interests. Whether or no he derived it in a general way from that background, or more directly from his peculiar material, must be a matter for conjecture.†

VI

John

St. John makes more references to the Divine Fatherhood than any of his predecessors—in all, round about one hundred and twenty;‡ and the vast majority are in Words of Jesus.

Few of them, however, require much discussion since nearly all are of the sort which by now we have become accustomed to call Messianic. For example, the first occurs in the well-known words at the beginning of the gospel, 'And the Word became flesh and dwelt among us (and we beheld his glory, glory as of the only begotten from the Father), full of grace and truth';§ and the last in the Commission to the Disciples at the end, 'Peace be unto you: as the Father hath sent me, even so send I you'.‖ In both of these examples 'the Father' is used absolutely, as frequently in this gospel; but it is plain from the context in either case that it is 'the Father' who is spoken of in relation to the Messianic Son, Jesus. And so normally.¶ Sometimes in Words of Jesus we find the variation 'my Father',[a] although this variation is comparatively rare.[b] And on three separate occasions Jesus addresses God as 'Father' in prayer.[c] All these instances, though, are patently Messianic.

---

* The references are $5^{16, 45, 48}$, $6^{1, 9, 14, 26, 32}$, $7^{11, 21}$, $10^{32, 33}$, 12^{50}, 15^{13}, 16^{17}, $18^{10, 14, 19, 35}$, 23^9.

† As with St. Luke's Parable of the Lost Son I have deliberately excluded St. Matthew's Parable of the Two Sons (Matt. 21^{28-32}) from this discussion. Once again, it is extremely questionable whether any analogy may legitimately be pressed.

‡ The vagueness of this statement is due to several uncertainties in the text—e.g., 10^{38} and 16^{27}.

§ Jn. 1^{14}.   ‖ Jn. 20^{21}.   ¶ E.g., Jn. 5^{26} and 15^9.   [a] E.g., Jn. 2^{16} and 5^{17}.
[b] There are altogether some thirty instances; but again it is impossible to be precise because of textual uncertainty—e.g., 10^{32} and 16^{10}.
[c] Jn. 11^{41}, $12^{27, 28}$, $17^{1, 5, 11, 21, 24, 25}$.

Interest consequently focuses on those passages where 'Father' occurs in the narrative, or in the mouths of persons other than Jesus, and also on three passages where it might at first sight be argued that the term had a wider application altogether.

The first narrative-passage has already been quoted—'the only begotten of the Father',* which is made more pointed a few verses later by a reference to 'the only begotten Son, which is in the bosom of the Father':† here there can be no doubt of the Messianic use of the term. At 5[18] the evangelist mentions a plot to kill Jesus because he called 'God his own Father': at 8[27] he comments 'they perceived not that he spake to them of the Father'; and again at the beginning of chapter 13 it is stated that Jesus knew 'that his hour was come that he should depart out of this world unto the Father', and 'that the Father had given all things into his hands'.‡ There is no reason to suppose that the term is to be understood in any of these instances (if read in their contexts) in any different sense from that in which it is to be understood in Words of Jesus. In this gospel, that is, its meaning for Jesus and its meaning for the evangelist are identical.

And the same is true of the occurrences in the mouths of persons other than Jesus. At 8[19] the Jews ask 'Where is thy Father?' and Jesus replies 'Ye know neither me nor my Father'. At 8[41, 42] the Jews claim that God is their Father—'we have one Father, even God'; but they are immediately rebuffed with the rejoinder 'If God were your Father, ye would love me, for I came forth and am come from God'—the term, we may say, means something else, and something more, for Jesus than it does for the Jews. And so also when Philip, at the Supper, comes forward with the demand 'Shew us the Father' he is at once rebuked with the words 'He that hath seen me hath seen the Father ... I am in the Father and the Father in me'.§ In both these last instances popular misconceptions of the Divine Fatherhood are being, as it were, exposed and corrected.

So too with the three passages where it might seem that 'Father' was being used more generally. At the Well of Sychar Jesus speaks to the Samaritan woman of 'worshipping the Father': but a distinction is immediately made between true and false worship, and true worship is shown to be the worship of the Messianic Age through the medium of the Messiah.‖ At 5[45] there is no need for Jesus to accuse the Jews 'to the Father': Moses will do that, 'for he wrote of me'. Again, at 6[45], 'Father' is not just a synonym for God, nor is the phrase 'everyone that hath

* Jn. 1[14].   † Jn. 1[18].   ‡ Jn. 13[1, 3].   § Jn. 14[8, 9].   ‖ Jn. 4[21-26].

heard from the Father and hath learned' to be taken merely in the light of Isaiah's prophecy 'they shall all be taught of God': on the contrary, it is distinctly affirmed that 'everyone that hath heard from the Father and hath learned cometh unto me', and 'no one can come to me except the Father which sent me draw him'.

This last affirmation provides the key to our understanding of St. John's whole presentation of the Divine Fatherhood. God is Father, St. John is saying, because He is the Father of His Son, the Messiah, Jesus. With this conception we are, of course, already familiar from the other evangelists, although none of them stresses it so forcibly and so consistently. Yet St. John does not stop there, as we might all too readily assume. For him, as for the other evangelists, God is Father of Christians too; but nowhere in the other gospels do we find the unique Messianic role of Jesus in bringing this relationship about emphasized to anything like the same degree. That is why we may easily miss this essential second element in St. John's presentation. Because it is overshadowed it inevitably tends to be overlooked.

In the other gospels the Messianic role of Jesus in relation to the evangelists' presentation of God as Father of Christians is implied. In John it is explicitly stated and explained. Jesus, and no one and nothing else, is the Door by which alone Man has access to God*; or, elsewhere, 'I am the way, and the truth, and the life', says Jesus, 'no one cometh unto the Father but by me'.† And all of this is something new. Although the Jews claim God as their Father, their claim is unfounded.‡ All who have come before Jesus are 'thieves and robbers'. § But now, through the advent of the Messianic Son a new way has been opened up: those who identify themselves with him are enabled, through him, to enter into a new, filial, relationship with God which was impossible before—'he came unto his own, and they that were his own received him not. But as many as received him, to them gave he the right to become children of God, even to them that believe on his name'.‖

This 'right' is, of course, the Christian's birth-right, given to him at his 'new birth' in Baptism,¶ and made effective in proportion as he 'eats the flesh' and 'drinks the blood' of 'the Son of man' in the Eucharist.ᵃ Yet the most important thing about it, once more, is that it is something new. It depends entirely on the unique Messianic role of Jesus, and is guaranteed by his Passion, his Resurrection, and his Ascension. This explains why there is

---

* Jn. 10[9].   † Jn. 14[6].   ‡ Jn. 8[41].   § Jn. 10[8].
‖ Jn. 1[11, 12].   ¶ Jn. 3[3].   ᵃ Jn. 6[53-57].

no reference to God as Father of anyone, except Jesus, until the very end of the gospel. 'Go unto my brethren', commands the Risen Jesus, 'and say to them, I ascend unto my Father and your Father, and my God and your God'—the solitary mention in Words of Jesus of God as Father of Christians anywhere in the gospel. And this is no accident. For only after Jesus is 'glorified' is the new way ready for use and the possibility of Divine sonship made available to Man.

VII

We are now in a position to summarize our results, to interpret them, and to relate them to the modern situation from which we started.

In the genuine text of Mark we saw that there were only three references to the Divine Fatherhood, and that all of them were Messianic. In the material shared in common by St. Matthew and St. Luke but not found in Mark there were at least five passages which came up for consideration (containing, in all, nine references): these passages represented God as Father, not only of Jesus, the Messianic Son, but also of the disciples of Jesus, to whom Jesus, as Messianic Son, willed to reveal Him. In Luke two of St. Mark's Messianic references were reproduced, as also were both the Messianic and the 'disciple' references from the common material: there were in addition six references in passages peculiar to Luke, all but one of which were Messianic. In Matthew there were forty-four references, found in sections derived from Mark, in sections derived from the common material, and in sections peculiar to Matthew: both the number of references in this gospel and the fact that several of them are clearly editorial additions makes it plain that St. Matthew had a special interest in the Divine Fatherhood; and, as previously, God is represented, not only as the Father of Jesus, but also as Father of the disciples of Jesus—in particular He is frequently referred to in the Rabbinic manner as 'my [your] Father which is in heaven'. In John there were some hundred and twenty references: apart from passages where the term occurs in the mouths of speakers other than Jesus, all except one are Messianic: the solitary exception is found at the very end of the gospel, when, after Messiah's 'glorification', those who 'receive him' and 'believe on his name' are given the 'right' to call themselves 'children of God' through him.

Two things stand out from this summary: (1) the varying frequency of the references in the different documents in relation to their dates; and (2) the extent of the agreement between the documents in the total picture presented.

It is apparent that the earliest document, Mark, has the fewest references, that the latest, John, has the most, and that the documents which intervene in date occupy intermediate positions as regards their number of references. This fact has already been observed by T. W. Manson, who explains it as 'an attempt' on the part of the later evangelists 'to bring out clearly what appeared to these writers to be the essence of the Gospel'.* I believe this explanation to be correct. Since all the documents agree in representing Jesus as speaking of God as Father, there is no justification for thinking that he did not do so. 'We may, if we choose, call' what the later evangelists have done 'interpretation rather than strict history, or exaggeration of one feature of the teaching of Jesus; but it is interpretation of something that is given and exaggeration of something real'.†

From this it follows that if we are to trust the evidence Jesus will have spoken of God as Father less often than a casual reading of the gospels might suggest, and certainly far less often than is popularly supposed. Manson accounts for this 'reticence of Jesus' by suggesting that the Fatherhood of God was not for Jesus 'a theological commonplace' but 'a personal religious experience of unparalleled depth and intensity', about which he naturally would not speak either lightly, or frequently, or to anyone but 'a chosen few'.‡ Again I think Manson is right. But I am doubtful whether he is also right in suggesting that Jesus only began to speak of God as Father after St. Peter's confession at Caesarea Philippi §—it is questionable if sufficient reliance can be placed on the contexts in which the evangelists have placed the Words of Jesus to make the suggestion anything more than an interesting speculation. However, whether this be true or no, we are safe in affirming that Jesus did speak of God as Father and that the evangelists regarded his teaching in this respect as so important as to merit repeated emphasis.

Yet in emphasizing they did not distort. Jesus, if we are to follow the earliest traditions, spoke of God as Father both of himself and of his disciples. And this dual aspect is as characteristic of Luke, Matthew, and John, as it is of Mark and the common

---

* T. W. Manson, *The Teaching of Jesus* (2nd edit., 1935), p. 100.

† T. W. Manson, *op. cit.*, p. 100. My former colleague, the Rev. J. G. Davies, suggests that the paucity of references to God as Father in Mark may be due to St. Mark's presentation of the Messiahship of Jesus as secret, and that the more frequent references in the later evangelists may be explained, at least in part, by their failure to appreciate St. Mark's presentation.

‡ *Ibid.*, pp. 101-9.   § *Ibid.*, pp. 109, 110: compare also pp. 95-8.

material. The total picture presented, that is, is the same throughout—God, in the first place, is the Father of Jesus because Jesus is the Messianic Son, but, in the second place, He is also Father of those who follow Jesus, who have perceived and acknowledged his Messianic status, and who are, in consequence, members of the Messianic (or Christian) community.

Such a statement as this, limiting, as it obviously does, the right to call God 'Father' to members of the Christian community, is bound to sound strange in modern ears. We have latterly become so accustomed to thinking of God as Creator, and of Man as the crowning glory of His Creation, that we tend automatically to interpret His Fatherhood in terms of His creational activity— hence the popular conception of God as the one Divine Father of the whole vast human 'family', all the members of which severally can claim to be 'children of God' in virtue of the fact that He has created them.

But whatever may be said in favour of this interpretation of the Divine Fatherhood from the point of view of Natural Theology— and there is a very great deal which may rightly be said from this point of view—our review of the evidence of the Gospels should make us chary of accepting it as the Christian interpretation, and even more chary of attributing it to Jesus. In spite of what is commonly supposed, there is no ground whatever for asserting that Jesus taught a Doctrine of 'the Fatherhood of God and the Brotherhood of Man'.* The bulk of his recorded references to God as Father are Messianic; and apart from one, at the best ambiguous, reference in Matthew,† all his references to God as Father of men are in passages where he is speaking to his disciples. There is no hint anywhere, either that he himself believed, or that he taught, a Doctrine of Universal Fatherhood. For Jesus, we may say, men were not 'sons of God' by nature, although they were capable of becoming so by Grace.

* A recent example of the popularization of this error is a placard which was exhibited outside the Church of the Messiah, Broad Street, Birmingham, during the early summer of 1951, and which announced:

Unitarians believe,
as Jesus did,
in the
Fatherhood of God
and the
Brotherhood of Man.

Unitarians may believe it, and legitimately believe it, in so far as they may be 'Natural' theologians; but they are not justified in claiming that Jesus was in agreement with them.

† Matt. 23⁹: see above, p. 253.

On this fundamental point the teaching of the evangelists is at one with the teaching of Jesus. So also is the teaching of St. Paul and of the other New Testament writers. Christians, for St. Paul, are not natural, but adopted, 'sons of God'; and it is only by reason of 'the spirit of adoption' which has been poured into their hearts, and which has the effect of making them 'heirs of God and joint-heirs with Christ', that they can dare to address God as 'Father' at all in the opening words of the pattern-prayer which their Lord himself has taught them.* Similarly, for St. Peter: the Christians to whom he is writing, and who 'call on' God as 'Father', have evidently only comparatively recently been 'redeemed' from 'the vain manner of life handed down from' their 'fathers':† they have been 'begotten again'‡ and are as 'new-born babes'. § There is no suggestion here of natural sonship, nor of God being represented as in any sense the Father of all men.

Accordingly, the distinctively Christian Doctrine of the Divine Fatherhood, as evidenced by the gospels and supported by the rest of the New Testament, is that God is the Father of those, and only of those, who acknowledge the Messianic sonship of Jesus, who are incorporated into his new Messianic community, and who are thereby entitled to claim that they are sons of God through him.

The twentieth century must inevitably suspect such a Doctrine. Even the Christian may find it unpalatable, since it smacks (he may say) of exclusiveness—it is a hard saying, who can hear it? Yet that is no excuse for the Christian's evading it, still less excuse for his misinterpreting it, in an effort to make it harmonize with current social theory. The Christian's contribution to the healing of the wounds of society is, and must remain, distinctive. In contradiction to the Humanist who works for the betterment of Man because he believes in the Brotherhood of Man, in contradistinction to the Theist who works for human betterment because he believes that all men everywhere are children of the one Universal Father, the Christian proclaims unashamedly that what Man needs is not so much 'betterment' as 'redemption', while he denies outright that any men anywhere are born naturally as 'sons of God'— they can only become so if they will condescend to be 'reborn'.

Consequently, the Christian is concerned with the redemption and rebirth of individuals rather than with the betterment of the mass. He will not, of course, despise or belittle the efforts and achievements of his non-Christian friends. Nor will he refuse to

* Rom. 8¹⁴⁻¹⁷: Gal. 4⁴⁻⁷.　　† I Pet. 1¹⁷, ¹⁸.　　‡ I Pet. 1²³.　　§ I Pet. 2².

co-operate with them inasmuch as he is able. But as he does so he cannot forget that as a Christian he starts from a different axiom and looks to a different end. His axiom is best expressed in the Word of Jesus, 'I am the way, and the truth, and the life: no one cometh unto the Father, but by me':* his end in the 'hope' of St. Paul 'that the creation itself also shall be delivered from the bondage of corruption into the liberty of the glory of the children of God'.†

* Jn, 14⁶.
† Rom. 8²¹.